MILADY'S STANDARD
Nail Technology

5th Edition

CATHERINE M. FRANGIE

DOUGLAS SCHOON

SUE ELLEN SCHULTES

DEBORAH BEATTY

JEWELL CUNNINGHAM

LIN HALPERN

NANCY KING

LACINDA HEADINGS

TERRI LUNDBERG

JANET MCCORMICK

REBECCA MORAN

GODFREY F. "OSCAR" MIX, D.P.M.

LAURA J. MIX

VICKI PETERS

THOMSON

DELMAR LEARNING

Australia   d Kingdom United States

THOMSON

™

DELMAR LEARNING

Milady's Standard: Nail Technology, Fifth Edition

President, Milady:
Dawn Gerrain

Managing Editor:
Robert Serenka

Product Manager:
Erik Herman

Editorial Assistant:
Jessica Burns

Director of Content and Media Production:
Wendy A. Troeger

Content Project Manager:
Nina Tucciarelli

Associate Content Project Manager:
Angela Iula

Director of Marketing:
Wendy Mapstone

Channel Manager:
Sandra Bruce

Marketing Coordinator:
Nicole Riggi

Text Design:
Essence of Seven

Library of Congress Cataloging-in-Publication Data

Milady's standard: nail technology / [editors], Catherine M. Frangie . . . [et al.]. --5th ed.
    p. cm.
  Includes index.
  ISBN-10: 1-4180-1615-2
  ISBN-13: 978-1-4180-1615-9
  1. Manicuring. 2. Nails (Anatomy)--Care and hygiene. 3. Fingernails.
  I. Frangie, Catherine M.
  TT958.3.M55 2006
  646.7'27--dc22

2006014854

NOTICE TO THE READER

Publisher does not warrant or guarantee any of the products described herein or perform any independent analysis in connection with any of the product information contained herein. Publisher does not assume, and expressly disclaims, any obligation to obtain and include information other than that provided to it by the manufacturer.

The reader is expressly warned to consider and adopt all safety precautions that might be indicated by the activities herein and to avoid all potential hazards. By following the instructions contained herein, the reader willingly assumes all risks in connection with such instructions.

The Publisher makes no representation or warranties of any kind, including but not limited to, the warranties of fitness for particular purpose or merchantability, nor are any such representations implied with respect to the material set forth herein, and the publisher takes no responsibility with respect to such material. The Publisher shall not be liable for any special, consequential, or exemplary damages resulting, in whole or part, from the readers' use of, or reliance upon, this material.

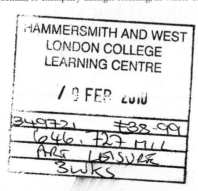

Contents in Brief

iii

Contents

Preface

TO THE STUDENT

Congratulations! You have chosen a career filled with unlimited potential, one that can take you in many directions and holds the possibility to make you a confident, successful professional. As a nail professional, you will play a vital role in the lives of your clients. They will come to rely on you to provide them with ongoing service, enabling them to look and feel their best.

Each year professional nail technicians perform more than $6 billion worth of manicuring, pedicuring, and artificial nail services for millions of fashion-conscious clients. The business of nails has grown enormously over the past several years and will continue to grow. Thus, the need for educated and competent nail technicians is expanding in the same way. *Milady's Standard: Nail Technology* is the complete first step to basic nail technology that all professional nail technicians need to kick off their career.

You are fortunate because you will learn from gifted instructors who will share their skills and experiences with you. You will meet other industry professionals at seminars, workshops, and conventions where you'll learn the latest techniques, specific product knowledge, and management procedures. All of the experiences in which you have the opportunity to participate will provide you with additional insights into the profession you have chosen. You will build a network of professionals to turn to for career advice, opportunity, and direction. Whatever direction you choose, we wish you a successful and enjoyable journey.

TO THE INSTRUCTOR

This edition of *Milady's Standard: Nail Technology* was prepared with the help of many instructors and professionals. Milady surveyed more than 40 instructors, practicing nail professionals, and state board officials, and received in-depth comments from a host of other experts to learn what needed to be changed, added, or deleted from this text.

Milady's Standard: Nail Technology contains new and updated information on many subjects, including communications and business skills, job seeking advice, life skills, electric filing, electricity, and sanitation and infection control.

You asked Milady to make your job easier by aligning overlapping editorial content between *Milady's Standard: Nail Technology* and *Milady's Standard: Cosmetology*, and we listened! This alignment includes the following chapters: History and Opportunities, Life Skills, Your Professional Image, Communicating for Success, Infection Control: Principles and and Practices, General Anatomy and Physiology, Skin Structure Growth, Nail Structure and Growth, Nail Diseases and Disorders, Basics of Chemistry, Basics of Electricity, Seeking Employment, On the Job, and Business Skills.

FEATURES OF THIS EDITION

In response to *your needs,* this exciting new edition of *Milady's Standard: Nail Technology* includes the following features:

○ *Chapters and Parts.* The book is divided into twenty-two chapters and four parts so it is very easy to use.

○ *Full-Color Art.* All art is in full color, with actual photographs to show you step-by-step procedures for manicuring, pedicuring, tips, wraps, acrylic nails, gels, and basic nail art.

○ *Learning Objectives and Review Questions.* Learning objectives provide goals for the students in each chapter. These objectives are reinforced by review questions that assess how well the student has mastered the goals established in the learning objectives. The answers to these review questions are conveniently located at the back of the book. They can be used by students to study for exams.

○ *Actual Photos of Nail Disorders.* Full-color photos are included to help students identify nail disorders more accurately.

○ *Client Consultation Guidelines.* A complete chapter focuses on client consultation and gives suggestions for identifying and meeting the needs of each individual client.

○ *Chemical Safety Coverage.* A complete chapter is devoted to the important topic of chemical safety in the nail salon. Students will learn to identify the chemicals commonly used in the nail salon, how they can cause harm, how to protect themselves and their clients, and how to read a Material Safety Data Sheet (MSDS).

○ *State Licensing Exam Topics.* The topics required for state licensing examinations are presented in a complete, easy-to-read fashion.

○ *Safety Cautions.* Highlighted safety cautions alert students to services that include potentially dangerous procedures. These cautions explain how to avoid dangerous situations and how to provide services in a safe, clean environment.

o *Sanitation Cautions.* Highlighted sanitation cautions give specific suggestions for maintaining proper sanitation at all times.

o *Tips.* These tips provide hints on the most efficient and effective way to complete step-by-step procedures and help students improve their nail technology skills.

o *Regulatory Agency Alerts.* Because state regulations vary, regulatory agency alerts remind students to check with their instructors for specific regulations in their state.

o *Business Tips:* These tips help nail technicians improve their business relations to achieve complete customer satisfaction.

SUPPLEMENTS FOR THE STUDENT AND INSTRUCTOR

Milady's Standard: Nail Technology, Fifth Edition, features these supplements:

Milady's Standard: Nail Technology Workbook

This workbook is a valuable student supplement that coordinates chapter-by-chapter with the textbook. It strengthens the students' understanding of nail technology by reinforcing the material covered in the textbook.

The workbook includes short answer, short essay, sentence completion, matching, definition, labeling, and word review activities. The workbook also includes a final exam review made up of multiple choice questions and a series of situational tests that ask students what they would do in difficult situations if they were the nail technician.

Milady's Standard: Nail Technology Course Management Guide

This step-by-step, simple-to-use course guide has been designed specifically to help the nail technology instructor set up and operate a successful nail technology training program. It includes

- guidelines for starting and implementing a nail technology program.
- detailed lesson plans for each chapter in the book.
- handouts ready for use in the classroom.
- transparency masters for easy-to-create visual aids.
- a Chemical Safety Program that can be implemented in the nail technology classroom.
- the answers to *Milady's Standard: Nail Technology Workbook*

Milady's Standard: Nail Technology Exam Review

This book of exam reviews contains questions similar to those found on state licensing exams for nail technology. It employs the multiple-choice type question, which has been widely adopted and approved by the majority of state licensing boards. Groups of questions are arranged under major subject areas.

Preparing for the Practical Exam: Nail Technology

This student supplement provides clear, detailed information on all procedures required by state boards for the practical exam. Not all state boards require that procedures be performed the same way, and this book provides options, so that students can be prepared for their particular state's methods.

Milady's Standard: Nail Technology Student CD-ROM

This interactive student product was designed to reinforce classroom learning, stimulate the imagination, and aid in preparation for board exams. Featuring video clips and graphical animations to demonstrate practices and procedures, this exciting educational tool also contains a test bank, learning games, and an audio glossary.

Milady's Standard: Nail Technology Course Management Guide—CD-ROM

Includes all the elements of the print version Course Management Guide and includes

- a computerized testbank for instant creation of review tests with answer keys
- an Image Library including all images in the text to be used in handouts, transparency slides, or PowerPoint® presentations

Milady's Standard: Nail Technology Instructor Support Slides

A complete PowerPoint® presentation for every chapter in the newly revised textbook.

Milady's Standard: Nail Technology DVDs

This brand new DVD series brings to life complete coverage of the practical applications of the textbook. This series will enhance classroom learning and is essential for remedial work and individual learning.

Advanced, Reference, and Continuing Education Material

- *Nail Structure and Product Chemistry,* Douglas D. Schoon—An informational guide for anyone interested in learning more about how and why professional nail products work; how to troubleshoot, understand and solve most common salon problems; why products sometimes don't work and how to avoid these problems; how to avoid product-related skin allergies; and more. The text contains an in-depth study of the natural nail, its various parts, and how they function together. In addition, it covers a wide range of topics helpful to the salon professional, including how to give clients trouble-free nails and nail services; nail polishes and treatments; the use of electric files; understanding and avoiding skin allergies; improving ventilation; and much, much more.
- *Guide to Owning and Operating a Nail Salon,* Joanne Wiggins—Includes well-organized, step-by-step tips for starting a salon, busi-

ness features specific to nail salons, and tips on developing a long-term plan.

- *Nail Q & A Book,* Vicki Peters—This book has over 500 questions and answers for nail technicians ranging from nail preparation to business practice tips.
- *The Professional's Reflexology Handbook,* Shelley Hess—This handbook offers a full spectrum of treatments using pressure points of the foot, hand, and ear. This guide provides clear, concise instructions and background on how reflexology treatments can be used in selected areas of service.
- *Spa Manicuring for the Salon and Spa,* Janet McCormick—This is the most complete and instructional source of information for any nail technician wishing to treat body, mind, and spirit. Easy to understand, concise, and inspiring, this book takes manicuring, and us as professionals, to a higher level of knowledge. It will change your concept of the spa service.
- *The Salon Professional's Guide to Foot Care,* Godfrey Mix, DPM—A licensed podiatrist offers invaluable information on the human foot and its care. Common foot problems and general foot diseases that can affect the foot are discussed. Knowing how and when to consult a medical professional or refer a client will help you better serve your clientele and increase loyalty.

About
the Authors

Catherine M. Frangie, Editor/Contributor

Catherine M. Frangie has been a dedicated and passionate beauty professional since 1982, when she first began her career as a licensed cosmetologist, salon owner, and beauty school instructor. Since then, Catherine has held prominent and dynamic positions throughout many facets of the professional beauty industry, including Marketing, Communications, and Education Vice President for a leading product company, Communications Director, Trade Magazine Editor/Publisher, and Textbook Editor and Author.

Catherine has addressed her beauty colleagues numerous times as a guest lecturer at the International Beauty Show in NYC and in other national venues. She has personally authored more than 125 feature length trade and consumer magazine articles and several books on beauty trends, fashion, and the business of the professional salon. Catherine holds a graduate degree in communications as well as undergraduate degrees in marketing and advertising.

Douglas Schoon, Contributor

With over thirty years experience as a research scientist, international lecturer, author and educator, Douglas Schoon heads up the most extensive nail research and development laboratory in existence today.

As the Vice President of Science and Technology for Creative Nail Design, Schoon spends much of his time leading a team of scientists working with high-tech, computerized testing equipment to produce state-of-the-art nail enhancement products and natural nail treatments, as well as world-renown spa products. With all of this expertise and technology, Creative Nail Design's research capabilities exceed even those found in many university laboratories.

For over sixteen years Schoon has led the Creative Nail Design's Research and Development program. He directs the Quality Assurance, Technical Services and Field Testing departments, as well. Schoon is the author of many books and video and audio training programs, as well as dozens of magazine articles on salon chemicals, chemical safety, and disinfection. He often serves as an expert witness in legal cases involving cosmetic safety and health. Additionally, dermatologists frequently call upon Schoon to assist them writing books and scientific papers concerning fingernails, proving, without a doubt, he is a world-leading expert on natural and artificial nail product, services, and salons. He is also a strong advocate for salon safety and represents the entire nail industry on scientific and technical issues in Europe, Canada, and the United States. Schoon first entered the nail industry in 1986 as the founder of Chemical Awareness Training Service, CATS, the beauty industry's first company focused on safety training programs for salons. So he has a long history of educating safe practices to nail professionals.

As a writer and speaker, Mr. Schoon is especially popular with the nail technicians because of his unique ability to make complex chemical theories and ideas seem simple, even easy, to understand. His natural nail health, safety, and disinfection lectures are also invaluable to anyone interested in product chemistry, safety, and health issues, as is his most popular book, *Nail Structure and Product Chemistry Simplified,* Second Edition, Delmar Thomson Learning.

In addition, Schoon is a Co-chair of the Safety and Standards Committee of Nail Manufacturers Council (NMC), as well as the holder of a Masters Degree in Chemistry from the prestigious University of California-Irvine. He currently resides in Dana Point, California.

Sue Ellen Schultes, Contributor

Sue Ellen Schultes is an award-winning nail artist, a licensed nail technician, and a former salon owner whose business was recognized as one of the top 100 nail salons in the country by *Nails* magazine ten years running. Sue is recognized as one of the leading nail art technology authorities in the United States and has taught extensively throughout the United States, conducting workshops and seminars via Notorious Nails Seminars. Sue serves as Competition Judge for various trade shows, both nationally and internationally. Besides acting as series editor and contributing author for Delmar Learning, Sue also contributes special interest articles to *Nails* magazine and several other publications. Sue was commissioned by the Smithsonian Institute's National Museum of American History to create a full set of nails commemorating the United States Presidential Inauguration

Deborah Beatty, Contributor

Deborah Beatty has over 32 years of industry experience, which has allowed her to gain and develop a wealth of knowledge that she shares during her educational seminars as well as in her classrooms. With 15 years experience in the educational sector, she enlightens and motivates cosmetologists, instructors, and students with her energetic and interactive approach to teaching. She is presently the Program Manager for the Cosmetology Department at a post-secondary college. In addition to being a Master Cosmetologist and Licensed Instructor, she also holds her Master Barber License, is a Licensed Practical Nurse, and is licensed by the Georgia Professional Standards Commission. Deborah is a book and product reviewer for Thomson Learning and is an educator for Milady's Career Institute. She is also a contributing editor for the revision of *Milady's Standard: Cosmetology* and *Milady's Standard: Nail Technology*. She is the author of the popular book *Preparing for the Practical Exam: Cosmetology* for students and instructors, as well as the author of *Preparing for the Practical Exam: Nail Technology* for students and instructors.

Deborah holds her Bachelor of Science Degree in Education for Technological Studies from the University of Georgia.

Jewell Cunningham, Contributor

Jewell Cunningham has been involved with the beauty industry for over 25 years. As a licensed nail technician, she competed in sculptured nail competitions from 1981 through 1986, winning 25 first place awards, an industry record, including International World Champion and National Champion. Jewell followed that success as a judge for national and international competitions, writing rules and regulations as well as directing competitions. In 1990, Jewell joined a manufacturer, where she developed over 75 items for the line and designed packaging as well. Jewell is the Nailpro Competition Director running all Nailpro competitions in the United States as well as world wide. She is a nationally recognized consultant to day spas, manufacturers, and salon owners, and continues to thrive in the beauty industry.

Lin Halpern, Contributor

A native New Yorker, Lin Halpern has been a nail technician for 42 years. Lin started her professional nail shop business in 1980 and expanded to a full service spa salon in 1981. From 1981 consecutively through 1999, worked as a consultant to four different nail product manufacturers developing acrylics, light-cure gels and nail coatings. Over the years she has developed numerous new and innovative products from fast drying topcoats, and easier to use controlled-flow acrylics to a unique Pink and White application using a three-dimensional nail tip for which she holds a U.S. Patent. Ms. Halpern has contributed technical articles to *Nails* and *Nailpro* magazines and has co-written and produced marketing design concepts for advertising photos and posters along with applying the model nails. Lin has judged international nail competitions, toured as an international educator on nail product knowledge and nail application techniques, and co-written and produced an interactive seminar on acrylic and gel nail product chemistry. Lin has been invited to join other notable nail technicians from varied companies to participate in open talk forums at beauty events around the world. Since closing her spa salon in 1989, she continues to service clients' daily as she develops new nail product chemistry to improve our every day work objective. In recent years Lin created a company that works exclusively on new and innovative polymer chemistry with top chemists in this field. She and her partners continue to bring the latest techniques and advanced chemistry's to both the professional and retail sides of our nail industry.

Nancy King, Contributor

Nancy King is an internationally recognized expert on safe salon practices and regulation. She has been an industry spokesperson to the media and was the technical advisor to the producers of the ABC's 20/20 and CNN nail stories on pedicure infections and salon chemical safety. A licensed nail technician, educator, and industry consultant, she has written articles and has been a cover artist for international trade publications. In 2000, Nancy became the Director of the AEFM, and took that organization to new heights in setting the industry standard for electric file education, both in the United States and internationally. Nancy is currently the Director of Education for *Nailpro* magazine.

LaCinda Headings, Contributor

LaCinda's passion for education has influenced her 18 years in the beauty industry as a cosmetologist specializing in nails. Her background includes 10 years in the salon, manufacturer's top trainer and consultant, school nail instructor, distribution, and presently admissions and marketing at one of the top cosmetology schools in the country. LaCinda has helped numerous nail technicians and salons start and grow their nail business. Her varied experience in the industry gives her a unique perspective that allows her to connect with nail technicians in every aspect of the business. LaCinda has inspired nail technicians all over the world with her motto of "Live, Laugh, Love and Learn."

Terri Lundberg, Contributor

Terri Lundberg has been a nail technology educator in both the professional arena and in the schools since 1990. A large part of her career was as the International Education Director for a nail product manufacturer. She not only trained company educators across the world, but developed a "train the trainer" method that is still used today. Terri also developed a mentoring program, creating a unique curriculum for mentoring nail technicians to a higher skill level, and authored and taught an advanced skills course. Terri stills teaches advanced classes but especially enjoys her work as a nail technology manager/instructor, in which she has developed an outstanding nail technician program, allowing students to be salon-ready at graduation.

Janet McCormick, Contributor

Janet McCormick, M.S., is a licensed nail technician and aesthetician, a former salon owner, seasoned instructor of nails and skin care skills, consultant, and author. Janet has achieved status as a CIDESCO diplomat and holds a master's degree in Allied Health Management. She speaks often at industry conferences and has authored over 300 skill and business articles in industry trade magazines. She is author of *Spa Manicuring for Salon and Spas,* published by Delmar Learning, describing a new, profitable focus for the industry: skin care based manicuring. Janet is owner of Spa Techniques Consulting, a spa consulting company in Frostproof, Florida.

Rebecca Moran, Contributor

Rebecca Moran has been a nail technologist, salon owner, licensed cosmetology, nail and esthetic instructor, director of education and an independent special education facilitator and researcher within our industry for over 14 years now. She has worked as a subject matter expert, expert reviewer and authored such other works as the *Milady's Standard: Nail Technology* CD ROM for Delmar Learning, as well as being a contributing author.

The proud mother of two "red-headed wild women," ages 11 and 9, she has broadened her focus and time in researching health, product, and safety issues affecting the service provider, our clients, and our industry as a whole. She has published articles in such publications as *Diabetes Health Magazine* and continues to work close with the medical and legal communities to both further her research and keep her finger on the pulse of "things yet to come" within ours and related industries.

Although stricken with an incurable illness, sometimes debilitating to the point of wheel chair-dependency, Rebecca continues to study, research, teach specialty student seminars, and write at every given opportunity. "My goal and intention is to help develop programs and publications to facilitate the most educated, professional, client and safety conscious service providers this industry has ever seen. We need to look to the future, develop working relationships with the medical community as service providers, and learn to protect ourselves and our clients from the ever developing and mutating viral, bacterial and other illnesses awaiting opportunity to spread. We all need to keep finding ways to work smarter, not harder."

Godfrey F. Mix, D.P.M., Contributor

Godfrey "Oscar" Mix is a Doctor of Podiatric Medicine, a member of the American Podiatric Medical Association, the California Podiatric Medical Association, and the Sacramento Valley Podiatric Medical Society, of which he is a past president. He is an Associate of the America College of Foot Surgeons and is Board Certified by the American Board of Podiatric Foot Surgery. Dr. Mix is the author of *The Salon Professional's Guide to Foot Care,* published by Delmar Learning, and currently writes on foot-related subjects for *Nail Pro* magazine, continuing to work as a manufacturer's consultant in the professional beauty industry. Dr. Mix is also on the *Nail Pro* advisory board.

Laura J. Mix, Contributor

Laura Mix began her career as a Clinical Laboratory Technician for a major metropolitan hospital in Sacramento California. After a number of years as a technician then as a full time homemaker, Laura returned to work with her husband, Dr. Oscar Mix, in his podiatry practice. The Mixes decided to offer pedicure services to patients, and so Laura began manicuring school in June of 1993. After obtaining her license, Laura continued working with her husband, providing pedicures and nail services. In November of 1998, she and Dr. Mix opened a specialty day spa, Footwork's, Inc., and also worked as a product educator for a fiberglass nail enhancement system. She has consulted as a subject matter expert for the Sacramento Bureau of Barbering and Cosmetology. Laura is now retired, but continues to keep her manicuring license current.

Vicki Peters, Contributor

As a nail technician, Vicki Peters has wowed the industry with her championship nails. As a cover artist and author, her work has been published worldwide, more than any other tech in the history of the nail business. As an educator, she has trained techs from Russia, Germany, Japan, Ireland, the United Kingdom, Canada, Mexico, Africa, Australia, and the United States. As an industry leader, she has mentored thousands. As a world-master nail technician, Peters, with her own line of products, will pioneer the industry to new levels.

Vicki Peters is a 25 year veteran nail technician, past competition champion, judge and competition director, technical educator and featured business speaker. She is also author of the *Nails Q&A Book, Drilltalk, The Competitive Edge* and *Novartis' Nail Healthy Guide.* Her nail artistry has been on the covers of *TV Guide, Dayspa, Nails, Nailpro, Nailpro Europe,* and numerous fashion magazines. Her expertise in the nail business ranges from salon work and hands on technical experience, to R&D, education and lecturing worldwide.

Acknowledgments

The staff of Delmar Learning wishes to acknowledge the many individuals and organizations who helped shape the fifth edition of *Milady's Standard: Nail Technology*. Their input enabled us to produce a book that will be a valuable resource for both students and professionals in the field of nail technology. To all those who contributed to this edition we extend our sincere thanks and appreciation.

Fifth Edition Reviewers

Melanie Thompson, The Nail Room, SC

Geeta Soogrim, Gloria Francis/New York Institute of Beauty, NY

Mary Lee Krantz, Design Associates Consulting, IL

Kenyatta Thompson, The Nail Academy, NY

Christina Player, Gadsen Correctional Facility, FL

Georgina Davis, Scot Lewis Schools, MN

Robin Hometchko, A Place in the Sun, MT

Lori Manicho, OPI Products, Inc., OH

Mark Ludewig, Jerry Lee Beauty College, CA

Vickie Y. Ledlow, OPI Products Inc., IL

Melissa A. Pechey, The Matrix Nail Lab & Spa, Wareham, MA

Nikki Birch

Tiffany Greco, HAIRADDIX, Carlsbad, CA

Leslie Randall, Entity Beauty College Inc., IL

Kristina Saindon, Denver, Colorado

Paul Bryson, Ph.D., Co-Director of Research and Development, OPI Products Inc., OH

Jean M. Harrity

Evonne Bennett, Evonne's Hair & Nail Salon, Dothan, AL

Linda Fishel, Iowa Cosmetology Educator, Nail Section, Cedar Rapids, Iowa

Paula Gilmore, Nail Industry Consultant

Frances L. Archer, Cosmetology Instructor, The Nail Clinic School of Manicuring, Columbia, SC

Ginger McQueen, School Account Consultant, OPI Products, Inc., OH

Clare Scott, Northeast Technology Center, Pryor, OK

Roseann H. Kinley, President, National-Interstate Council of State Boards of Cosmetology, Inc.(NIC), SC

Donn Kerr, Esthetics International School, Columbia, SC

Photography and Location

Salon Location:

Kimberley's… A Day Spa, Ltd., Latham, NY

Sue Ellen Schultes Notorious Nails, Green Brook, NJ

All location photos:

Paul Castle, Castle Photography, Inc., Troy, NY (www.castlephotographyinc.com)

Michael Dzaman Photography ©Michael Dzaman/Dzaman Photography (www.dzamanphoto.com)

Part 1: inset photo, Castle Photography.

Chapter 1: chapter opener photo, Castle Photography, Figs. 1-1 and 1-2, Corbis. Figs. 1-3 and 1-6, PhotoDisc. All other photos by Michael Dzaman.

Chapter 2: chapter opener photo, Comstock Premium/Alamy, Fig. 2-1 Michael Dzaman. Figs. 2-2 and 2-5, Corbis. Fig. 2-3, Getty Images. Fig. 2-4, 2-6 and 2-8, Delmar Learning. Fig. 2-7, Ed Hille. Fig. 2-9 Paul Castle.

Chapter 3: chapter opener photo, Getty Images, Fig. 3-4, 3-6, Delmar Learning. Figs. 3-7 Larry Hamill. All other photos by Paul Castle.

Chapter 4: chapter opener photo, Castle Photography, Fig. 4-2, Michael Dzaman. Fig. 4-6, Getty Images. All other photos by Paul Castle.

Part 2: inset photo, Getty Images.

Chapter 5: chapter opener photo, Dzaman Photography, Figs. 5-1 thru 5-6, Delmar Learning. Fig. 5-7, courtesy of Robert A. Silverman, MD, Clinical Associate Professor, Department of Pediatrics, Georgetown University. Fig. 5-8, Kimberley's A Day Spa, Ltd. Figs.5-18 and 5-19, Michael Dzaman. Fig. 5-20, Larry Hamill. All other photos by Paul Castle.

Chapter 6: chapter opener photo, Getty Images, Anatomy illustrations by Joe Chovan, Health Care Visuals.

Chapter 7: chapter opener photo, Getty Images, Figs. 7-7, 7-8, 7-11, 7-12, 7-13, 7-15, 7-17 thru 7-25, reprinted with permission from American Academy of Dermatology. All rights reserved. Figure 7-9, photo courtesy of Timothy Berger, MD, Associate Clinical Professor, University of California San Francisco. Fig. 7-14, Larry Hamill. Fig. 7-16, courtesy of Center for Disease Control and Prevention (CDC). Fig. 7-26, Getty Images. Illustrations owned by Delmar Learning.

Chapter 8: chapter opener photo, Getty Images, Fig. 8-1, 8-3, Delmar Learning. Fig. 8-2, courtesy of Godfrey F. Mix, DPM, Sacramento, CA.

Chapter 9: chapter opener photo, Castle Photography, Fig. 9-2, 9-14, 9-17, 9-22, courtesy of Robert Baran, MD (France). Fig. 9-4, 9-5, 9-7, 9-8, 9-10 and 9-15, courtesy of Godfrey F. Mix, DPM, Sacramento, CA. Fig. 9.6, Paul Castle. Fig. 9-12 and 9-13, 9-16 Michael Dzaman. Fig. 9-16, Paul Castle. Fig. 9-21, reprinted with permission from American Academy of Dermatology. All rights reserved.

Chapter 10: chapter opener photo, Getty Images.

Chapter 11: chapter opener photo, Dzaman Photography.

Chapter 12: chapter opener photo, Getty Images.

Part 3: inset photo, Getty Images.

Chapter 13: chapter opener photo, Getty Images, Fig. 13-6, 13-10, 13-65, Paul Castle. Figure 13-45, courtesy of Paul Rollins. All other photos by Michael Dzaman.

Chapter 14: chapter opener photo, Getty Images, Figs. 14-2 and 14-28, Paul Castle. All other photos by Michael Dzaman.

Chapter 15: chapter opener photo, courtesy of Vicki Peters, KUPA Inc., Figs. 15-1 thru 15-11, photos courtesy of Nancy King.

Chapter 16: chapter opener photo, Castle Photography, Figs. 16-2, 16-5, Paul Castle. All other photos by Michael Dzaman.

Chapter 17: chapter opener photo, Dzaman Photography, Figs. 17-1, 17-2, 17-3, 17-5, 17-7 thru 17-19, photos courtesy of Nail Systems International (NSI). Figs. 17-4, 17-20 thru 17-26, Paul Castle.

Chapter 18: chapter opener photo, Dzaman Photography, Figs. 18-1, 18-3 thru 18-8, 18-10 thru 18-16, photos courtesy of Nail Systems International (NSI). Fig. 18-2, Paul Castle. Fig 18-13, Michael Dzaman.

Chapter 19: chapter opener photo, Dynamic Graphics Group/Creatas/Alamy.

Chapter 20: chapter opener photo, Getty Images, Fig. 20-2, Getty Images. Fig. 20-5, Jerry Kelon Carter, CC'S Cosmetology College, Tulsa, OK. Fig. 20-6, Kimberley's Day Spa. Fig. 20-7, Ed Hille. All other photos by Paul Castle.

Chapter 21: chapter opener photo, Dzaman Photography, All photos in chapter by Paul Castle.

Chapter 22: chapter opener photo, Getty Images, Fig. 22-1, 22-2, 22-3, 22-5, Kimberley's Day Spa, photos taken by Paul Castle. Fig. 22-4, Getty Images. Fig. 22-7, Zanos Salon, Chicago, IL. Fig. 22-9, Tom Stock. Fig. 22-12, Stephen Ciuccoli.

For their generous assistance with supplies, tools, and apparel:

Gavson Salon Classics Quality Salon Apparel, Garland, TX
www.gavsonsalon.com

Bianco Brothers International Hand-honed instruments for the medical
and beauty industries, Brooklyn, NY

Essie Cosmetics, Ltd., Astoria, NY www.essieltd.com

Emiliani Enterprises, Union, NJ www.beauty-net.com

AromaTouch, Encino, CA

For participation as models in the photo shoot:

Alison Banks-Moore	Brian McGrath
Brian Banks	Austen Miller
Shanon Brouillette	Allison Parker
Shannon Bruce	C. Cole Pflegl
Melanie Buck	Valerie Erceg Pietryak
Nicole Cedeno	Mylene Quines
Shannon Ciasulli	April Rich
Eileen M. Clawson	Lois S. Robinson
Barbara L. Diaz	Ronda Robinson
Guy Erceg	Corinne Santiago
Michael P. Fredrick	Gladys Schalet
Carolyn Gillish	Raymond E. Schultes
Sarah Ginsberg	Nicole Smith
Marcus Jury	Eric Strife
Suzanne M. Kendall	Elizabeth Tinsley
Joy Kocsis	Nina Tucciarelli
Robert Lartaud	Courtney VanAuskas
Kurt Manz	Elizabeth Wenk
Lisa Manz	Jamie Wetzel
Stacy Masucci	

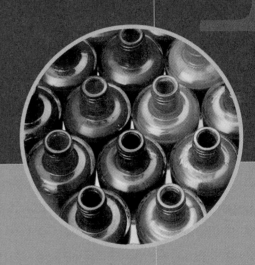

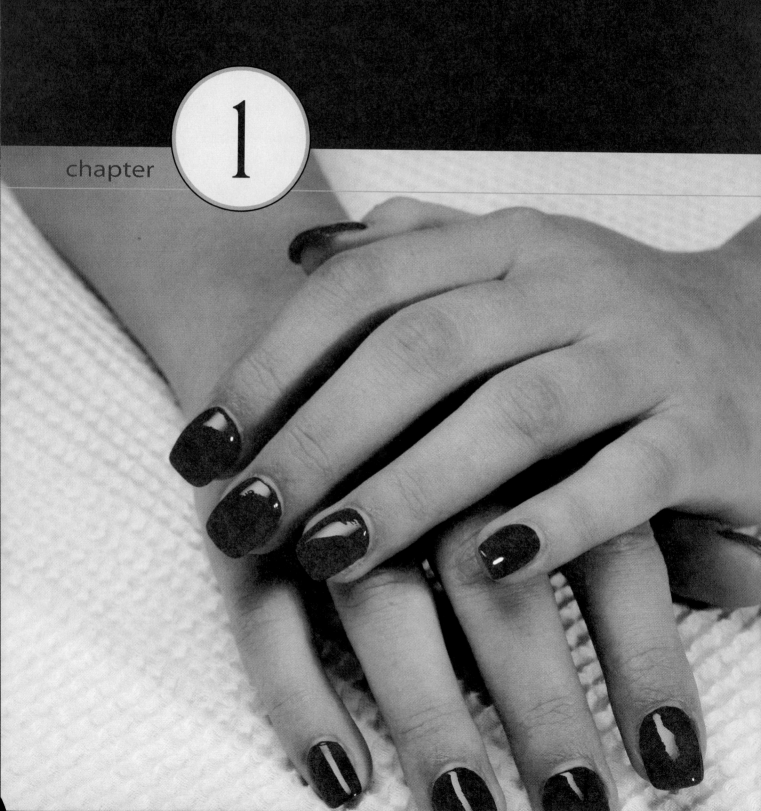

History and Opportunities

LEARNING OBJECTIVES

After completing this chapter, you will be able to:

1. Describe the origins of appearance enhancement.

2. Describe the advancements made in cosmetology during the 19th, 20th, and early 21st centuries.

3. List the career opportunities available to a licensed nail technician.

BRIEF HISTORY OF COSMETOLOGY

Cosmetology is a term used to encompass a broad range of specialty areas, including hairstyling, nail technology, and esthetics. Cosmetology defined is "the art and science of beautifying and improving the skin, nails, and hair, and the study of cosmetics and their applications." The term comes from the Greek word *kosmetikos*, meaning "skilled in the use of cosmetics." Archeological studies reveal that personal beautification was practiced in some form as early as the Ice Age.

The simple but effective grooming implements used at the dawn of history were shaped from sharpened flints, oyster shells, or bone. Animal sinew or strips of hide were used to tie the hair back or as adornment. Ancient people around the world used coloring matter on their hair, skin, and nails, and practiced tattooing. Pigments were made from berries, tree bark, minerals, insects, nuts, herbs, leaves, and other materials. Many of these colorants are still used today.

Egyptians

The Egyptians were the first to cultivate beauty in an extravagant fashion, and to use cosmetics as part of their personal beautification habits, religious ceremonies, and preparing the deceased for burial.

As early as 3000 BC, Egyptians used minerals, insects and berries to create makeup for their eyes, lips, and skin, and henna to stain their hair and nails a rich, warm red. They were also the first civilization to infuse essential oils from the leaves, bark, and blossoms of plants for use as perfumes and for purification purposes. Queen Nefertiti (1400 BC) stained her nails red by dipping her fingertips in henna, wore lavish makeup designs, and used custom-blended essential oils as signature scents. Queen Cleopatra (50 BC) took this dedication to beauty to an entirely new level by erecting a personal cosmetics factory next to the Dead Sea.

Ancient Egyptians are also credited with creating kohl makeup—originally made from a mixture of ground galena (a black mineral), sulfur, and animal fat—to heavily line the eyes, alleviate eye inflammations, and protect the eyes from the glare of the sun.

In both ancient Egypt and Rome, military commanders stained their nails and lips in matching colors before important battles.

Chinese

History also shows that during the Shang Dynasty (1600 BC), Chinese aristocrats rubbed a tinted mixture of gum arabic, gelatin, beeswax, and egg whites onto their nails to turn them crimson or ebony. Throughout the Chou Dynasty (1100 BC), gold and silver were the royal colors. During this early period in Chinese history, nail tinting was so closely tied to social status that commoners caught wearing a royal nail color faced a punishment of death.

Greeks

During the Golden Age of Greece (beginning in 500 BC), hairstyling became a highly developed art. The ancient Greeks made lavish use of perfumes and cosmetics in their religious rites, in grooming, and for medicinal purposes. They built elaborate baths and developed excellent methods of dressing the hair and caring for the skin and nails. Greek women applied preparations of white lead on their faces, kohl on their eyes, and vermilion on their cheeks and lips. The brilliant red pigment was made by grinding cinnabar, a mineral that is the chief source of mercury, to a fine powder. It was mixed with ointment or dusted on the skin in the same way as modern cosmetics are applied today.

Romans

Roman women made lavish use of fragrances and cosmetics. Facials made of milk and bread or fine wine were popular. Other facials were made of corn, flour, and milk, or flour and fresh butter. A mixture of chalk and white lead was used as a facial cosmetic. Women used hair color to indicate their class in society. Noblewomen tinted their hair red, middle-class women colored their hair blonde, and poor women colored their hair black.

Middle Ages

The Middle Ages is the period of European history between classical antiquity and the Renaissance, beginning with the downfall of Rome in 476 AD, and lasting until about 1450. Beauty culture is evidenced by tapestries, sculptures, and other artifacts from this period. All show towering headdresses, intricate hairstyles, and the use of cosmetics on skin and hair. Women wore colored makeup on their cheeks and lips, but not on their eyes or nails. Around 1000 AD, a Persian physician and alchemist named Avicenna refined the process of steam distillation. This ushered in the modern era of steam distilled essential oils that we use today.

Renaissance

This is the period in history during which Western civilization made the transition from medieval to modern history. Paintings and written records tell us a great deal about the grooming practices of the time. One of the most unusual practices was the shaving of the eyebrows and the hairline to show a greater expanse of forehead. A bare brow was thought to give women a look of greater intelligence. During this period, both men and women took great pride in their physical appearance and wore elaborate elegant clothing. Fragrances and cosmetics were used, although highly colored preparations for the lips, cheeks, eyes and nails were discouraged.

Victorian Age

The reign of Queen Victoria of England between 1837 and 1901 was known as the Victorian Age. Fashions in dress and personal grooming were drastically influenced by the social mores of this austere and restrictive period in history. To preserve the health and beauty of the skin, women used beauty masks and packs made from honey, eggs, milk, oatmeal, fruits, vegetables, and other natural ingredients. Victorian women are said to have pinched their cheeks and bitten their lips to induce natural color rather than use cosmetics such as rouge or lip color.

20th Century

In the early 20th century, the invention of motion pictures coincided with an abrupt shift in American attitudes. As viewers saw pictures of celebrities with flawless complexions, beautiful hairstyles, and manicured nails, standards of feminine beauty began to change. This era also signaled the onset of industrialization, which brought a new prosperity to the United States, and all forms of beauty began to follow trends.

1901–1910

In 1904 Max Faktor emigrated from Lodz, Poland to the United States. By 1908, he had Americanized his name to Max Factor and moved to Los Angeles, where he began by making and selling to movie stars makeup that wouldn't cake or crack, even under hot studio lights.

On October 8, 1906, Karl Nessler debuted the first permanent wave machine.

In 1909, French chemist Eugene Schueller developed the first commercial hair dye. Two years later, Schueller named his company L'Oreal. That same year, Florence Graham and cosmetologist Elizabeth Hubbard opened a salon on Fifth Avenue in New York City that was eventually renamed "Elizabeth Arden." T.J. Williams founded Maybelline in 1914 and introduced the first mascara, in the form of a cake and brush, to an adoring female public. Lipstick in cylindrical metal tubes was introduced in 1915. Prior to that lipstick came in a cosmetic pan and was applied using the pinky finger.

1920's

The cosmetics industry grew rapidly during the 1920s. Advertising expenditures in radio alone went from $390,000.00 to $3.2 million between 1927 and 1930. At first, many women's magazines refused advertisements for cosmetics—deeming them improper—but by the end of the 1920s, cosmetics provided one of their largest sources of advertising revenue.

1930's

In 1932—nearly 4,000 years after the first recorded nail color craze—Charles Revson of Revlon fame marketed the first nail polish—as opposed to a nail stain—using formulas that were borrowed from the automobile paint industry. This milestone marked a dramatic shift in nail cosmetics, as women finally had an array of nail lacquers available to them. Early screen sirens, Jean Harlow and Gloria Swanson glamorized this hip new nail fashion in silent pictures and early talkies by appearing in films wearing matching polish on their fingers and toes.

Also in 1932, Lawrence Gelb, a New York Chemist introduced the first permanent hair color product and founded a company called Clairol. In 1935, Max Factor created pancake makeup to make actors' skin look natural on color film. In 1938, Arnold F. Willatt invented the cold wave that used no machines or heat. The cold wave is considered to be the precursor to the modern perm.

1940's

Although commercial progress definitely came to a crawl due to World War II, the beauty industry did benefit from a major breakthrough when aerosol cans were invented. This eventually led to the first hair sprays. Shiny lips also came into vogue for the first time when women began applying petroleum jelly over their lipstick.

1951-2000

The second half of the 20th century saw the introduction of tube mascara, improved hair care and nail products, and the boom and then death of the weekly salon appointment. In the late 1960's, Vidal Sassoon turned the hairstyling world on its ear with his revolutionary geometric cuts. The 1970's saw a new era in highlighting when French hairdressers introduced the art of "hair weaving," using aluminum foil. In the 1980's makeup went full circle, from being barely there to cat-eyes and the heavy use of eye shadows and blush. In the 1990's hair color became gentler, allowing all ethnicities to enjoy being blondes, brunettes, or redheads. In 1998, Creative Nail Design introduced the first spa pedicure system to the professional beauty industry.

Juliet wraps, a paper nail wrapping system, was the first nail strengthening system performed by nail technicians. Juliet wraps were applied with model airplane glue, and wrapped across the free edge and tucked under the bottom edge of the nail. Juliet Wraps were the precursor of today's silk and linen wraps and provided a booming business for many nail technicians until the mid 1970's, when artificial nail enhancements completely took over the industry. Juliet wraps are also credited with establishing the now familiar bi-monthly maintenance appointments.

Until plastic nail tips became widely distributed in the early 1970's, human nail clippings were used to restore length to broken nails. When clients broke nails, they were asked to bring their separated nail tips to their nail appointments for reattachment. Because broken nails were often shattered or lost, nail technicians carefully collected client nail clippings. These clippings were filed into the proper shape, attached to the clients' natural nails with glue, and then strengthened with either a Juliet paper wrap or (later) a tough plastic strip.

In the mid-1970's, plastic nail tips became widely available, along with artificial nail enhancements that were originally made from porcelain and purchased from the dental industry. The practice of using porcelain was quickly banned, and the acrylic nail business was born.

The original acrylic formulations were difficult to apply, required vigorous filing, discolored easily, and had a tendency to lift away from the nail plate. By comparison, today's formulations are nothing short of modern marvels! The same holds true of nail tips that have evolved from being straight, unnatural-looking, and difficult to fit, to the natural, easy-fitting tips we have today.

Jeff Pink, American nail icon and founder of Orly nail care products, created the first iconic nail look in 1975, when he introduced the original French Manicure , which is characterized by natural looking nail beds and clean white tips. Mr. Pink is also credited with creating ridge filler—a product that makes ridged nails appear smooth—and fiber nail strengtheners that add strength to brittle, flexible and peeling nails.

21st Century

Today, hairstylists have far gentler, no-fade hair color, and estheticians can noticeably rejuvenate the face, as well as keep disorders such as sunspots and mild acne at bay. The beauty industry has also entered the age of specialization, where cosmetologists frequently specialize in either hair color or haircutting; estheticians specialize in esthetic or medical-esthetic services; and nail technicians can either offer a full array of services, or specialize in artificial nail enhancements, natural nail care, or even pedicures.

In terms of products, nail technicians now work with advanced acrylic (methacrylate), UV-light and no-light gel artificial nail enhancement products that never yellow, are much easier to apply, and are far more durable than formulations available just 10 years ago. Silk and linen wraps have become tougher and far more natural looking. Unlike all but the last few years of the 20th century, when the most beneficial nail service was a hot oil manicure, there are now a bevy of professional products to promote beautiful hands and feet.

Nail polish formulations have also evolved to embody chip-resistant, fade-resistant characteristics that retain a lustrous finish for up to two weeks. Manicuring implements have also reached a zenith in terms of ergonomics and performance, and the number of natural nail services and products available on the professional market is both staggering and exciting.

Since the late 1980's, the salon industry has evolved to include day spas, a name that was first coined by beauty legend Noel DeCaprio. Day spas now represent an excellent employment opportunity for nail technicians who wish to do in-depth manicures and pedicures that use sophisticated natural-based products with beneficial botanical extracts and essential oils. Men's-only specialty spas and barber spas have also grown in popularity, providing new opportunities for men's nail care specialists. The pedicure phenomenon has also catapulted the nail care industry into the forefront of beauty. Because our culture now views nail care as an essential part of grooming, even moderately priced family salons now typically employ nail technicians. All of these areas of growth combined have created a job surplus, making nail technicians one of the most sought-after practitioners in the beauty industry.

CAREER PATHS FOR A NAIL TECHNICIAN

To become part of this exciting and growing profession, make the most out of your school experience, eagerly embrace new information, push the limits of your creativity, and explore all your career options to find out which choices are right for you.

Nail Technician

Today, clients are eagerly requesting a variety of services that require a combination of skills. Natural nail services—luxurious manicures and pedicures, as well as natural nail-strengthening treatments—acrylic nail enhancements, the latest gel nail services, and silk nail wraps are all very popular in salons and day spas (Figure 1–1).

Salon Management

If business is your calling, you will find that management opportunities in the salon and spa environment are quite diverse. They include inventory manager, department head, educator, special events manager (promotions),

Figure 1–1 The demand for nail services has quadrupled over the past 5 years.

assistant manager, and general manager. With experience, you can also add "salon owner" to this list of career possibilities. To ensure your success, it is wise to enroll in business classes to learn more about managing products, departments, and, above all, people.

While you will most likely begin your career in a salon, your career choices do not end there. Just a few career possibilities outside the salon follow:

○ Product educator for a manufacturer or distributor

○ Distributor sales representative

○ Freelance editorial nail technician for photo shoots, film, and more

○ Beauty school instructor and, eventually, supervisor of a school

○ Retail sales and management

Beyond defining your area of expertise, you must also decide whether you want to work in one or more of the following environments in your career:

○ Nail salon

○ Full-service salon (hair, skin, and nail services)

○ Day spa (skin, body, nail, and hair services that emphasize beauty and wellness) (Figure 1–2)

To learn more about all types of salon business models, see Chapter 20. There you will find a wealth of choices, including national and regional chains, and independent opportunities.

Figure 1–2 A day spa may offer nail, hair, body, and skin services.

A BRIGHT FUTURE

Clearly, the field of cosmetology has broadened to encompass areas of specialization including esthetics and nail technology. As the cosmetology industry continues to grow, opportunities for professionals also grow. To make each day in school positively impact your future, focus on your studies, read trade publications cover to cover, become a member of relevant trade associations, and attend workshops outside of school. Remember, your license will unlock countless doors, but it is your personal dedication and passion that will fuel your career.

REVIEW **QUESTIONS**

1. What are the origins of appearance enhancement?
2. Name the advancements made in cosmetology during the 19th, 20th, and early 21st centuries.
3. List some of the career opportunities available to licensed nail technicians.

CHAPTER **GLOSSARY**

cosmetology	The art and science of beautifying and improving the skin, nails, and hair, and the study of cosmetics and their applications.

Life Skills

CHAPTER OUTLINE

- The Psychology of Success
- Motivation and Self-Management
- Managing Your Career
- Goal Setting
- Time Management
- Study Skills
- Ethics
- Personality Development and Attitude

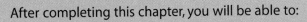

LEARNING OBJECTIVES

After completing this chapter, you will be able to:

1. List the principles that contribute to personal and professional success.

2. Explain the concept of self-management.

3. Create a mission statement.

4. Explain how to set long- and short-term goals.

5. Discuss the most effective ways to manage time.

6. Describe good study habits.

7. Define ethics.

8. List the characteristics of a healthy, positive attitude.

KEY **TERMS**

Page number indicates where in the chapter the term is used.

W hile going through beauty school has its own set of challenges, staying on course for your entire career can be difficult without having great life skills. This is particularly true of cosmetology since the hard-and-fast rules that apply to more structured industries are frequently absent in the salon business. By nature, the salon is a creative workplace where you are expected to exercise your artistic talent. It is also a highly social atmosphere that requires strong self-discipline and excellent people skills. Besides making a solid connection with each client, you must always stay focused, and feel both competent and enthusiastic about taking care of every client's need—no matter how you feel, or how many hours you have already worked. Your livelihood, as well as your own personal feelings of success, depend on how well you do this.

There are a great many life skills that can lead to a more satisfying and productive beauty career. Some of the most important life skills include:

Being genuinely caring and helpful to others.

Successfully adapting to different situations.

Sticking to a goal and seeing a job to completion.

Being consistent in your work.

Developing a deep reservoir of common sense.

Making good friends.

Feeling good about yourself.

Maintaining a cooperative attitude.

Defining your own code of ethics, and living within your definition.

Approaching all your work with a strong sense of responsibility.

Mastering techniques that will help you become more organized.

Having a sense of humor to bring you through difficult situations.

Acquiring one of the greatest virtues: patience.

Always striving for excellence.

Rules for Success

To be successful, you must take ownership of your education. While your instructors can create motivational circumstances and an environment to assist you in the learning process, the ultimate responsibility for learning is *yours*. To get the greatest benefits from your education, commit yourself to the following "rules" that will take you a long way down the road of success:

- Attend all classes.

- Arrive for class early.

- Have all necessary materials ready.

- Listen attentively to your instructor.

- Highlight important points.

- Take notes for later review.

- Pay close attention during summary and review sessions.

- When something is not clear, ask, ask, ask.

Continually seek further education. Never stop learning. The cosmetology industry is always changing. There are always new trends, techniques, products, and information. Read industry magazines, books, and attend trade shows and advanced educational classes throughout your career.

THE PSYCHOLOGY OF SUCCESS

Are you passionate about studying? Do you see yourself sustaining this passion 1 year, 5 years, or even 10 years from now? While beauty school is definitely challenging, it becomes much easier when you put that extra amount of effort, enthusiasm, and excitement into your studies. If your talent is not fueled by the passion necessary to sustain you over the course of your career, you can have all the talent in the world and still not be successful (Figure 2–1).

Guidelines for Success

Defining success is a very personal thing. There are some basic principles, however, that form the foundation of all personal and business success. You can begin your path to success right now by examining and putting these principles into practice.

Build self-esteem. Self-esteem is based on inner strength and begins with trusting your ability to reach your goals. It is essential that you begin working on improving your self-esteem while you are still a student.

Visualize. Imagine yourself working in your dream salon, competently handling clients, and feeling at ease and happy with your situation. The more you practice visualization, the easier you can turn the possibilities in your life into realities.

Figure 2–1 Loving your work is critical to your success.

Figure 2–2 Spend time on the things you do well.

Build on your strengths. Practice doing whatever it is that helps you maintain a positive self-image. If you are good at doing something (e.g., playing the guitar, running, cooking, gardening, or singing), the time you invest in this activity will allow you to feel good about yourself (Figure 2–2). Also remember that there may be things you are good at that you cannot see. You could be a good listener, for instance, or a caring and considerate friend.

Be kind to yourself. Put a stop to self-critical or negative thoughts that can work against you. If you make a mistake, tell yourself that it is okay and you will do your best next time.

Define success for yourself. Do not depend on other people's definitions of success; be a success in your own eyes. What is right for your father or sister, for instance, may not be right for you.

Practice new behaviors. Because creating success is a skill, you can help develop it by practicing positive new behaviors such as speaking with confidence, standing tall, or using good grammar.

Keep your personal life separate from your work. Talking about yourself and others at work is personally counterproductive, and causes the whole salon to suffer.

Keep your energy up. Successful nail technicians do not run themselves ragged, nor do they eat, sleep, and drink beauty. They take care of their personal needs by spending time with family and friends, having hobbies, enjoying recreational activities, and so on.

Respect others. Make a point of relating to everyone you know with a conscious feeling of respect. Exercise good manners with others by using words like "please," "thank you," and "excuse me." Do not interrupt people and practice being a good listener.

Stay productive. There are three bad habits that can keep you from maintaining peak performance: (1) **procrastination**, (2) **perfectionism**, and (3) lack of a **game plan**. You will see an almost instant improvement when you work on eliminating these troublesome habits.

○ **Procrastination** is putting off until tomorrow what you can do today. This destructive, yet common habit is a characteristic of poor study habits ("I'll study tomorrow"). It may also be a symptom of taking on too much, which, in turn, is a symptom of faulty organization.

○ **Perfectionism** is the unhealthy compulsion to do things perfectly. Success is not measured by always doing things right. In fact, someone who never makes a mistake may not be trying hard enough. A better definition of success is to not give up, even when things get really tough.

○ Lacking a **game plan.** Having a game plan is the conscious act of planning your life, instead of just letting things happen. While an overall game plan is usually organized into large blocks of time (5 or 10 years ahead), it is just as important to set daily, monthly, and yearly goals. Where do you want to be in your career 5 years from now? What do you have to do this week, this month, and this year to get closer to your goal?

MOTIVATION AND SELF-MANAGEMENT

Motivation propels you to do something; self-management is a well-thought-out process for the long haul. When you are hungry, for example, you are motivated to eat. But it is self-management that helps you to decide how you will get food. A motivated student finds it much easier to learn. The best motivation for you to learn comes from an inner desire to grow your skills as a professional—a lifelong pursuit that is motivated by the ever-changing world of professional beauty.

If you are personally drawn to cosmetology, then you are likely to be interested in the material you will be studying in school. If your motivation comes from some external source—for instance, your parents, friends, or a vocational counselor—you will have a difficult time finishing school and jump-starting your beauty career. To achieve success, you need more than an external push; you must feel a sense of personal excitement and a good reason for staying the course. You are the one in charge of managing your own life and learning. To do this successfully, you need good self-management skills.

Your Creative Capability

One self-management skill we can draw on is creativity. Creativity means having a talent such as painting, acting, or doing artificial nail enhancements. Creativity is also an unlimited inner resource of ideas and solutions. To enhance your creativity, keep these guidelines in mind:

Do not be self-critical. Criticism blocks the creative mind from exploring ideas and discovering solutions to challenges.

Do not look to others for motivation. Tapping into your own creativity will be the best way to manage your own success.

Change your vocabulary. Build a positive vocabulary by using active problem solving words like "explore," "analyze," "determine," and so on.

Do not try to go it alone. In today's hectic and pressured world, many talented people find that they are more creative in an environment where people work together and share ideas. This is where the value of a strong salon team comes into play (Figure 2–3).

MANAGING YOUR CAREER

No matter how creative, talented, or motivated you are, as you navigate your beauty career, you will come up against shallow spots, rocks, swift currents, and even an occasional iceberg. Knowing how to manage your career will make all the difference in staying afloat.

Figure 2–3 Build strong relationships for support.

Figure 2–4 An example of a personal mission statement.

Design a Mission Statement

Every successful business has a business plan. An essential part of this plan is the **mission statement** that establishes the values the business wants to live by, as well as future goals (Figure 2–4). If you are going to succeed in life, you also need a well thought-out sense of purpose and a reason for being.

Try to prepare a mission statement in one or two sentences that communicates who you are, and what you want for your life. One example of a simple, yet thoughtful mission statement is: "I am dedicated to pursuing a successful career with dignity, honesty, and integrity." Whatever you want for your future will be based on the mission statement you make now. It will point you in a solid direction, and help you feel secure when things are temporarily not working out as planned. For reinforcement, keep a copy of your mission statement where you can see it and read it every day.

GOAL SETTING

Some people never have a fixed goal in their minds. They go through life one day at a time without really deciding what they want, where they can find it, or how they are going to live their lives once they get it. They drift from one activity to the next with no direction. Does this describe you? Or do you have drive, desire, and a dream? If so, do you have a reasonable idea of how to go about meeting your goal?

Goal setting helps you decide what you want out of your life. When you know what you want, you can draw a circle around your destination and chart the best course to get you there. By mapping out your goal, you will see where you need to focus your attention, and what you need to learn in order to fulfill your dreams.

How Goal Setting Works

There are two types of goals: short term and long term. An example of a short-term goal is to get through a competency exam successfully. Another short-term goal would be your graduation from cosmetology school. Short-term goals are usually those you wish to accomplish in a year or less.

Long-term goals are measured in larger sections of time such as 5 years, 10 years, or even longer. An example of a long-term goal is telling yourself that in 5 years you will own your own salon.

Once you have organized your thinking around your goals and written them down in "short-term" and "long-term" columns, divide each set of goals into workable segments. In this way, reaching your goals will not seem out of sight or overwhelming. For example, one of your biggest goals at the moment should be getting your license to practice your chosen career path. At first, the prospect of getting this license might seem to require a huge amount of time and effort. When you separate this goal into short-term goals (such as going to class on time, completing homework assignments, and mastering techniques), you begin to see how you can accomplish each one without too much difficulty.

The important thing to remember about goal setting is to have a plan and re-examine it often to make sure that you are staying on track. Even after successful people have accumulated fame, fortune, and respect, they still set goals for themselves. While they may adjust their goals and action plans as they go along, they never lose sight of the fact that their goals are what keep them going.

TIME MANAGEMENT

Many experts have researched how to make time more manageable. One thing they all agree on is that each of us has an "inner organizer." When we pay attention to our natural rhythms, we can learn how to manage our time most efficiently and reach our goals faster and with less frustration. Here are some tips from the experts.

○ Learn to **prioritize** by making a list of tasks that need to be done in the order of most-to-least important.

○ When designing your own time management system, make sure it will work for you. For example, if you are a person who needs a fair amount of flexibility, schedule in some blocks of unstructured time.

○ Never take on more than you can handle. Learn to say "no" firmly but kindly, and mean it. You will find it easier to complete your tasks if you limit your activities, and not spread yourself too thin.

○ Learn problem-solving techniques that will save you time and needless frustration.

○ Give yourself some down time whenever you are frustrated, overwhelmed, worried, or feeling guilty about something. You lose valuable time and energy when you are in a negative state of mind.

Figure 2–5 Keep a schedule for yourself and be sure to refer to it on a frequent basis.

Unfortunately, there may be situations—like being in the classroom—when you cannot get up and walk away. To handle these difficult times, try practicing the technique of deep breathing. Just fill your lungs as much as you can and exhale slowly. After about 5 to 10 breaths, you will find that you have calmed down, and your inner balance has been restored.

○ Carry a notepad or an organizer with you at all times. You never know when a good idea might strike. Write it down before it slips your mind!

○ Make daily, weekly, and monthly schedules for study and exam times, and any other regular commitments. Plan your leisure time around these commitments, and not the other way around (Figure 2–5).

○ Identify the times of day when you are highly energetic, and when you just want to relax. Plan your schedule accordingly.

○ Reward yourself with a special treat or activity for work well done and time managed efficiently.

○ Do not neglect physical activity. Remember that exercise and recreation stimulate clear thinking and planning.

○ Schedule at least one additional block of free time each day. This will be your hedge against events that come up unexpectedly like car trouble, baby-sitting problems, a friend in need, and so on.

○ Understand the value of to-do lists for the day and week. They can help you prioritize your tasks and activities, which is key to organizing your time efficiently (Figure 2–6).

○ Make time management a habit.

STUDY SKILLS

If you find studying overwhelming, focus on small tasks at a time. For example, instead of trying to study for 3 hours at a stretch and suffering a personal defeat when you fold after 40 minutes, set the bar lower by studying in smaller chunks of time. If your mind tends to wander in class, try writing down key words or phrases as your instructor discusses them. Any time you lose your focus, you can stay after class and ask questions based on your notes.

Another way to get a better handle on studying is to find other students who are open to being helpful and supportive. The more you discuss new material with others, the more comfortable you will become with it, and the more successful you will be. If possible, study together (Figure 2–7).

Establishing Good Study Habits

Part of developing consistently good study habits is knowing where, when, and how to study.

◎ focus on...

THE GOAL

Determine whether your goal-setting plan is a good one by asking yourself these key questions:

• Are there specific skills I will need to learn in order to meet my goals?

• Is the information I need to reach my goals readily available?

• Would I be willing to seek out a mentor or a coach to enhance my learning?

• What is the best method or approach that will allow me to accomplish my goals?

• Am I always open to finding better ways of putting my plan into practice?

Where

○ Establish a comfortable, quiet spot where you can study uninterrupted.

○ Have everything you need—books, pens, paper, proper lighting, and so on—before you begin studying.

○ Remain as alert as possible by sitting upright. Reclining will make you sleepy!

When

○ Start out by estimating how much study time you need.

○ Study when you feel most energetic and motivated.

○ Make good use of your time by planning to study while you are waiting in the doctor's office, taking a bus across town, and so on.

How

○ Study a section of a chapter at a time, instead of the entire chapter at once.

○ Make a note of key words and phrases as you go along.

○ Test yourself on each section to ensure that you understand and remember the key points of each chapter.

Remember that every effort you make to follow through on your education is an investment in your future. The progress you make with your learning will increase your confidence and self-esteem across the board. In fact, when you have mastered a range of information and techniques, your self-esteem will soar right along with your grades.

To do today

Laundry
Workout - lift weights today?
Call Marcy - set up a time to study
Ask teacher about the chemistry project!!!
Do homework 3 - 5:30
Movie tonight with Sharon and Joey

Figure 2–6 An example of a to-do list.

Figure 2–7 Studying with a friend can be effective and fun.

focus on...

PROFESSIONAL ETHICS

Ethics are the moral principles by which we live and work. In cosmetology, each state board sets the ethical standards for sanitation and safety that all nail technicians working in that state must follow. In the salon setting, ethics also entail the role you assume with your clients and fellow employees. When your actions show that you are respectful, courteous, and helpful, you are behaving in an ethical manner.

Here are five ways to show that you are an ethical person:

1. Provide skilled and competent services.

2. Be honest, courteous, and sincere.

3. Never share what clients have told you privately with others—even your closest friend.

4. Participate in ongoing education and stay on track with new information, techniques, and skills.

5. Always give correct information to clients about treatments and any products that they may want to purchase.

ETHICS

Self-care. Many service providers suffer from stress and eventual burnout because they focus most of their energy and time on other people and very little on themselves. If you are to be truly helpful to others, it is essential to take care of yourself. Try the self-care test to see how you rate (Figure 2–8).

Integrity. Maintain your integrity by making sure that your behavior and actions match your values. For example, if you believe that it is unethical to sell products just to make money, then do not do so. On the other hand, if you feel that a client needs products and additional services, it would be unethical not to give the client that information.

Discretion. Do not share your personal problems with clients. Likewise, never *breach confidentiality* by repeating personal information that clients have shared with you.

Communication. Your responsibility and ethical behavior extend to your communication with your customers and the other people with whom you work.

The Self-Care Test

Some people know intuitively when they need to stop, take a break, or even take a day off. Other people forget when to eat. You can judge how well you take care of yourself by noting how you feel physically, emotionally, and mentally. Here are some questions to ask yourself to see how you rate on the self-care scale.

1. Do you wait until you are exhausted before you stop working?
2. Do you forget to eat nutritious food and substitute junk food on the fly?
3. Do you say you will exercise and then put off starting a program?
4. Do you have poor sleep habits?
5. Are you constantly nagging yourself about not being good enough?
6. Are your relationships with people filled with conflict?
7. When you think about the future are you unclear about the direction you will take?
8. Do you spend most of your spare time watching TV?
9. Have you been told you are too stressed and yet you ignore these concerns?
10. Do you waste time and then get angry with yourself?

Score 5 points for each yes. A score of 0-15 says that you take pretty good care of yourself, but you would be wise to examine those questions you answered yes to. A score of 15-30 indicates that you need to rethink your priorities. A score of 30-50 is a strong statement that you are neglecting yourself and may be headed for high stress and burnout. Reviewing the suggestions in these chapters will help you get back on track.

Figure 2–8 Self-care test.

Some occupations require less interaction with people than others. For example, if you are a computer programmer, you may not be exposed to all different sorts of people every day. As a nail technician however, dealing with people from all walks of life is a major aspect of your work. It is useful, therefore, to have some sense of how different personalities and attitudes can affect your performance.

PERSONALITY DEVELOPMENT AND ATTITUDE

Refer often to the following ingredients of a healthy, well-developed attitude to see if they match your recipe.

Diplomacy. Being assertive is a good thing because it helps people know where you are coming from. However, it is a short step from being assertive to becoming aggressive, and even bullying. Take your attitude temperature to see how well you practice the art of tact. Being tactful means being straightforward, not critical. This is called "diplomacy."

Tone of voice. Here is a good example of an inborn personality trait that you can modify by softening the sound of your voice and speaking

Figure 2–9 Being receptive is an important personal skill.

 focus on...

THE WHOLE PERSON

An individual's personality is the sum total of her or his inborn characteristics, attitudes, and behavioral traits. While you may not be able to alter most of your inborn characteristics, you certainly can work on your attitude. This is a process that continues throughout your life. In both your business and personal life, a pleasing attitude gains more associates, clients, and friends.

clearly. Also, if you have a positive attitude, you can deliver your words more pleasantly.

Emotional stability. Our emotions are important. Some people, though, have no control over their feelings, and may express themselves excessively or inappropriately. When they are happy, they get almost frantic; when they are angry, they fly into a rage. Learning how to handle a confrontation, as well as sharing how you feel without going overboard, are important indicators of maturity.

Sensitivity. Sensitivity is a combination of understanding, empathy, and acceptance. Being sensitive means being compassionate and responsive to other people.

Values and goals. Neither values nor goals are inborn characteristics; we acquire them as we move through life. They show us how to behave, and what to aim toward.

Receptivity. To be receptive means to be interested in other people, and to be responsive to their opinions, feelings, and ideas. Receptivity involves taking the time to really listen, instead of pretending to do so (Figure 2–9).

Communication skills. People with a warm, caring personality have an easy time talking about themselves and listening to what others have to say. When they want something, they can ask for it clearly and directly.

REVIEW **QUESTIONS**

1. How do you personally define success?

2. List and explain 10 basic guidelines for personal and professional success.

3. What are three common habits that can prevent people from being productive?

4. List at least three steps that you can take to enhance your creativity.

5. In one to five sentences, write a mission statement for yourself.

6. List three short-term and three long-term goals you have set for yourself.

7. Define "game plan" and how it can keep your career on target.

8. Why is it so important to learn how to manage your time?

9. List seven characteristics of a healthy, well-developed attitude.

10. List the qualities and characteristics of professional ethics.

CHAPTER **GLOSSARY**

ethics	Principles of good character, proper conduct, and moral judgment, expressed through personality, human relation skills, and professional image.
game plan	The conscious act of planning your life rather than just letting things happen.
goal setting	The identification of long- and short-term goals.
mission statement	A statement that sets forth the values that an individual or institution lives by and that establishes future goals.
perfectionism	A compulsion to do things perfectly.
prioritize	To make a list of tasks that need to be done in the order of most to least important.
procrastination	Putting off until tomorrow what you can do today.

Your Professional Image

LEARNING OBJECTIVES

After completing this chapter, you will be able to:

1. Understand professional hygiene.

2. Explain the concept of dressing for success.

3. Use appropriate methods to ensure personal health and well-being.

4. Demonstrate an understanding of ergonomic principles and ergonomically correct postures and movement.

KEY **TERMS**

Page number indicates where in the chapter the term is used.

ergonomics
pg. 31

physical presentation
pg. 31

professional image
pg. 30

stress
pg. 31

personal hygiene
pg. 28

Because you are in the image business, how you look and present yourself has a big influence on whether you will be successful working in your chosen career path within the field of cosmetology. If you are talking style, then you need to look stylish; if you are advising your clients about makeup, then your makeup must be current and beautifully applied. If you are recommending hand care services, it is critical that your hands and nails are well manicured. When your appearance and the way that you conduct yourself are in harmony with the beauty business, your chances of being successful in any area of cosmetology increase by as much as 100 percent! After all, when you look great, your clients will assume that you can make them look great, too (Figure 3–1).

Figure 3–1 Project a professional image.

BEAUTY AND WELLNESS

Personal Hygiene

Being well groomed begins with looking and smelling fresh. This is especially important in the beauty business where practitioners are frequently only inches away from their clients during services. It is a given that you should shower or bathe every day, use deodorant before going to work, and generally be neat and clean. Beyond that, though, there are special considerations when working in a salon.

One weak moment of drinking coffee right before performing a service, for instance, or wearing something that needs laundering because you did not plan ahead, could spell disaster. Rather than telling you that you smell offensive, most clients will simply not return for another service. Equally distressing, they will typically tell three of their friends about the bad experience they had while sitting in your chair.

Personal hygiene is the daily maintenance of cleanliness by practicing good sanitary habits (Figure 3–2). Working as a stylist behind the chair, or doing makeup, nail care, or skin care means that you must be extremely meticulous about your hygiene.

One of the best ways to ensure that you always smell fresh and clean is to create a hygiene pack to keep in your station or locker. Your hygiene pack should include:

Toothbrush and toothpaste

Floss

Mouthwash

Deodorant or antiperspirant

Sanitizing hand wipes or liquid to freshen your hands between clients

Your hygiene pack will be useful in following these guidelines:

Wash your hands throughout the day as required, including at the beginning of each service.

Use deodorant or antiperspirant.

Brush and floss your teeth, and use mouthwash or breath mints throughout the day as needed.

Do self-checks periodically to ensure that you smell and look fresh.

If you smoke cigarettes, *do not* smoke during work hours. If you cannot wait until after work, make sure to smoke in a well-ventilated area at least 30 minutes before seeing your next client. Always brush your teeth, use mouthwash, and wash your hands after smoking if you are still servicing clients!

Figure 3–2 Practice meticulous personal hygiene every day.

LOOKING GOOD

Naturally, in the line of work that you have chosen, an extremely important element of your image is having well-groomed hair, skin, and nails that serve as an advertisement for your commitment to professional beauty. Make sure that you:

o Put thought into your appearance every day.

o Keep your haircut and color in tip-top shape.

o Keep your skin well groomed. Determine the best length and grooming for your nails and meticulously maintain their appearance.

o Change your style frequently, or as often as you feel comfortable, to keep up with trends.

Personal Grooming

Many salon owners and managers view appearance, personality, and poise as being just as important as technical knowledge and skills. One of the most vital aspects of good personal grooming is the careful maintenance of your wardrobe. First and foremost, your clothes must be clean—not simply free of the dirt that you can see, but stain free, a feat that is sometimes difficult to achieve in a salon environment. Because you are constantly coming into contact with products and chemicals that can stain fabric in a nanosecond, it is a good idea to invest in an apron or smock to wear while handling such products. Be mindful about spills and drips when using chemicals, and avoid leaning on counters in the work area—particularly in the dispensary.

safety caution!

PERFUME

Many salons have a no-fragrance policy for staff members during work hours because a significant number of people are sensitive or allergic to a variety of chemicals, including perfume oils. Whether or not your salon has a no-fragrance policy, perfume should be saved for after work.

Figure 3–3 Be guided by your salon's dress code.

Dress for Success

If you want to go out on the weekend and wear something wild and crazy, this is your choice. But while you are at your place of employment, you will need to consider whether your wardrobe selection expresses a **professional image** that is consistent with the image of the salon. Common sense as well should rule when it comes to choosing clothes to wear at work. When shopping for work clothes, you should always visualize how you would look in them while performing professional client services. Is the image you present one that is acceptable to your clients?

To a large degree, your clothing should reflect the fashions of the season by embodying current styles, colors, textures, and so forth. Depending on where you work, you may be encouraged to wear stylish torn jeans and faded tees, or they may be expressly forbidden. Just remember to "tune in" to your salon's energy and clientele so that you can make the best clothing choices that promote your career as a promising stylist nail technician.

You should always be guided by your salon's dress code with regard to these matters, but the following guidelines are generally appropriate (Figure 3–3).

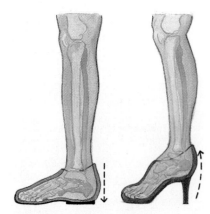

Figure 3–4 Working in high heels can throw off the body's balance.

- Make sure that your clothing is clean, fresh, and in step with fashion.

- Choose clothing that is functional, as well as stylish.

- Accessorize your outfits, but make sure that your jewelry does not clank and jingle while working. This can be irritating to fellow professionals and drive clients to distraction.

- Wear shoes that are comfortable, have a low heel, and good support. Ill-fitting shoes, and any type with high heels, are not the best choices to wear when performing pedicures and portable services within the salon. (Figure 3–4).

The Art of Makeup

Makeup is an exciting category for beauty professionals. It helps promote your professional image, and is an area where some of your most lucrative sales can be made. You should always use makeup to accentuate your best features, and mask your less flattering ones. With that said, it is vital to always wear makeup at work. A freshly scrubbed face may look great for a leisurely day at the beach, but it does nothing to promote your image as a beauty professional while at work. Likewise, unless you are working in a trendy urban salon, things like heavily blackened eyes are generally best left to the club scene. Let the salon's image be your guide on the right makeup choices to wear for work (Figure 3–5).

YOUR PHYSICAL PRESENTATION

Posture

Good posture is a very important part of your **physical presentation**. It shows off your figure to its best advantage, and conveys an image of confidence. From a health standpoint, it can also prevent fatigue and many other physical problems. When you work within the field of cosmetology, sitting improperly can put a great deal of **stress** on your neck, shoulders, back, and legs. Having good posture, on the other hand, allows you to get through your day feeling good, and doing your best work (Figure 3–6).

Some guidelines for achieving and maintaining good work posture follow:

o Keep the neck elongated and balanced directly above the shoulders.

o Lift your upper body so that your chest is out and up (do not slouch).

o Hold your shoulders level and relaxed, not scrunched up.

o Sit with your back straight.

o Pull your abdomen in so that it is flat.

Ergonomics

Each year, hundreds of cosmetology professionals report musculoskeletal disorders, including carpal tunnel syndrome and back injuries. Beauty professionals expose their bodies to potential injury on a daily basis. Many have to stand or sit all day and hold their bodies in unnatural positions for long periods of time. They are susceptible to problems of the hands, wrists, shoulders, neck, back, feet, and legs. If not attended to, these problems can become career threatening.

Prevention is the key to alleviating these problems. An awareness of your body posture and movements, coupled with better work habits and proper tools and equipment, will enhance your health and comfort. An understanding of **ergonomics** is useful as well. Ergonomics is the study of how a workplace can best be designed for comfort, safety, efficiency, and productivity. It attempts to fit the job to the person, rather than the other

Figure 3–5 Expertly applied makeup is part of having a professional image.

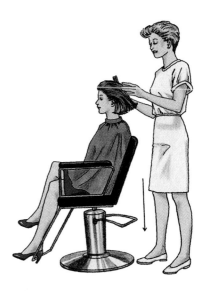

Figure 3–6 Good physical presentation.

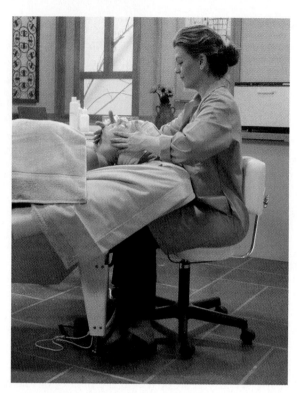

Figure 3–7 Proper positioning of the client on the facial bed.

Figure 3–8 Improper haircutting position.

Figure 3–9 Correct wrist and hand position for haircutting.

way around. One example is a nail technician's stool that can be raised or lowered to accommodate different heights. Another is having ergonomically designed nippers and clippers.

Stressful repetitive motions have a cumulative effect on the muscles and joints. Monitor yourself as you work to see if you are:

○ Gripping or squeezing implements too tightly.

○ Bending the wrist up or down constantly when using the tools of your profession.

○ Holding your arms away from your body as you work.

○ Holding your elbows more than a 60-degree angle away from your body for extended periods of time (Figure 3–7).

○ Bending forward and/or twisting your body to get closer to your client.

Try the following measures to avoid some of the problems discussed above:

Keep your wrists in a straight or neutral position as much as possible (Figure 3–8 and 3–9).

When giving a manicure, do not reach across the table; have the client extend her hand across the table to you (Figure 3–10).

Use ergonomically designed implements.

Keep your back and neck straight.

If you work in an environment that has any physical discomfort built into it, as most places do, try to counter the problem by including regular

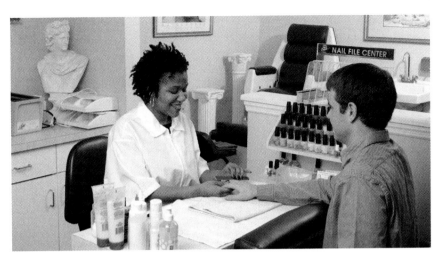

Figure 3–10 Follow proper ergonomic techniques when giving nail services.

stretching intervals to break up the repetitiveness of the motions you use. And, in every aspect of your work, always put your health first and then the task at hand. It will serve you well in the beauty business, and ensure a long, injury-free career.

REVIEW **QUESTIONS**

1. Define image. List the elements of professional image.
2. List three basic habits of personal hygiene.
3. Identify what is included in a "hygiene pack." Where is it kept?
4. How often should you freshen up throughout the day?
5. List the general guidelines of dressing for success.
6. What is the role of posture in good health?
7. Assess your own work posture. How can it be improved?
8. Define the term "ergonomics."
9. List ergonomic features for tools.
10. List ergonomic features for equipment.

CHAPTER **GLOSSARY**

ergonomics	Study of how a workplace can best be designed for comfort, safety, efficiency, and productivity.
personal hygiene	Daily maintenance of cleanliness by practicing good sanitary habits.
physical presentation	Person's physical posture, walk, and movements.
professional image	Impression projected by a person engaged in any profession, consisting of outward appearance and conduct exhibited in the workplace.
stress	Inability to cope with a threat, real or imagined, to our well-being, which results in a series of responses and adaptations by our minds and bodies; tension caused by a situation.

Communicating for Success

chapter **4**

LEARNING OBJECTIVES

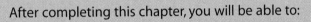

After completing this chapter, you will be able to:

1. List the golden rules of human relations.

2. Explain the importance of effective communication.

3. Conduct a successful client consultation.

4. Handle delicate communications with your clients.

5. Build open lines of communication with coworkers and salon managers.

KEY TERMS

Page number indicates where in the chapter the term is used.

clarify	**client consultation**	**communication**	**reflective listening**
pg. 46	pg. 41–46	pg. 39	pg. 45

D o you have outstanding technical skills? Artistic talents? If you do, you are definitely on your way to becoming successful in your chosen career path within the field of cosmetology.. It is important to realize, though, that technical and artistic skills can only take you so far. In order to have a thriving clientele, you must also master the art of communication (Figure 4–1). Effective human relations and communication skills build lasting client relationships, aid in your growth as a salon practitioner, and help prevent misunderstandings and unnecessary tension in the workplace.

HUMAN RELATIONS

No matter where you work, you will not always get along with everyone. It is not possible to always understand what people need, even when you know them well. Even if you do think you understand what people want, you cannot always be sure that you will satisfy them. This can lead to tension and misunderstanding.

The ability to understand people is the key to operating effectively in many professions. It is especially important in cosmetology where customer service is central to success. Most of your interactions will depend on your ability to communicate successfully with a wide range of people: your boss, coworkers, clients, and the different vendors who come into the salon to sell products. When you clearly understand the motives and needs of others, you are in a better position to do your job professionally and easily.

The best way to understand others is to begin with a firm understanding of yourself. When you know what makes you tick, it is easier to appreciate others and to help them get what they need. Basically, we all have the same needs. When we are treated with respect and people listen to us, we feel good about them and ourselves. When we create an atmosphere where customers and staff have confidence in us, we will get the respect we deserve. Good relationships are built on mutual respect and understanding. Here is a brief look at the basics of human relations along with some practical tips for dealing with situations that you are likely to encounter.

○ A fundamental factor in human relations has to do with how secure we are feeling. When we feel secure, we are happy, calm, and confident, and we act in a cooperative and trusting manner. When we feel

Figure 4–1 Communication is part of building lasting practitioner/client relationships.

insecure, we become worried, anxious, overwhelmed, perhaps angry and suspicious, and usually we do not behave very well. We might be uncooperative, hostile, or withdrawn.

o Human beings are social animals. When we feel secure, we like to interact with other people. We enjoy giving our opinions, we take pleasure from having people help us, and we take pride in our ability to help others. When people feel secure with us, they are a joy to be with. You can help people feel secure around you by being respectful, trustworthy, and honest.

o No matter how secure you are, there will be times when you will be faced with people and situations that are difficult to handle. You may already have had such experiences. There are always some people who create conflict wherever they go. They can be rude, insensitive, or so full of themselves that being considerate just does not enter their minds. Even though you may wonder how anyone could be so unfeeling, just try to remember that this person at this particular time feels insecure or he/she wouldn't be acting this way.

To become skilled in human relations, learn to make the best of situations that could otherwise drain both your time and your energy. Here are some good ways to handle the ups and downs of human relations.

Respond instead of reacting. A fellow was asked why he did not get angry when a driver cut him off. "Why should I let someone else dictate my emotions?" he replied. A wise fellow, don't you think? He might have even saved his own life by not reacting with "an eye for an eye" mentality.

Believe in yourself. When you do, you trust your judgment, uphold your own values, and stick to what you believe is right. It is easy to believe in yourself when you have a strong sense of self-worth. It comes with the knowledge that you are a good person and you deserve to be successful. Believing in yourself makes you feel strong enough to handle almost any situation in a calm, helpful manner.

Talk less, listen more. There is an old saying that we were given two ears and one mouth for a reason. You get a gold star in human relations when you listen more than you talk. When you are a good listener, you are fully attentive to what the other person is saying. If there is something you do not understand, ask a question to gain understanding.

Be attentive. Each client is different. Some are clear about what they want, others are aggressively demanding, while others may be hesitant. If you have an aggressive client, instead of trying to handle it by yourself, ask your manager for advice. You will likely be told that what usually calms difficult clients down is agreeing with them and then asking what you can do to make the service more to their liking. This approach is virtually guaranteed to work (Figure 4–2).

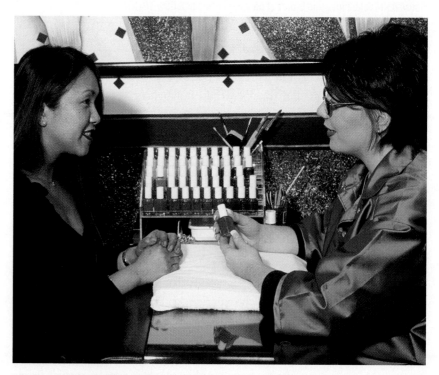

Figure 4–2 Be attentive to your client's needs.

Take your own temperature. If you are tired or upset about a personal problem, or have had an argument with a fellow student, you may be feeling down about yourself and wish you were anywhere but in school. If this feeling lasts a short time, you will be able to get back on track easily enough and there is no cause for alarm. If, however, you begin to notice certain chronic behaviors about yourself once you are in a job, pay careful attention to what is happening. An important part of being in a service profession is taking care of yourself first and resolving whatever conflicts are going on so that you can take care of your clients. Trust can be lost in a second without even knowing it—and, once lost, trust is almost impossible to regain.

To conclude, human relations can be rewarding or demoralizing. It all depends on how willing you are to give.

The Golden Rules of Human Relations

Keep the following guidelines in mind for a crash course in human relations that will always keep you in line and where you should be:

- Communicate from your heart; problem solve from your head.

- A smile is worth a million times more than a sneer.

- It is easy to make an enemy; it is harder to keep a friend.

- See what happens when you ask for help instead of just reacting.

- Show people you care by listening to them and trying to understand their point of view.

- Tell people how great they are (even when they are not acting so great).

- Being right is different from acting righteous.

- For every service you do for others, do not forget to do something for yourself.

- Laugh often.

- Show patience with other people's flaws.

- Build shared goals; be a team player and a partner to your clients.

- Always remember that listening is the best relationship builder.

COMMUNICATION BASICS

Communication is the act of successfully sharing information between two people, or groups of people so that it is effectively understood. You can communicate through words, voice inflections, facial expressions, body language and visual tools (e.g., a portfolio of your work). When you and your client are both communicating clearly about an upcoming service, your chances of pleasing that person soar.

Meeting and Greeting New Clients

One of the most important communications you will have with a client is the first time you meet that person. Be polite, genuinely friendly, and inviting (which you will continue to be in all your encounters), and remember that your clients are coming to you for services for which they are paying hard-earned cash (Figure 4–3). This means you need to court them every time they come to see you; otherwise, you may lose them to another nail technician or salon.

To earn clients' trust and loyalty, you need to:

o Always approach a new client with a smile on your face. If you are having a difficult day or have a problem of some sort, keep it to yourself. The time you are with your client is for her needs, not yours.

o Always introduce yourself. Names are powerful and they are meant to be used. Many clients have had the experience of being greeted

Figure 4–3 Welcome your client to the salon.

by the receptionist, ushered back to the service area, and when the service has been performed and the appointment is over, they have not learned the name of a single person.

o Set aside a few minutes to take new clients on a quick tour of the salon.

o Introduce them to people they may have interactions with while in the salon, including potential service providers for other services such as skin care or makeup.

o Be yourself. Do not try to trick your clients into thinking you are someone or something that you are not. Just be who you are. You will be surprised at how well this will work for you.

Intake Form

An intake form—also called a "client questionnaire" or "consultation card"—should be filled out by every new client prior to sitting at your nail station. Whether in the salon or in school, this form can prove to be extremely useful (Figure 4–4).

Some salon intake forms ask for a lot of detailed information, and some do not. In cosmetology school, the consultation form may be accompanied by a release statement in which the client acknowledges that the service is being provided by a student who is still learning. This helps protect the school and the student from any legal action by a client who may be unhappy with the service.

How to Use the Client Intake Form

The client intake form can be used from the moment a new client calls the salon to make an appointment. When scheduling the appointment, let her know that you and the salon will require some information before you can begin the service, and that it is important for her to arrive 15 minutes prior to her appointment time to fill out a brief form. You will also have to allow time in your schedule to do a 5-minute to 20-minute **client consultation**, depending on the type of service you will be performing and the needs of the client.

THE CLIENT CONSULTATION

The client consultation is the verbal communication that determines the desired results. It is the single most important part of any service and should always be done *before* beginning any part of the service. Some professionals skip the client consultation altogether, or they make time for it only on a client's first visit to the salon. These professionals are making a serious mistake. A consultation should be performed, to some degree, as part of every single service and salon visit. It keeps good communication going, and allows you to keep your clients looking current and feeling satisfied with your services.

Client Consultation Card

Dear Client,

Our sincerest hope is to serve you with the best hair care services you've ever received! We not only want you to be happy with today's visit but we also want to build a long-lasting relationship with you—we want to be your hair care salon. In order for us to do so, we would like to learn more about you, your hair care needs and your preferences. Please take a moment now to answer the questions below as completely and as accurately as possible.

Thank you, and we look forward to building a "beautiful" relationship!

Name: _____

Address: _____

Address: _____

Phone Number: (day)_____ (evening)_____

Sex: _____ Male   _____ Female   Age:_____

How did you hear about our salon?

If you were referred, who referred you?

Please answer the following questions in the space provided. Thanks!

1.   Approximately when was your last salon visit?

2.   In the past year have you had any of the following services either in or out of a salon? (Please indicate the date on which you had it.)

_____ Haircut   _____ Waxing (what type?)

_____ Hair color   _____ Manicure

_____ Permanent Wave or Texturizing Treatment   _____ Artificial nail services (please describe)

_____ Chemical Relaxing or Straightening Treatment _____ Pedicure

_____ Highlighting or Lowlighting   _____ Facial/Skin Treatment

_____ Full head lightening   _____ Other (please any other services you've enjoyed

_____ Haircolor correction   at a salon that may not be listed here).

3.   Are you currently taking any medications? (Please list.)

4.   What is your natural hair color shade?

5.   How would you describe your hair's texture?

6.   How would you describe your hair's condition?

7.   How would you describe the condition of your scalp?

8.   What type of skin do you have? _____Dry _____Oily _____Normal _____Combination

9.   What type of skin care regimen do you follow? (Please explain) _____

      _____

10.   How would you characterize your nails? _____normal _____brittle _____flexible

11.   Do you have any of the following nail services? (Check all that apply) _____ Silk Wraps _____Porcelain
      _____Acrylic wraps _____Glue manicure _____Natural manicure _____Paraffin hand treatments

12.   Do you have any of the following foot services? (Check all that apply)
      _____Basic Pedicure _____Spa Pedicure _____Paraffin foot treatments

13.   Do you ever experience dry, itchy skin? _____Scalp? If so, how often?

14.   Do you notice your ability to manage your hair, skin, or nail regimens change with the change in climate? How so?

Figure 4–4 A typical client consultation card.

15. How often do you shampoo your hair?

16. How often do you condition your hair?

17. Once cleansed and conditioned, how do you style your hair?

18. Please list all of the products that you use on your hair, skin, and nails regularly.

19. On average, how much time do you spend each day styling your hair?

20. Are you now or have you ever been allergic to any of the products, treatments or chemicals you've received during any salon service—hair, nails or skin? (Please explain)

21. What is your biggest complaint concerning your hair?

22. What is your biggest complaint concerning your skin?

23. What is your biggest complaint concerning your nails?

24. What do you like about your hair?

25. What do you like about your complexion?

26. What do you like about your nails?

27. Please describe the best hairstyle you've ever had and explain why you felt it was the best.

28. What is the one thing that you want your stylist to know about you/your beauty regimens?

NOTE: If this card were used in a beauty school setting, it would include a release form at the bottom such as the one below.

Statement of Release: I hereby understand that cosmetology students render these services for the sole purpose of practice and learning and that, by signing this form, I recognize and agree not to hold the school, its employees or the student liable for my satisfaction or the service outcome.

Client signature _____ Date _____

Service Notes

Today's Date:

Today's Services:

Notes:

Today's Date:

Today's Services:

Notes:

Today's Date:

Today's Services:

Notes:

Today's Date:

Today's Services:

Notes:

Today's Date:

Today's Services:

Notes:

Figure 4–4, cont'd

focus on...

UNDERSTANDING THE TOTAL LOOK CONCEPT

While the enhancement of your client's image should always be your primary concern, it is important to remember that the nails, skin and hair adorn the body and are reflective of an entire lifestyle. How can you help a client make choices that reflect a personal sense of style? Start the process by doing a little research. Look for books or articles that describe different fashion styles, and become familiar with them. This exercise is useful for developing a profile of the broad fashion categories that you can refer to when consulting with clients.

For example, a person may be categorized as having a "classic" style if simple and sophisticated clothing, monochromatic colors, and no bright patterns are preferred. A person who prefers a classic styling in her clothing would likely want a simple, elegant, and sophisticated look with respect to her nails, makeup, and hair services as well.

Someone who prefers a more dramatic look, on the other hand, will choose nail designs, hairstyles, and , clothing and accessories that demand greater attention and allow for more options. These clients are likely to be more willing to try a variety of new products and spend more time having additional services that will help achieve the desired look (Figures 4–5 and 4–6).

Figure 4–5   A "classic" look.

Figure 4–6   A "dramatic" look.

Preparing for the Client Consultation

In order for your time to be well spent during the client consultation, it is important to be prepared. To facilitate the consultation process, you should have certain important items on hand. These include clippings from beauty magazines, particularly close-ups of hand/foot models that have beautiful nails. If you are stressing artificial nail enhancements in your future practice, always include clippings from trade magazines that show beautiful silk, gel, and acrylic (methacrylate) enhancements. You should also take photos of your best work to use as a communication tool and client confidence builder during client consultations. Equally important, have at the ready drawings of different nail shapes that are identified by name: square, round, oval, squoval, and pointed.

The Consultation Area

Presentation counts for a lot in a business that is concerned with style and appearance. Once you have brought the client to your station to begin the consultation process, make sure she is comfortable. You and she are about to begin an important conversation that will clue you in to her needs and preferences. Your work area needs to be freshly cleaned and uncluttered. Have your photos, magazine clippings, nail shape drawings, and all other appropriate aids for the desired service available. You should read the intake form carefully, and refer to it often during the consultation process. Throughout the consultation, and especially once a course of action is decided on, make notes on the intake form. Record any formulations or products that you use and include any specific techniques you follow or goals you are working toward, so that you can remember them for future visits.

10-Step Consultation Method

Every complete consultation needs to be structured in such a way that you cover all the key points that consistently lead to a successful conclusion. While this may seem like a lot of information to memorize, it will become second nature as you become more experienced and have many consultations under your belt. Depending on the service requested, the consultation will vary to some degree. For example, a full set of gel nails with tips will require a more detailed consultation than a plain manicure. To ensure that you always cover your bases, keep a list of the following 10 key points at your station for referral and modify it as needed for the actual service.

This Method is highly effective prior to caring for new nail clients, and before every new nail service.

1. **Review.** Review the intake form your client has filled out and feel free to make comments to break the ice and get the consultation going.

2. **Assess your client's nails.** Are they long, short, or somewhere in-between? Are the nails healthy and strong? Brittle and weak? Are the edges peeling?

3. **Preference.** Always ask clients what they like or dislike about their nails. Delve into their nail history to learn which nail services they've had in the past (e.g. artificial nail enhancements, etc.) and the outcome of those services.

4. **Analyze.** Analyze and determine the ideal length and shape based on the shape of the fingertips and nail bed, and personal preferences.

5. **Lifestyle.** Always ask clients about their career and personal lifestyles.
   - Does your client spend a great deal of time outdoors? Does she swim everyday?
   - Is your client an executive in a conservative industry? An artist? A stay-at-home parent?
   - Does your client have a strong personal style that she wishes to project?
   - How much time is she willing to invest on nail grooming?

6. **Show and tell**. Encourage her to flip through your photo collections and point out finished looks that she likes and why. This is a good time to get a real grasp on whether or not she not only understands, but accepts any personal limitations. Reiterating what she tells you using specific terms and reinforcing your words, with both pictures and your hands, are critical to having a clear understanding of what both of you are really saying. Listening to the client and then repeating, in your own words, what you think the client is telling you is known as **reflective listening**. Mastering this listening skill will help you to always be on target with your services, and build a deep trust with your clients.

7. **Suggest.** Once you have enough information, you can make valid style suggestions. Narrow your selections to lifestyle and other characteristics applicable to the desired service such as hair type, nail characteristics, or face and body shapes, and so on.

   When making suggestions, **clarify** them by referencing the above parameters. Tactfully discuss any unreasonable expectations she may have shared with you by picking out photos that are unrealistic based on her characteristics and personal needs.

8. **Additional services.** Never hesitate to suggest additional services to make the new look complete or better in some way. For example, you may have only provided a nail service; however, recommending the client for another service such as color or texture (with you or another practitioner) could help the client achieve the total desired look.

9. **Upkeep.** Counsel every client on the salon maintenance, lifestyle limitations, and home maintenance commitments needed to keep nails looking their best at all times.

10. **Repeat.** Reiterate everything that you have agreed on. Make sure to speak in measured, precise terms and use visual tools to demonstrate the end result. This is the most critical step of the consultation process because it determines the ultimate service(s). Take your time and be thorough.

Concluding the Service

Once the service is finished and the client has let you know whether or not she is satisfied, take a few more minutes to record the results on the record card. Ask for her reactions and record them. Note anything you did that you might want to do again, as well as anything that does not bear repeating. Also, make note of the final results and any retail products that you recommended. Be sure to date your notes and file them in the proper place.

SPECIAL ISSUES IN COMMUNICATION

Although you may do everything in your power to communicate effectively, you will sometimes encounter situations that are beyond your control. The solution is not to try to control the circumstances, but to communicate past the issue. Your reactions to situations, and your ability to communicate in the face of problems, are critical to being successful in a "people" profession such as the beauty industry.

Handling Tardy Clients

Tardy clients are a fact of life in every service industry. Because nail technicians are so dependent on appointments and scheduling to maximize working hours, a client who is very late for an appointment, or one who is habitually late, can cause problems. One tardy client can make you late for every other client you service that day, and the pressure involved in making up for lost time can take its toll. You also risk inconveniencing the rest of your clients who are prompt for their appointments.

Here are a few guidelines for handling late clients:

○ Know and abide by the salon's tardy or late policy. Many salons set a limited amount of time they allow a client to be late before they require them to reschedule. Generally, if clients are more than 15 minutes late, they should be asked to reschedule. Most will accept responsibility and be understanding about the rule, but you may come across a few clients who insist on being serviced immediately. Explain that you have other appointments and are responsible to those clients as well. Also explain that rushing through the service is unacceptable to both of you.

○ If your tardy client arrives and you have the time to take her without jeopardizing other clients' appointments, let your client know why you are taking her even though she is late. You can deliver this information and still remain pleasant and upbeat. Say, "Oh, Ms. Lee, we're in luck! Even though you're a bit late, I can still take you because my next appointment isn't for two hours. Isn't it great that it worked out?" This lets her know that being late is not acceptable under normal circumstances, but that if you can accommodate her, you will.

○ As you get to know your clients, you will learn who is habitually late. You may want to schedule such clients for the last appointment of the day or ask them to arrive earlier than their actual appointments. In other words, if a client is always 30 minutes late, schedule her for 2:30 but tell her to arrive at 2:00!

○ Imagine this scenario. In spite of your best efforts, you are running late. You realize that no matter what has happened in the salon that day, your clients want and deserve your promptness. If you have your clients' telephone numbers, call them and let them know about the delays. Give them the opportunity to reschedule, or to come a little later than their scheduled appointments. If you cannot reach them beforehand, be sure to approach them when they come into the salon and let them know that you are delayed. Tell them how long you think the wait will be, and give them the option of changing their appointment. Apologize for the inconvenience and show a little extra attention by personally offering them a beverage. Even if these clients are not happy about the delay, or they need to change their appointment, at least they will feel informed and respected.

Handling Scheduling Mix-Ups

We are all human, and we all make mistakes. Chances are you have gone to an appointment on a certain day, at a certain time, only to discover that you are in the wrong place, at the wrong time. The way you are treated at that moment will determine if you ever patronize that business again. The number-one thing to remember when you, as a professional, get involved with a scheduling mix-up is to be polite and never argue about who is correct. Being right may sound good, but this kind of situation is not about being right; it is about preserving your relationship with your client. If you handle the matter poorly, you run the risk of never seeing that client again.

Even if you know for sure that she is mistaken, tell yourself that the client is always right. Assume the blame if it helps keep her happy. *Do not, under any circumstances, argue the point with the client.*

Once you have the chance to consult your appointment book, you can say, "Oh, Mrs. Montez, I have you in my appointment book for 10:00, and unfortunately I have already scheduled other clients for 11:00 and 12:00. I'm so sorry about the mix-up. Can I reschedule you for tomorrow at 10:00?" Even though the client may be fuming, you need to stay disengaged. Your focus is to move the conversation away from who is at fault, and squarely in the direction of resolving the confusion. Make another appointment for the client and be sure to get her telephone number so that you can call and confirm the details of the appointment in advance (Figure 4–7).

Handling Unhappy Clients

No matter how hard you try to provide excellent service to your clients, once in a while you will encounter a client who is dissatisfied with the service. The way you and the salon handle this difficult situation will have lasting effects on you, the client, and the salon, so you need to know how best to proceed.

Once again, it is important to remember the ultimate goal: make the client happy enough to pay for the service and return for more of the same. Here are some guidelines to follow:

Figure 4–7 Accommodate an unhappy client promptly and calmly.

○ Try to find out why the client is unhappy. Ask for specifics. If she has a difficult time expressing herself, break the service down for her piece by piece until you determine exactly what has caused the dissatisfaction.

○ If it is possible to change what she dislikes, do so immediately. If that is not possible, look at your schedule to see how soon you can do it. You may need to enlist the help of the receptionist in rescheduling your other appointments. If the client seems open to the suggestion, ask her to return to the salon at a time when you are free. If this is not possible, explain that you will begin her service, but will need to take your next client and will be relying on help from another practitioner. Do whatever you have to do to make her happy, and explain along the way who will be working with her and what the other practitioner will be doing.

○ If you cannot change what the client does not like, or it is simply impossible to change ("It's too short!"), you must honestly and tactfully explain the reason why you cannot make any changes. The client will not be happy, but you can offer any options that may be available.

o Again, never argue with the client or try to force your opinion. Unless you can change what has caused the dissatisfaction, this will just fuel the fire.

o Do not hesitate to call on a more experienced nail technician or your salon manager for help. They have encountered a similar situation at some point in their careers and have insights that can help you.

o If, after you have tried everything, you are unable to satisfy the client, defer to your manager's advice on how to proceed. The client may be too upset to handle the situation maturely, and it may be easier for her to deal with someone else. This does not mean that you have failed; it simply means that another approach is needed.

o Confer with your salon manager after the experience. A good manager will not hold the event against you, but view it instead as an inevitable fact of life from which you can learn. Follow your manager's advice and move on to your next client. Use whatever you may have learned from the experience to perform future client consultations and services better.

Getting Too Personal

Sometimes when a client forms a bond of trust with her nail technician she may have a hard time differentiating between a professional and a personal relationship. That will be *her* problem, but you must not make it *your* problem. Your job is to handle your client relationships tactfully and sensitively. You cannot become your clients' counselor, career guide, parental sounding board, or motivational coach. Your job and your relationship with your clients are very specific: the goal is to advise and service clients with their beauty needs, and nothing more.

IN-SALON COMMUNICATION

Behaving in a professional manner is the first step in making this meaningful communication possible. Unfortunately, many beauty professionals act immaturely and get overly involved in the salon rumor mill.

The salon community is usually a close-knit one in which people spend long hours working side by side. For this reason, it is important to maintain boundaries around what you will and will not do or say at the salon. Remember, the salon is your place of business and, as such, must be treated respectfully and carefully.

Communicating with Coworkers

As with all communication, there are basic principles that must guide your interactions. In a work environment, you will not have the opportunity to handpick your colleagues. There will always be people you like or relate to

focus on...

COMMUNICATION

At some point in your career you will no doubt have a disgruntled client who is unhappy about something that was done either during the service or in scheduling. No matter how well you communicate, handling a situation like this can be difficult. The best way to prepare is to practice. Role-play with a classmate, taking turns being the client and the practitioner. Role playing both sides of the issue will give you a better understanding of the entire situation.

focus on...

PROFESSIONALISM

A long-time client reveals to you one day that she and her husband are going through a messy divorce. You care for her and try to be understanding as she reveals increasingly personal details. Other practitioners and their clients are soon listening to every word of this conversation. You want to be helpful and supportive, but this is not the right time or place. What can you do?

Try this: Tell her you understand the situation is very difficult, but while she is in the salon, you want to do everything in your power to give her a break from it. Let her know that while she is in your care, you should both concentrate on her enjoyment of the services and not on the things that are stressing her.

She will appreciate the suggestion, and you will have put her back on the track of her real reason for coming to see you.

better than others, and people whose behaviors or opinions you find yourself in conflict with. These people can try your patience and your nerves, but they are your colleagues and are deserving of your respect.

Here are some guidelines to keep in mind as you interact and communicate with fellow staffers.

Treat everyone with respect. Regardless of whether you like someone, your colleagues are professionals who service clients who bring revenue into the salon. And, as practicing professionals, they have information they can offer you. Look at these people as having something to teach you, and hone in on their talents and their techniques.

Remain objective. Different types of personalities working side by side over long and intense hours are likely to breed some degree of dissension and disagreement. In order to learn and grow, you must make every effort to remain objective and resist being pulled into spats and cliques. When one or two people in the salon behave disrespectfully toward one another, the entire team suffers because the atmosphere changes. Not only will this be unpleasant for you , but it will also be felt by the clients who may decide to take their business elsewhere if they find the atmosphere in your salon too tense.

Be honest and be sensitive. Many people use the excuse of being honest as a license to say anything to anyone. While honesty is always the best policy, using unkind words or actions with regard to your colleagues is never a good idea. Be sensitive. Put yourself in the other person's place and think through what you want to say before you say it. That way, any negative or hurtful words can be suppressed.

Remain neutral. Undoubtedly, there will come a time when you are called on to make a statement or to "pick a side." Do whatever you can to avoid getting drawn into the conflict. If you have a problem with a colleague, the best way to resolve it is to speak with her or him directly and privately.

Speaking to, or gossiping with, others about someone never resolves a problem. It only makes it worse and is often as damaging to you as it is to the object of your gossip.

Seek help from someone you respect. If you find yourself in a position where you are at odds with a coworker, you may want to seek out a third party—someone who is not involved and who can remain objective—such as the manager or a more experienced practitioner. Ask for advice about how to proceed and really listen to what this mentor has to say. Since this person is not involved, he or she is more likely to see the situation as it truly is and can offer you valuable insights.

Do not take things personally. This is often easier said than done. How many times have you had a bad day, or been thinking about something totally unrelated, when a person asks you what's wrong, or wonders if you are mad at them? Just because someone is behaving in a

certain manner and you happen to be there, do not interpret the words
or behaviors as being meant for you. If you are confused or concerned
by someone's actions, find a quiet and private place to ask the person
about it. The person may not even realize she was giving off any
signals.

Keep your private life private. There is a time and a place for
everything, but the salon is never the place to discuss your personal life
and relationships. It may be tempting to engage in that kind of conversation, especially if others in the salon are doing so, and to solicit advice
and opinions, but that is why you have friends. Coworkers can become
friends, but those whom you selectively turn into friends are different
from the ones whose chairs happen to be next to yours.

Communicating with Managers

Another very important relationship for you within the salon is the one
you will build with your manager. The salon manager is generally the person who has the most responsibility for how the salon is run in terms of
daily maintenance and operations and client service. The manager's job is a
very demanding one. Often, in addition to running a hectic salon, she also
has a clientele that she personally services.

Your manager is likely to be the one who hired you and is responsible for your training and for how well you move into the salon culture.
Therefore, your manager has a vested interest in your success. As a salon
employee, you will see the manager as a powerful and influential person,
but it is also important to remember that she is a human being. She is-
n't perfect, and she will not be able to do everything you think should
be done in every instance. Whether she personally likes you or not, her
job is to look beyond her personal feelings and make decisions that are
best for the salon as a whole. The best thing you can do is to try to understand the decisions and rules that she makes whether you agree with
them or not.

Many salon professionals utilize their salon managers in inappropriate
ways by asking them to solve personal issues between staff members.

Inexperienced managers, hoping to keep everything flowing smoothly,
may make the mistake of getting involved in petty issues. You and your
manager must both understand that her job is to make sure the business is
running smoothly, not to baby-sit temperamental practitioners.

Here are some guidelines for interacting and communicating with your
salon manager.

Be a problem solver. When you need to speak with your manager
about some issue or problem, think of some possible solutions beforehand. This will indicate that you are working in the salon's best interest
and are trying to help, not make things worse.

Get your facts straight. Make sure that all your facts and information are accurate before you speak to your salon manager. This way you
will avoid wasting time solving a "problem" that really does not exist.

Be open and honest. When you find yourself in a situation you do not understand or do not have the experience to deal with, tell your salon manager immediately and be willing to learn.

Do not gossip or complain about colleagues. Going to your manager with gossip or to "tattle" on a coworker tells your manager that you are a troublemaker. If you are having a legitimate problem with someone and have tried everything in your power to handle the problem yourself, then it is appropriate to go to your manager. But you must approach her with a true desire to solve the problem, not just to vent.

Check your attitude. The salon environment, although fun and friendly, can also be stressful, so it is important to take a moment between clients to "take your temperature." Ask yourself how you are feeling. Do you need an attitude adjustment? Be honest with yourself.

Be open to constructive criticism. It is never easy to hear that you need improvement in any area, but keep in mind that part of your manager's job is to help you achieve your professional goals. She is supposed to evaluate your skills and offer suggestions on how to increase them. Keep an open mind and do not take her criticism personally.

Communicating During an Employee Evaluation

Salons that are well run will make it a priority to conduct frequent and thorough employee evaluations. Sometime in the course of your first few days of work, your salon manager will tell you when you can expect your first evaluation. If she does not mention it, you might ask her about it and request a copy of the form she will use or the criteria on which you will be evaluated.

Take some time to look over this document. Be mindful that the behaviors and/or activities most important to the salon are likely to be the ones on which you will be evaluated. This is very useful information. You can begin to watch and rate yourself in the weeks and months ahead so you can assess how you are doing. Remember, everything you are being evaluated on is there for the purpose of helping you improve. Make the decision to approach these communications positively. As the time draws near for the evaluation, try filling out the form yourself. In other words, give yourself an evaluation, even if the salon has not asked you to do so. Be objective, and carefully think out your comments. Then, when you meet with the manager, show her your evaluation and tell her you are serious about your improvement and growth. She will appreciate your input and your desire. And, if you are being honest with yourself, there should be no surprises (Figure 4–8).

Before your evaluation meeting, write down any thoughts or questions you may have so you can share them with your manager. Do not be shy. If you want to know when you can take on more services, when your pay scale will be increased, or when you might be considered for promotion, this meeting is the appropriate time and place to ask. Many beauty professionals never take advantage of this crucial communication opportunity to

Figure 4–8 Your employee evaluation is a good time to discuss your progress with your manager.

discuss their future because they are too nervous, intimidated, or unprepared. Do not let that happen to you. Participate proactively in your career and in your success by communicating your desires and interests.

At the end of the meeting, thank your manager for taking the time to do an evaluation and for the feedback and guidance she has given you.

REVIEW **QUESTIONS**

1. List the golden rules of human relations.
2. Define communication.
3. How should you prepare for a client consultation?
4. What is the "total look" concept?
5. List and describe the 10 elements of a successful client consultation.
6. Name some types of information that should go on a client consultation card.
7. How should you handle tardy clients?
8. How should you handle a scheduling mix-up?
9. How should you handle an unhappy client?
10. List at least five things to remember when communicating with your coworkers.
11. List at least four guidelines for communicating with salon managers.

CHAPTER **GLOSSARY**

clarify	To make clear.
client consultation	Verbal communication with a client to determine desired results.
communication	The act of accurately sharing information between two people, or groups of people.
reflective listening	Listening to the client and then repeating, in your own words, what you think the client is telling you.

GENERAL SCIENCES

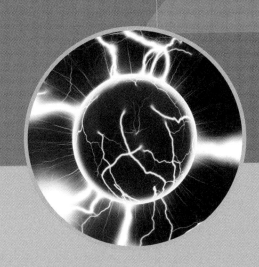

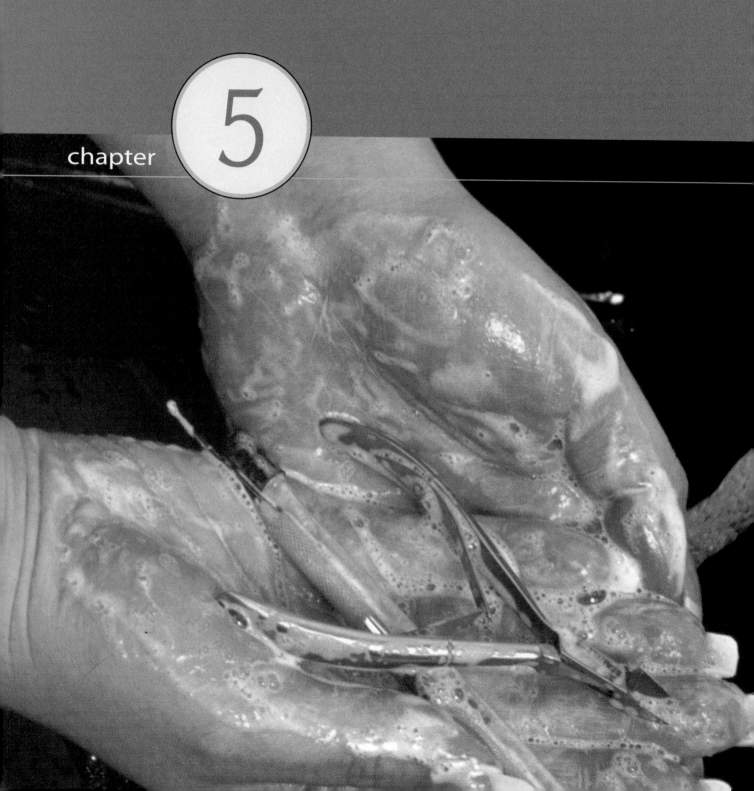

Infection Control:
Principles And Practice

chapter **5**

LEARNING OBJECTIVES

After completing this chapter, you will be able to:

1. Understand state laws and rules.

2. List the types of disinfectants and how they are used.

3. Define hepatitis and HIV and explain how they are transmitted.

4. Describe how to safely clean and disinfect salon tools and equipment.

5. Explain the differences between cleaning, disinfection and sterilization.

6. Discuss Universal Precautions and your responsibilities as a salon professional.

KEY TERMS

Page number indicates where in the chapter the term is used.

AIDS
pg. 67

allergy
pg. 66

antiseptics
pg. 79

bacteria
pg. 63

bactericidal
pg. 62

bloodborne pathogens
pg. 67

contagious disease
pg. 65

diagnosis
pg. 66

disease
pg. 66

disinfectable
pg. 74

disinfectants
pg. 59, 70

disinfection
pg. 70

efficacy
pg. 71

fungi
pg. 62, 68

fungicidal
pg. 62

hepatitis
pg. 67

HIV
pg. 65, 67

infection
pg. 65

infectious
pg. 62

inflammation
pg. 65

microorganism
pg. 63

mildew
pg. 68

MSDS
pg. 59

nonpathogenic
pg. 63

occupational disease
pg. 66

parasite
pg. 68

pathogenic
pg. 63

pediculosis capitis
pg. 69

phenolics
pg. 72

porous
pg. 72, 74

quaternary ammonium compounds (quats)
pg. 72

sanitation
pg. 69

sodium hypochlorite
pg. 72

sterilization
pg. 69

toxins
pg. 68

tuberculocidal
pg. 59

tuberculosis
pg. 59

Universal Precautions
pg. 80

virucidal
pg. 62

virus
pg. 62, 65

Editor's Note: Please notice that the words sanitation or sanitizing simply mean cleaning, and that they may be used interchangeably throughout the chapter.

When reading this chapter, you may wonder if you are required to be part scientist or chemist to be a professional in the field of nail technology. It is not important that you know the chemistry of the products that you use, or that you memorize medical terms, or that you know how to pronounce germs that disinfectants will kill – what is important is that you know what to do and when to do it to keep clients safe. Understanding the basics of cleaning and disinfecting and following state rules will ensure that you have a long and successful career in the field of nail technology.

REGULATION

Many different state and federal agencies regulate the practice of nail technology. Federal agencies set guidelines for manufacturing, sale, and use of equipment and chemical ingredients, and for safety in the workplace. State agencies regulate licensing, enforcement, and your conduct when working in the salon.

Federal Agencies

OSHA

The Occupational Safety and Health Administration (OSHA) was created as part of the U.S. Department of Labor to regulate and enforce safety and health standards to protect the employee in the workplace. Regulating employee exposure to potentially toxic substances and informing employees about possible hazards of materials used in the workplace are key points of the Occupational Safety and Health Act of 1970. This regulation created the Hazard Communication Act, which requires that chemical manufacturers and importers assess the hazards associated with their products. Material Safety Data Sheets (MSDSs) are a result of this law.

The standards set by OSHA are important to the nail industry because of the products used in salons. These standards address issues relating to handling, mixing, storing, and disposing of products, general safety in the workplace, and, most important, your right to know the hazardous ingredients in the products you use.

Material Safety Data Sheet

Both state and federal laws require that manufacturers supply a Material Safety Data Sheet (MSDS) for all products sold (Figure 5-1). **MSDS** sheets include information about hazardous ingredients, safe use and handling procedures, precautions to reduce the risk of harm and overexposure, flammability and data in case of a fire, proper disposal guidelines, and medical information should anyone have a reaction to the product. When necessary, the MSDS can be sent to a doctor, so that any reaction can be properly treated. OSHA and state regulatory agencies require that MSDSs be kept available in the salon for all products that can cause harm. State inspectors can issue fines for the salon not having these available.

You can get MSDSs from the products' manufacturers, download them from the product manufacturer or distributor's website, or from distributors. Not having an MSDS poses a health risk to anyone in a salon who is exposed to hazardous materials and is a violation of federal regulations. Take the time to read all of this information to be certain that you are protecting yourself and your clients to the best of your ability.

Environmental Protection Agency (EPA)

The EPA licenses different types of **disinfectants**. The two types that are used in salons are hospital and **tuberculocidal**. Hospital products are safe for cleaning blood and body fluids in hospitals.

Tuberculocidal disinfectants are proven to kill the **bacteria** that causes **tuberculosis**, which is more difficult to kill (these products are also hospital products). This does not mean that you should use a tuberculocide; in fact, these products can be harmful to salon tools and equipment and they require special methods of disposal. Check the rules in your state to be sure that the product that you choose complies with requirements.

It is against Federal Law to use any disinfecting product contrary to its labeling. This means that if you do not follow the instructions for mixing,

Material Safety Data Sheet

May be used to comply with
OSHA's Hazard Communication Standard,
29 CFR 1910.1200. Standard must be
consulted for specific requirements.

U.S. Department of Labor

Occupational Safety and Health Administration
(Non-Mandatory Form)
Form Approved
OMB No. 1218-0072

IDENTITY *(As Used on Label and List)*

Note: Blank spaces are not permitted. If any item is not applicable or no
information is available, the space must be marked to indicate that.

Section I

Manufacturer's Name	Emergency Telephone Number
Address *(Number, Street, City, State, and ZIP Code)*	Telephone Number for information
	Date Prepared
	Signature of Preparer *(optional)*

Section II — Hazardous Ingredients/Identity Information

Hazardous Components (Specific Chemical Identity; Common Names(s))	OSHA PEL	ACGIH TLV	Other Limits Recommended	% *(optional)*

Section III — Physical/Chemical Characteristics

Boiling Point		Specific Gravity (H$_2$O - 1)	
Vapor Pressure (mm Hg.)		Melting Point	
Vapor Density (Air - 1))		Evaporation Rate (Butyl Acetate - 1)	
Solubility in Water			
Appearance and Odor			

Section IV — Fire and Explosion Hazard Data

Flash Point (Method Used)	Flammable Limits	LEL	UEL
Extinguishing Media			
Special Fire Fighting Procedures			
Unusual Fire and Explosion Hazards			

(Reproduce locally)

OSHA 174, Sept. 1985

Figure 5–1 A sample MSDS.

Material Safety Data Sheet (MSDS)

Section V — Reactivity Data

Stability	Unstable		Conditions to Avoid
	Stable		

Incompatibility (Materials to Avoid)

Hazardous Decomposition or Byproducts

Hazardous Polymerization	May Occur		Conditions to Avoid
	Will Not Occur		

Section VI — Health Hazard Data

Route(s) of Entry: Inhalation?   Skin?   Ingestion?

Health Hazards *(Acute and Chronic)*

Carcenogenicity: NTP?   IARC Monographs   OSHA Regulated?

Signs and Symptoms of Exposure

Medical Conditions
Generally Aggravated by Exposure

Emergency and First Aid Program

Section VII — Precautions for Safe Handling and Use

Steps to Be Taken in Case Material is Released or Spilled

Waste Disposal Method

Precautions to Be Taken in Handling and Storing

Other Precautions

Section VIII — Control Measures

Respiratory Protection (Specify Type)

Ventilation	Local Exhaust	Special
	Mechanical (General)	Other

Protective Gloves	Eye Protection

Other Protective Clothing or Equipment

Work/Hygienic Practices

Page 2

Figure 5–1, cont'd

? DID YOU **KNOW...**

The term Hospital Grade is a myth. The EPA does not 'grade' disinfectants; a product is approved for use in a hospital or it is not.

? DID YOU **KNOW...**

A single practitioner can put many of their clients at risk if she does not practice stringent cleaning and disinfection guidelines. A case in point was the spread of a bacterium called Mycobacterium fortuitum furunculosis (MY-koh-bak-TIR-ee-um for-TOO-i-tum fur-UNK-yoo-LOH-sis), a germ that normally exists in tap water and, in small numbers, is completely harmless. In 2000, over 100 clients from one California salon had serious skin infections in their legs after getting pedicures. The infection caused stubborn, ugly sores that lingered for months, required the use of strong antibiotics, and, in some cases, caused scarred legs. The source of the infection was traced to the salon's whirlpool foot spas. Salon staff did not clean the foot spas properly, which resulted in a build-up of hair and debris in the foot spas, which created the perfect breeding ground for bacteria.

The outbreak was a catalyst for change in the industry. As a result, the state of California issued specific requirements for pedicure equipment in the hope of preventing another outbreak in the future. In spite of their efforts at that time, there have been other outbreaks affecting hundreds of women since then, and not only in California. Although rare, there are several documented deaths (and several people have had lengthy hospital stays) resulting from pedicures in 2006. This has enlightened the industry to some very important facts about cleanliness, especially for pedicure equipment.

contact time, and the type of surface the disinfecting product can be used on, you have broken federal Law.

State Regulatory Agencies

State regulatory agencies exist to protect the consumers' health, safety, and welfare while receiving services in the salon. These include licensing agencies, state boards of Cosmetology, Commissions, and health departments. They do this by requiring that everyone working in a salon or spa follow specific procedures. Enforcement of the rules through inspections and investigations of consumer complaints is also part of the agency's responsibility. The agency can issue penalties against both the salon owner and the operator's license ranging from warnings to fines, probation, and suspension or revocation of licenses. It is vital that you understand and follow the laws and rules in your state at all times - your license and your client's safety depend on it.

Laws and Rules - what is the difference?

Laws are written by the legislature and determine scope of practice (what each license allows the holder to do) and establish guidelines for regulatory agencies to make rules. **Laws** are also called **statutes. Rules** (also called **regulations**) are more specific than laws. Rules are written by the regulatory agency or board and determine how the law will be applied. Rules establish specific standards of conduct, and can be changed or updated frequently.

● PRINCIPLES OF PREVENTION

Being a salon professional is fun and rewarding, but it is also a great responsibility. One careless action could cause injury or **infection,** and you could lose your license to practice. Fortunately, preventing the spread of infections is easy if you know what to do and you practice what you have learned at all times. Safety begins and ends with YOU (Figure 5-2).

Infection Control

There are three types of potentially **infectious** microorganisms that are important to practitioners of nail technology. These are **bacteria, fungi, and viruses.** Remember, we are not seeking to treat any **disease** or condition; we are taking steps so that the tools and equipment we use are safe to use on clients. These steps are designed to prevent infection or disease. Disinfectants used in salons must be **bactericidal** (back-teer-uh-SYD-ul), **fungicidal** (fun-jih- SYD-ul), and **virucidal** (vy-rus-SYD-ul), meaning that when they are mixed and used according to the instructions on the labels, they will kill potentially infectious bacteria, fungi and viruses.

Dirty salon tools and equipment may spread infections from client to client. You have an obligation to provide safe services and prevent consumers from harm by practicing safely. If they are infected or harmed be-

Figure 5–2 A sparkling clean salon gains your clients' confidence.

cause you did not correctly perform the services, you may be found legally responsible for their injury or infection.

Bacteria

Bacteria are one-celled microorganisms (my-kroh-OR-gah-niz-ums) with both plant and animal characteristics. Bacteria can exist almost anywhere: skin, water, air, decayed matter, body secretions, clothing, or under the free edge of finger nails. Bacteria are so small they can only be seen with a microscope. In fact, 1500 rod-shaped bacteria will fit comfortably on the head of a pin!

Types of Bacteria

There are thousands of different kinds of bacteria that fall into two primary types: pathogenic and nonpathogenic. Most bacteria are **nonpathogenic** (completely harmless; do not cause disease). They can perform many useful functions. In the human body, nonpathogenic bacteria help the body break down food, protect against infection, and stimulate the immune system. **Pathogenic** (path-uh-JEN-ik) bacteria are considered harmful because they may cause disease or infection when they invade the body. Preventing the spread of pathogenic **microorganisms** is why salons and schools must maintain sanitary standards. Table 5–1 presents terms and definitions related to pathogens.

Bacteria have distinct shapes that help to identify them (Figure 5-3).

Bacterial Growth and Reproduction

Bacteria generally consist of an outer cell wall containing liquid called protoplasm.

TABLE 5-1 ● DEFINITIONS RELATING TO CAUSES OF DISEASE

Term	Definition
bacteria (singular: bacterium)	One-celled microorganisms with both plant and animal characteristics. Some are harmful, some harmless, but all are also known as microbes or germs.
infectious	Infection can be spread from one person to another person or from one infected body part to another.
microbes/germs	Synonyms for any microorganisms.
microorganism	Microscopic plant or animal.
parasite	An organism that lives on or in another organism and draws its nourishment from that organism.
toxin	Any of the various poisonous substances produced by some microorganisms.
virus (plural: viruses)	An infectious microorganism smaller than bacteria and capable of infesting almost all plants and animals, including bacteria; continues to live and reproduce only by penetrating cells and becoming part of them.

Cells manufacture their own food from what they can absorb from the surrounding environment.

They give off waste products, grow, and reproduce. The life cycle of bacteria consists of two distinct phases: the active stage, and the inactive or spore-forming stage.

Active Stage. During the active stage, bacteria grow and reproduce. Bacteria multiply best in warm, dark, damp, or dirty places where food is available. When conditions are favorable, bacteria grow and reproduce. When they reach their largest size, they divide into two new cells. This division is called **mitosis** (my-TOH-sis). The cells that are formed are called daughter cells. When conditions become unfavorable and difficult for them to thrive, the bacteria either die or become inactive.

Inactive or Spore-forming Stage. Certain bacteria, such as the anthrax and tetanus bacilli, coat themselves with wax outer shells that are able to withstand long periods of famine, dryness, and unsuitable temperatures. In this stage, spores can be blown about and are not harmed by disinfectants, heat, or cold.

When favorable conditions are restored, the spores change into the active form and begin to grow and reproduce. Although spores are dangerous

Figure 5–3 Some general forms of bacteria.

if they enter the body during a surgical procedure and become active, they pose little or no risk to clients in a salon.

Bacterial Infections

An **infection** occurs when body tissues are invaded by disease-causing or pathogenic bacteria.

There can be no bacterial infection without the presence of pathogenic bacteria. So if they are eliminated, clients can not become infected. **Pus** is a fluid created by tissue **inflammation** and contains white blood cells (Chapter 6), bacteria, and dead cells. The presence of pus is a sign of a bacterial infection. Staphylococci ("staph") are among the most common human bacteria, and are normally carried by about a third of the population. Staph can be picked up on doorknobs, countertops, and other surfaces, but are more frequently spread through skin-to-skin contact, such as shaking hands or using unclean implements. If these bacteria get into the wrong place they can be very dangerous.

Staph is responsible for food poisoning and a wide range of diseases, like toxic shock syndrome.

Staph infections occur most frequently among persons who have weakened immune systems, but can occur in otherwise healthy people. The symptoms usually appear as skin infections, such as pimples and boils that can be very difficult to cure and have resulted in death. Some bacteria are resistant to certain antibiotics.

Because of these highly resistant strains, it is important to clean and disinfect all tools and equipment used in the salon. You owe it to yourself and your clients!

A **local infection,** such as a pimple or abscess, is one that is confined to a particular part of the body and is indicated by a lesion containing pus. When a disease spreads from one person to another by contact, it is said to be **contagious** (kon-TAY-jus) or communicable (kuh-MYOO-nih-kuh-bul). Some of the more common **contagious diseases** that will prevent a salon professional from servicing a client are common cold, ringworm, conjunctivitis (pinkeye), and viral infections. The chief sources for spreading these infections are dirty hands and implements, open sores, pus, mouth and nose discharges, and shared drinking cups, telephone receivers, and towels. Uncovered coughing or sneezing and spitting in public also spread germs.

Table 5–2 lists general terms and definitions that are important for an understanding of disease in general.

Viruses

A **virus** (VY-rus) is a microorganism capable of infecting almost all plants and animals, including bacteria. They are so small that they can only be seen under the most sophisticated and powerful microscopes available. They cause common colds and other respiratory and gastrointestinal (digestive tract) infections. Other viruses that plague humans are measles, mumps, chicken pox, smallpox, rabies, yellow fever, hepatitis, polio, influenza, and **HIV,** which causes **AIDS.**

TABLE 5-2 ● GENERAL TERMS RELATING TO DISEASE

Term	Definition
allergy	An immune system response to certain foods, chemicals, product ingredients, or other normally harmless substances that is caused by repeated exposure to that substance.
contagious disease	A disease that is communicable or easily spread by contact.
contamination	The presence, or the reasonably anticipated presence, of blood or other potentially infectious materials on an item surface or visible debris/residues such as dusts, hair, skin, etc.
diagnosis	Determination of the nature of the disease from its symptoms. Diagnosing is medical practice and MUST only be done by a doctor. It is against federal law for salon professionals to diagnose any medical condition, including nail or skin infections.
disease	Abnormal condition of all or part of the body, organ, or mind that makes it incapable of carrying on normal function.
exposure incident	Contact with non-intact skin, blood, body fluid or other potentially infectious materials that results from the performance of an employee's duties (previously called Blood Spill).
infectious disease	Disease caused by pathogenic microorganisms that are easily spread.
inflammation	Condition in which a part of the body reacts to protect itself from injury, irritation, or infection, characterized by redness, heat, pain, and swelling.
occupational disease	Illnesses resulting from conditions associated with employment, i.e. prolonged and repeated exposure to certain products or ingredients.
parasitic disease	Disease is caused by vegetable or animal parasites, such as lice and ringworm.
pathogenic disease	disease produced by disease-causing organisms, i.e. bacteria, virus and fungi.
systemic disease	Disease that affects the body generally, often due to under or over functioning glands.

One difference between viruses and bacteria is that a virus can live and reproduce only by penetrating other cells and becoming part of them, while bacteria can live and reproduce on their own. Bacterial infections can usually be treated with specific antibiotics while viruses are hard to kill without harming the body in the process. Viruses are not affected by antibiotics. Vaccinations prevent viruses from growing in the body but are not available for all viruses.

Bloodborne Pathogens

Disease-causing bacteria or viruses that are carried through the body in the blood or body fluids, such as hepatitis and HIV, are called **bloodborne pathogens**. If you accidentally cut a client who is HIV-positive, or is infected with **hepatitis,** and you continue to use the implement without cleaning and disinfecting it, you risk puncturing your skin or cutting another client with a contaminated tool. The spread of bloodborne pathogens is possible through shaving, nipping, clipping, facial treatments, waxing, or tweezing any time the skin is broken. Use great care to avoid damaging clients' skin during any type of service.

Hepatitis

A bloodborne virus causes hepatitis, a disease that damages the liver. It is easier to contract hepatitis than HIV since it can be present in all body fluids. Unlike HIV, hepatitis can live on a surface outside the body for long periods of time. It is vital that all surfaces that contact a client are thoroughly cleaned, especially if someone sneezes or coughs on them. Be sure to clean hands after coughing or sneezing.

There are three types of hepatitis that are of concern within the salon: hepatitis A, hepatitis B, and hepatitis C. Hepatitis B is the most difficult to kill on a surface, so check the label of the disinfectant you use to be sure that the product is effective against it. Those who work closely with the public can be vaccinated against hepatitis. You may want to check with your doctor to see if this is an option for you.

HIV/AIDS

HIV (Human Immunodeficiency Virus) is the virus that causes **AIDS** (Acquired Immune Deficiency Syndrome). AIDS is a disease that breaks down the body's immune system. HIV is spread from person to person through blood and less often through other body fluids, such as semen and vaginal secretions. A person can be infected with HIV for many years without having symptoms, but testing can determine if a person is infected within six months after exposure to the virus. Sometimes, people who are HIV-positive have never been tested and do not know they are infecting other people. The HIV virus is spread mainly through the sharing of needles by intravenous (IV) drug users, and less often by unprotected sexual contact or accidents with needles in healthcare settings. The virus is less likely to enter the bloodstream through cuts and sores. It is *not spread* by holding hands, hugging, kissing, sharing food or household items like the telephone, or even toilet seats. There are no documented cases of the virus being spread by food handlers, insects, casual contact, or hair, skin and nail salon services.

Parasites

Parasites are plant or animal organisms that live in, or on, another living organism and draw their nourishment from that organism (referred to as a host). They must have a host to survive.

Fungi (FUN-jI), which include molds, **mildews,** and yeasts, can produce contagious diseases, such as ringworm. Hair stylists must clean and disinfect clipper blades to avoid spreading scalp and skin infections. *Tinea barbae* (Barber's Itch) is the most frequently encountered infection resulting from hair services, but others can occur. This infection affects the coarse hairs in the mustache and beard area, or around the neck and scalp, usually in men. Cleaning clippers of all visible hair, then disinfecting properly reduces the risk of spreading skin and scalp infections. Using compressed air to clean clipper blades is very effective and saves time.

Nail fungus can be spread by using dirty implements or by not properly preparing the surface of the natural nail before enhancement products are applied. Although it is not as common on the hands, nail fungus is usually a chronic condition that is localized to one or two fingers or toes, but can be spread to other nails, or from client to client if implements are not properly cleaned and disinfected. The FDA has determined that topical treatments applied directly to the fingernails, skin, and toenails are not effective in eliminating fungal infections. The FDA prohibits sale of antifungal products for finger and toenails without a medical prescription. If the client is concerned about an infection of the nails, she should seek the advice of a doctor (Figure 5-4).

How Pathogens Enter the Body

Pathogenic bacteria or viruses or fungi can enter the body through:

- broken skin, such as a cut or scratch; intact skin is an effective barrier to infection.

- the mouth (contaminated water, food or fingers).

- the nose (inhaling dusts).

- the eyes or ears (less likely, but possible).

- unprotected sex.

The body prevents and controls infections with:

- healthy, unbroken skin, the body's first line of defense.

- body secretions, such as perspiration and digestive juices.

- white blood cells within the blood that destroy bacteria.

- antitoxins that counteract the **toxins** produced by bacteria and viruses.

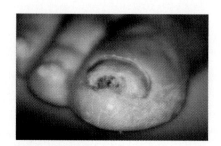

Figure 5–4 Nail fungus.

Parasites

Head lice are another type of parasite responsible for contagious diseases and conditions (Figure 5-5). A skin disease caused by an infestation of head lice is called **pediculosis capitis** (puh-dik-yuh-LOH-sis). **Scabies** (SKAYbeez) is another contagious skin disease that is caused by the itch mite, which burrows under the skin. Contagious diseases and conditions caused by parasites should only be treated by a doctor. Contaminated countertops, tools, and equipment should be thoroughly cleaned and then disinfected for 10 minutes with an EPA-registered disinfectant or bleach solution.

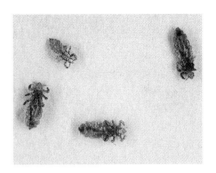

Figure 5–5 Head lice.

Immunity

Immunity is the ability of the body to destroy and resist infection. Immunity against disease can be either natural or acquired, and is a sign of good health. **Natural immunity** is partly inherited and partly developed through healthy living. **Acquired immunity** is immunity that the body develops after overcoming a disease, or through inoculation (such as flu vaccinations).

Decontamination

There are three steps to decontamination. These are **sanitation, disinfection** and **sterilization**. Because of the low risk of infection compared to medical facilities, salons are only concerned with the first two.

Sanitation

Sanitation or **sanitizing** is simply **cleaning.** Removing all visible dirt and debris is sanitizing. When a surface is properly cleaned, the number of germs on the surface is greatly reduced, as is the risk of infection. The vast majority of contaminants and pathogens can be washed from the surface through proper cleaning. This is why cleaning is the most important part of processing salon tools and equipment. A surface must be properly cleaned, or it cannot be properly disinfected. Using a disinfectant without cleaning first is like using mouthwash without brushing your teeth - it just does not work properly!

Cleaned surfaces can still harbor pathogens, but they are much less likely to spread infections.

Putting antiseptics on your skin or washing your hands is another example of sanitation. Your hands may appear clean when you are finished but there are still germs on them. Do not underestimate the importance of cleaning. It the most powerful and important way to prevent the spread of infection.

Methods of Cleaning
o Scrubbing with a brush

o Using an ultrasonic unit

o Using a solvent (i.e. on metal bits for electric files)

Disinfection

The second step of decontamination is **disinfection.** Disinfection is the process that kills most, but not necessarily all, microorganisms on non-living surfaces. In the salon setting, disinfection is extremely effective in controlling microorganisms on surfaces such as shears, nippers, and other multi-use tools and equipment.

Disinfectants are chemical agents that destroy all bacteria, fungi, and viruses, but not spores, on surfaces. *Disinfectants are not for use on human skin, hair, or nails.* Never use disinfectants as hand cleaners. All disinfectants clearly state on the label to avoid skin contact. This means avoid contact with your skin as well as the client's. Do not put your fingers directly into any disinfecting solution. These are pesticides and can be harmful to the skin if absorbed through the skin. If you mix a disinfectant in a container that is not labeled by the manufacturer, it must be labeled with the contents and the date mixed.

Sterilization

The word "sterilize" is often used incorrectly. Sterilization is the complete elimination of all microbial life, including spores, and is necessary only when surgical instruments cut into the vascular layers of the body (this does not mean an accidental cut). Methods of sterilization include high-pressure steam or dry heat autoclaves, and some chemicals. Simply exposing instruments to steam, is not enough. To be effective against disease causing pathogens, the steam must be pressurized, i.e. an autoclave. Dry heat forms of sterilization are less efficient and require longer times at higher temperatures. Estheticians must sterilize reusable needles and probes that lance the skin, but it is better to use pre-sterilized disposable items for these procedures. Most people without medical training do not realize that the proper use of any autoclave requires cleaning, sterile rinse, *and* disinfection for 10 minutes in an EPA registered hospital germicide before sterilizing. Since surgical procedures are not performed in salons, sterilization of salon tools and equipment is not necessary.

Read Labels Carefully!

Manufacturers take great care to develop safe and highly effective systems. However, just because something is safe does not mean that it cannot be dangerous if used improperly. Any professional salon product can be dangerous if used incorrectly. Like all chemicals, disinfectants must always be used exactly as the label instructs. **Important!** Disinfectants must be registered with the Environmental Protection Agency (EPA). Look for an EPA reg. number on the label.

Choosing a Disinfectant

To use a disinfectant properly, you must read and follow the manufacturer's instructions. Mixing ratios (dilution) and contact time are very important. Not all disinfectants have the same concentration, so be sure to mix the correct amount according to the instructions on the label. If the label does not have the word "concentrate" on it, the product is already mixed and must be used as is. All EPA disinfectants, even aerosol spray products for clippers, require 10-minute contact on pre-cleaned, hard, non-porous surfaces. Alcohol (70% or higher) is also used to disinfect abrasive nail files and buffers used on healthy nails.

Disinfectants must have **efficacy** claims on the label. This is a list of the specific germs the product is proven to kill when used according to the label instructions. Salons pose a very low infection risk when compared to hospitals. In hospitals, cleaning and disinfection standards are much stricter than in salons, and for good reason. Some types of disinfectants (such as glutaraldehyde) are much too dangerous for use in the salon environment, especially since the risk of causing serious infection is extremely low. There is some risk of spreading certain types of infections to salon clients, therefore, it is important to clean and disinfect correctly. Fortunately, any EPA registered liquid hospital disinfectant will be more than enough for salons. Hospital infection control guidelines now include the use of an EPA-registered **hospital** liquid disinfectant or bleach solution for cleanup of blood or body fluid. For this reason, when salon implements accidentally contact blood, body fluids, or unhealthy conditions, they should be cleaned and then completely immersed in an EPA-registered hospital disinfectant solution or 10% bleach solution.

Proper Use of Disinfectants

All implements must be thoroughly cleaned of all visible matter or residue before soaking in disinfectant solution because residue can interfere with the disinfectant. Implements and tools must be completely immersed in disinfectant solution for 10 minutes. Complete immersion means enough liquid to cover all surfaces of the item, including the handles (Figure 5-6).

Disinfectant Tips

1. Use only on precleaned hard non-porous surfaces – not abrasive files or buffers.

2. Dilute according to the label of the product.

3. Contact time for 10 minutes (according to the label of the product).

4. If a solution is sprayed on a clean surface, the solution must remain there for the time required by the product label (merely spraying and wiping is cleaning - NOT considered proper disinfection).

5. If the product label states 'complete immersion', this product cannot be used to disinfect by spraying.

6. Any use other than that on the label is a violation of Federal Law.

7. If using an EPA registered disinfectant in a whirlpool pedicure spa, the solution MUST be circulated for the time required by the label (the solution must go where the water was and remain there for the specified time), especially if the label states to disinfect by complete immersion.

safety caution!

Improperly mixing disinfectants, to be weaker or more concentrated than the manufacturer's instructions, can dramatically reduce their effectiveness. Always add the disinfectant concentrate to the water when mixing. Quats contain detergents that will foam if you add water to the concentrate, which can result in an incorrect mixing ratio.

The use of safety glasses and gloves is recommended.

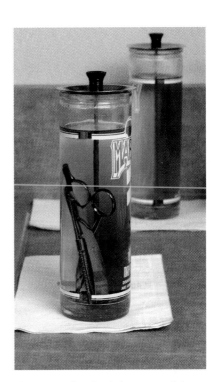

Figure 5–6 Completely immerse tools in disinfectant.

NOTE: Absorbent nail files must be disposed of if they accidentally break the client's skin or contact unhealthy skin or nails.

Types of Disinfectants

Quats. **Quaternary ammonium compounds** (KWAT-ur-nayr-ree uh-MOH-neeum), commonly called "quats," are very safe and useful disinfectants. The most advanced type of these formulations are called "dual quats" because they contain sophisticated blends of quats that work together to dramatically increase the effectiveness of these disinfectants. Quat solutions disinfect implements usually in 10 minutes. These formulas contain anti-rust ingredients, but leaving tools in the solution for longer can cause damage. Complete immersion means enough liquid to cover all surfaces of the item being disinfected. Spraying is not adequate disinfection unless the solution saturates the surface and remains wet for the time specified by the product label.

Phenolics. **Phenolics** (fi-NOH-lik) are powerful tuberculocidal disinfectants. Phenolics have a very high pH and can cause damage to the skin and eyes, and some can be harmful to the environment. Phenolics have been used reliably over the years to disinfect salon tools; however, they do have some drawbacks. Phenol can damage plastic and rubber (phenolics should never be used to disinfect pedicure equipment) and can cause certain metals to rust. Extra care should be taken to avoid skin contact with phenolics.

Alcohol and Bleach. The word "alcohol" is often misunderstood. There are many different chemical compounds that are classified as alcohols. Two types of alcohol used as disinfectants in the salon are ethyl (ETH-ul) alcohol (ethanol or grain alcohol), and isopropyl (eye-soh-PROH-pul) alcohol (isopropanol or rubbing alcohol). When used properly, both of these alcohols are considered to be useful and powerful disinfectants. Alcohol can be used to disinfect some items used in the salon, especially **porous** and absorbent items. To be effective, the concentration of ethyl and isopropyl alcohol must be 70 percent or higher. Since alcohol was used as a disinfectant long before there was an EPA, it does not need an EPA registration number.

Caution: Alcohol should never be used to clean up blood or to disinfect any item that has contact with blood, body fluid, or any unhealthy condition.

Household bleach (5.25% **sodium hypochlorite**) (SOH-dee-um hy-puh- KLOR-ite) is an effective disinfectant for all uses in the salon. Bleach has been used extensively as a disinfectant, long before the EPA existed, so it is not required to have an EPA registration number. Using too much bleach can damage some metals and plastics, so be sure to read the label for safe use. Bleach can be corrosive to metals and plastics, and can cause skin irritation. To mix bleach solution, add 3/4 cup of household bleach to one gallon (128 ounces) of water. Store this solution away from heat and light.

Fumigants. Years ago, formalin tablets were used as fumigants in dry cabinet "sanitizers". This was before EPA disinfectants came to market and before it was known that formaldehyde vapors may cause cancer in high concentrations. But the greater risk of using these tablets is the potential for

safety caution!

Bleach is not magic! Like all disinfectants, bleach is inactivated (less effective) in the presence of materials such as oils, lotions, creams, and biological residue. If bleach is used to disinfect pedicure equipment, it is critical to use a detergent first to remove any residue from pedicure products.

developing allergic sensitivity in nail professionals who constantly breathe these vapors. Fumigants are no longer used in the salon for several reasons: first, the label clearly requires that these be kept in an airtight container and it takes 24 hours to kill one fungus (remember that liquid disinfectants kill all fungi in 10 minutes); second, the vapors are poisonous and are extremely irritating to the eyes, nose, throat, and lungs and can cause skin allergies, irritation, dryness, and rash; third, using the product without following the label instructions is against federal law; and last, long-term exposure to formaldehyde vapors can aggravate existing lung problems and may create other symptoms similar to those seen in people with chronic bronchitis or asthma.

Caution: Fumigant tablets should *never* be left open in drawers or cabinets in the salon!

Glutaraldehyde is a dangerous chemical used to sterilize surgical instruments in hospitals. It is not safe for salon use.

Disinfectant Safety

Disinfectants are pesticides (poison) and may cause serious skin and eye damage. Some disinfectants appear clear, while others are a little cloudy, especially phenolics. A good rule to remember is always *use caution* when handling these products and avoid skin contact!

Safety Tips for Disinfectants

○ always wear gloves and safety glasses when mixing disinfectants. (Figure 5-7).

○ always add disinfectant to water, not water to disinfectant. Disinfectants contain detergents and will foam when water is added to them; this can result in an incorrect mixing ratio.

○ use tongs, gloves, or a draining basket to remove implements from disinfectants.

○ always keep disinfectants out of reach of children.

○ never pour quats, phenols, formalin, alcohol, or any other disinfectant over your hands. If you get disinfectants on your skin, immediately wash your hands with soap and warm water and dry them thoroughly.

○ carefully weigh and measure all products according to label instructions.

○ never place any disinfectant or other product in an unmarked container (Figure 5-8).

○ always follow the manufacturer's instructions for mixing and using, and disposal of disinfectants.

○ change disinfectants every day, or more often if the solution becomes soiled or contaminated.

Figure 5–7 Wear gloves and safety goggles while handling disinfectants.

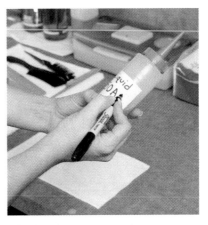

Figure 5–8 All containers should be labeled.

Jars or containers used to disinfect implements are often incorrectly called wet sanitizers. The purpose of these containers is to disinfect. Disinfectant

Figure 5–9 Carefully pour disinfectant into the water when preparing disinfectant solution.

containers must be covered but not airtight. Remember to clean the container every day as well. Always follow manufacturer's label instructions for disinfecting products.

Disinfect or Dispose

How can you tell which items in the salon can be disinfected and used more than once? If the process of cleaning and disinfecting damages the item or changes its condition, it is a single use item. There are two types of items used in salons; there are **multi-use** or reusable, and **single-use** or **disposable** items.

Multi-use items can be cleaned, disinfected and used on more than one person, even if the item is exposed to blood or body fluid. Examples of these are nippers, shears, combs, pushers, some nail files and buffers. Another word for these items is "**disinfectable,** " meaning these items can be disinfected.

Porous means made or constructed of an absorbent material. Some porous items can be safely cleaned, disinfected, and used on more than one client. Examples of these are towels, chamois, and some nail files and buffers. NOTE: If a porous item contacts broken skin, blood, body fluid or any unhealthy conditions, it must be discarded immediately. Do not try to disinfect it. If you are not sure if an item can be safely cleaned, disinfected and used again, throw it out. Remember, **when in doubt, throw it out!**

Single-use disposable items cannot be used more then once, either because these cannot be cleaned of all visible residue (such as pumice stones used for pedicures), or because cleaning and disinfecting damages them. Examples of disposable items are orangewood sticks, cotton balls, gauze, tissues, paper towels, and some nail files and buffers.

Disinfection Procedures

Tools and equipment must be cleaned and disinfected after each time they are used and before they may be used on another client. Be certain to dilute and mix disinfectants according to label of the product that you choose. Mix disinfectants according to manufacturer's directions, always adding disinfectant to the water (Figure 5-9).

Towels, Linens and Capes. Clean towels and linens must be used for each client. Once a towel or linen has been used on a client, it must not be used again until it has been properly laundered. Store soiled linens and towels separately from clean linens and towels. It is not necessary to store clean towels in a closed container unless your regulatory agency requires it. Whenever possible, use disposable towels, especially in rest rooms. Use disposable neck strips or towels to keep capes from cutting, or shampooing and chemical services from touching the client's skin. If a cape touches skin, do not use it again until it has been cleaned.

Work Surfaces. Before beginning service for each client, all work surfaces (manicure tables, workstations, esthetic tables, etc.) must be cleaned by wiping with a clean disposable towel. It is not necessary to disinfect tables and

safety caution!

Ultraviolet (UV) sanitizers are useful storage containers but they do not disinfect or sterilize.

PROCEDURE 5-1

DISINFECTING NON-ELECTRICAL TOOLS AND EQUIPMENT

These include combs, brushes, rollers, picks, styling tools, scissors, tweezers, nail clippers, and multi-use abrasive nail files

1. Clean tools and equipment to remove all visible matter and residue (Figure 5-10).

2. Rinse thoroughly, and pat dry with a clean towel.

3. Completely immerse implements in a properly mixed disinfecting solution for 10 minutes (Figure 5-11) or per the manufacturer's directions.

4. Remove implements with tongs, basket, or gloves to avoid skin contact (Figure 5-12).

5. Rinse and dry tools thoroughly.

6. Store disinfected implements. Store disinfected implements in a clean container and sanitary manner between uses. A clean drawer can be used for storage of tools if only clean items are in it. Never seal tools inside a closed airtight container or they may not completely dry, which can promote bacterial growth.

Figure 5–10 Remove all visible debris and residue from tools and implements.

Figure 5–11 Submerge combs and brushes in disinfectant solution for 10 minutes.

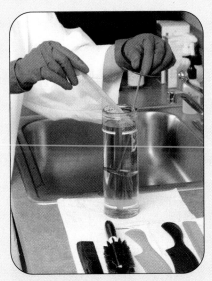

Figure 5–12 Remove implements with tongs, gloves, or a draining basket.

chairs unless the customers touch them with their skin, but they certainly need to be cleaned regularly (Figure 5-13). Clean doorknobs and handles daily to reduce germs on hands.

Individual Client Packs

You may save client packs with items like nail files and buffers as long as each item in the pack is cleaned, disinfected, and dried before being placed in the pack. Do not put single-use items in client packs stored between services. Never use bags or containers with an airtight seal to store tools or implements. Saving client tools to avoid cleaning and disinfecting is NOT safe and violates state rules. Remember, state rules require ALL tools and equipment be cleaned and disinfected before each use - even if used on the same person! This also applies to clients that bring their tools with them to the salon - before you use it, you must clean and then disinfect each item for 10 minutes! Remember, it is *your* license that is at risk if there is a problem, even if your client brings her tools with her. This practice should be vehemently discouraged.

Disinfecting Foot Spas and Pedicure Equipment

All equipment that holds water for pedicures, including whirlpool spas, "pipe-less" units, foot baths, basins, tubs, sinks, and bowls, must be cleaned and disinfected after every pedicure. Inspectors can issue fines if there is no logbook. Most pedicure spas hold 5 gallons of water; check with the manufacturer so that you use the correct amount of disinfectant. Remember: 128 ounces = 1 gallon.

Figure 5–13 Clean manicure tables.

PROCEDURE 5-2

DISINFECTING FOOT SPAS AFTER EACH CLIENT

1. **Drain and remove debris.** Drain all water and remove all visible debris from the foot spa or basin; if there is a footplate or impeller, remove it and clean the areas behind and underneath.

2. **Thoroughly clean.** Clean the surfaces and walls of the foot spas or basin with liquid soap and a brush to remove all visible debris, and rinse with clean, clear water; remember to clean and disinfect the brush.

3. **Disinfect basin.** Disinfect the foot basin with an EPA-registered liquid hospital disinfectant for 10 minutes. If it is a whirlpool unit, the solution must be circulated. The solution must go every place the water was and stay there for 10 minutes (or as indicated on the product label). Until then the unit is not properly disinfected!

4. **Dry basin.** Wipe dry with a disposable towel. Cloth towels can transmit pathogens if they are not properly laundered between clients.

5. Record the time and date these procedures were performed in the pedicure log book, if required by your state regulatory agency.

PROCEDURE 5-3

DISINFECTING FOOT SPAS AT THE END OF EACH DAY

1. Remove the screen. Clean the screen and the area behind the screen of all visible residue and trapped materials with a brush and liquid soap and water. Replace the screen.

2. Fill the basin with warm water and chelating liquid soap; flush the spa system for 5 minutes, then rinse and drain.

3. Fill the basin with water and the correct amount of an EPA-registered liquid hospital disinfectant. Circulate this solution through the basin for 10 minutes, then drain and rinse.

4. Allow the unit to completely dry overnight.

5. Make a record of the date and time of this cleaning and disinfecting in the salon pedicure log book, if required by your state regulatory agency.

Foaming: If the disinfectant foams while it circulates, run the unit for about 90 seconds and turn off the jets. Leave the solution in the basin for the remainder of 10 minutes; then drain.

PROCEDURE 5-4

DISINFECTING FOOT SPAS AT LEAST ONCE EACH WEEK

1 Drain all water and remove all debris from the foot spa or basin; if there is a footplate or impeller, remove it and clean the areas behind and underneath.

2 Clean the surfaces and walls of the foot spas or basin with liquid soap and a brush to remove all visible debris, and rinse with clean, clear water; remember to clean and disinfect the brush.

3 Disinfect the foot basin with an EPA-registered liquid hospital disinfectant for 10 minutes. If it is a whirlpool unit, the solution must be circulated to ensure proper disinfection.

4 Do not drain the disinfectant solution. Turn off the unit and leave the solution in the unit overnight (6-10 hours).

5 In the morning, drain and rinse.

6 Record this procedure in the salon pedicure logbook, if required by your state regulatory agency.

Note: Never place client's feet in water that contains a disinfectant.

Detergents and Soaps. Using **chelating surfactant** soaps or detergents, which work to sequester debris, is very important for removing the residue from pedicure products like scrubs, salts, and masques. These detergents work in all types of water, are low-sudsing, and are especially formulated to work in the areas where hard water is prevalent. Check with your local distributor for pedicure cleaners that contain chelating detergents.

Additives, Powders and Tablets. There is no additive, powder, or tablet that eliminates the need for you to clean and disinfect. You cannot replace proper cleaning and disinfection with a shortcut. These products cannot be used instead of EPA registered liquid disinfectant solutions. For example, be wary of products containing Chloramine-T because this chemical is not recognized as an effective disinfectant for use in the United States.

Dispensary

The dispensary must be kept clean and orderly, with the contents of all containers clearly marked. Store products according to manufacturers' instructions and away from heat. Keep MSDSs for all chemicals used in the salon.

PROCEDURE 5-5
WASHING HANDS

1. Wet your hands with warm water.

2. Using liquid soap and a clean, disinfected soft bristle nail brush, scrub your hands together and work up a good lather for at least 20 seconds. Give particular attention to the areas between the fingers, the nails, both sides of the hands, and the exposed portions of the arms (Figure 5-14). Be sure to use the nail brush to carefully scrub the underside of the nail plate where bacteria can hide.

3. Thoroughly rinse soap residue from your hands with warm water.

4. Dry your hands using a disposable paper towel, air blower or clean cloth towel.

Figure 5–14 Proper hand-washing technique.

Handling Disposable Supplies. All items designed to be disposed of after a single use, such as orangewood sticks, cotton, gauze, neck strips, nail wipes, and paper towels, should be thrown away after one use. Anything exposed to blood, including skincare treatment debris, must be double-bagged and marked with a biohazard sticker or disposed of according to OSHA standards (separated from other waste and disposed of according to federal, state, and local regulations). Puncture-proof containers should be used for disposal of all sharps.

Remember: Disinfect or Discard.

Washing Hands

Hand washing is one of the most important actions to prevent spreading germs from one person to another. Hand washing removes germs from the folds and grooves of the skin and from under the free edge of the nail plate by lifting and rinsing them from the surface. In the salon, hands, both yours and the clients, should be thoroughly washed with soap and water before each service. Medical studies suggest that antimicrobial and antibacterial soaps are no more effective than regular soaps or detergents and may actually promote the growth of resistant strains.

The use of a moisturizing hand lotion can help prevent dry skin, which can be caused by repeated hand washing.

Waterless Hand Sanitizers

Antiseptics (ant-ih-SEP-tiks) are agents formulated for use on skin. Antiseptics can contain either alcohol or benzalkonium chloride (less drying to

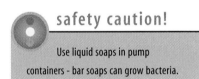

safety caution!

Use liquid soaps in pump containers - bar soaps can grow bacteria.

the skin than alcohol). Both types of antiseptics are effective for cleaning (sanitizing) hands if soap and water are not available, but should not replace washing with soap, soft bristle, brush and water. These agents are not the same as surface or implement disinfectants, so never use an antiseptic to disinfect instruments or other surfaces.

UNIVERSAL PRECAUTIONS

Universal Precautions are a set of guidelines published by OSHA that require the employer and the employee to assume that all human blood and body fluids are infectious for bloodborne pathogens. Because it is impossible to identify clients with infectious diseases, the same infection control practices should be used with all clients. In most instances, clients who are infected with Hepatitis B Virus or other bloodborne pathogens are **asymptomatic,** which means that they show no symptoms or signs of infection. Bloodborne pathogens are more difficult to kill than germs that live outside the body.

OSHA sets safety standards and precautions that protect employees when they are potentially exposed to bloodborne pathogens. Precautions include hand-washing, wearing gloves, and proper handling and disposal of sharp instruments and items that have been contaminated by blood or other body fluids. It is important that specific procedures are followed if blood or body fluid is present.

Contact with Blood or Body Fluid

Accidents happen. If a client's skin is cut during a salon service, blood or body fluid can be present. If this should occur, follow these steps for the safety of both you and the client:

1. If a cut occurs during service, stop the service.

2. Wear gloves to protect yourself against contact with the client's blood.

3. Clean the injured area with an antiseptic. Each salon must have a first aid kit.

4. Bandage the cut with an adhesive bandage.

5. Clean workstation as necessary.

6. Discard contaminated objects. Discard all disposable contaminated objects such as wipes or cotton balls by double-bagging (place the waste in a plastic bag and then in a trash bag). Use a biohazard sticker (red or orange), or a container for contaminated waste. Deposit sharp disposables in a sharps box (Figure 5–15).

7. Disinfect tools and implements. Remember, before removing your gloves, all tools and implements that have come into contact with blood or body fluids must be thoroughly cleaned and completely immersed in an EPA-registered hospital disinfectant

Figure 5–15 A sharps box.

solution or 10% bleach solution for ten minutes. Because blood can carry pathogens, you should never touch an open sore or wound.

8. Remove your gloves. Wash your hands with soap and warm water before returning to the service.

THE PROFESSIONAL SALON IMAGE

Cleanliness should be a part of your normal routine as well as those who work with you. This way, you and your coworkers can project a steadfast professional image. The following are some simple guidelines that will keep the salon looking its best:

1. Keep floors clean. Sweep hair after every client. Mop floors and vacuum carpets every day.

2. Keep trash in a waste receptacle; covered containers may be necessary by mandate of your state regulatory agency and to reduce chemical odors and look more professional.

3. Control dust, hair and other debris.

4. Clean fans, ventilation systems, and humidifiers at least once each week.

5. Keep all work areas well lit.

6. Keep rest rooms clean, including door handles.

7. Provide toilet tissue, paper towels, liquid soap, and clean, soft bristle nail brushes in the rest room.

8. Do not allow the salon to be used for cooking or living quarters.

9. Never place food in refrigerators used to store salon products.

10. Prohibit eating, drinking, and smoking in areas where services are performed or where product mixing occurs, i.e. back bar area.

11. Empty waste receptacles regularly throughout the day. A metal waste receptacle with a self-closing lid works best.

12. Make sure all containers are properly marked and properly stored.

13. Never place any tools or implements in your mouth or pockets.

14. Properly clean and disinfect all tools after each use.

15. Store clean and disinfected tools in a clean container or sanitary manner. Clean drawers may be used for storage if only clean items are stored in them.

16. Avoid touching your face, mouth, or eye areas during services.

17. Clean all work surfaces after every client. This includes manicure tables, esthetic chairs and tables, workstations, and shampoo bowls.

18. Always use clean linens on clients and use disposable towels and linens. Keep soiled linens separate from clean linens. Use neck strips or towels to avoid skin contact with shampoo capes and cutting or chemical protection gowns.

19. Use exhaust systems in the salon. Replacing the air in the salon with fresh air at least 4 times every hour is recommended. This will ensure proper air quality in the salon.

Your Professional Responsibility

You have many responsibilities as a salon professional, but none is more important than protecting your clients' health and safety. Never take shortcuts for cleaning and disinfection. You can't afford to skip steps or save money when it comes to safety.

Remember, it is *your* responsibility to follow state laws and rules. Keep your license current and notify the licensing agency if you move, or change your name. Check the state website weekly for any changes to the rules.

REVIEW **QUESTIONS**

1. What is sanitation? Why is this important?

2. What is the primary purpose of regulatory agencies?

3. What is an exposure incident?

4. List the steps for cleaning and disinfecting electrical equipment.

5. List the three types of microorganisms that are important to nail technology.

6. What is complete immersion?

7. Is HIV a risk in the salon? Why or why not?

8. What is a contagious or communicable disease?

9. How often should disinfectant solutions be changed?

10. Describe the procedure for taking care of blood or body fluid in the salon.

11. How do you know if an item is disinfectable?

12. Can porous items be disinfected?

13. What is an MSDS? Where can you get these?

14. List the steps for cleaning and disinfecting pedicure equipment after each client.

15. Explain how to clean and disinfect the following: implements for haircutting and styling; nail implements; linens and capes; electrical tools that cannot be immersed.

16. List at least six precautions to follow when using disinfectants.

17. What are Universal Precautions?

CHAPTER **GLOSSARY**

AIDS	Acquired immunodeficiency syndrome, a disease caused by the HIV virus, which breaks down the body's immune system; not a transmission risk to consumers in the salon.
allergy	is an immune system response to certain foods, chemicals, or other normally harmless substances that is caused by repeated exposure to that substance.
antiseptics	Chemical germicides formulated for use on skin, registered and regulated by the FDA.
bacteria	One-celled microorganisms; some are harmful, most are harmless.
bactericidal	Capable of destroying bacteria.
bloodborne pathogens	Disease-causing microorganisms carried in the body by blood or body fluids.
contagious disease	Disease that can be easily spread to others by contact.
diagnosis	Determining the nature of a disease or infection; must be done by a physician. Federal regulations prohibit salon professionals from performing any medical diagnosis.
disease	Abnormal condition of all or part of the body, organ, or mind that makes it incapable of carrying on normal function.

disinfectable	An item that can be disinfected.
disinfectants	Chemical products that destroy most bacteria and viruses, but not spores, on surfaces.
disinfection	The process that eliminates most microorganisms, but is not effective against bacterial spores.
efficacy	The effectiveness with which a disinfecting solution kills germs when used according to the label.
fungi (singular: fungus)	Microscopic plant parasites, including molds, mildews, and yeasts.
fungicidal	Capable of destroying fungi.
hepatitis	A bloodborne virus that causes disease affecting the liver.
HIV	Human immunodeficiency virus; virus that can cause AIDS.
infection	The invasion of body tissues by pathogens.
infectious	Infection that can be spread from one person to another person or from one infected body part to another.
inflammation	The body's response to injury or infection with redness, heat, pain, and swelling.
microorganism	A microscopic plant or animal.
mildew	A type of fungus that affects plants or grows on inanimate objects, but does not cause human infections in the salon setting.
MSDS	Material Safety Data Sheet; safety information about products compiled by a manufacturer.
nonpathogenic	Not harmful; organisms that may perform useful functions.
occupational disease	Illness resulting from conditions associated with employment.
parasite	Plant or animal organism that derives its nutrition from another organism.
pathogenic	Causing disease; may cause harmful conditions or illnesses in humans.
pediculosis capitis	Skin disease caused by infestation of head lice.
phenolics	Powerful tuberculocidal disinfectants.
porous	Absorbent; having pores or openings.
quaternary ammonium compounds	A type of disinfectant solution safe for all uses in the salon; commonly called quats.
sanitation or sanitizing	Cleaning to remove all visible residue and matter.
sodium hypochlorite	Common household bleach; disinfectant for salon use.
sterilization	The process that completely destroys all microbial life, including spores.
toxins	Poisonous substances, some of which can be produced by certain microorganisms.
tuberculocidal	Disinfectants that kill the bacteria that can cause tuberculosis.

tuberculosis	A disease caused by a bacteria that is only transmitted through coughing.
Universal Precautions	A set of guidelines published by OSHA that require the employer and the employee to assume that all human blood and body fluids are infectious for bloodborne pathogens.
virucidal	Capable of destroying viruses.
virus	A tiny organism that can invest plants and animals; lives and reproduces by penetrating cells and becoming part of them.

General Anatomy and Physiology

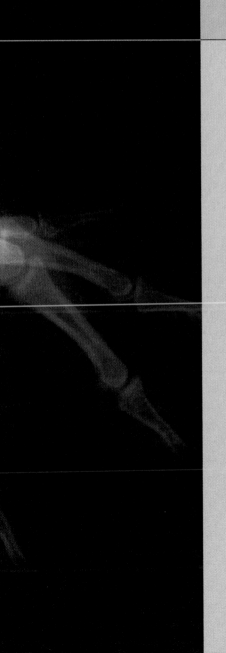

CHAPTER OUTLINE

LEARNING OBJECTIVES

After completing this chapter, you will be able to:

1. Explain the importance of anatomy and physiology to the cosmetology profession.
2. Describe cells, their structure, and their reproduction.
3. Define tissue and identify the types of tissues found in the body.
4. Name the 10 main body systems and explain their basic functions.

KEY **TERMS**

Page number indicates where in the chapter the term is used.

abductor
pg. 96

abductor hallucis
pg. 97

adductor
pg. 97

anabolism
pg. 91

anatomy
pg. 89

anterior tibial artery
pg. 103

anterior tibial nerve
pg. 100

artery
pg. 101

atrium
pg. 100

autonomic nervous system
pg. 98

axon
pg. 99

belly (muscle)
pg. 95

bicep
pg. 96

blood
pg. 102

blood vascular system
pg. 100

body systems
pg. 92

brain
pg. 98

capillary
pg. 102

cardiac muscle
pg. 95

carpus
pg. 94

catabolism
pg. 91

cell membrane
pg. 90

cells
pg. 90

central nervous system
pg. 98

circulatory system
pg. 100

common peroneal nerve
pg. 100

connective tissue
pg. 91

cytoplasm
pg. 90

deep peroneal nerve
pg. 100

deltoid
pg. 96

dendrites
pg. 99

diaphragm
pg. 104

digestive system
pg. 103

digit
pg. 94

digital nerve
pg. 99

dorsal
pg. 100

dorsal cutaneous nerve
pg. 100

dorsalis pedis artery
pg. 103

endocrine (ductless) glands
pg. 103

endocrine system
pg. 103

epithelial tissue
pg. 91

excretory system
pg. 104

exhalation
pg. 104

exocrine (duct) glands
pg. 103

extensor
pg. 96

extensor digitorum brevis
pg. 97

extensor digitorum longus
pg. 97

femur
pg. 94

fibula
pg. 94

flexor
pg. 96

flexor digitorum brevis
pg. 97

gastrocnemius
pg. 97

gland
pg. 103

heart
pg. 100

hemoglobin
pg. 102

histology
pg. 89

hormone
pg. 103

humerus
pg. 94

inhalation
pg. 104

insertion
pg. 95

integumentary system
pg. 104

joint
pg. 94

latissimus dorsi
pg. 96

liquid tissue
pg. 91

lungs
pg. 104

lymph
pg. 100

lymph node
pg. 103

lymph vascular system
pg. 100

median nerve
pg. 99

metabolism
pg. 91

metacarpus
pg. 94

metatarsal
pg. 94

mitosis
pg. 91

motor nerve
pg. 99

muscular system
pg. 95

muscular tissue
pg. 92

musculo-cutaneous nerve
pg. 100

myology
pg. 95

nerve
pg. 99

nerve tissue
pg. 92

nervous system
pg. 98

neuron
pg. 99

neurology
pg. 98

nonstriated muscle
pg. 95

nucleus
pg. 90

organ
pg. 92

origin
pg. 95

os
pg. 92

osteology
pg. 92

patella
pg. 94

A side from medical practitioners, few professionals are licensed to actually touch people as part of their services. When performing nail services, you are touching your clients in ways that few other people have ever done.

While understanding the overall concept of human anatomy is important, nail technology is primarily restricted to the muscles, nerves, circulatory system, and bones of the arms, hands, lower legs, and feet.

WHY STUDY ANATOMY?

As a beauty professional, an overview of human anatomy and physiology will enable you to:

Understand how the human body functions as an integrated whole.

Recognize changes from the norm.

Determine a scientific basis for the proper application of services and products such as scalp manipulations, facials, and hand and arm massages.

Anatomy is the study of the structures of the human body that can be seen with the naked eye, and what they are made up of. It is the science of the structure of organisms, or of their parts.

Physiology (fiz-ih-OL-oh-jee) is the study of the functions and activities performed by the body structures.

Histology (his-TAHL-uh-jee) is the study of the tiny structures found in living tissue, that is, microscopic anatomy.

CELLS

Cells are the basic units of all living things, from bacteria to plants and animals, and including human beings. Without cells, life does not exist. As a basic functional unit, the cell is responsible for carrying on all life processes. There are trillions of cells in the human body, and they vary widely in size, shape, and purpose.

Basic Construction of the Cell

The cells of all living things are composed of a substance called **protoplasm** (PROH-toh-plaz-um), a colorless jelly-like substance in which food elements such as proteins, fats, carbohydrates, mineral salts, and water are present. You can visualize the protoplasm of a cell as being similar to the white of a raw egg. In addition to protoplasm, most cells also include the following (Figure 6–1):

> The **nucleus** (NOO-klee-us) is the dense, active protoplasm found in the center of the cell. It plays an important part in cell reproduction and metabolism. You can visualize the nucleus as the yolk of a raw egg.

> The **cytoplasm** (sy-toh-PLAZ-um) is all the protoplasm of a cell that surrounds the nucleus. It is the watery fluid that cells need for growth, reproduction, and self-repair.

> The **cell membrane** acts like a balloon to contain the protoplasm and allows certain types of substances to pass through its walls.

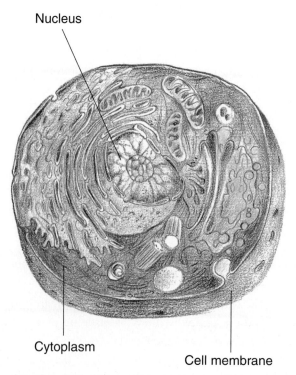

Nucleus

Cytoplasm

Cell membrane

Figure 6–1 Anatomy of the cell.

Cell Reproduction and Division

Cells have the ability to reproduce, thus providing new cells for the growth and replacement of worn or injured ones. Most cells reproduce by dividing into two identical cells called daughter cells. This reproduction process is known as **mitosis** (my-TOH-sis). As long as conditions are favorable, the cell will grow and reproduce. This is true of human cells, plant cells, and single-cell creatures such as bacteria. Favorable conditions include an adequate supply of food, oxygen, and water; suitable temperatures; and the ability to eliminate waste products. If conditions become unfavorable, the cell will become impaired or may die. Unfavorable conditions include toxins (poison) and disease.

Cell Metabolism

Metabolism (muh-TAB-uh-liz-um) is a chemical process that takes place in living organisms, whereby the cells are nourished and carry out their activities. Metabolism has two phases.

> **Anabolism** (uh-NAB-uh-liz-um) is constructive metabolism, the process of building up larger molecules from smaller ones. During this process, the body stores water, food, and oxygen for the time when these substances will be needed for cell growth, reproduction or repair.

> **Catabolism** (kuh-TAB-uh-liz-um) is the phase of metabolism that involves the breaking down of complex compounds within the cells into smaller ones. This process releases energy that has been stored.

> Anabolism and catabolism are carried out simultaneously and continually within the cells as part of their normal processes.

TISSUES

A **tissue** (TISH-oo) is a collection of similar cells that perform a particular function. Each tissue has a specific function and can be recognized by its characteristic appearance. Body tissues are composed of large amounts of water, along with various other substances. There are five types of tissue in the body.

o **Connective tissue** serves to support, protect, and bind together other tissues of the body. Examples of connective tissue are bone, cartilage, ligaments, tendons, fascia (which separates muscles), and fat or adipose tissue.

o **Epithelial tissue** (ep-ih-THEE-lee-ul) is a protective covering on body surfaces. Skin, mucous membranes, and the lining of the heart, digestive, and respiratory organs, and glands are all examples of epithelial tissue.

o **Liquid tissue**, such as blood and lymph, carries food, waste products, and hormones through the body.

○ **Muscular tissue** contracts and moves the various parts of the body.

○ **Nerve tissue** carries messages to and from the brain and controls and coordinates all bodily functions. Nerve tissue is composed of special cells known as neurons, which make up the nerves, brain, and spinal cord.

ORGANS AND BODY SYSTEMS

Organs are groups of tissues designed to perform a specific function. Table 6–1 lists some of the most important organs of the body.

Body systems are groups of bodily organs acting together to perform one or more functions. The human body is composed of 10 major **systems** (Table 6–2).

THE SKELETAL SYSTEM

The **skeletal system** is the physical foundation of the body. It is composed of 206 bones that vary in size and shape and are connected by movable and immovable joints. **Osteology** (ahs-tee-AHL-oh-jee) is the study of anatomy, structure, and function of the bones. **Os** means "bone," and is used as a prefix in many medical terms, such as osteoarthritis, a joint disease.

Except for the tissue that forms the major part of the teeth, bone is the hardest tissue in the body. It is composed of connective tissue consisting of about one-third organic matter, such as cells and blood, and two-thirds minerals, mainly calcium carbonate and calcium phosphate.

TABLE 6-1 ○ SOME MAJOR BODY ORGANS AND THEIR FUNCTIONS	
Organ	**Function**
Brain	Controls the body
Eyes	Control vision
Heart	Circulates the blood
Kidneys	Excrete water and waste products
Lungs	Supply oxygen to the blood
Liver	Removes waste created by digestion
Skin	External protective coating that covers the body
Stomach and intestines	Digest food

TABLE 6-2 ● BODY SYSTEMS AND THEIR FUNCTIONS

System	Function
Circulatory	Controls the steady circulation of the blood through the body via the heart and blood vessels
Digestive	Changes food into nutrients and wastes; consists of mouth, stomach, intestines, salivary and gastric glands, and other organs
Endocrine	Affects the growth, development, sexual activities, and health of the entire body; consists of specialized glands
Excretory	Purifies the body by the elimination of waste matter; consists of kidneys, liver, skin, intestines, and lungs
Integumentary	Serves as a protective covering and helps in regulating the body's temperature; consists of skin, accessory organs such as oil and sweat glands, sensory receptors, hair, and nails
Muscular	Covers, shapes, and supports the skeleton tissue; also contracts and moves various parts of the body; consists of muscles
Nervous	Controls and coordinates all other systems and makes them work harmoniously and efficiently; consists of brain, spinal cord, and nerves
Reproductive	Responsible for processes by which plants and animals produce offspring
Respiratory	Enables breathing, supplying the body with oxygen, and eliminating carbon dioxide as a waste product; consists of lungs and air passages
Skeletal	Physical foundatio

The primary functions of the skeletal system are to:

Give shape and support to the body.

Protect various internal structures and organs.

Serve as attachments for muscles and act as levers to produce body movement.

Help produce both white and red blood cells (one of the functions of bone marrow).

Store most of the body's calcium supply as well as phosphorus, magnesium, and sodium.

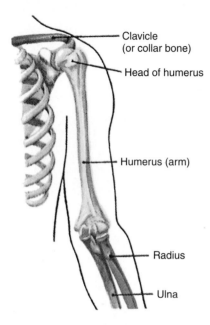

Figure 6–2 Bones of the arm.

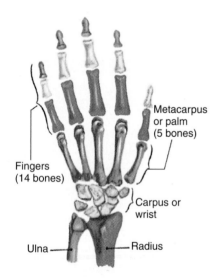

Figure 6–3 Bones of the hand.

A **joint** is the connection between two or more bones of the skeleton. There are two types of joints: movable, such as elbows, knees, and hips; and immovable, such as the pelvis or skull, which allows little or no movement.

Bones of the Arms and Hands

The important bones of the shoulder, arms, and hands that you should know about (Figures 6–2 and 6–3) include the following:

Humerus (HYOO-muh-rus). Uppermost and largest bone of the arm, extending from the elbow to the shoulder.

Ulna (UL-nuh). Inner and larger bone of the forearm (lower arm), attached to the wrist and located on the side of the little finger.

Radius (RAY-dee-us). Smaller bone in the forearm (lower arm) on the same side as the thumb.

Carpus (KAR-pus). The wrist; flexible joint composed of a group of eight small, irregular bones (carpals) held together by ligaments.

Metacarpus (met-uh-KAR-pus). Bones of the palm of the hand; parts of the hand containing five bones between the carpus and phalanges.

Phalanges (fuh-LAN-jeez). Bones in the fingers, or **digits** (also the toes), consisting of three bones in each finger and two in each thumb, totaling 14 bones.

Bones of the Leg and Foot

The **femur** (FEE-mur) is a heavy, long bone that forms the leg above the knee.

The **tibia** (TIB-ee-ah) is the larger of the two bones that form the leg below the knee. The tibia may be visualized as a "bump" on the big-toe side of the ankle.

The **fibula** (FIB-ya-lah) is the smaller of the two bones that form the leg below the knee. The fibula may be visualized as a "bump" on the little-toe side of the ankle.

The **patella** (pah-TEL-lah), also called the accessory bone, forms the knee cap joint (Figure 6–4).

The ankle joint is made up of three bones. The ankle joint is formed by the tibia, fibula, and the **talus** (TA-lus) or ankle bone of the foot.

The foot is made up of 26 bones. These can be subdivided into three general categories: seven **tarsal** (TAHR-sul) bones (talus, calcaneous, navicular, three cuneiform bones, and the cuboid), and five **metatarsal** (met-ah-TAHR-sul) bones, which are long and slender, like the metacarpal bones of the hand, and 14 bones called **phalanges**, which compose the toes.

The phalanges are similar to the finger bones. There are three phalanges in each toe, except for the big toe, which has only two (Figure 6–5).

THE MUSCULAR SYSTEM

The **muscular system** is the body system that covers, shapes, and supports the skeleton tissue. It contracts and moves various parts of the body.

The nail technician must be concerned with the voluntary muscles that control movements of the arms, hands, lower legs, and feet. It is important to know where these muscles are located and what they control.

Myology (my-AHL-uh-jee) is the study of the structure, function, and diseases of the muscles. The human body has over 600 muscles, which are responsible for approximately 40 percent of the body's weight. Muscles are fibrous tissues that have the ability to stretch and contract according to demands of the body's movements. There are three types of muscular tissue.

Striated muscles (STRY-ayt-ed), also called skeletal muscles, are attached to the bones and are voluntary or consciously controlled. Striated (skeletal) muscles assist in maintaining the body's posture, and protect some internal organs (Figure 6–6).

Nonstriated muscles, or smooth muscles, are involuntary and function automatically, without conscious will. These muscles are found in the internal organs of the body, such as the digestive or respiratory systems (Figure 6–7).

Cardiac muscle is the involuntary muscle that is the heart. This type of muscle is not found in any other part of the body (Figure 6–8).

A muscle has three parts. The **origin** is the part that does not move; it is attached to the skeleton and is usually part of a skeletal muscle. The **insertion** is the part of the muscle at the more movable attachment to the skeleton. The **belly** is the middle part of the muscle. Pressure in massage is usually directed from the insertion to the origin.

Muscular tissue can be stimulated by:

o Massage (hand or electric vibrator)

o Electrical current (high frequency or faradic current)

o Light (infrared or ultraviolet)

o Dry heat (heating lamps or heating caps)

o Moist heat (steamers or moderately warm steam towels)

o Nerve impulses (through the nervous system)

o Chemicals (certain acids and salts)

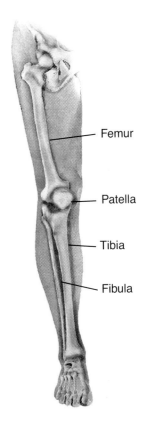

Figure 6–4 Bones of the leg.

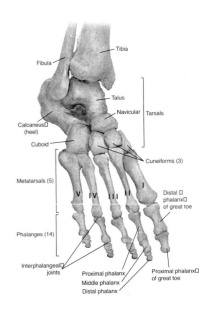

Figure 6–5 Bones of the foot and ankle.

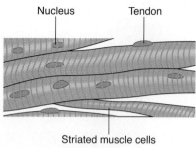

Figure 6–6 Striated muscle cells.

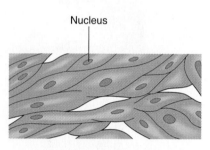

Figure 6–7 Nonstriated muscle cells.

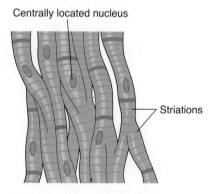

Figure 6–8 Cardiac muscle cells.

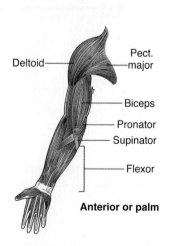

Figure 6–9a Muscles of the shoulder and arm.

Muscles That Attach the Arms to the Body

These muscles are briefly summarized below.

> **Latissimus dorsi** (lah-TIS-ih-mus DOR-see). Broad, flat superficial muscle covering the back of the neck and upper and middle region of the back, controlling the shoulder blade and the swinging movements of the arm.

> **Pectoralis major** (pek-tor-AL-is) and **pectoralis minor.** Muscles of the chest that assist the swinging movements of the arm.

> **Serratus anterior** (ser-RAT-us an-TEER-ee-or). Muscle of the chest that assists in breathing and in raising the arm.

> **Trapezius** (trah-PEE-zee-us). Muscle that covers the back of the neck and upper and middle region of the back; rotates and controls swinging movements of the arm.

Muscles of the Shoulder and Arm

There are three principal muscles of the shoulders and upper arms (Figure 6–9a and 6–9b):

> **Bicep** (BY-sep). Muscle producing the contour of the front and inner side of the upper arm; they lift the forearm and flex the elbow.

> **Deltoid** (DEL-toyd). Large, triangular muscle covering the shoulder joint that allows the arm to extend outward and to the side of the body.

> **Tricep** (TRY-sep). Large muscle that covers the entire back of the upper arm and extends the forearm.

The forearm is made up of a series of muscles and strong tendons. As a cosmetologist, you will be concerned with:

> **Extensors** (ik-STEN-surs). Muscles that straighten the wrist, hand, and fingers to form a straight line.

> **Flexors** (FLEK-surs). Extensor muscles of the wrist, involved in bending the wrist.

> **Pronators** (proh-NAY-tohrs). Muscles that turn the hand inward so that the palm faces downward.

> **Supinator** (SOO-puh-nayt-ur). Muscle of the forearm that rotates the radius outward and the palm upward.

Muscles of the Hand

The hand is one of the most complex parts of the body, with many small muscles that overlap from joint to joint, providing flexibility and strength to open and close the hand and fingers. Important muscles to know include the:

> **Abductors** (ab-DUK-turz). Muscles that separate the fingers (Figure 6–10).

Adductors (ah-DUK-turz). Muscles at the base of each finger that draw the fingers together.

Muscles of the Lower Leg and Foot

As a nail technician, you will use your knowledge of the muscles of the foot and leg during a pedicure. The muscles of the foot are small and provide proper support and cushioning for the foot and leg (Figure 6–11).

The **extensor digitorum longus** (eck-STEN-sur dij-it-TOHR-um LONG-us) bends the foot up and extends the toes.

The **tibialis anterior** (tib-ee-AHL-is an-TEHR-ee-ohr) covers the front of the shin. It bends the foot upward and inward.

The **peroneus longus** (per-oh-NEE-us LONG-us) covers the outer side of the calf and inverts the foot and turns it outward.

The **peroneus brevis** (BREV-us) originates on the lower surface of the fibula. It bends the foot down and out.

The **gastrocnemius** (gas-truc-NEEM-e-us) is attached to the lower rear surface of the heel and pulls the foot down.

The **soleus** (SO-lee-us) originates at the upper portion of the fibula and bends the foot down.

The muscles of the feet include the **extensor digitorum brevis** (ek-STEN-sur dij-it-TOHR-um BREV-us), **abductor hallucis** (ab-DUK-tohr ha-LU-sis), **flexor digitorum brevis** (FLEKS-or dij-it-TOHR-um BREVus) and the **abductor**. The foot muscles move the toes and help maintain balance while walking and standing (Figure 6–12).

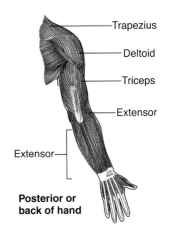

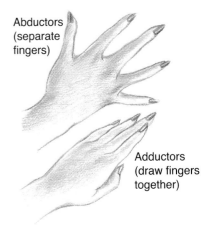

Figure 6–9b Muscles of the shoulder and arm. (Continued)

Figure 6–10 Muscles of the hand.

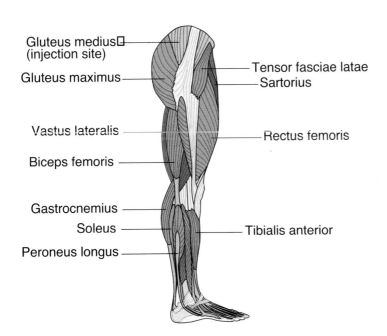

Figure 6–11 Muscles of the lower leg and foot.

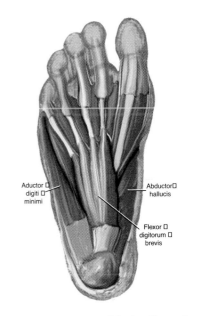

Figure 6–12 Muscles of the foot (bottom).

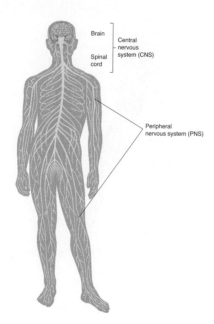

Brain
Central nervous system (CNS)
Spinal cord
Peripheral nervous system (PNS)

Figure 6–13 Principal parts of the nervous system.

THE NERVOUS SYSTEM

The **nervous system** is an exceptionally well-organized system that is responsible for coordinating all the many activities that are performed both inside and outside of the body. Every square inch of the human body is supplied with fine fibers known as nerves; there are over 100 billion nerve cells, known as neurons, in the body. The scientific study of the structure, function, and pathology of the nervous system is known as **neurology** (nuh-RAHL-uh-jee).

An understanding of how nerves work will help you perform services in a more proficient manner when administering massages or shampoos. It will also help you understand the effects that these treatments have on the body as a whole.

Divisions of the Nervous System

The principal components of the nervous system are the brain, spinal cord, and the nerves themselves (Figure 6–13). The nervous system as a whole is divided into three main subdivisions.

The **central nervous** system consists of the brain, spinal cord, spinal nerves, and cranial nerves. It controls consciousness and many mental activities, voluntary functions of the five senses (seeing, hearing, feeling, smelling, and tasting), and voluntary muscle actions, including all body movements and facial expressions.

The **peripheral nervous system** (puh-RIF-uh-rul) is a system of nerves that connects the peripheral (outer) parts of the body to the central nervous system; it has both sensory and motor nerves. Its function is to carry impulses, or messages, to and from the central nervous system.

The **autonomic nervous system** (aw-toh-NAHM-ik) is the part of the nervous system that controls the involuntary muscles; it regulates the action of the smooth muscles, glands, blood vessels, and heart.

The Brain and Spinal Cord

The **brain** is the largest and most complex nerve tissue in the body. The brain is contained in the cranium and weighs a little less than 3 pounds, on average. It controls sensation, muscles, activity of glands, and the power to think, sense, and feel. It sends and receives messages through 12 pairs of cranial nerves that originate in the brain and reach various parts of the head, face, and neck.

The **spinal cord** is the portion of the central nervous system that originates in the brain, extends down to the lower extremity of the trunk, and is protected by the spinal column. Thirty-one pairs of spinal nerves extending from the spinal cord are distributed to the muscles and skin of the trunk and limbs.

Nerve Cell Structure and Function

A **neuron** (NOO-rahn), or nerve cell, is the primary structural unit of the nervous system (Figure 6–14). It is composed of the cell body and nucleus; **dendrites** (DEN-dryts), tree-like branchings of nerve fibers extending from the nerve cell that receive impulses from other neurons; and the **axon** (AK-sahn) and axon terminal, which send impulses away from the cell body to other neurons, glands, or muscles.

Nerves are whitish cords made up of bundles of nerve fibers held together by connective tissue through which impulses are transmitted. Nerves have their origin in the brain and spinal cord and send their branches to all parts of the body.

Types of Nerves

Sensory nerves carry impulses or messages from the sense organs to the brain, where sensations of touch, cold, heat, sight, hearing, taste, smell, pain, and pressure are experienced. Sensory nerve endings called receptors are located close to the surface of the skin. As impulses pass from the sensory nerves to the brain and back through the motor nerves to the muscles, a complete circuit is established, resulting in movement of the muscles.

Motor nerves carry impulses from the brain to the muscles. The transmitted impulses produce movement.

A **reflex** (REE-fleks) is an automatic nerve reaction to a stimulus that involves the movement of an impulse from a sensory receptor along the sensory nerve to the spinal cord, and a responsive impulse is sent along a motor neuron to a muscle, causing a reaction (e.g., the quick removal of the hand from a hot object). Reflexes do not have to be learned; they are automatic.

Nerves of the Arm and Hand

The principal nerves supplying the superficial parts of the arm and hand are as follows (Figure 6–15):

> **Digital nerve** (DIJ-ut-tul) (sensory-motor), with its branches, supplies the fingers.
>
> **Radial nerve** (RAY-dee-ul) (sensory-motor), with its branches, supplies the thumb side of the arm and back of the hand.
>
> **Median nerve** (MEE-dee-un) (sensory-motor), smaller nerve than the ulnar and radial nerves that, with its branches, supplies the arm and hand.
>
> **Ulnar nerve** (UL-nur) (sensory-motor), with its branches, affects the little finger side of the arm and palm of the hand.

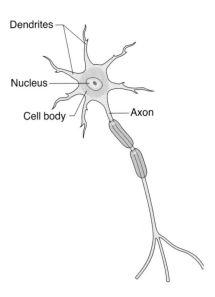

Figure 6–14 A neuron or nerve cell.

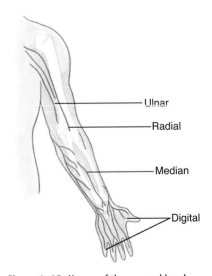

Figure 6–15 Nerves of the arm and hand.

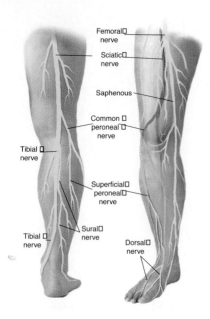

Figure 6–16 Nerves of the lower leg and foot.

Nerves of the Lower Leg and Foot

The **tibial** (TIB-ee-al) **nerve**, a division of the sciatic nerve, passes behind the knee. It subdivides and supplies impulses to the knee, the muscles of the calf, the skin of the leg, and the sole, heel, and underside of the toes.

The **common peroneal** (per-oh-NEE-al) **nerve**, also a division of the sciatic nerve, extends from behind the knee to wind around the head of the fibula to the front of the leg where it divides into two branches. The **deep peroneal nerve**, also known as the **anterior tibial nerve**, extends down the front of the leg, behind the muscles. It supplies impulses to these muscles and also to the muscles and skin on the top of the foot and adjacent sides of the first and second toes. The **superficial peroneal nerve**, also known as the **musculo-cutaneous nerve**, extends down the leg, just under the skin, supplying impulses to the muscles and the skin of the leg, as well as to the skin and toes on the top of the foot, where it is called the **dorsal** (DOOR-sal) or **dorsal cutaneous nerve**.

> The **saphenous** (sa-FEEN-us) **nerve** supplies impulses to the skin of the inner side of the leg and foot.
>
> The **sural nerve** supplies impulses to the skin on the outer side and back of the foot and leg.
>
> The **dorsal** (DOOR-sal) **nerve** supplies impulses to the skin on top of the foot (Figure 6–16).

● THE CIRCULATORY SYSTEM

The **circulatory system**, also referred to as the cardiovascular or vascular system, controls the steady circulation of the blood through the body by means of the heart and blood vessels. The circulatory system is made up of two divisions:

> The **blood vascular system**, which consists of the heart, arteries, veins, and capillaries for the distribution of blood throughout the body.
>
> The **lymph vascular system** (LIMF VAS-kyoo-lur) or lymphatic system, which acts as an aid to the blood system and consists of the lymph, lymphatics (lymph vessels), lymph nodes, and other structures. **Lymph** is a clear yellowish fluid that circulates in the lymphatics of the body. It carries waste and impurities away from the cells.

The Heart

The **heart** is often referred to as the body's pump. It is a muscular cone-shaped organ that keeps the blood moving within the circulatory system. It is enclosed by a membrane known as the **pericardium** (payr-ih-KAR-deeum).

The heart is the approximate size of a closed fist, weighs approximately 9 ounces, and is located in the chest cavity. The heartbeat is regulated by the vagus (tenth cranial) nerve and other nerves in the autonomic nervous system. In a normal resting state, the heart beats 72 to 80 times per minute.

The interior of the heart contains four chambers and four valves. The upper, thin-walled chambers are the right **atrium** (AY-tree-um) and left atrium. The lower, thick-walled chambers are the right **ventricle**

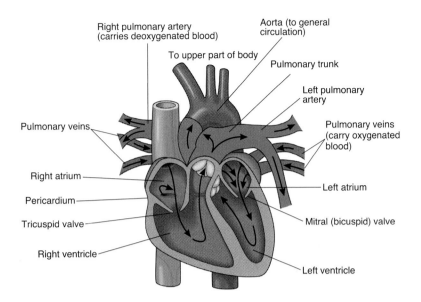

Right pulmonary artery
(carries deoxygenated blood)

To upper part of body

Aorta (to general circulation)

Pulmonary trunk

Left pulmonary artery

Pulmonary veins

Pulmonary veins (carry oxygenated blood)

Right atrium

Left atrium

Pericardium

Tricuspid valve

Mitral (bicuspid) valve

Right ventricle

Left ventricle

Figure 6–17 Anatomy of the heart.

(VEN-truh-kul) and left ventricle. **Valves** between the chambers allow the blood to flow in only one direction. With each contraction and relaxation of the heart, the blood flows in, travels from the atria (plural of atrium) to the ventricles, and is then driven out, to be distributed all over the body (Figure 6–17).

The blood is in constant and continuous circulation from the time that it leaves the heart until it returns to the heart. Two systems attend to this circulation. **Pulmonary circulation** sends the blood from the heart to the lungs to be purified. **Systemic circulation** or general circulation carries the blood from the heart throughout the body and back to the heart. The following is an overview of how these systems work.

1. Blood flows from the body into the right atrium.

2. From the right atrium, it flows through the tricuspid valve into the right ventricle.

3. The right ventricle pumps the blood to the lungs, where it releases waste gases and receives oxygen. The blood is then considered to be oxygen rich.

4. The oxygen-rich blood returns to the heart, entering the left atrium.

5. From the left atrium, the blood flows through the mitral valve into the left ventricle.

6. The blood then leaves the left ventricle and travels to all parts of the body.

Blood Vessels

The blood vessels are tube-like structures that include the arteries, capillaries, and veins. The function of these vessels is to transport blood to and from the heart, and then on to various tissues of the body.

Arteries are thick-walled, muscular, flexible tubes that carry oxygenated blood away from the heart to the capillaries. The largest artery in the body is the aorta.

Blood flow toward the heart

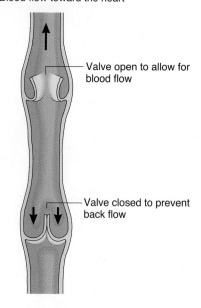

Valve open to allow for blood flow

Valve closed to prevent back flow

Figure 6–18 Valves in the veins.

Capillaries are tiny, thin-walled blood vessels that connect the smaller arteries to the veins. They bring nutrients to the cells and carry away waste materials.

Veins are thin-walled blood vessels that are less elastic than arteries. They contain cuplike valves that prevent backflow and carry blood containing waste products from the various capillaries back toward the heart for cleaning and to pick up oxygen. Veins are located closer to the outer skin surface of the body than arteries (Figure 6–18).

The Blood

Blood is a nutritive fluid circulating through the circulatory system. There are approximately 8 to 10 pints of blood in the human body, which contribute about 1/20th of the body's weight. Blood is approximately 80 percent water. It is sticky and salty, with a normal temperature of 98.6° Fahrenheit (36° Celsius). It is bright red in the arteries (except for the pulmonary artery) and dark red in the veins. The color change occurs with the exchange of carbon dioxide for oxygen as the blood passes through the lungs, and the exchange of oxygen for carbon dioxide as the blood circulates throughout the body. Red blood is oxygen rich; blue blood is oxygen poor.

Composition of the Blood

Blood is composed of red and white cells, platelets, plasma, and hemoglobin.

Red blood cells are produced in the red bone marrow. They contain **hemoglobin** (HEE-muh-gloh-bun), a complex iron protein that binds to oxygen, which is the function of red blood cells, to carry oxygen to the body cells.

White blood cells, also called white corpuscles or leukocytes (LOO-koh-syts), perform the function of destroying disease-causing microorganisms.

Platelets are much smaller than red blood cells. They contribute to the blood-clotting process, which stops bleeding.

Plasma (PLAZ-muh) is the fluid part of the blood in which the red and white blood cells and platelets flow. It is about 90 percent water and contains proteins and sugars. The main function of plasma is to carry food and other useful substances to the cells and to take carbon dioxide away from the cells.

Chief Functions of the Blood

Blood performs the following critical functions:

○ Carries water, oxygen, and food to all cells of the body.

○ Carries away carbon dioxide and waste products to be eliminated through the lungs, skin, kidneys, and large intestines.

○ Helps to equalize the body's temperature, thus protecting the body from extreme heat and cold.

○ Works with the immune system to protect the body from harmful microorganisms.

○ Seals leaks found in injured blood vessels by forming clots, thus preventing further blood loss.

The Lymph Vascular System

The lymph vascular system, also known as the lymphatic system, acts as an aid to the blood system. Lymph is circulated through the lymphatic vessels and filtered by the **lymph nodes**, which are found inside the lymphatic vessels. They filter the blood and help to fight infections.

The primary functions of the lymph vascular system are to:

Carry nourishment from the blood to the body cells.

Act as a defense against invading microorganisms and toxins.

Remove waste material from the body cells to the blood.

Provide a suitable fluid environment for the cells.

Blood Supply of the Arm and Hand

The ulnar and radial arteries are the main blood supply of the arms and hands (Figure 6–19). The **ulnar artery** and its numerous branches supply the little-finger side of the arm and palm of the hand. The **radial artery** and its branches supply the thumb side of the arm and the back of the hand.

While the arteries are found deep in the tissues, the veins lie nearer to the surface of the arms and hands.

Blood Supply to the Lower Leg and Foot

There are several major arteries that supply blood to the lower leg and foot.

The **popliteal** (pop-lih-TEE-ul) **artery** divides into two separate arteries known as the **anterior tibial** (TIB-ee-al) and the **posterior tibial**. The anterior tibial goes to the foot and becomes the **dorsalis pedis** which supplies the foot with blood.

As in the arm and hand, the important veins of the lower leg and foot are almost parallel with the arteries and take the same names (Figure 6–20).

THE ENDOCRINE SYSTEM

The **endocrine system** (EN-duh-krin) is made up of a group of specialized glands that affect the growth, development, sexual activities, and health of the entire body. **Glands** are specialized organs that remove certain elements from the blood to convert them into new compounds.

There are two main types of glands:

Exocrine glands (EK-suh-krin) or duct glands produce a substance that travels through small tube-like ducts. Sweat and oil glands of the skin and intestinal glands belong to this group.

Endocrine glands or ductless glands release secretions called **hormones** directly into the bloodstream, which in turn influence the welfare of the entire body. Hormones, such as insulin, adrenaline, and estrogen, stimulate functional activity or secretion in other parts of the body. These hormones can also affect your moods, feelings, and emotions.

THE DIGESTIVE SYSTEM

The **digestive system**, also called the gastrointestinal (gas-troh-in-TES-tunul) system, is responsible for breaking down food into nutrients and waste.

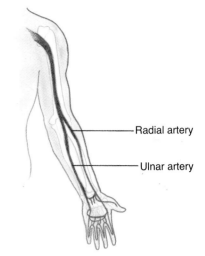

Figure 6–19 Arteries of the arm and hand.

Radial artery

Ulnar artery

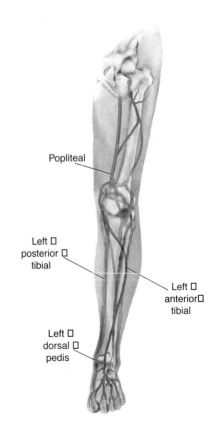

Popliteal

Left ☐ posterior ☐ tibial

Left ☐ anterior☐ tibial

Left ☐ dorsal ☐ pedis

Figure 6–20 Arteries of the lower leg and foot.

Digestive enzymes (EN-zymz) are chemicals that change certain kinds of food into a form that can be used by the body. The food, now in soluble form, is transported by the bloodstream and used by the body's cells and tissues. The entire food digestion process takes about 9 hours to complete.

THE EXCRETORY SYSTEM

The **excretory system** (EK-skre-tor-ee) is responsible for purifying the body by eliminating waste matter. The metabolism of body cells forms various toxic substances that, if retained, could poison the body.

Each of the following organs plays a crucial role in the excretory system:

The kidneys excrete waste containing urine.

The liver discharges waste containing bile.

The skin eliminates waste containing perspiration.

The large intestine eliminates decomposed and undigested food.

The lungs exhale carbon dioxide.

THE RESPIRATORY SYSTEM

The **respiratory system** enables breathing (**respiration**) and consists of the lungs and air passages. The **lungs** are spongy tissues composed of microscopic cells in which inhaled air is exchanged for carbon dioxide during one breathing cycle. The respiratory system is located within the chest cavity and is protected on both sides by the ribs. The **diaphragm** is a muscular wall that separates the thorax from the abdominal region and helps control breathing (Figure 6–21).

With each breathing cycle, an exchange of gases takes place. During **inhalation** (in-huh-LAY-shun), or breathing in, oxygen is passed into the blood. During **exhalation** (eks-huh-LAY-shun), or breathing outward, carbon dioxide (collected from the blood) is expelled from the lungs.

Oxygen is more essential than either food or water. Although people may survive for more than 60 days without food, and several days without water, if they are deprived of oxygen, they will die within a few minutes.

THE INTEGUMENTARY SYSTEM

The **integumentary system** is made up of the skin and its various accessory organs, such as the oil and sweat glands, sensory receptors, hair, and nails. (Skin anatomy and physiology are discussed in detail in Chapter 7.)

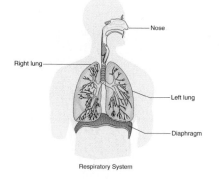

Nose

Right lung

Left lung

Diaphragm

Respiratory System

Figure 6–21 Respiratory system.

REVIEW **QUESTIONS**

1. Define anatomy, physiology, and histology.

2. Why is the study of anatomy, physiology, and histology important to the cosmetologist?

3. Name and describe the basic structures of a cell.

4. Explain cell metabolism and its purpose.

femur	A heavy, long bone that forms the leg above the knee.
fibula	The smaller of the two bones that form the leg below the knee. The fibula may be visualized as a "bump" on the littletoe side of the ankle.
flexor	Extensor muscle of the wrist involved in flexing the wrist.
flexor digitorum brevis	Muscle of the foot that moves the toes and help maintain balance while walking and standing.
gastrocnemius	Muscle that is attached to the lower rear surface of the heel and pulls the foot down.
gland	Specialized organ that removes certain constituents from the blood to convert them into new substances.
heart	Muscular cone-shaped organ that keeps the blood moving within the circulatory system.
hemoglobin	Coloring matter of the blood; and iron-containing protein in red blood cells that binds to oxygen.
histology	Science of the minute structures of organic tissues; microscopic anatomy.
hormone	Secretion produced by one of the endocrine glands and carried by the bloodstream or body fluid to another part of the body to stimulate a specific activity.
humerus	Uppermost and largest bone in the arm, extending from the elbow to the shoulder.
inhalation	The breathing in of air.
insertion	Part of the muscle at the more movable attachment to the skeleton.
integumentary system	The skin and its accessory organs, such as the oil and sweat glands, sensory receptors, hair, and nails.
joint	Connection between two or more bones of the skeleton.
latissimus dorsi	Broad, flat superficial muscle covering the back of the neck and upper and middle region of the back, controlling the shoulder blade and the swinging movements of the arm.
liquid tissue	Body tissue that carries food, waste products, and hormones (i.e., blood and lymph).
lungs	Organs of respiration; spongy tissues composed of microscopic cells in which inhaled air is exchanged for carbon dioxide.
lymph	Clear yellowish fluid that circulates in the lymph spaces (lymphatic) of the body; carries waste and impurities away from the cells.
lymph nodes	Special structures found inside the lymphatic vessels that filter lymph.
lymph vascular system	Body system that acts as an aid to the blood system and consists of the lymph spaces, lymph vessels, and lymph glands.
median nerve	Nerve that supplies the arm and hand.
metabolism	Chemical process taking place in living organisms whereby the cells are nourished and carry out their activities.
metacarpus	Bones of the palm of the hand; parts of the hand containing five bones between the carpus and phalanges.
metatarsal	One of three subdivisions of the foot comprised of five bones, which are long and slender, like the metacarpal bones of the hand, help make-up the foot. The other two subdivisions are the tarsal and phalanges. All three subdivisions comprise 26 bones.
mitosis	Cells dividing into two new cells (daughter cells); the usual process of cell reproduction of human tissues.
motor nerves	Nerves that carry impulses from the brain to the muscles.
muscular system	Body system that covers, shapes, and supports the skeleton tissue; contracts and moves various parts of the body.
muscular tissue	Tissue that contracts and moves various parts of the body.

musculo-cutaneous nerve	See "superficial peroneal nerve".
myology	Science of the nature, structure, function, and diseases of the muscles.
nerve	Whitish cord made up of bundles of nerve fibers held together by connective tissue, through which impulses are transmitted.
nerve tissue	Tissue that controls and coordinates all body functions.
nervous system	Body system composed of the brain, spinal cord, and nerves; controls and coordinates all other systems and makes them work harmoniously and efficiently.
neurology	Science of the structure, function, and pathology of the nervous system.
neuron	Nerve cell; basic unit of the nervous system, consisting of cell body, nucleus, dendrites, and axon.
nonstriated muscle	Also called involuntary or smooth muscle; muscle that functions automatically without conscious will.
nucleus	Dense, active protoplasm found in the center of the cell; plays an important part in cell reproduction and metabolism.
organs	In plants and animals, structures composed of specialized tissues and performing specific functions.
origin	Part of the muscle that does not move; it is attached to the skeleton and is usually part of a skeletal muscle.
os	Bone.
osteology	The study of anatomy, structure, and function of the bones.
patella	Also called the accessory bone, forms the knee cap joint.
pectoralis major, pectoralis minor	Muscles of the chest that assist the swinging movements of the arm.
pericardium	Double-layered membranous sac enclosing the heart.
peripheral nervous system	System of nerves and ganglia that connects the peripheral parts of the body to the central nervous system; it has both sensory and motor nerves.
peroneus brevis	Muscle that originates on the lower surface of the fibula. It bends the foot down and out.
peroneus longus	Muscle that covers the outer side of the calf and inverts the foot and turns it outward.
phalanges	Bones of the fingers or toes (singular: phalanx).
physiology	Study of the functions or activities performed by the body's structures.
plasma	Fluid part of the blood and lymph that carries food and secretions to the cells.
platelet	Blood cell that aids in the forming of clots.
popliteal artery	Divides into two separate arteries known as the anterior tibial (TIB-ee-al) and the posterior tibial. The anterior tibial goes to the foot and becomes the dorsalis pedis which supplies the foot with blood.
pronator	Muscle that turns the hand inward so that the palm faces downward.
protoplasm	Colorless jelly-like substance found inside cells in which food elements such as protein, fats, carbohydrates, mineral salts, and water are present.
pulmonary circulation	Blood circulation from heart to lungs and back to heart.
radial artery	Artery that supplies blood to the thumb side of the arm and the back of the hand; supplies the muscles of the skin, hands, fingers, wrist, elbow, and forearm.
radial nerve	Supplies the thumb side of the arm and back of the hand.
radius	Smaller bone in the forearm on the same side as the thumb.
red blood cells	Blood cells that carry oxygen from the lungs to the body cells and transport carbon dioxide from the cells back to the lungs.
reflex	Automatic nerve reaction to a stimulus that involves the movement of specific muscles as a response to impulses carried along a motor neuron to a muscle, causing a spontaneous reaction.

reproductive system	Body system responsible for processes by which plants and animals produce offspring.
respiration	Act of breathing; the exchange of carbon dioxide and oxygen in the lungs and within each cell.
respiratory system	Body system consisting of the lungs and air passages; enables breathing, supplying the body with oxygen and eliminating carbon dioxide wastes.
saphenous	Supplies impulses to the skin of the inner side of the leg and foot.
sensory (afferent) nerve	Nerve that carries impulses or messages from the sense organs to the brain, where sensations of touch, cold, heat, sight, hearing, taste, smell, pain, and pressure are experienced.
serratus anterior	Muscle of the chest that assists in breathing and in raising the arm.
skeletal system	Physical foundation of the body, comprised of 206 bones that vary in size and shape and are connected by movable and immovable joints.
soleus	Muscle that originates at the upper portion of the fibula and bends the foot down.
spinal cord	Portion of the central nervous system that originates in the brain, extends down to the lower extremity of the trunk, and is protected by the spinal column.
superficial peroneal nerve	A nerve that extends down the leg, just under the skin, supplying impulses to the muscles and the skin of the leg, as well as to the skin and toes on the top of the foot.
striated muscle	Also called voluntary or skeletal muscle; muscle that is consciously controlled.
supinator	Muscle of the forearm that rotates the radius outward and the palm upward.
sural nerve	Supplies impulses to the skin on the outer side and back of the foot and leg.
system	Comprised of a group of bodily organs acting together to perform one or more functions.
systemic circulation	Circulation of blood from the heart throughout the body and back again to the heart; also called general circulation.
talus	One of three bones that comprise the ankle joint. The other two bones are the tibia and fibula.
tarsal	One of three subdivisions of the foot comprised of seven bones (talus, calcaneous, navicular, three cuneiform bones, and the cuboid). The other two subdivisions are the metatarsal and the phalanges. All three subdivisions comprise 26 bones.
tibia	The larger of the two bones that form the leg below the knee. The tibia may be visualized as a "bump" on the big-toe side of the ankle.
tibial nerve	A division of the sciatic nerve that passes behind the knee. It subdivides and supplies impulses to the knee, the muscles of the calf, the skin of the leg, and the sole, heel, and underside of the toes.
tibialis anterior	Muscle that covers the front of the shin. It bends the foot upward and inward.
tissue	Collection of similar cells that perform a particular function.
trapezius	Muscle that covers the back of the neck and upper and middle region of the back; rotates and controls swinging movements of the arm.
tricep	Large muscle that covers the entire back of the upper arm and extends the forearm.
ulna	Inner and larger bone of the forearm, attached to the wrist and located on the side of the little finger.
ulnar artery	Artery that supplies blood to the muscle of the little finger side of the arm and palm of the hand.
ulnar nerve	Nerve that affects the little finger side of the arm and palm of the hand.
valve	Structure that temporarily closes a passage, or permits flow in one direction only.
vein	Thin-walled blood vessel that is less elastic than an artery; veins contain cup-like valves to prevent backflow and carry impure blood from the various capillaries back to the heart and lungs.
ventricle	One of the two lower chambers of the heart.
white blood cells	Blood cells that perform the function of destroying disease-causing microorganisms.

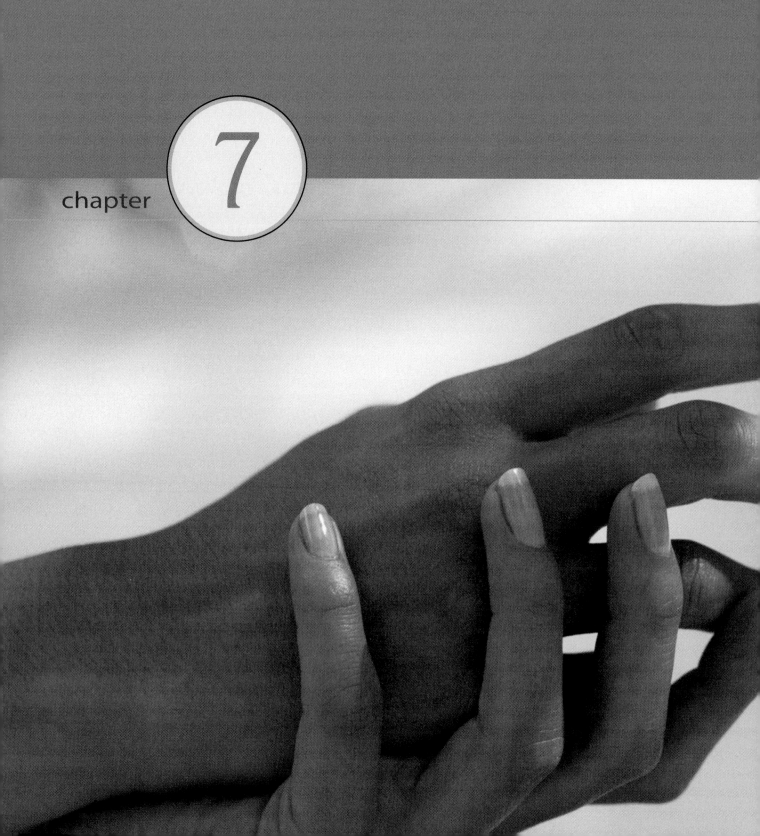

Skin Structure and Growth

LEARNING OBJECTIVES

After completing this chapter, you will be able to:

1. Describe the structure and composition of the skin.

2. List the functions of the skin.

3. Describe the aging process and the factors that influence aging of the skin.

4. Define important terms relating to skin disorders.

5. Discuss which skin disorders may be handled in the salon, and which should be referred to a physician.

KEY TERMS

Page number indicates where in the chapter the term is used.

albinism
pg. 126

anhidrosis
pg. 125

basal cell carcinoma
pg. 128

basal cell layer
pg. 113

bromhidrosis
pg. 125

bulla (plural: bullae)
pg. 123

chloasma
pg. 127

collagen
pg. 118

comedo (comedone)
pg. 119

crust
pg. 125

cyst
pg. 123

dermatitis
pg. 126, 128

dermatologist
pg. 113

dermatology
pg. 113

dermis
pg. 115

eczema
pg. 126

elastin
pg. 118

epidermis
pg. 113

esthetician
pg. 113

excoriation
pg. 125

fissure
pg. 125

histamine
pg. 131

hyperhidrosis
pg. 126

hypertrophy
pg. 127

keloid
pg. 125

keratin
pg. 114

keratoma
pg. 127

lentigenes
pg. 127

lesion
pg. 123

leukoderma
pg. 127

macule (plural: maculae)
pg. 123

malignant melanoma
pg. 128

melanin
pg. 116

melanocyte
pg. 114

miliaria rubra
pg. 126

mole
pg. 128

nevus
pg. 127

overexposure
pg. 129

papillary layer
pg. 115

papule
pg. 123

psoriasis
pg. 126

pustule
pg. 124

reticular layer
pg. 115

retinoic acid
pg. 133

scale
pg. 125

scar or cicatrix
pg. 125

sebaceous gland
pg. 118

sensitization
pg. 129

skin tag
pg. 128

squamous cell carcinoma
pg. 128

stain
pg. 127

stratum corneum
pg. 114

stratum germinativum
pg. 113

stratum granulosum
pg. 114

stratum lucidum
pg. 114

stratum spinosum
pg. 114

subcutaneous tissue
pg. 116

sudoriferous glands
pg. 118

tactile corpuscles
pg. 115

tan
pg. 127

telangiectasia
pg. 122

tubercle
pg. 124

tumor
pg. 124

ulcer
pg. 125

verruca
pg. 128

vesicle
pg. 124

vitiligo
pg. 127

wheal
pg. 124

C lear glowing skin is one of today's most important hallmarks of beauty. With all the latest high-performance ingredients and state-of-the-art delivery systems, 21st-century skin care has entered the realm of high technology with products and services that truly help protect, nourish, and preserve the health and beauty of the skin.

No matter how advanced the latest skincare technology may be, though, knowing how to care for skin begins with understanding its underlying structure and basic needs. As a licensed service provider, you also must recognize adverse conditions, including inflamed skin conditions, diseases, and infectious skin disorders.

ANATOMY OF THE SKIN

The medical branch of science that deals with the study of skin—its nature, structure, functions, diseases, and treatment—is called **dermatology**.

A **dermatologist** is a physician engaged in the science of treating the skin, its structures, functions, and diseases. An **esthetician** is a specialist in the cleansing, preservation of health, and beautification of the skin and body.

The skin is the largest organ of the body. If the skin of a typical 150-pound (68-kilogram) adult male were stretched out flat, it would cover about two square yards (1.7 square meters) and weigh about 9 pounds (4 kilograms). Our skin protects the network of muscles, bones, nerves, blood vessels, and everything else inside our bodies. It is our only barrier against the environment.

Healthy skin is slightly moist, soft, and flexible with a texture (feel and appearance) that ideally is smooth and fine-grained. The surface of healthy skin is slightly acidic and its immune responses react quickly to organisms that touch or try to enter it. Appendages of the skin include hair, nails, and sweat and oil glands.

Our eyelids have the thinnest skin; the soles of our feet have the thickest skin.

Continued pressure on any part of the skin can cause it to thicken and develop into a callus. The skin of the scalp is constructed similarly to the skin elsewhere on the human body, but the scalp has larger and deeper hair follicles to accommodate the longer hair of the head.

The skin is composed of two main divisions: epidermis and dermis (Figure 7–1).

The **epidermis** (ep-uh-DUR-mis) is the outermost layer of the skin. This layer, also called the cuticle (KYOO-tih-kul), is the thinnest layer of skin and forms a protective covering for the body. It contains no blood vessels, but has many small nerve endings. The epidermis is made up of the layers discussed below.

The **basal cell layer,** also referred to as the **stratum germinativum** (jer-mih-nah-TIV-um), is the deepest layer of the epidermis. It is composed of several layers of differently shaped cells. It is the live layer of the

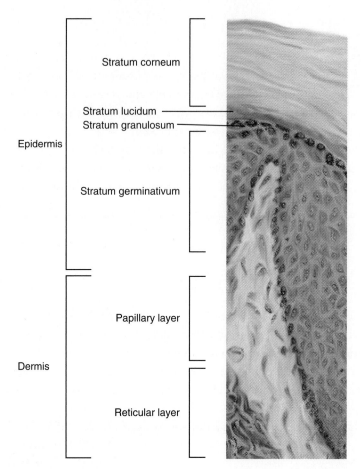

Figure 7–1 Layers of the skin.

epidermis, which produces new epidermal skin cells and is responsible for the growth of the epidermis. It also contains special cells called **melanocytes** (muh-LANuh-syts), which produce a dark skin pigment, called melanin, that protects the sensitive cells in the dermis below from the destructive effects of excessive ultraviolet rays of the sun or those from an ultraviolet lamp. The type of melanin produced also determines skin color.

The spiny layer, also referred to as the **stratum spinosum**, is just above the basal cell layer. It is in the spiny layer that the beginning of the process that causes skin cells to shed begins.

The **stratum granulosum** (gran-yoo-LOH-sum), or granular layer, consists of cells that look like distinct granules. These cells are almost dead and are pushed to the surface to replace cells that are shed from the skin surface layer.

The **stratum lucidum** (LOO-sih-dum) is the clear, transparent layer just under the skin surface; it consists of small cells through which light can pass.

The **stratum corneum** (STRAT-um KOR-nee-um), or horny layer, is the outer layer of the epidermis. The corneum is the layer we see when we look at the skin, and the layer treated by the practitioner. Its scale-like cells are continually being shed and replaced by cells coming to the surface from underneath. These cells are made up of **keratin**, a fiber protein that is also the principal component of hair and nails. The cells combine with lipids or fats produced by the skin to help make the stratum corneum a protective, waterproof layer.

The **dermis** (DUR-mis) is the underlying or inner layer of the skin. It is also called the derma, corium (KOH-ree-um), cutis (KYOO-tis), or true skin. This highly sensitive layer of connective tissue is about 25 times thicker than the epidermis. Within its structure, there are numerous blood vessels, lymph vessels, nerves, sweat glands, oil glands, and hair follicles, as well as arrector pili muscles (small muscles that work in connection with the hair follicles and cause "goose pimples") and papillae (small cone-shaped projections of elastic tissue that point upward into the epidermis). The dermis is comprised of two layers: the papillary or superficial layer, and the reticular or deeper layer (Figure 7–2).

The **papillary layer** (PAP-uh-lair-ee) is the outer layer of the dermis, directly beneath the epidermis. Here you will find the dermal papillae (puh-PIL-eye), which are small, cone-shaped elevations at the bottom of the hair follicles. Some papillae contain looped capillaries and others contain small structures called **tactile corpuscles** (TAK-tile KOR-pusuls), with nerve endings that are sensitive to touch and pressure. This layer also contains melanocytes, the pigment-producing cells. The top of the papillary layer where it joins the epidermis is called the epidermal–dermal junction.

The **reticular layer** (ruh-TIK-yuh-lur) is the deeper layer of the dermis that supplies the skin with oxygen and nutrients. It contains the following structures within its network:

Fat cells

Sweat glands

Blood vessels

Hair follicles

Lymph vessels

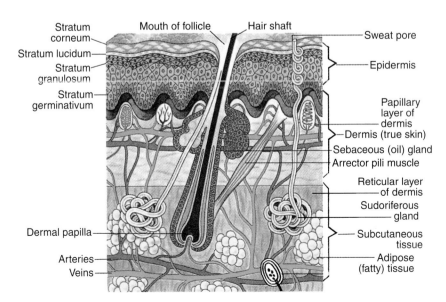

Figure 7–2 Structures of the skin.

Arrector pili muscles

Oil glands

Subcutaneous tissue (sub-kyoo-TAY-nee-us) is a fatty layer found below the dermis that some specialists regard as a continuation of the dermis. This fat tissue is also called **adipose** (AD-uh-pohs) or **subcutis** (sub-KYOO-tis) tissue, and varies in thickness according to the age, gender, and general health of the individual. It gives smoothness and contour to the body, contains fats for use as energy, and also acts as a protective cushion for the outer skin.

How the Skin Is Nourished

Blood supplies nutrients and oxygen to the skin. Nutrients are molecules from food, such as protein, carbohydrates, and fats. These nutrients are necessary for cell life, repair, and growth.

Lymph, the clear fluids of the body that resemble blood plasma but contain only colorless corpuscles, bathe the skin cells, remove toxins and cellular waste, and have immune functions that help protect the skin and body against disease. Networks of arteries and lymph vessels in the subcutaneous tissue send their smaller branches to hair papillae, hair follicles, and skin glands .

Nerves of the Skin

The skin contains the surface endings of the following nerve fibers:

Motor nerve fibers are distributed to the arrector pili muscles attached to the hair follicles. These muscles can cause goose bumps when a person is frightened or cold.

Sensory nerve fibers react to heat, cold, touch, pressure, and pain. These sensory receptors send messages to the brain.

Secretory nerve fibers are distributed to the sweat and oil glands of the skin. Secretory nerves, which are part of the autonomic nervous system, regulate the excretion of perspiration from the sweat glands and control the flow of sebum (a fatty or oily secretion of the sebaceous glands) to the surface of the skin.

Sense of Touch

The papillary layer of the dermis houses the nerve endings that provide the body with the sense of touch. These nerve endings register basic sensations such as touch, pain, heat, cold, and pressure. Nerve endings are most abundant in the fingertips. Complex sensations, such as vibrations, seem to depend on the sensitivity of a combination of these nerve endings.

Skin Color

The color of the skin—whether fair, medium, or dark—depends primarily on **melanin**, the tiny grains of pigment (coloring matter) deposited into cells in the basal cell layer of the epidermis and the papillary layers of the dermis. The color of the skin is a hereditary trait and varies among races and nationalities. Genes determine the amount and type of pigment produced in an individual.

The body produces two types of melanin: pheomelanin, which is red to yellow in color, and eumelanin, which is dark brown to black. People with light-colored skin mostly produce pheomelanin, while those with dark-colored skin mostly produce eumelanin. In addition, individuals differ in the size of melanin particles (Figure 7–3).

Melanin protects sensitive cells against strong light rays. Daily use of a sunscreen with a sun protection factor (SPF) of 15 or higher can help the melanin in the skin protect it from burning, and from receiving damage that can lead to skin cancer or premature aging.

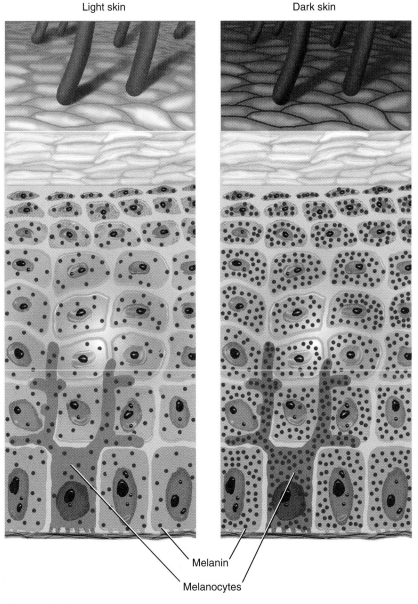

Light skin   Dark skin

Melanin

Melanocytes

Figure 7–3 Melanocytes in the epidermis produce melanin.

Strength and Flexibility of the Skin

The skin gets its strength, form, and flexibility from two specific structures composed of flexible protein fibers found within the dermis. These two structures, which make up 70 percent of the dermis, are called collagen and elastin.

Collagen is a fibrous protein that gives the skin form and strength. This fiber makes up a large portion of the dermis and helps give structural support to the skin by holding together all the structures found in this layer.

When collagen fibers are healthy, they allow the skin to stretch and contract as necessary. If collagen fibers become weakened due to a lack of moisture in the skin, environmental damage such as sun tanning or routine unprotected sun exposure, or frequent changes in weight, the skin will begin to lose its tone and suppleness. Wrinkles and sagging are often the result of collagen fibers losing their strength.

Collagen fibers are interwoven with **elastin**, a protein base similar to collagen that forms elastic tissue. This fiber gives the skin its flexibility and elasticity. Elastin helps the skin regain its shape, even after being repeatedly stretched or expanded.

Both of these fibers are important to the overall health and appearance of the skin. As we age, gravity causes these fibers to weaken, resulting in some degree of elasticity loss or skin sagging.

A majority of scientists now believe that most signs of skin aging are caused by sun exposure over a lifetime. Keeping the skin healthy, protected, moisturized, and free of disease will slow the weakening process and help keep the skin looking young longer.

Glands of the Skin

The skin contains two types of duct glands that extract materials from the blood to form new substances: the **sudoriferous glands** (sood-uh-RIF-uhrus) or **sweat glands**, and the **sebaceous glands** (sih-BAY-shus) or **oil glands** (Figure 7–4).

Sudoriferous (Sweat) Glands

The sudoriferous or sweat glands, which excrete sweat from the skin, consist of a coiled base, or **secretory coil**, and a tube-like duct that ends at the skin surface to form the sweat pore. Practically all parts of the body are supplied with sweat glands, which are more numerous on the palms, soles, and forehead, and in the armpits.

The sweat glands regulate body temperature and help to eliminate waste products from the body. The evaporation of sweat cools the skin surface. Their activity is greatly increased by heat, exercise, emotions, and certain drugs.

The excretion of sweat is controlled by the nervous system. Normally, one to two pints of liquids containing salts are eliminated daily through sweat pores in the skin.

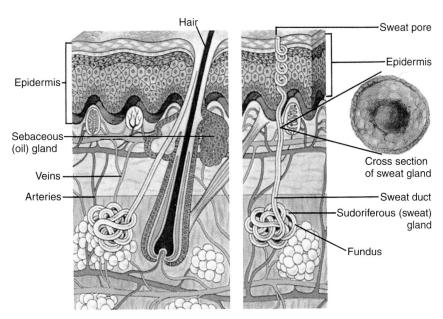

Figure 7–4 Sweat gland and oil gland.

Sebaceous (Oil) Glands

The sebaceous or oil glands of the skin are connected to the hair follicles. They consist of little sacs with ducts that open into the follicles. These glands secrete sebum, a fatty or oily secretion that lubricates the skin and preserves the softness of the hair. With the exception of the palms and soles, these glands are found in all parts of the body, particularly in the face and scalp, where they are larger.

Ordinarily, sebum flows through the oil ducts leading to the mouths of the hair follicles. However, when the sebum hardens and the duct becomes clogged, a pore impaction or **comedo** is formed, which may lead to an acne papule or pustule.

Functions of the Skin

The principal functions of the skin are protection, sensation, heat regulation, excretion, secretion, and absorption.

Protection. The skin protects the body from injury and bacterial invasion. The outermost layer of the epidermis is covered with a thin layer of sebum, and fatty lipids between the cells produced through the cell renewal process, which render it essentially waterproof. This outermost layer is resistant to wide variations in temperature, minor injuries, chemically active substances, and many forms of bacteria.

Sensation. By stimulating different sensory nerve endings, the skin responds to heat, cold, touch, pressure, and pain. When the nerve endings are stimulated, a message is sent to the brain. You respond by saying "ouch" if you feel pain, by scratching an itch, or by pulling away when you touch something hot. Sensory nerve endings are located near hair follicles (Figure 7–5).

Heat regulation. This means that the skin protects the body from the environment. A healthy body maintains a constant internal temperature of

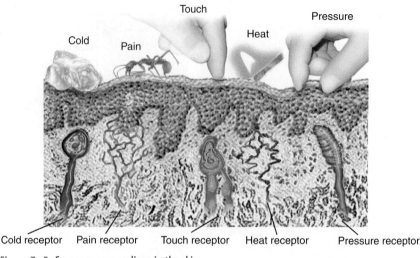

Figure 7–5 *Sensory nerve endings in the skin.*

about 98.6° Fahrenheit (37° Celsius). As changes occur in the outside temperature, the blood and sweat glands of the skin make necessary adjustments to allow the body to be cooled by the evaporation of sweat.

Excretion. Perspiration from the sweat glands is excreted through the skin. Water lost through perspiration takes salt and other chemicals with it.

Secretion. Sebum, or oil, is secreted by the sebaceous glands. This oil lubricates the skin, keeping it soft and pliable. Oil also keeps hair soft. Emotional stress and hormone imbalances can increase the flow of sebum.

Absorption. Absorption is limited, but it does occur. Female hormones, when used as an ingredient of a face cream, can enter the body through the skin and influence it to a minor degree. Fatty materials, such as those used in many advanced skin care formulations, may be absorbed between the cells, and through the hair follicles and sebaceous gland openings.

AGING OF THE SKIN

Aging of the skin is a process that takes many years and can be influenced by many different factors. One does not necessarily age as one's parents have.

Many outside factors such as the sun, environment, health habits, and general lifestyle greatly influence the signs of skin aging to such a great extent that it has been estimated that heredity may be responsible for only 15 percent of the factors that determine how skin ages.

The Sun and Its Effects

The sun and its ultraviolet (UV) rays have the greatest impact on how our skin ages. Approximately 80 to 85 percent of our skin's aging is caused by the rays of the sun. As we age, the collagen and elastin fibers of the skin naturally weaken. This weakening happens at a much faster rate when the skin is frequently exposed to ultraviolet rays without proper protection. The UV rays of the sun reach the skin in two different forms, as UVA and UVB rays.

Each of these types of rays influences the skin at a different level. UVA rays, also called the "aging rays," are deep-penetrating rays that can even go through a glass window. These rays weaken the collagen and elastin fibers, causing wrinkling and sagging in the tissues.

UVB rays, also referred to as the "burning rays," cause sunburns and tanning of the skin by affecting the melanocytes, the cells of the epidermis that are responsible for producing melanin, the skin pigment. Melanin is designed to help protect the skin from the sun's UV rays, but can be altered or destroyed when large, frequent doses of UV light are allowed to penetrate the skin. Although UVB penetration is not as deep as UVA, these rays are equally damaging to the skin and can damage the eyes as well. On a positive note, UVB rays contribute to the body's synthesis of vitamin D and other important minerals. However, the amount of sun exposure necessary for vitamin D synthesis is minimal, not to mention the fact that you can get vitamin D from fortified milk or orange juice.

As a consultant to your clients, it is appropriate that you advise them about the necessary precautions to take when they are exposed to the sun:

○ On a daily basis, wear a moisturizer or protective lotion with a sunscreen of at least SPF 15 on all areas of potential exposure.

○ Avoid prolonged exposure to the sun during peak hours, when UV exposure is highest. This is usually between 10 AM and 3 PM.

○ Sunscreen should be applied at least 30 minutes before sun exposure to allow time for absorption. Many people make the mistake of applying sunscreen after they have been exposed to the heat and sun's rays for 30 minutes or more. The already inflamed skin is more likely to react to the sunscreen chemicals when applied after sun exposure.

○ Apply sunscreen liberally after swimming or any activities that result in heavy perspiration. If the skin is exposed to hours of sun, such as during a boat trip or day at the beach, sunscreen should be applied periodically throughout the day as a precaution.

○ All sunscreen used for protection should be full or broad spectrum to filter out UVA and UVB rays. Check expiration dates printed on the bottle to make sure that the sunscreen has not expired.

○ Avoid exposing children younger than 6 months to the sun.

○ If prone to burning frequently and easily, wear a hat and protective clothing when participating in outdoor activities. Redheads and blue-eyed blondes are particularly susceptible to sun damage.

○ In addition to following the above precautions, clients should be advised to regularly see a physician specializing in dermatology for checkups of the skin, especially if any changes in coloration, size, or shape of a mole are detected, or if the skin bleeds unexpectedly or a lesion or scrape does not heal quickly.

○ Home self-examinations can also be an effective way to check for signs of potential skin cancer between scheduled doctor visits. When

FYI

The American Cancer Society recommends using the ABCD Cancer Checklist to help make potential skin cancer easier to recognize. When checking existing moles, look for changes in any of the following:

A: asymmetry - one half of the mole does not match the other half.

B: border irregularity - the edges of the mole are ragged or notched.

C: color - the color of the mole is not the same all over. There may be shades of tan, brown, or black, and sometimes patches of red, blue, or white.

D: diameter - the mole is wider than about 1/4 inch (although doctors are now finding more melanomas that are smaller).

Changes to any of these should be examined by a physician. For more information, contact the American Cancer Society at www.cancer.org or (800) ACS-2345.

performing a self-care exam, clients should be advised to check for any changes in existing moles and pay attention to any new visible growths on the skin.

Skin Aging and the Environment

While the sun may play the major role in how the skin ages, changes in our environment also greatly influence this aging process. Pollutants in the air from factories, automobile exhaust, and even secondhand smoke can all influence the appearance and overall health of our skin. While these pollutants affect the surface appearance of the skin, they can also change the health of the underlying cells and tissues, thereby speeding up the aging process.

The best defense against these pollutants is the simplest one: follow a good daily skin care routine. Routine washing and exfoliating (removing dead surface skin cells) at night helps to remove the buildup of pollutants that have settled on the skin's surface throughout the day. The application of daily moisturizers, protective lotions, and even foundation products all help to protect the skin from airborne pollutants.

Aging and Lifestyle

Aging of the skin cannot be blamed entirely on the outside influences of the sun and other environmental factors. What we choose to put into our bodies also has a profound effect on the overall aging process. The impact of poor choices can be seen most visibly on the skin. Smoking, drinking, drug abuse, and making poor dietary choices all greatly influence the aging process. It is the responsibility of the practitioner to be aware of how these habits affect the skin and to tactfully point out these effects to clients.

Smoking and tobacco use may not only cause cancer, but have also been linked to premature aging and wrinkling of the skin. Nicotine in tobacco causes contraction and weakening of the blood vessels and small capillaries that supply blood to the tissues. In turn, this contraction and weakening causes decreased circulation to the tissues. Eventually, the tissues are deprived of essential oxygen, and the effect of this becomes evident on the skin's surface. The skin may appear yellowish or gray in color and can have a dull appearance.

The use of illegal drugs affects the skin as much as smoking does. Some drugs have been shown to interfere with the body's intake of oxygen, thus affecting healthy cell growth. Some drugs can even aggravate serious skin conditions, such as acne. Others can cause dryness and allergic reactions on the skin's surface.

The overuse of alcohol has an opposite, yet equally damaging effect on the skin. Heavy or excessive intake of alcohol over-dilates the blood vessels and capillaries. Over time, this constant over-dilation and weakening of the fragile capillary walls will cause them to become distended. These dilated capillaries, called **telangiectasias (te-lanj-ec-tay-jas)** may also be caused by tobacco use, sun exposure, or other environmental factors. Alcohol can also dehydrate the skin by drawing essential water out of the tissues, which causes the skin to appear dull and dry.

Both smoking and drinking contribute to the aging process on their own, but the combination of the two can be devastating to the tissues. The constant dilation and contraction that occur on the tiny capillaries and blood vessels, as well as the constant deprivation of oxygen and water to the tissues, quickly make the skin appear lifeless and dull. It is very difficult for the skin to adjust and repair itself. Usually, the damage done by these lifestyle habits is hard to reverse or diminish.

Like any other organ of the body, the skin is susceptible to a variety of diseases, disorders, and ailments. In your work as a nail technician you will often see skin disorders, so you must be prepared to recognize certain common skin conditions and know what you can and cannot do with them. Some skin disorders can be treated in cooperation with, and under the supervision of, a physician. Medicinal preparations, available only by prescription, must be applied in accordance with the physician's directions. If a client has a skin condition that you do not recognize as a simple disorder, refer the client to a physician.

It is very important that a beauty salon does not serve a client who is suffering from an inflamed skin disorder, infectious or not. The cosmetologist should be able to recognize these conditions, and sensitively suggest that proper measures be taken to prevent more serious consequences.

DISORDERS OF THE SKIN

Listed below are a number of important terms relating to skin, scalp, and hair disorders that you should be familiar with.

Skin Lesions

A **lesion** (LEE-zhun) is a mark on the skin. Certain lesions could indicate an injury or damage that changes the structure of tissues or organs. There are three types of lesions: primary, secondary, and tertiary. The nail technician is concerned with primary and secondary lesions only. If you are familiar with the principal skin lesions, you will be able to distinguish between conditions that may or may not be treated in a salon (Figure 7–6).

The terms for different lesions listed below often indicate differences in the area of the skin layers affected, and the size of the lesion.

Primary Lesions

Primary lesions are briefly summarized below.

Bulla (BULL-uh) (plural: bullae). A large blister containing a watery fluid; similar to a vesicle but larger (Figure 7–7).

Cyst (SIST). A closed, abnormally developed sac, containing fluid, pus, semifluid, or morbid matter, above or below the skin.

Macule (MAK-yool) (plural: maculae) (MAK-yuh-ly). A spot or discoloration on the skin, such as a freckle. Macules are neither raised nor sunken.

Papule (PAP-yool). A pimple; small circumscribed elevation on the skin that contains no fluid but may develop pus.

Bulla:
Same as a vesicle only
greater than 0.5 cm
Example:
Contact dermatitis, large
second-degree burns,
bulbous impetigo, pemphigus

Macule:
Localized changes in skin
color of less than 1 cm
in diameter
Example:
Freckle

Tubercle:
Solid and elevated; however,
it extends deeper than
papules into the dermis or
subcutaneous tissues, 0.5-2 cm
Example:
Lipoma, erythema, nodosum,
cyst

Papule:
Solid, elevated lesion less
than 0.5 cm in diameter
Example:
Warts, elevated nevi

Pustule:
Vesicles or bullae that
become filled with pus,
usually described as less
than 0.5 cm in diameter
Example:
Acne, impetigo, furuncles,
carbuncles, folliculitis

Ulcer:
A depressed lesion of
the epidermis and upper
papillary layer of the dermis
Example:
Stage 2 pressure ulcer

Tumor:
The same as a nodule only
greater than 2 cm

Example:
Carcinoma (such as advanced
breast carcinoma); **not** basal cell
or squamous cell of the skin

Vesicle:
Accumulation of fluid between
the upper layers of the skin;
elevated mass containing
serous fluid; less than 0.5 cm
Example:
Herpes simplex, herpes
zoster, chickenpox

Wheal:
Localized edema in the
epidermis causing irregular
elevation that may be red
or pale
Example:
Insect bite or a hive

Figure 7–6 Primary skin lesions.

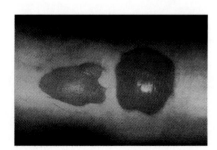

Figure 7–7 Bullae.

Pustule (PUS-chool). An inflamed pimple containing pus (Figure 7–8).

Tubercle (TOO-bur-kul). An abnormal rounded, solid lump above, within, or under the skin; larger than a papule.

Tumor (TOO-mur). A swelling; an abnormal cell mass resulting from excessive multiplication of cells, varying in size, shape, and color. Nodules are also referred to as tumors, but are smaller.

Vesicle (VES-ih-kel). A small blister or sac containing clear fluid, lying within or just beneath the epidermis. Poison ivy and poison oak, for example, produce vesicles (Figure 7–9).

Wheal (WHEEL). An itchy, swollen lesion that lasts only a few hours; caused by a blow, the bite of an insect, urticaria (skin allergy), or the sting of a nettle. Examples include hives and mosquito bites.

Secondary Lesions

Secondary skin lesions develop in the later stages of disease (Figure 7–10). These lesions include the following:

Crust. Dead cells that form over a wound or blemish while it is healing; an accumulation of sebum and pus, sometimes mixed with epidermal material. An example is the scab on a sore.

Excoriation (ek-skor-ee-AY-shun). A skin sore or abrasion produced by scratching or scraping.

Fissure (FISH-ur). A crack in the skin that penetrates the dermis, such as chapped hands or lips.

Keloid (KEE-loyd). A thick scar resulting from excessive growth of fibrous tissue (Figure 7–11).

Scale. Any thin plate of epidermal flakes, dry or oily. An example is abnormal or excessive dandruff.

Scar or **cicatrix** (SIK-uh-triks). Light-colored, slightly raised mark on the skin formed after an injury or lesion of the skin has healed.

Ulcer (UL-sur). An open lesion on the skin or mucous membrane of the body, accompanied by pus and loss of skin depth.

Disorders of the Sudoriferous (Sweat) Glands

Anhidrosis (an-hih-DROH-sis). Deficiency in perspiration, often a result of fever or certain skin diseases. It requires medical treatment.

Bromhidrosis (broh-mih-DROH-sis). Foul-smelling perspiration, usually noticeable in the armpits or on the feet.

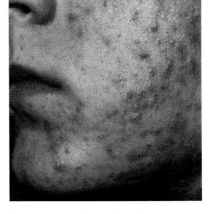

Figure 7–8 Papules and pustules.

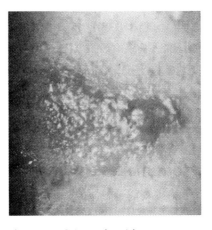

Figure 7–9 Poison oak vesicles.

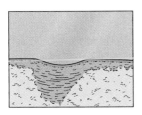

Scar

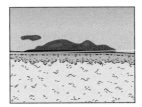

Crust

Scale

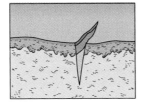

Fissure

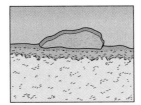

Excoriation

Figure 7–10 Secondary skin lesions.

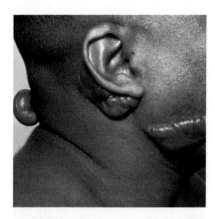

Figure 7–11 Keloids.

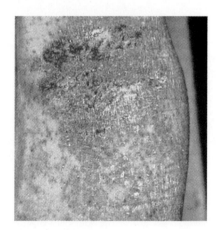

Figure 7–12 Eczema.

Hyperhidrosis (hy-per-hy-DROH-sis). Excessive sweating, caused by heat or general body weakness. Medical treatment is required.

Miliaria rubra (mil-ee-AIR-ee-ah ROOB-rah). Prickly heat; acute inflammatory disorder of the sweat glands, characterized by the eruption of small red vesicles and accompanied by burning, itching skin. It is caused by exposure to excessive heat.

Skin Inflammations

Dermatitis (dur-muh-TY-tis). Inflammatory condition of the skin. The lesions come in various forms, such as vesicles or papules.

Eczema (EG-zuh-muh). An inflammatory, painful itching disease of the skin, acute or chronic in nature, presenting many forms of dry or moist lesions. There are several different types of eczema. All cases of eczema should be referred to a physician for treatment. Eczema is not contagious (Figure 7–12).

Psoriasis (suh-RY-uh-sis). A skin disease characterized by red patches, covered with silver-white scales usually found on the scalp, elbows, knees, chest, and lower back. Psoriasis is caused by the skin cells turning over faster than normal. It rarely occurs on the face. If irritated, bleeding points occur. Psoriasis is not contagious (Figure 7–13).

Pigmentation Disorders

Pigment can be affected by internal factors such as heredity or hormonal fluctuations, or by outside factors such as prolonged exposure to the sun. Abnormal coloration accompanies every skin disorder and many systemic disorders. A change in pigmentation can also be observed when certain drugs are being taken internally. The following terms relate to changes in the pigmentation of the skin.

Albinism (AL-bi-niz-em). Congenital leukoderma, or absence of melanin pigment of the body, including the skin, hair, and eyes (Figure 7–14). Hair is silky white. The skin is pinkish white and will not tan. The eyes are pink, and the skin is sensitive to light and ages early.

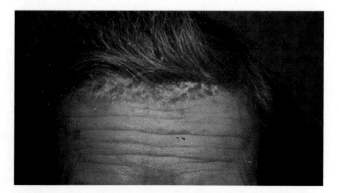

Figure 7–13 Psoriasis.

Chloasma (kloh-AZ-mah). Condition characterized by increased pigmentation on the skin, in spots that are not elevated. Chloasma is also called liver spots. They have nothing to do with the liver. They are generally caused by cumulative sun exposure.

Lentigines (len-TIJ-e-neez) (singular: lentigo) (len-TY-goh). Technical term for freckles. Small yellow- to brown-colored spots on skin exposed to sunlight and air.

Leukoderma (loo-koh-DUR-muh). Skin disorder characterized by light abnormal patches; caused by a burn or congenital disease that destroys the pigment-producing cells. It is classified as vitiligo and albinism.

Nevus (NEE-vus). Small or large malformation of the skin due to abnormal pigmentation or dilated capillaries; commonly known as a birthmark.

Stain. Abnormal brown or wine discoloration of the skin with a circular and irregular shape (Figure 7–15). Its permanent color is due to the presence of darker pigment. Stains occur during aging; after certain diseases; and after the disappearance of moles, freckles, and liver spots. The cause is unknown.

Tan. Change in pigmentation of skin caused by exposure to the sun or ultraviolet rays.

Vitiligo (vih-til-EYE-goh). Milky-white spots (leukoderma) of the skin. Vitiligo is hereditary, and may be related to thyroid conditions (Figure 7–16). Must be protected from overexposure to the sun.

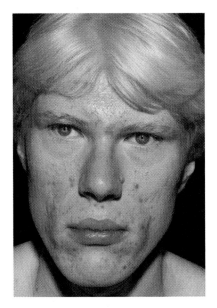

Figure 7–14   Albinism.

Hypertrophies of the Skin

A **hypertrophy** (hy-PUR-truh-fee) of the skin is an abnormal growth of the skin. Many hypertrophies are benign, or harmless.

Keratoma (kair-uh-TOH-muh). An acquired, superficial, thickened patch of epidermis commonly known as callus, caused by pressure or friction on the hands and feet. If the thickening grows inward, it is called a corn.

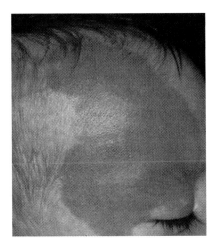

Figure 7–15   Port wine stain.

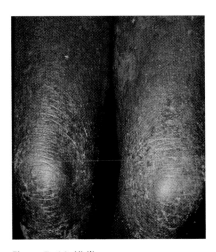

Figure 7–16   Vitiligo.

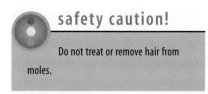

Figure 7–17 Skin tags.

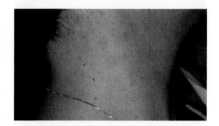

Figure 7–18 Basal cell carcinoma.

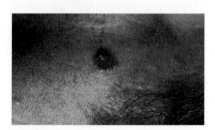

Figure 7–19 Squamous cell carcinoma.

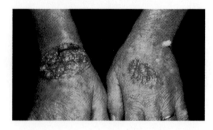

Figure 7–20 Malignant melanoma.

Mole. A small, brownish spot or blemish on the skin, ranging in color from pale tan to brown or bluish black. Some moles are small and flat, resembling freckles; others are raised and darker in color. Large dark hairs often occur in moles. Any change in a mole requires medical attention.

Skin tag. Small brown or flesh-colored outgrowth of the skin (Figure 7–17). Skin tags occur most frequently on the neck of an older person. They can be easily removed by a dermatologist.

Verruca (vuh-ROO-kuh). Technical term for wart; hypertrophy of the papillae and epidermis. It is caused by a virus and is infectious. It can spread from one location to another, particularly along a scratch in the skin.

Skin Cancer

Skin cancer—primarily caused from overexposure to the sun—comes in three distinct forms, varying in severity. Each is named for the type of cells that it affects.

Basal cell carcinoma (BAY-zul SEL kar-sin-OH-muh) is the most common type and the least severe. It is often characterized by light or pearly nodules (Figure 7–18). **Squamous** (SKWAY-mus) **cell carcinoma** is more serious than basal cell carcinoma, and often is characterized by scaly red papules or nodules (Figure 7–19). The third and most serious form of skin cancer is **malignant melanoma** (muh-LIG-nent mel-uh-NOH-muh), which is often characterized by black or dark brown patches on the skin that may appear uneven in texture, jagged, or raised (Figure 7–20).

Malignant melanomas often appear on individuals who do not receive regular sun exposure, and are most commonly located on areas of the body that are not regularly exposed. They are often nicknamed the "city person's cancer." Malignant melanoma is the least common, but most dangerous type of skin cancer.

If detected early, anyone with any of these three forms of skin cancer has a good chance for survival. It is important for a cosmetologist to be able to recognize the appearance of serious skin disorders in order to better serve clients. It also important to remember that a nail technician should not attempt to diagnose a skin disorder, but should sensitively suggest that the client seek the advice of a dermatologist.

PREVENTING SKIN PROBLEMS IN SALON

Skin problems are common in every facet of the professional salon industry. Nail, skin, and hair services all can cause problems for the sensitive client. Fortunately, the vast majority of fingernail-related problems can be easily avoided—if you understand how!

Dermatitis

Dermatitis is a medical term for abnormal skin inflammation. There are many kinds of dermatitis, but only one is important in the salon. **Contact**

dermatitis is the most common skin disease for nail technicians. Contact dermatitis is caused by touching certain substances to the skin. This type of dermatitis can be short term or long term. Contact dermatitis can have several causes. When the skin is irritated by a substance, it is called **irritant contact dermatitis**. It is also possible to become allergic to an ingredient in a product, which is known as **allergic contact dermatitis**.

Prolonged or Repeated Contact

Allergic reactions are caused by prolonged or repeated direct skin contact. This type of skin problem does not occur overnight. Acrylic (methacrylate) liquids, wraps, and UV light gels are all capable of causing allergic reactions. In general, it takes from 4 to 6 months of repeated exposure before sensitive clients show symptoms.

As a nail technician, you are also at risk. Prolonged, repeated, or longterm exposures can cause anyone to become sensitive. This is usually caused by **overexposure**. Simply touching monomers does not cause sensitivities. It usually requires months of improper handling and overexposure. Some likely places for allergies to occur are:

1. Between a technician's thumb and pointer finger

2. On the nail technician's wrist or palm or on the back of the hand

3. On the nail technician's face, especially the cheeks

4. On the client's cuticles, fingertips, or the sensitive tissues of the underlying nail bed

If you examine the area where the problem occurs, you can usually determine the cause. For example, nail technicians often smooth wet brushes with their fingers. This is both prolonged and repeated contact!

Eventually the area becomes sore and inflamed. The same occurs when technicians lay their arms on the towels contaminated with UV gel, monomer, or filings. The palms are overexposed by picking up containers that have traces of monomer on the outside. Small amounts of product on your hands are often transferred to the cheeks or face. Direct product contact to the skin is the cause of these facial irritations, not the vapors. Nail enhancement product vapors will not cause a skin allergy.

Touching a client's skin with any monomer or UV gel has the same effect. This is the most common reason for client sensitivities. With each service the risk of sensitization increases. **Sensitization** is a greatly increased or exaggerated sensitivity to products. It is extremely important that you always leave a tiny, free margin (approximately 1/16") between the product and the skin. The most important rule of being a good nail technician is: *Never touch any nail enhancement product to the skin.*

Improper product consistency is the second most common reason for allergy. If too much liquid monomer is used, the result is an overly wet bead. Many technicians do not realize that the initiator in the polymer powder can only harden a certain amount of the liquid monomer. Wet beads are incorrectly balanced. Beads with too wet of a consistency will harden with monomer trapped inside. This extra monomer eventually works its way down to the nail bed and may cause an allergic reaction. It is very important that only the powders designed to work with the monomer liquids of your choice should be used. Using the wrong powder with your monomer liquid will probably result in improper cure, which may lead to service breakdown and an increased risk of adverse skin reactions. The same type of problems can occur with UV gel enhancements. In fact, many things can cause UV gels to improperly cure (harden), including:

Applying product too thickly

Too short of a time under the light

Dirty bulbs in the lamp unit

Old bulbs that should be changed

Several thin coatings and long exposures lead to the best and most complete cure. If the UV bulb is dirty or old, it does not give enough energy to fully cure the enhancement. UV bulbs will remain blue for years, but they will lose effectiveness after 4 to 6 months. They should be cleaned daily, and UV lamps will work best if the UV bulbs are replaced with new bulbs at least three times per year. The enhancement product will set more thoroughly, last longer, and be less likely to cause an allergy if you take these precautions. Filings can also be too rich in uncured UV gel or liquid monomer. Also, always use the UV lamp that was designed for the UV gel system of your choice. It is incorrect to believe that just because the UV lamp has the same wattage as another, that they are the same. They are not, and different types of lamps will produce difference amounts of UV energy. Depending on the quality and design, some UV lamps may require the bulbs to be changed more often, such as five to six times per year to maintain the proper level of UV light. Each type of UV lamp will behave differently than another type, and they should not be used interchangeably with different UV gel systems. There is no such thing as a UV lamp that works for all UV gel systems. If the incorrect UV lamp is used, service breakdown and adverse skin reactions become much more likely. Thus, it is important to use the proper UV lamp; otherwise, you cannot ensure the success of the services and you may put your clients or yourself at increased risk of developing skin irritations or allergies. Also, if the nail technician's arm, wrist, hands, or fingers are overexposed to dusts from undercured artificial nails, the potential for developing allergic reactions becomes more likely.

It is critical to use medium-consistency beads. Never use a wet consistency. Beads that flatten out or have a ring of liquid around them are much too wet. A proper consistency bead should form a smooth dome when placed on the natural nail or tip. It should not flatten out, nor should it be runny.

The gooey layer on top of UV gel enhancements is mostly uncured gel. It must never come in contact with soft tissue. Also, never dip back into the dappen dish to get more liquid or clean up around the cuticle with monomer. Never use the powder that was not designed specifically for use with the monomer liquid of your choice. If you do, chances are that your clients will begin to develop skin problems in those areas. Avoid using extra-large or oversize brushes. They usually make overly wet beads that are difficult to control. The belly of these large brushes can carry enough liquid for *four* normal size beads.

Brushes that are too large do not save time—they cause allergic reactions. Mixing product lines or custom blending your own "special" mixture can also create chemical imbalances, which lead to allergic reactions. Do not take unnecessary risks. Always use products exactly as instructed and never mix your own products. If you do, do not be surprised when you or your clients develop skin problems.

Skin disorders of the hands affect more than 30 percent of all nail technicians sometime during their careers. Skin problems and allergies force many good nail technicians to give up successful careers. Unfortunately, once you or a client become allergic to an ingredient, you are sensitive for the rest of your life. This is especially upsetting, because it is completely avoidable.

No one should suffer from any work-related allergy or irritation.

Irritant Contact Dermatitis

Irritating substances will temporarily damage the epidermis. Corrosive substances are examples of irritants. When the skin is damaged by irritating substances, the immune system springs into action. It floods the tissue with water, trying to dilute the irritant. This is why swelling occurs.

The body is trying to stop things from getting any worse. The immune system also tells the blood to release chemicals, called **histamines**, which enlarge the vessels around the injury. Blood can then rush to the scene more quickly and help remove the irritating substance.

You can see and feel all the extra blood under the skin. The entire area becomes red, warm, and may throb. It is the histamines that cause the itchy feeling that often accompanies contact dermatitis. After everything calms down, the swelling will go away. The surrounding skin is often left damaged, scaly, cracked, and dry. Fortunately, irritations are not permanent. If you avoid repeated and/or prolonged contact with the irritating substance, the skin will usually quickly repair itself. However, continued or repeated exposure may lead to permanent allergic reactions.

Surprisingly, tap water is a very common salon irritant. Hands that remain damp for long periods often become sore, cracked, and chapped. Avoiding the problem is simple. Always completely dry the hands. Regularly use moisturizing hand creams to compensate for loss of skin oils.

Frequent hand washing, especially in hard water, can further damage the skin. Do not wash your hands excessively. Washing your hands more than 10 or 15 times a day can cause them to become irritated and damaged. Cleansers and detergents worsen the problem. They increase damage by stripping away sebum and other natural skin chemicals that protect the skin. Prolonged or repeated contact with many solvents will strip away skin oils, leaving the skin dry or damaged. Sometimes it is difficult to determine the cause of the irritation. One way to identify the irritant is by observing the location of the reaction. Symptoms are always isolated to the contact area. The cause will be something that you are doing to this part of the skin.

Remember the following precautions:

Never smooth the enhancement surface with more liquid monomer.

Never use monomer to "clean up" the edges, under the nail, or side walls.

Never touch any monomer liquids, UV gels, or adhesives to the skin.

Never touch the bristles of the brush with your fingers.

Never mix your own special product blends.

Always follow instructions—exactly!

Once a client becomes allergic, things will only get worse if you continue using the same products and techniques. It is best to discontinue use until you figure out what you are doing wrong. Otherwise, more clients will eventually be affected. Medications and illness do not make clients sensitive to nail products. These are just excuses. Only prolonged and repeated contact causes these allergies.

Protect Yourself

Take extreme care to keep brush handles, containers, and tabletops clean and free from product dusts and residues. Repeatedly handling these items will cause overexposure if the items are not kept clean. Enhancement products are not designed for skin contact! If you avoid contact, neither you nor your client will ever develop an allergic reaction.

Many serious problems can be related to contact dermatitis. Do not fall into the trap of developing bad habits.

MAINTAINING SKIN HEALTH

For your own benefit, as well as the benefit of your clients, you should have a basic understanding of how best to maintain healthy skin. In order to keep the skin and the body healthy, the old adage "you are what you eat" still holds true. Proper dietary choices help to regulate hydration (maintaining a healthy level of water in the body), oil production, and overall function of the cells. Eating foods found in all three basic food groups—fats, carbohydrates, and proteins—is the best way to support the health of the skin.

Vitamins and Dietary Supplements

Vitamins play an important role in the skin's health, often aiding in healing, softening, and fighting diseases of the skin. Vitamins such as A, C, D, and E have all been shown to have positive effects on the skin's health when taken internally. Although experts agree that taking vitamins internally is still the best way to support the health of the skin, some external applications of vitamins have also been found to be useful in nourishing the skin. The following vitamins relate to the skin in particularly significant ways:

Vitamin A supports the overall health of the skin. This vitamin aids in the health, function, and repair of skin cells. Vitamin A is an antioxidant that can help prevent certain types of cancers, including skin cancer, and has been shown to improve the skin's elasticity and thickness. In its topical acid form as the prescription cream called **retinoic acid** or by its trade name, Retin-A®, vitamin A can be used to treat many different types of acne.

Vitamin C, also known as ascorbic acid or another topical form, magnesium ascorbyl phosphate, is an important element needed for proper repair of the skin and various tissues. This vitamin aids in, and even speeds up, the healing processes of the body. Vitamin C is also vitally important in fighting the aging process and promotes the production of collagen in the skin's dermal tissues, keeping the skin healthy and firm.

Vitamin D promotes the healthy and rapid healing of the skin. The best source of this vitamin is sunlight (in limited amounts). Vitamin D can also be obtained from fortified milk or orange juice. Because vitamin D helps to support the bone structure of the body, it has been made readily available in many fortified foods and dietary supplements.

Vitamin E, or tocopherol, used in conjunction with vitamin A, helps fight against, and protect the skin from, the harmful effects of the sun's rays. Vitamin E also helps to heal damage to the skin's tissues when used both internally and externally. When used externally in topical lotions or creams, vitamin E can help heal structural damage on the skin including severe burns and stretch marks.

Ideally, the nutrients the body needs for proper functioning and survival should come primarily from the foods we eat. If a person's daily food consumption is lacking in nutrients, an effective way to provide them is to take vitamins and mineral supplements (providing that the recommended daily allowance is not exceeded).

Clients will occasionally ask you about nutrition and their skin. While it is important that the professional know the basics of nutrition, nail technicians are not registered dieticians, and should never give nutritional advice. Instead, refer the client to a registered dietician.

Water and the Skin

There is one essential nutrient that no person can live without, and that is water. In order to function properly, the body and skin both rely heavily on the benefits of water. Water composes 50- to 70-percent of body weight.

Drinking pure water is essential to the health of the skin and body because it sustains the health of the cells, aids in the elimination of toxins and waste, helps regulate the body's temperature, and aids in proper digestion. All these functions, when performing properly, help keep the skin healthy, vital, and attractive.

The amount of water needed by an individual varies, depending on body weight and the level of daily physical activity. The following is an easy formula to help you determine how much water you need every day for maximum physical health: Take your body weight and divide by 2. Divide this number by 8. The resulting number approximates how many 8-ounce glasses of water you should drink every day. For instance, if you weigh 160 pounds, you should drink 10 glasses of water a day. If intense physical activity is performed daily, add two extra glasses of water to the final number. This will help replace extra fluids lost while exercising (Figure 7–21).

Figure 7–21 Water is essential for healthy skin.

REVIEW **QUESTIONS**

1. Briefly describe healthy skin.

2. Name the main divisions of the skin and the layers within each division.

3. How is the skin nourished?

4. List the three types of nerve fibers found in the skin.

5. What is collagen?

6. Name the two types of glands contained within the skin and describe their functions.

7. What are the six important functions of the skin?

8. List the factors that contribute to aging of the skin.

9. Explain the effect of overexposure to the sun on the skin.

10. Define dermatology.

11. What is a skin lesion?

12. Name and describe at least five disorders of the sebaceous glands.

13. Name and describe at least five changes in skin pigmentation.

14. List at least six skin conditions and disorders that should be referred to a physician.

15. Name and describe the three forms of skin cancer.

CHAPTER **GLOSSARY**

acne	Skin disorder characterized by chronic inflammation of the sebaceous glands from retained secretions and *Propionibacterium acnes* (*P. acnes*) bacteria.
albinism	Congenital leukoderma or absence of melanin pigment of the body, including the hair, skin, and eyes.
anhidrosis	Deficiency in perspiration, often a result of fever or certain skin diseases.
basal cell carcinoma	Most common and least severe type of skin cancer; often characterized by light or pearly nodules.
basal cell layer	The bottom, live layer of the epidermis where cell divides and begins the keratinization process.
bromhidrosis	Foul-smelling perspiration, usually noticeable in the armpits or on the feet.
bulla (plural: bullae)	Large blister containing a watery fluid; similar to a vesicle but larger.
chloasma	Condition characterized by increased pigmentation on the skin, in spots that are not elevated.
collagen	Fibrous protein that gives the skin form and strength.
comedo (plural: comedones)	Hair follicle filled with keratin and sebum. When the sebum of the comedone is exposed to the environment, it oxidizes and turns black (blackheads); when the follicle is closed and not exposed to the environment, comedones are a white or cream color (whiteheads).
crust	Dead cells that form over a wound or blemish while it is healing; an accumulation of sebum and pus, sometimes mixed with epidermal material.
cyst	Closed, abnormally developed sac, containing fluid, semifluid, or morbid matter, above or below the skin.
dermatitis	Inflammatory condition of the skin.
dermatitis venenata	Also known as contact dermatitis, an eruptive skin infection caused by contact with irritating substances such as chemicals or tints.
dermatologist	Physician engaged in the science of treating the skin—its structures, functions, and diseases.
dermatology	Medical branch of science that deals with the study of skin and its nature, structure, functions, diseases, and treatment.
dermis	Underlying or inner layer of the skin; also called the derma, corium, cutis, or true skin.
eczema	Inflammatory, painful itching disease of the skin, acute or chronic in nature, presenting many forms of dry or moist lesions.
elastin	Protein base similar to collagen that forms elastic tissue.
epidermis	Outermost layer of the skin; also called cuticle.
esthetician	Specialist in cleansing, preservation of health, and beautification of the skin and body; one who gives therapeutic facial treatments.

excoriation	Skin sore or abrasion produced by scratching or scraping.
fissure	Crack in the skin that penetrates the dermis, such as chapped hands or lips.
histamine	Chemicals released in the blood that enlarge the vessels around an injury to speed removal of any irritating substance.
hyperhidrosis	Excessive sweating, caused by heat or general body weakness.
hypertrophy	Abnormal growth of the skin.
keloid	Thick scar resulting from excessive growth of fibrous tissue.
keratin	Fiber protein that is the principal component of hair and nails.
keratoma	Acquired, superficial, thickened patch of epidermis commonly known as callus, caused by pressure or friction on the hands and feet.
lentigines	Technical term for freckles.
lesion	Mark on the skin; certain lesions could indicate an injury or damage that changes the structure of tissues or organs.
leukoderma	Skin disorder characterized by light abnormal patches; caused by a burn or congenital disease that destroys the pigment-producing cells.
macule (plural: maculae)	Spot or discoloration on the skin, such as a freckle.
malignant melanoma	Most serious form of skin cancer; often characterized by black or dark brown patches on the skin that may appear uneven in texture, jagged, or raised.
melanin	Tiny grains of pigment (coloring matter) deposited in the basal cell layer of the epidermis and papillary layers of the dermis.
melanocytes	Melanin-forming cells.
miliaria rubra	Prickly heat; acute inflammatory disorder of the sweat glands, characterized by the eruption of small red vesicles and accompanied by burning, itching skin.
mole	Small brownish spot or blemish on the skin, ranging in color from pale tan to brown or bluish black.
Nevus	Small or large malformation of the skin due to abnormal pigmentation or dilated capillaries; commonly known as birthmark.
overexposure	Prolonged, repeated, or long-term exposure that can cause sensitivity.
papillary layer	Outer layer of the dermis, directly beneath the epidermis.
papule	Pimple; small circumscribed elevation on the skin that contains no fluid but may develop pus.
psoriasis	Skin disease characterized by red patches, covered with silver-white scales usually found on the scalp, elbows, knees, chest, and lower back, and rarely on the face.
pustule	Inflamed lesion containing pus.
reticular layer	Deeper layer of the dermis that supplies the skin with oxygen and nutrients; contains cells, vessels, glands, nerve endings, and follicles.

retinoic acid	Retin-A®; prescription cream for acne.
scale	Any thin plate of epidermal flakes, dry or oily, such as abnormal or excessive dandruff.
scar or cicatrix	Light-colored, slightly raised mark on the skin formed after an injury or lesion of the skin has healed.
sebaceous gland	Oil gland of the skin connected to hair follicles.
sensitization	Greatly increased or exaggerated sensitivity to products.
skin tag	Small brown or flesh-colored outgrowth of the skin.
squamous cell carcinoma	Type of skin cancer more serious than basal cell carcinoma; often characterized by scaly red papules or nodules.
stain	Abnormal brown or wine-colored skin discoloration with a circular and irregular shape.
stratum corneum	Outer layer of the epidermis.
stratum germinativum	Deepest layer of the epidermis; also known as the basal layer.
stratum granulosum	Granular layer of the epidermis.
stratum lucidum	Clear, transparent layer of the epidermis under the stratum corneum.
stratum spinosum	The spiny layer just above the basal cell layer.
subcutaneous tissue	Fatty layer found below the dermis that gives smoothness and contour to the body, contains fat for use as energy, and also acts as a protective cushion for the outer skin; also called adipose or subcutis tissue.
sudoriferous glands	Sweat glands of the skin.
tactile corpuscles	Small epidermal structures with nerve endings that are sensitive to touch and pressure.
tan	Change in pigmentation of skin caused by exposure to the sun or ultraviolet rays.
telangiectasia	Dilation of surface blood vessels.
tubercle	Abnormal rounded, solid lump above, within, or under the skin; larger than a papule.
tumor	A swelling; abnormal cell mass resulting from excessive multiplication of cells, varying in size, shape, and color.
ulcer	Open lesion on the skin or mucous membrane of the body, accompanied by pus and loss of skin depth.
verruca	Technical term for wart; hypertrophy of the papillae and epidermis.
vesicle	Small blister or sac containing clear fluid, lying within or just beneath the epidermis.
vitiligo	Milky-white spots (leukoderma) of the skin. Vitiligo is hereditary, and may be related to thyroid conditions.
wheal	Itchy, swollen lesion that lasts only a few hours; caused by a blow, the bite of an insect, urticaria, or the sting of a nettle.

Nail Structure and Growth

LEARNING OBJECTIVES

After completing this chapter, you will be able to:

1. Describe the structure and composition of nails.
2. Discuss how nails grow.

W hen most people think of nail services, they immediately envision pleasurable manicures, pedicures, and nail enhancements that produce strong gorgeous nails. While your goal for cosmetology school should be to learn how to expertly groom, strengthen, and beautify the nails, it is equally important to understand their physiology. Technically speaking, the natural nail is the hard protective plate. It is made of a protein called keratin and located at the end of the finger or toe. It is an appendage of the skin and is, therefore, part of the integumentary system. The nail plates protect the tips of the fingers and toes, and their appearance can reflect the general health of the body. To provide professional services and care for your clients, you must educate yourself about the natural nail's structure and growth.

THE NATURAL NAIL

The natural nail is composed mainly of keratin, the same protein found in skin and hair. The keratin in natural nails is harder than the keratin in hair or skin. A healthy nail should be whitish and translucent in appearance, with the pinkish color of the nail bed below showing through. The nail plate is relatively porous to water, allowing it to pass much more easily than it will pass through normal skin of equal thickness. The water content of the nail is related to the relative humidity of the surrounding environment. A healthy nail may look dry and hard, but it actually has a water content of between 15 and 25 percent. The water content directly affects the nail's flexibility. The lower the water content, the more rigid the nail becomes. Using an oil-based nail conditioner, or nail polish to coat the plate, can reduce water loss and improve flexibility.

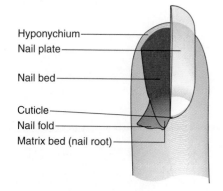

Hyponychium —
Nail plate —

Nail bed —

Cuticle —
Nail fold —
Matrix bed (nail root) —

Figure 8–1 Structure of the natural nail.

NAIL ANATOMY

The natural **nail unit** consists of several basic parts (Figures 8–1 and 8–2).

Nail Bed

The **nail bed** is the portion of living skin on which the nail plate sits. Because it is richly supplied with blood vessels, the area under the nail plate has a pinkish appearance in the area that extends from the lunula to the area just before the free edge of the nail. The nail bed is supplied with many nerves, and is attached to the nail plate by a thin layer of tissue called the **bed epithelium** (ep-ih-THEE-lee-um). That bed epithelium helps guide the nail plate along the nail bed as it grows.

Matrix

The **matrix** is where the natural nail is formed. The matrix is composed of matrix cells that produce other cells that become the nail plate. The matrix area contains nerves, lymph, and blood vessels to nourish the matrix cells. The matrix will continue to create new nail cells as long as it is nourished and is kept in healthy condition. The matrix extends from under the nail fold at the base of the nail plate. The visible part of the matrix that extends from underneath the living skin is called the **lunula** (LOO-nuh-luh). The lighter color of the lunula shows the true color of the matrix.

Growth of the nails can be affected if an individual is in poor health, a nail disorder or disease is present, or there has been an injury to the matrix.

Nail Plate

The **nail plate** is the most visible and functional part of the nail module. It is a hardened keratin plate that sits on and slides across the nail bed. It is formed by the matrix cells whose sole job is to create nail plate cells. The nail plate may appear to be one piece, but is actually constructed of about 100 layers of nail cells. The **free edge** is the part of the nail plate that extends over the tip of the finger or toe.

The **cuticle** (KYOO-tih-kul) is the dead colorless tissue attached to the nail plate. The cuticle comes from the underside of the skin that lies above the natural nail plate. This tissue is incredibly sticky and difficult to remove from the nail plate. Its job is to seal the space between the natural nail plate and living skin above to prevent entry of foreign material and microorganisms, thus helping to prevent injury and infection. The **eponychium** (ep-oh-NIK-eeum) is the living skin at the base of the nail plate covering the matrix area. The eponychium is sometimes confused with the cuticle. They are not the same. The cuticle is the dead tissue on the nail plate, where as the eponychium is living tissue. The cuticle comes from the underside of this area, where it becomes strongly attached to the new growth of nail plate and is pulled free to form a seal between the natural nail plate and the eponychium. The **hyponychium** (hy-poh-NIK-eeum) is the slightly thickened layer of skin that lies underneath the free edge of the nail plate. It creates a seal under the nail plate to prevent microorganisms from invading and infecting the nail bed.

Specialized Ligaments

A **ligament** is a tough band of fibrous tissue that connects bones or holds an organ in place. Specialized ligaments attach the nail bed and matrix bed

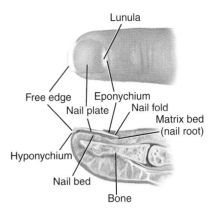

Figure 8–2 Cross-section of the nail.

to the underlying bone. They are located at the base of the matrix and around the edges of the nail bed.

Nail Folds

The **nail folds** are folds of normal skin that surround the nail plate. These folds form the **nail grooves**, the slits or furrows on the sides of the nail on which it moves as it grows.

NAIL GROWTH

The growth of the nail plate is affected by nutrition, exercise, and a person's general health.

A normal nail grows forward from the matrix and extends over the tip of the finger. Normal, healthy nails can grow in a variety of shapes, depending on the shape of the matrix (Figure 8–3). The length, width, and curvature of the matrix determine the thickness, width, and curvature of the natural nail plate. For example, a longer matrix produces a thicker nail plate and a highly curved matrix creates a highly curved free edge.

The average rate of nail growth in the normal adult is about 1/10" (3.7 mm) per month. Nails grow faster in the summer than they do in the winter. Children's nails grow more rapidly, whereas those of elderly persons grow at a slower rate. The nail of the middle finger grows fastest and the thumbnail grows the slowest. Nail growth rates increase dramatically during the last trimester of pregnancy due to hormonal changes in the body. The nail growth rate decreases dramatically after delivery and return to normal, as do hormone levels in the body. It is a myth that this is due to taking prenatal care vitamins. Nail growth rates will accelerate whether or not a woman takes these vitamins. Although toenails grow slower than fingernails, they are thicker and harder.

Nail Malformation

If disease, injury, or infection occurs in the matrix, the shape or thickness of the nail plate can change. The natural nail will continue to grow as long as the matrix is healthy and undamaged. Ordinarily, replacement of the natural nail takes about 4 to 6 months. Toenails take 9 months to a year to be

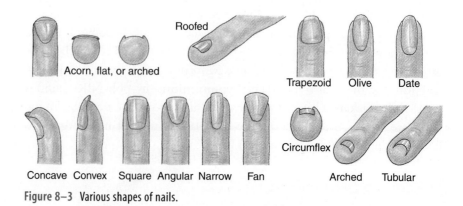

Figure 8–3 Various shapes of nails.

fully replaced. It should be noted that nails are not shed automatically or periodically, as is the case with hair.

KNOW YOUR NAILS

Many nail care professionals are interested in nails because of the creative opportunities they present. As with every other area of cosmetology, this creativity must be grounded in a full awareness of the structure and physiology of the nails and the surrounding tissue.

Working on good, strong, healthy nails can be a pleasure.

REVIEW **QUESTIONS**

1. Describe the appearance of a normal healthy nail.

2. What is the technical term for the nail?

3. What material is the nail plate made from?

4. Name six basic parts of the nail unit.

5. What part of the nail unit contains the nerve and blood supply?

CHAPTER **GLOSSARY**

bed epithelium	Thin layer of tissue between the nail plate and the nail bed.
cuticle	Dead tissue that tightly adheres to the natural nail plate.
eponychium	Living skin at the base of the nail plate covering the matrix area.
free edge	Part of the nail plate that extends over the tip of the finger or toe.
hyponychium	Thickened skin between the fingertip and free edge of the nail plate, which forms a protective barrier that keeps pathogens from infecting the nail bed.
ligament	Tough bank of fibrous tissue that connects bones or holds an organ in place.
lunula	Whitish, half-moon shape at the base of the nail plate, caused by the reflection of light off the surface of the matrix.
matrix	Area where the nail plate cells are formed; this area is composed of matrix cells that make up the nail plate.
nail bed	Portion of the skin that supports the nail plate as it grows toward the free edge.
nail fold	Fold of normal skin that surrounds the nail plate.
nail groove	Slit or furrow on the sides of the nail.
nail plate	Hardened keratin plate covering the nail bed.
nail unit	All the anatomical parts of the fingernail necessary to produce the natural nail plate.

Nail Diseases and Disorders

Name:

Home address:

Home phone:

est hours for appointment:

ENT PROFILE

What type of work do you do?

Do you have any hobbi

you part

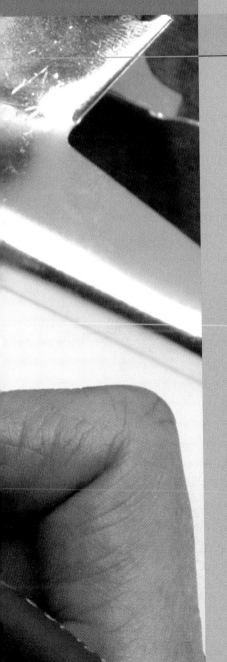

CHAPTER OUTLINE

- ● Nail Disorders
- ● Nail Diseases

LEARNING OBJECTIVES

After completing this chapter, you will be able to:

1. List and describe the various disorders and irregularities of nails.

2. Recognize diseases of the nails that should not be treated in the salon.

KEY **TERMS**

Page number indicates where in the chapter the term is used.

T o give clients professional and responsible service and care, you need to learn about not only the structure and growth of the nail as you did in Chapter 8, but you must also know when it is safe to work on a client. Nails are an interesting and surprising part of the human body. They are small mirrors of the general health of the entire body. You must be able to recognize conditions you may encounter while servicing clients. Many of these conditions are easily treated in the salon—hangnails, for instance, or bruising—but others are infectious and should not be treated by salon professionals. A select few may even signal serious health problems that warrant the attention of a doctor. Carefully studying this chapter will vastly improve your expertise in caring for nails. It will also help ensure that you are protecting your clients, rather than promoting the spread of disease.

A normal healthy nail is firm and flexible, and should be shiny and slightly pink in color, with more yellow tones in some races. Its surface should be smooth and unspotted, without any pits or splits. Certain health problems in the body can show up in the nails as visible disorders or poor nail growth.

NAIL DISORDERS

A **nail disorder** is a condition caused by injury or disease. Most, if not all, of your clients have experienced one or more types of common nail disorder at some time in their lives. The technician should recognize normal and abnormal nail conditions, and understand what to do. You may be able to help your clients with nail disorders in one of two ways.

You can tell clients that they may have a disorder and refer them to a physician, if required.

You can cosmetically improve certain nail plate conditions if the problem is cosmetic and not a medical disorder.

It is your professional responsibility and a requirement of your license to know which option to choose. A client whose nail or skin is infected, inflamed, broken, or swollen should not receive services. Instead, the client should be referred to a physician, if you feel that is an appropriate recommendation, based on the condition.

Bruised nails are a condition in which a blood clot forms under the nail plate, forming a dark purplish spot. These discolorations are usually due to small injuries to the nail bed. The dried blood absorbs into the bed epithelium on the underside of the nail plate and grows out with it. Treat this injured nail gently and advise your clients to be more careful with their nails if they want to avoid this problem in the future. Advise them to treat their nails like "jewels" and not "tools"!

Ridges running vertically down the length of the natural nail plate, are caused by uneven growth of the nails, usually the result of age. Older clients are more likely to have these ridges, and unless they become very deep and weaken the nail plate, the are perfectly normal. When manicuring a client with this condition, carefully buff the nail plate to minimize the appearance of these ridges. This helps to remove or minimize the ridges, but great care must be taken not to overly thin the nail plate, which could lead to nail plate weakness and additional damage. Ridge filler is less damaging to the natural nail plate, and can be used with colored polish to give a smooth appearance to the plate while keeping it strong and healthy.

Eggshell nails are noticeably thin, white nail plates that are much more flexible than normal. Eggshell nails are normally weaker and can curve over the free edge (Figure 9–1A and B). The condition is usually caused by improper diet, hereditary factors, internal disease, or medication. Be very careful when manicuring these nails because they are fragile and can break easily. Use the fine side of an abrasive board (240 grit or higher) to file them gently and remove as little of the nail plate as possible. Do not use heavy pressure with a pusher at the base of the nail plate, where it is thinnest and most likely to be punctured.

Beau's lines are visible depressions running across the width of the natural nail plate (Figure 9–2). These usually result from major illness or injury that has traumatized the body, such as pneumonia, adverse drug reaction, surgery, heart failure, massive injury, and high fever. Beau's lines occur because the matrix slows down in producing nail cells for an extended period of time, say a week or a month. This causes the nail plate to grow thinner for a period of time. The nail plate thickness usually returns to normal after the illness or condition is resolved.

Hangnail or **agnail** (AG-nayl) is a condition in which the living skin splits around the nail (Figure 9–3). Dryness of the skin or cutting this living tissue can result in hangnails. Advise the client that proper nail care, such as hot oil manicures, will aid in correcting the condition. Also, never cut the living skin around the natural nail plate. It is against state board regulations and can lead to serious infections for which you and the salon may be legally liable. If not properly cared for, a hangnail can become infected.

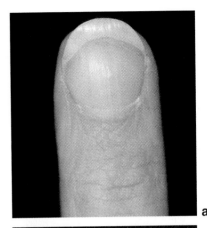
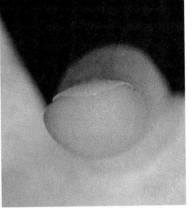

a

b

Figure 9–1 **A:** Eggshell nail, front view.
B: Eggshell nail, end view.

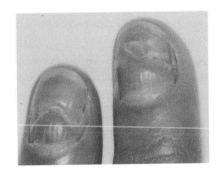

Figure 9–2 Beau's lines.

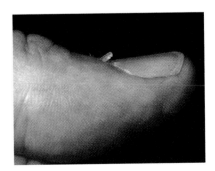

Figure 9–3 Hangnail.

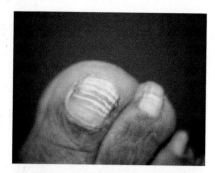

Figure 9–4 Leukonychia spots.

Figure 9–5 Melanonychia.

Clients with symptoms of infections in their fingers should be referred to a physician. Signs of infection are redness, pain, swelling, or pus.

Leukonychia spots (loo-koh-NIK-ee-ah), or white spots, are a whitish discoloration of the nails, usually caused by injury to the nail matrix. They are not a symptom of any vitamin or mineral deficiency. Instead, they are results of minor damage to the matrix. It is a myth that these result from calcium or zinc deficiency (Figure 9–4). They appear frequently in the nails but do not indicate disease. As the nail continues to grow, the white spots eventually disappear.

Melanonychia (mel-uh-nuh-NIK-ee-uh) is darkening of the fingernails or toenails. It may be seen as a black band within the nail plate, extending from the base to the free edge. In some cases, it may affect the entire nail plate. A localized area of increased pigment cells (melanocytes), usually within the matrix bed, is responsible for this condition. As matrix cells form the nail plate, melanin is laid down within the plate by the melanocytes. This is a fairly common occurrence and considered normal in African Americans, but could be indicative of a disease condition in Caucasians (Figure 9–5).

Onychophagy (ahn-ih-koh-FAY-jee), or bitten nails, is the result of a habit that prompts the individual to chew the nail or the hardened, damaged skin surrounding the nail plate (Figure 9–6). Advise the client that frequent manicures and care of the hardened eponychium can often help to overcome this habit, while improving the health and appearance of the hands. Sometimes, the application of nail enhancements can beautify deformed nails and discourage the client from biting the nails.

Onychorrhexis (ahn-ih-koh-REK-sis) refers to split or brittle nails that also have a series of lengthwise ridges giving a rough appearance to the surface of the nail plate. This condition is usually caused by injury to the matrix, excessive use of cuticle removers, harsh cleaning agents, nail polish removers, aggressive filing techniques, or hereditary causes. Nail services can be performed only if the nail is not split and exposing the nail bed. This condition may be corrected by softening the nails with a conditioning treatment, that is, hot oil manicures, and discontinuing the use of harsh detergents, cleaners, polish removers, or improper filing (Figure 9–7). These

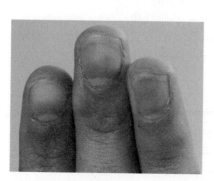

Figure 9–6 Bitten nails.

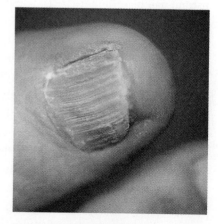

Figure 9–7 Onychorrhexis.

nail plates often lacked sufficient moisture, so twice daily treatments with a high-quality, penetrating nail oil can be very beneficial.

Plicatured nail (plik-a-CHOORD) literally means "folded nail" (Figure 9–8), and is a type of highly curved nail plate often caused by injury to the matrix, but may be inherited. This condition often leads to ingrown nails.

Nail pterygium (teh-RIJ-ee-um) is an abnormal condition that occurs when skin is stretched by the nail plate. This disorder is usually caused by serious injury, such as burns or an adverse skin reaction to chemical nail enhancement products. (Figure 9–9). The terms "cuticle" and "pterygium" are not the same thing, and they should never be used interchangeably. Nail pterygium is abnormal, that is, damage to the eponychium or hyponychium.

Do not treat nail pterygium by pushing the extension of skin back with an instrument. Doing so will cause more injury to the tissues and will make the condition worse. The gentle massage of conditioning oils or creams into the affected area may be beneficial. Hot oil manicures may be very helpful. If this condition becomes painful or show signs of infection, recommend that the client see a physician.

Increased Curvature Nails

Nails plates with a deep or sharp curvature at the free edge have this shape because of the matrix. The greater the curvature of the matrix, the greater the curvature of the free edge. Increased curvature can range from mild to severe pinching of the soft tissue at the free edge. In some cases, the free edge pinches the sidewalls into a deep curve. This is known as a plicatured nail. The nail can also curl in upon itself (Figure 9–10) or may only be deformed only on one sidewall. In each of these cases, the natural nail plate should be carefully trimmed and filed. Extreme or unusual cases should be referred to a qualified medical doctor or podiatrist. A brief summary of nail disorders is found in Table 9–1.

Nail Fungus

Fungi (FUN-jy) (singular fungus, FUNG-gus) are parasites, which under some circumstances may cause infections of the feet and hands. Nail fungi are of concern to the salon because they are contagious and can be transmitted through unsanitary implements. Fungi can spread from nail to nail on the client's feet, but it is much less likely that these pathogens will cause fingernail infections. Fungi infections prefer to grow in conditions where the skin is warm, moist, and dark, that is, feet inside shoes. It is extremely unlikely that a nail technician could become infected from a client, but it is possible to transmit fungal infections from one client's foot or toe to another client.

With proper sanitation and disinfection practices the transmission of fungal infections can be very easily avoided. Clients with suspected nail fungal infection must be referred to a physician.

It Is Not a Mold!

In the past, discolorations of the nail plate (especially those between the plate and artificial enhancements) were incorrectly referred to as "molds."

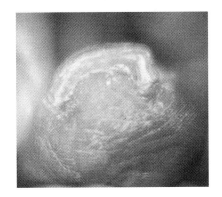
Figure 9–8 Plicatured nail.

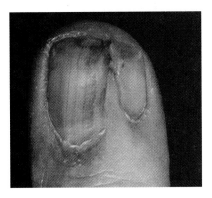
Figure 9–9 Nail pterygium.

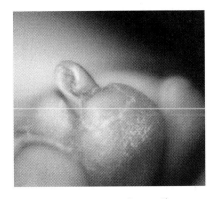
Figure 9–10 Trumpet or pincer nail

TABLE 9-1 ● OVERVIEW OF NAIL DISORDERS

Disorder	Signs or Symptoms
Discolored nails	Nails turn variety of colors; may indicate a systemic disorder, poor blood circulation.
Bruised nails	Dark purplish spots, usually due to injury.
Ridged nails	Wavy ridges seen in normal aging.
Eggshell nails	Noticeably thin, white plate, more flexible than normal; usually caused by improper diet, hereditary factors, internal disease, or medication.
Beau's lines	Depressions running across the width of the nail plate; a result of serious illness or injury.
Hangnail	Living skin around the nail plate (often the eponychium) becomes split or torn.
Infected finger	Redness, pain, swelling, or pus; refer to physician.
Leukonychia spots	Whitish discoloration of the nails; usually caused by minor injury to the nail matrix. Not related to health.
Melanonychia	Darkening of the fingernails or toenails.
Onychophagy	Bitten nails.
Onychorrhexis	Abnormal surface roughness on the nail plate.
Plicatured nails	Sharp bend in one corner of the nail plate creating increased curvature.
Nail pterygium	Abnormal stretching of skin around the nail plate; usually from serious injury or an allergic skin reaction.
Nails psoriasis	Nail surface pitting, roughness, onycholysis, and bed discolorations.
Pincer nails	A form of dramatically increased nail curvature.
Trumpet nails	A form of dramatically increased nail curvature.

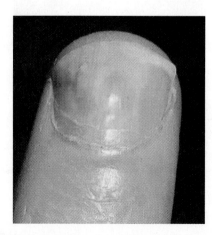

Figure 9–11 *Pseudomonas aeruginosa.*

This term should not be used when referring to infections of the fingernails or toenails. The discoloration is actually a bacterial infection that is caused by several types of *Pseudomonas aeruginosa* bacteria. These naturally occurring skin bacteria can grow out of control and cause an infection, if conditions are correct for growth (Figure 9–11). Bacterial infections are more often seen on the hands. Bacteria do not need the same growing conditions as fungal organisms, and can thrive on fingernails more easily. Infection can be caused by the use of implements that are contaminated with large numbers of these bacteria. These infections are not a result of moisture trapped between the natural nail and artificial nail enhancements. This is a myth! Water does not cause infections. Infections are caused by large numbers of bacteria or fungal organisms on a surface. This is why proper cleansing and preparation of the natural nail plate, as well as sanitation and disinfection of implements, are so important. If these pathogens are not present, infections cannot occur. A typical bacterial infection on the nail plate can be identified in the early stages as a yellow-green spot that becomes darker in its advanced stages. The color usually changes from yellow to green to brown to black.

You should not provide nail services for a client who has a nail fungal or bacterial infection.

NAIL DISEASES

There are several nail diseases that you may come across. A brief summary of nail diseases is found in Table 9–2. Any nail disease that shows signs of infection or inflammation (redness, pain, swelling, or pus) should not be treated in the salon. Medical treatment is required for all nail diseases.

A person's occupation can cause a variety of nail infections. For instance, infections develop more readily in people who regularly place their hands in a harsh cleaning solutions. Natural oils are removed from the skin by frequent exposure to soaps, solvents, and many other types of substances. The nail technician's hands are exposed daily to professional products. These products should be used according to manufacturer's instructions to ensure that they

Figure 9–12 Always practice strict sanitation when working with the nails.

TABLE 9-2 ● **OVERVIEW OF NAIL DISEASES**	
Disease	**Signs or Symptoms**
Onychia	Inflammation of the matrix and shedding of the nail.
Onychocryptosis	Ingrown nails.
Onycholysis	Separation of the nail plate and bed, often due to physical injury or allergic reactions.
Onychomadesis	Separation and falling off of a nail from the nail bed.
Onychomycosis	Fungal infection of the natural nail plate.
Paronychia	Bacterial inflammation of the tissues around the nail plate, causing pus, swelling, and redness.
Pyogenic granuloma	Severe inflammation of the nail in which a lump of red tissue grows up from the nail bed to the nail plate.
Tinea pedis	Red itchy patches of skin on the bottom of feet and/or between the toes.

are being used correctly and safely. If those instructions or warnings tell you to avoid skin contact, you should take heed and follow such advice. If the manufacturer recommends that you wear gloves, make sure that you do so to protect your skin. Contact the product manufacturer if you are not sure how to use the product safely. Product manufacturers can always provide you with additional information and guidance. Call them whenever you have any questions related to safe handling and proper use.

Onychosis (ahn-ih-KOH-sis) any deformity or disease of the nails.

Onychia (uh-NIK-ee-uh) is an inflammation of the nail matrix followed by shedding of the natural nail plate. Any break in the skin surrounding the nail plate can allow pathogens to infect the matrix. Be careful to avoid injuring sensitive tissue, and make sure that all implements are properly sanitized and disinfected. Improperly sanitized and disinfected nail implements can cause this and other diseases, if an accidental injury occurs.

Onychocryptosis (ahn-ih-koh-krip-TOH-sis), or ingrown nails, can affect either the fingers or toes (Figure 9–13). In this condition, the nail grows into the sides of the tissue around the nail. The movements of walking can press the soft tissues up against the nail plate, contributing to the problem. If the tissue around the nail plate is not infected, or if the nail is not deeply imbedded in the flesh, you can carefully trim the corner of the nail in a curved shape to relieve the pressure on the nail groove. You may not work on infected or deeply ingrown nails. Refer the client to a physician, if appropriate.

Onycholysis (ahn-ih-KAHL-ih-sis) is the lifting of the nail plate from the bed without shedding, usually beginning at the free edge and continuing toward the lunula area (Figure 9–14). This is usually the result of physical injury, trauma, or allergic reaction of the nail bed, and less often related to a health disorder. It often occurs when the natural nails are filed too aggressively or artificial nails are improperly removed. If there is no indication of an infection or open sores, a basic pedicure or manicure may be given. The nail plate should be short to avoid further injury, and the area underneath the nail plate should be kept clean and dry. If the trauma that caused the onycholysis is removed, the area will begin to slowly heal itself. Eventually, the nail plate will grow off the free edge and the hyponychium will

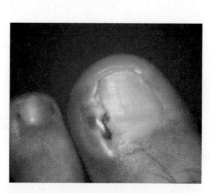

Figure 9–13 Onychocryptosis.

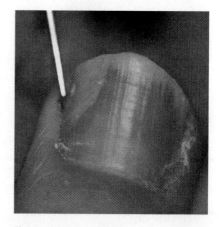

Figure 9–14 Onycholysis.

reform the seal that provides a natural barrier against infection.(Figure 9–15).

Onychomadesis (ahn-ih-koh-muh-DEE-sis) is the separation and falling off of a nail plate from the bed. It can affect fingernails and toenails (Figure 9–16). In most cases, the cause can be traced to a localized infection, injuries to the matrix, or a severe systemic illness. Drastic medical procedures such as chemotherapy may also be the cause.

Whatever the reason, once the problem is resolved, a new nail plate will eventually grow again. If onychomadesis is present, do not apply enhancements to the nail plate. If there is no indication of an infection or open sores, a basic manicure or pedicure service may be given.

Nail psoriasis often causes tiny pits or severe roughness on the surface of the nail plate. Sometimes these pits occur randomly, and sometimes they appear in evenly spaced rows. Nail psoriasis can also cause the surface of the plate to look like it had been filed with the course abrasive, or may create a ragged free edge or all of the above (Figure 9–17). People with skin psoriasis will often experience these nail disorders. Nail psoriasis can also affect the nail bed, causing it to develop yellowish to reddish spots underneath the nail plate, called salmon patches. Onycholysis is also much more prevalent in people with nail psoriasis. When all of these symptoms are present on the nail unit at the same time, nail psoriasis becomes a likely cause of the client's problem nails and they should be referred to a physician for diagnoses.

Paronychia (payr-uh-NIK-ee-uh) is a bacterial inflammation of the tissues surrounding the nail (Figure 9–18). Pus and swelling are usually seen in the skin fold adjacent to the nail plate.

Individuals who work with their hands in water, such as dishwashers and bartenders, or who must wash their hands continually, such as health care workers and food processors, are more susceptible, since their hands are often very dry or chapped from excessive exposure to water, detergents, and so on. This makes them much more likely to develop infections.

Toenails, because they spend a lot of time in a warm, moist environment, are often more susceptible to paronychia infections as well (Figure 9–19). Use moisturizing hand lotions to keep skin healthy and keep feet clean and dry.

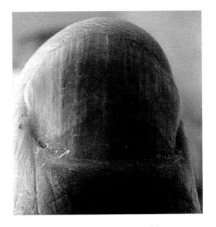

Figure 9–15 Onycholysis caused by trauma.

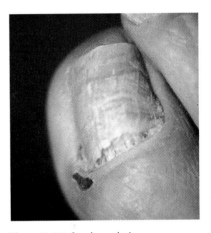

Figure 9–16 Onychomadesis.

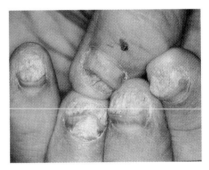

Figure 9–17 Nail psoriasis.

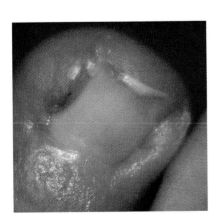

Figure 9–18 Chronic paronychia.

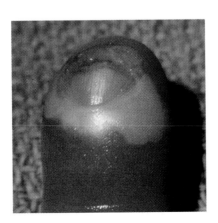

Figure 9–19 Paronychia.

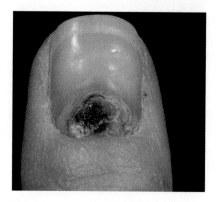

Figure 9–20   Pyogenic granuloma.

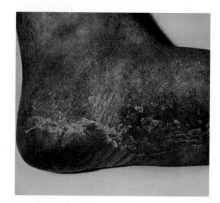

Figure 9–21   Tinea pedis.

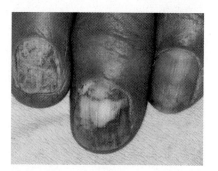

Figure 9–22   Onychomycosis.

Pyogenic granuloma (py-oh-JEN-ik gran-yoo-LOH-muh) is a severe inflammation of the nail in which a lump of red tissue grows up from the nail bed to the nail plate (Figure 9–20).

Tinea pedis is the medical term for fungal infections of the feet. These infections can occur on the bottoms of the feet and often appear as a red itchy rash in the spaces between the toes, most often between the fourth and fifth toe. There is sometimes a small degree of scaling of the skin. The client should be advised to wash their feet every day and dry them completely. This will make it difficult for the infection to live or grow. Advise clients to wear cotton socks and change them at least twice per day. They should also avoid wearing the same pair of shoes each day, since it can take up to 24 hours for a pair of shoes to completely dry. Over-the-counter antifungal powders can help keep feet dry and may help speed healing (Figure 9–21).

Onychomycosis (ahn-ihkoh- my-KOH-sis) is a fungal infection of the nail plate (Figure 9–22). A common form is whitish patches that can be scraped off the surface of the nail. Another common type of infection shows long whitish or pale yellowish streaks within the nail plate. A third common form causes the free edge of the nail to crumble and may even affect the entire plate. These types of infection often invade the free edge and spread toward the matrix.

REVIEW **QUESTIONS**

1. What conditions do fungal organisms favor for growth?

2. Name two common causes of onycholysis.

3. In what situation should a nail service not be performed?

4. What is *Pseudomonas aeruginosa*? Why is it important to learn about it?

5. Name at least eight nail disorders and describe their appearance.

6. What is the most effective way to avoid transferring infections among your clients?

CHAPTER **GLOSSARY**

Beau's lines	Visible depressions running across the width of the natural nail plate.
bruised nail	Condition in which a blood clot forms under the nail plate, forming a dark purplish spot, usually due to injury.
eggshell nail	Noticeably thin, white nail plate that is more flexible than normal.
hangnail or agnail	Condition in which the eponychium or other living tissue surrounding the nail plate becomes split or torn.
leukonychia spot	Whitish discoloration of the nails, usually caused by injury to the matrix area; white spot.
melanonychia	Darkening of the fingernails or toenails; may be seen as a black band under or within the nail plate, extending from the base to the free edge.
nail disorder	Condition caused by an injury or disease of the nail unit.
nail pterygium	An abnormal growth of the skin that stretches into a winglike structure, on the nail plate, it may be a result of severe injury or allergic reaction.
nail psoriasis	A condition that affects the surface of the natural nail plate, causing it to appear rough and pitted, as well as causing reddish color spots on the nail bed, and onycholysis.
onychia	Inflammation of the matrix of the nail with shedding of the nail.
onychocryptosis	Ingrown nails; nail grows into the living tissue around the nail.
onycholysis	Separation of the nail plate from the nail bed, often caused by injury or allergic reactions.
onychomadesis	The separation and falling off of a nail from the nail bed; can occur on fingernails and toenails.
onychomycosis	Fungal infection of the natural nail plate.
onychophagy	Bitten nails.
onychorrhexis	Abnormal brittleness with deep, rough grooves in the nail plate.
onychosis	Any disease or disorder of the natural nails.
paronychia	Bacterial inflammation of the tissues surrounding the nail; pus, redness, and swelling are usually present.
plicatured nail	Disorder in which one or both of the edges of the plate are folded at a sharp 90-degree (or more) angle down into the soft -tissue.
Pseudomonas aeruginosa	One of several common bacteria that can cause nail infection.
pyogenic granuloma	Severe inflammation of the nail in which a lump of red tissue grows up from the nail bed to the nail plate.
ridges	Vertical lines running the length of the natural nail plate, usually related to normal aging.
pincer nail	Increased crosswise curvature throughout the nail plate caused by an increased curvature of the matrix.
tinea pedis	Medical term for the condition known as athlete's foot.
trumpet nail	Disorder in which the edges of the nail plate curl around to form the shape of a trumpet or sharp cone at the free edge.

Basics of Chemistry

LEARNING OBJECTIVES

After completing this chapter, you will be able to:

1. Explain the difference between organic and inorganic chemistry.
2. Discuss the different forms of matter: elements, compounds, and mixtures.
3. Explain the difference between solutions, suspensions and emulsions.
4. Explain pH and the pH scale.
5. Describe oxidation and reduction (redox) reactions.

KEY TERMS

Page number indicates where in the chapter the term is used.

acid
pg. 168

alkali
pg. 168

alkanolamines
pg. 166

ammonia
pg. 166

atom
pg. 159

chemical change
pg. 161

chemical properties
pg. 158

chemistry
pg. 169

combustion
pg. 160

compound molecules
pg. 160

element
pg. 159

elemental molecules
pg. 160

emulsion
pg. 163

exothermic
pg. 169

glycerin
pg. 166

hydrophilic
pg. 163

immiscible
pg. 163

inorganic chemistry
pg. 159

ion
pg. 166

ionization
pg. 166

lipophilic
pg. 163

matter
pg. 159

miscible
pg. 163

molecule
pg. 159

**oil-in-water (O/W)
emulsion**
pg. 163

organic chemistry
pg. 158

oxidation
pg. 169

oxidizing agent
pg. 169

pH
pg. 167

physical change
pg. 160

physical mixture
pg. 162

physical properties
pg. 161

pure substance
pg. 162

redox
pg. 169

reduction
pg. 169

silicones
pg. 166

solute
pg. 162

solution
pg. 162

solvent
pg. 162

surfactants
pg. 163

suspension
pg. 163

C osmetology services in a modern salon would not be possible without the use of chemicals. To use professional products effectively and safely, all cosmetology professionals need to have a basic understanding of chemistry. This chapter will provide you with the overview you need.

CHEMISTRY

Chemistry is the science that deals with the composition, structures, and properties of matter and how matter changes under different conditions.

Organic chemistry is the study of substances that contain carbon. Organic substances burn because they contain carbon. All living things, or things that were once alive, whether they are plants or animals, contain carbon. Although the term "organic" is often misused to mean "natural," because of its association with living things, not all organic substances are natural or healthy.

You may be surprised to learn that gasoline, motor oil, plastics, synthetic fabrics, pesticides, and fertilizers are all organic substances. All hair-coloring products, chemical hair texturizers, shampoos, conditioners, and styling aids are organic. All artificial nail enhancements and nail polishes are organic. These products are manufactured from natural gas and oil, which are the remains of plants and animals that died millions of years ago. So, remember, "organic" does not mean "natural".

Inorganic chemistry is the study of substances that do not contain carbon. Inorganic substances do not burn, because they do not contain carbon. Inorganic substances are not, and never were, alive. Metals, minerals, water, and air are inorganic substances. Hydrogen peroxide and hydroxide hair relaxers are examples of inorganic substances.

MATTER

Matter is any substance that occupies space and has mass (weight). All matter has physical and chemical properties, and exists in the form of a solid, liquid, or gas. Although matter has physical properties that we can touch, taste, smell, or see, not everything that we can see is matter. For instance, we can see visible light and electric sparks, but these are forms of energy, and energy is not matter.

Energy does not occupy space or have mass (weight). We will discuss energy in chapter 12.

Elements

An **element** is the simplest form of matter and cannot be broken down into a simpler substance without a loss of identity. There are 90 naturally occurring elements, each with its own distinctive physical and chemical properties. All matter in the universe is made up of these 90 different elements.

Each element is identified by a letter symbol, such as O for oxygen, C for carbon, H for hydrogen, N for nitrogen and S for sulfur.

Atoms

Atoms are the particles from which all matter is composed. Atoms are the structural units that make up the elements. Different elements are different from one another because the structure of their atoms is different. An atom is the smallest particle of an element that retains the properties of that element. Atoms cannot be divided into simpler substances by ordinary chemical means.

Molecules

Just as words are made by combining letters, **molecules** are made by combining atoms. A molecule is a chemical combination of two or more atoms. Elemental molecules are a chemical combinations of atoms of the same element.

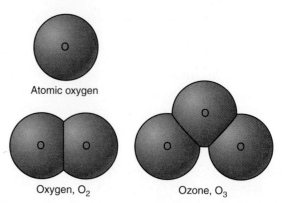

Figure 10–1 Elemental molecules contain atoms of the same element.

Atmospheric oxygen, in the air we breathe, is an **elemental molecule** containing two atoms of the element oxygen and is written as O_2. Ozone is a very dangerous form of oxygen and a major component of smog, it contains three atoms of the element oxygen, and is written as O_3 (Figure 10-1).

Compound molecules are chemical combinations of two or more atoms of different elements (Figure 10-2). Sodium chloride (NaCl), or common table salt, is a compound molecule that contains one atom of the element sodium (Na) and one atom of the element chlorine (Cl).

States of Matter

All matter exists in one of three different physical forms: (1) solid, (2) liquid, or (3) gas.

These three forms are called the "states of matter." Matter assumes one of these states, depending on its temperature (Figure 10-3).

Like many other substances, water (H_2O) can exist in all three states of matter, depending on its temperature. For instance, when water freezes, it turns to ice. When ice melts, it turns to water. When water boils, it turns to steam. When the steam cools, it turns back into water. The form of the water physically changes according to changes in the temperature, but it is still water (H_2O). It does not become a different chemical. It stays the same chemical, but in a different physical form. This is called a **physical change**.

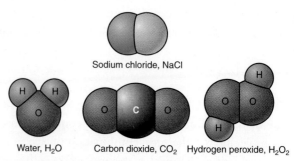

Figure 10–2 Compound molecules contain atoms of different elements.

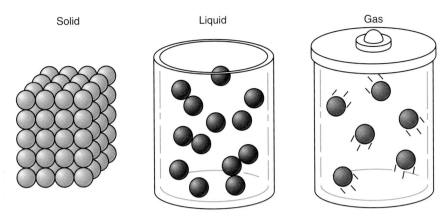

Figure 10–3 Solids, liquids, and gases.

The three different states of matter have the following distinct characteristics:

o Solids have a definite shape and volume. Ice is an example of a solid.

o Liquids have a definite volume, but not a definite shape. Water is an example of a liquid.

o Gases do not have a definite volume or shape. Steam is an example of a gas.

Physical and Chemical Properties

Every substance has unique properties that allow us to identify it. The two different types of properties are physical and chemical.

Physical properties are those characteristics that can be determined without a chemical reaction and do not involve a chemical change. Physical properties include color, size, weight and hardness.

Chemical properties are those characteristics that can only be determined by a chemical reaction and a chemical change in the substance. Chemical properties include the ability of iron to rust and wood to burn. In both of these examples, oxidation is the chemical reaction that causes a chemical change in the substance.

Physical and Chemical Changes

Matter can be changed in two different ways. Physical forces cause physical changes and chemical reactions cause chemical changes.

A **physical change** is a change in the form, or physical properties of a substance, without a chemical reaction or the creation of a new substance. A physical change is the result of physical forces that only change the physical properties of a substance, no chemical reaction is involved, and no new chemicals are formed. Solid ice undergoes a physical change when it melts into liquid water (Figure 10-4). A physical change occurs with the application of non-oxidation (temporary) haircolor or nail polish.

A **chemical change** is a change in the chemical and physical properties of a substance by a chemical reaction that creates a new substance or

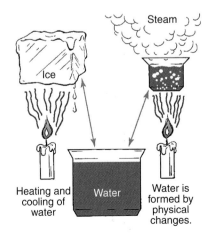

Figure 10–4 Physical changes.

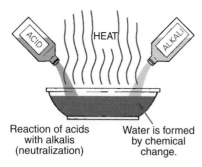

Reaction of acids
with alkalis
(neutralization)

Water is formed
by chemical
change.

Figure 10–5 Chemical changes.

substances. A chemical change is the result of a chemical reaction that creates new chemicals that have new chemical and physical properties. (Figure 10-5). Examples of a chemical change are the oxidation of haircolor and the polymerization of acrylic (methacrylate) nail enhancements.

Pure Substances and Physical Mixtures

All matter can be classified as either a pure substance or a physical mixture.

A **pure substance** is a chemical combination of matter, in definite proportions. Pure substances have unique properties. All atoms, elements, elemental molecules and compound molecules are pure substances. Water is a pure substance that results from the chemical combination of two atoms of the element hydrogen and one atom of the element oxygen, in definite proportions. The properties of water (a liquid) are not the properties of hydrogen and oxygen (both gases). Pure substances include oxygen, ozone, water and salt. Few of the products cosmetologists or manicurists use are pure substances.

A **physical mixture** is a physical combination of matter, in any proportions. The properties of a physical mixture are the combined properties of the substances in the mixture. Salt water is a physical mixture of salt and water, in any proportions. The properties of salt water are the properties of salt and water. Salt water is salty and wet. Most of the products a cosmetologist or manicurist uses are physical mixtures. (Figure 10-6). See Table 10-1 for a summary of the differences between pure substances and physical mixtures.)

Solutions, Suspensions, and Emulsions

Solutions, suspensions, and emulsions are all physical mixtures. The differences among solutions, suspensions, and emulsions are determined by the size of the particles and the solubility of the substances.

A **solution** is a stable mixture of two or more mixable substances. The **solute** is the substance that is dissolved in a solution. The **solvent** is the substance that dissolves the solute to form a solution.

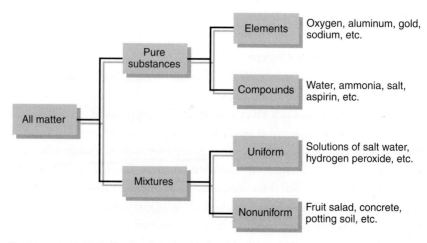

Figure 10–6 Pure substances and physical mixtures.

TABLE 10-1 ◯ PURE SUBSTANCES AND PHYSICAL MIXTURES	
Pure Substances	**Physical Mixtures**
Combined chemically in definite (fixed) proportions	**Combined physically** in any proportions
Have unique chemical and physical properties	Have combined chemical and physical properties.
salt (NaCl) and water (H_2O) are examples.	salt water is a physical mixture of salt, NaCl, and water, H20.

Miscible (MIS-uh-bul) liquids are mutually soluble, meaning that they can be mixed into stable solutions. Water and alcohol are examples of miscible liquids.

Immiscible liquids are not capable of being mixed into stable solutions. Water and oil are examples of immiscible liquids.

Solutions contain small particles that are invisible to the naked eye. Solutions are usually transparent, although they may be colored. They do not separate on standing. Salt water is a solution of a solid dissolved in a liquid. Water is the solvent that dissolves the salt (solute) and holds it in solution.

A **suspension** is an unstable mixture of undissolved particles in a liquid. Suspensions contain larger and less miscible particles than solutions. The particles are generally visible to the naked eye but not large enough to settle quickly to the bottom. Suspensions are not usually transparent and may be colored. Suspensions are unstable and separate over time.

Oil and vinegar salad dressing is an example of a suspension, with tiny oil droplets suspended in the vinegar. The suspension will separate on standing and must be shaken well before using. Some lotions are suspensions and need to be shaken or mixed well before use. Calamine lotion and nail polish are examples of suspensions.

An **emulsion** is an unstable mixture of two or more immiscible substances united with the aid of an emulsifier. The term "emulsify" means "to form an emulsion." Although emulsions have a tendency to separate slowly over time, a properly formulated emulsion that is stored correctly should be stable for at least three years. Table 10-2 offers a summary of the differences among solutions, suspensions, and emulsions.

Surfactants are substances that act as a bridge to allow oil and water to mix, or emulsify. The term "surfactant" (sur-FAK-tant) is a contraction for "surface active agent." A surfactant molecule has two distinct parts (Figure 10-7). The head of the surfactant molecule is **hydrophilic** (hy-drah-FIL-ik), meaning water-loving, and the tail is **lipophilic** (ly-puh-FIL-ik), meaning oil-loving. Since "like dissolves like," the hydrophilic head dissolves in water and the lipophilic tail dissolves in oil. So a surfactant molecule mixes with and dissolves in both oil and water and temporarily joins them together to form an emulsion.

In an **oil-in-water emulsion (O/W)**, oil droplets are emulsified in water. The droplets of oil are surrounded by surfactants with their lipophilic

? DID YOU KNOW...

Soaps were the first surfactants. Soaps were made about 4500 years ago by boiling oil or animal fat with wood ashes. Modern soaps are made from animal, vegetable, or synthetic fats or oils. Traditional soaps are highly alkaline and combine with the minerals in hard water to form an insoluble film that coats and dulls the hair. Modern synthetic surfactants have overcome these disadvantages and are superior to soaps.

TABLE 10-2 ○ SOLUTIONS, SUSPENSIONS, AND EMULSIONS

Solutions	Suspensions	Emulsions
Miscible	Slightly miscible	Immiscible
No surfactant	No surfactant	Surfactant
Small particles	Larger particles	Largest particles
Stable mixture	Unstable mixture	Limited stability
Usually clear	Usually cloudy	Usually a solid color
Solution of Calamine	Calamine lotion	Hair conditioners

Figure 10–7 A surfactant molecule.

tails pointing in. Tiny oil droplets form the internal portion of an O/W emulsion because the oil is completely surrounded by water (Figure 10-8). Oil-in-water emulsions do not feel as greasy as water-in-oil emulsions because the oil is "hidden" and water forms the external portion of the emulsion.

Mayonnaise is an example of an oil-in-water emulsion of two immiscible liquids. Although oil and water are immiscible, the egg yolk in mayonnaise emulsifies the oil droplets and distributes them uniformly in the water. Without the egg yolk as an emulsifying agent, the oil and water would separate. Most of the emulsions used in a salon are oil-in-water. Haircoloring, shampoos, conditioners, and hand creams are oil-in-water emulsions.

In a water-in-oil emulsion (W/O), water droplets are emulsified in oil. The droplets of water are surrounded by surfactants with their hydrophilic heads pointing in (Figure 10-9). Tiny droplets of water form the internal portion of a W/O emulsion because the water is completely surrounded by oil. Water-in-oil emulsions feel more greasy than oil-in-water emulsions because

activity ▶

Have you ever heard the saying, "Oil and water don't mix"? Pour some water into a glass, and then add a little cooking oil (or other oil). What happens? Stir the water briskly with a spoon, and then observe for a minute or two. What does the oil do?

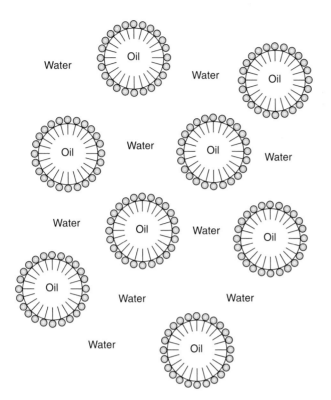

Figure 10–8 Oil-in-water emulsions.

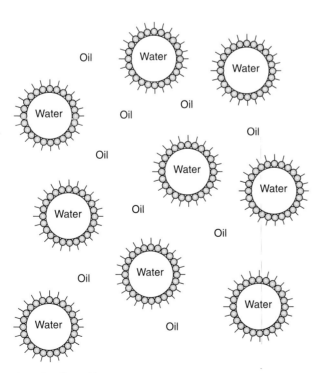

Figure 10–9 Water-in-oil emulsions.

the water is "hidden" and oil forms the external portion of the emulsion. Cold cream and styling creams are examples of a water-in-oil emulsion.

Other Physical Mixtures

Ointments, pastes, pomades, and styling waxes are semisolid mixtures made with any combination of petrolatum (petroleum jelly), oil, and wax.

Powders are a physical mixture of one or more types of solids. Off the scalp powdered hair lighteners are physical mixtures that may separate during shipping and storage and should be thoroughly mixed before each use.

Common Product Ingredients

Some of the most common chemical ingredients used in salon products are described below.

Most people are familiar with volatile (VAHL-uh-tul) alcohols (those that evaporate easily) such as isopropyl alcohol (rubbing alcohol) and ethyl alcohol (alcoholic beverages). But there are many other types of alcohols, from free flowing liquids to hard, waxy solids. Fatty alcohols, such as cetyl alcohol and cetearyl alcohol, are nonvolatile waxes that are used as hair conditioners.

Alkanolamines (al-kan-oh-LAH-mynz) are substances used to neutralize acids or raise the pH of many hair products. They are often used in place of ammonia, because there is less odor associated with their use.

Ammonia (uh-MOH-nee-uh) is a colorless gas with a pungent odor, composed of hydrogen and nitrogen. It is used to raise the pH in hair products to allow the solution to penetrate the hair shaft. Ammonium hydroxide and ammonium thioglycolate are examples of ammonia compounds that are used to raise the pH.

Glycerin (GLIS-ur-in) is a sweet, colorless, oily substance. It is used as a solvent and as a moisturizer in skin and body creams.

Silicones are a special type of oil used in hair conditioners and as water-resistant lubricants for the skin. Silicones are less greasy than other oils and form a "breathable" film that does not cause comedones (blackheads). Silicones also impart a silky smooth feel on the skin and great shine to hair.

Volatile organic compounds (VOCs) are compounds that contain carbon (organic) and evaporate very quickly (volatile). For example, a common VOC used in hairsprays is SD alcohol (ethyl alcohol).

POTENTIAL HYDROGEN (PH)

Although pH is often discussed with regard to salon products, it is one of the least understood chemical properties. Understanding what pH is and how it affects the skin and hair is essential to understanding all salon services.

Water and pH

We cannot understand pH without first learning about ions. An **ion** (EYE-ahn) is an atom or molecule that carries an electrical charge. **Ionization**

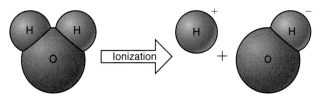

Figure 10–10 The ionization of water.

(eye-ahn-ih-ZAY-shun) causes an atom or molecule to split in two, creating a pair of ions with opposite electrical charges. An ion with a negative electrical charge is an anion (AN-eye-on). An ion with a positive electrical charge is a cation (KAT-eye-un).

In water, some of the water molecules (H_2O) naturally ionize into hydrogen ions and hydroxide ions. The pH scale measures these ions. The hydrogen ion (H^+) is acidic, and the more hydrogen ions the substance has, the more acidic it will be. The hydroxide ion (OH) is alkaline, and the more hydroxide ions the substance has, the more alkaline it will be. pH is only possible because of this ionization of water. Only products that contain water can have a pH.

In pure water, each water molecule that ionizes produces one hydrogen ion and one hydroxide ion (Figure 10-10). Pure water has a neutral pH because it contains the same number of hydrogen ions as hydroxide ions. Pure water is not neutral because it doesn't have a pH. Pure water is neutral because it is an equal balance of both acid and alkaline. The pH of any substance is always a balance of both acidity and alkalinity. As acidity increases, alkalinity decreases. The opposite is also true; as alkalinity increases, acidity decreases. Even the strongest acid also contains some alkalinity. (Figure10-11) Pure water is 50% acidic and 50% alkaline.

The pH Scale

The **pH** scale measures the acidity and alkalinity of a substance. Notice that the term pH is written with a small p (which represents a quantity) and a capital H (which represents the hydrogen ion.) The symbol pH represents the quantity of hydrogen ions.

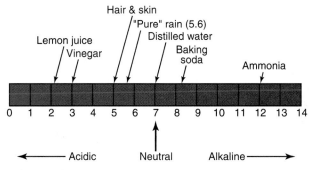

Figure 10–11 The pH scale.

The pH scale has a range from 0 to 14. A pH of 7 indicates a neutral solution; a pH below 7 indicates an acidic solution; and a pH above 7 indicates an alkaline solution.

The term logarithm (LOG-ah-rhythm) means multiples of ten. Since the pH scale is a logarithmic scale, a change of one whole number represents a tenfold change in pH. That means that a pH of 8 is 10 times more alkaline than a pH of 7. A change of two whole numbers represents a change of 10 times 10, or a one-hundredfold change. That means that a pH of 9 is 100 times more alkaline than a pH of 7. A small change on the pH scale indicates a large change in the pH.

pH is always a balance of both acidity and alkalinity. Pure water has a pH of 7, which is an equal balance of acid and alkaline. Although a pH of 7 is neutral on the pH scale, it is not neutral compared to the hair and skin which has an average pH of 5. Pure water, with a pH of 7, is 100 times more alkaline than a pH of 5. Pure water is 100 times more alkaline than your hair and skin. Pure water can cause the hair to swell as much as 20 percent and is drying to the skin.

Acids and Alkalis

All **acids** owe their chemical reactivity to the hydrogen ion (H^+). Acids have a pH below 7.0 and turn litmus paper from blue to red. Acids contract and harden the hair. One such acid, thioglycolic acid, is used in permanent waving.

All **alkalis** (AL-kuh-lyz) owe their chemical reactivity to the hydroxide (OH-) ion. The terms "alkali" and "base" are interchangeable. Alkalis have a pH above 7.0, and turn litmus paper from red to blue. They feel slippery and soapy on the skin. Alkalis soften and swell the hair and skin. Sodium hydroxide, commonly known as lye, is a very strong alkali used in drain cleaners and chemical hair relaxers.

Acid-Alkali Neutralization Reactions

The same reaction that naturally ionizes water (H_2O) into hydrogen (H^+) ions and hydroxide ions (OH), also runs in reverse. When acids (H^+) and alkalis (OH^-) are mixed together in equal proportions, they neutralize each other to form water (H_2O) (Figure 10-12). The neutralizing shampoos and normalizing lotions used to neutralize hydroxide hair relaxers work by creating an acid-alkali neutralization reaction

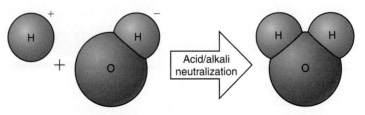

Figure 10–12 Acid/alkali neutralization reaction.

OXIDATION-REDUCTION (REDOX) REACTIONS

Oxidation-reduction (redox) reactions are responsible for the chemical changes created by hair colors, hair lighteners, permanent wave solutions, and neutralizers. The chemical services that we take for granted would not be possible without oxidation-reduction (redox) reactions.

Oxidation Reactions

Oxidation is a chemical reaction that combines a substance with oxygen to produce an oxide. Chemical reactions that produce heat are called **exothermic** (ek-soh-THUR-mik). All oxidation reactions are exothermic.

Combustion (kum-BUS-chun) is the rapid oxidation of a substance, accompanied by the production of heat and light. Lighting a match is an example of rapid oxidation. Since oxygen is needed, there cannot be a fire without air.

Reduction Reactions

When oxygen is added to a substance, the substance is oxidized. When oxygen is subtracted from a substance, the substance is reduced, and the chemical reaction is called **reduction**. An **oxidizing agent** is a substance that releases oxygen. Hydrogen peroxide (H_2O_2) is an example of an oxidizing agent. Hydrogen peroxide can be thought of as water (H_2O) with an "extra" atom of oxygen. When hydrogen peroxide is mixed with an oxidation hair color, oxygen is added to the hair color and the hair color is oxidized. At the same time, oxygen is subtracted from the hydrogen peroxide and the hydrogen peroxide is reduced. In this example, hair color is a reducing agent.

Redox Reactions

Oxidation and reduction reactions always occur at the same time, and are referred to as redox reactions. **Redox** is a contraction for reduction-oxidation. Redox reactions involve a transfer between the oxidizing agent

Did you know that you can easily and safely test the pH of a solution? Litmus papers (pH test papers) can be used to indicate the pH of any salon product that contains water. You can test hair color, permanent waving solution, neutralizer, shampoo and conditioner, skin care, or nail care products.

You will need litmus papers (pH test papers), several small open containers, bottled drinking water, stirring sticks, and some white towels. Place the product you want to test in a small, open cup or bowl. If the product is a powder or is extremely thick, add a small amount of bottled water and stir thoroughly. Dip the litmus paper into the product.

Immediately place the paper on a white towel and compare the color obtained to the color on the package to determine the pH. Test anything you can think of, but it must contain water in order to have a pH. Be creative! What you discover may surprise you!

OXIDATION	REDUCTION
+ Oxygen	− Oxygen
− Hydrogen	+ Hydrogen

Figure 10–13 Chart for Oxidation/ Reduction reactions.

and the reducing agent. The oxidizing agent is reduced, and the reducing agent is oxidized.

Redox reactions can also take place without oxygen. Oxidation can also occur when hydrogen is subtracted from a substance. So, oxidation is the result of either the addition of oxygen, or the subtraction of hydrogen. Reduction can also occur when hydrogen is added to a substance. So, reduction is the result of either the loss of oxygen or the addition of hydrogen (Figure 10-13).

YOU HAVE THE VALUE

There are many benefits for the client who takes advantage of the various salon services that use chemical products. While the use of chemical products has great benefits, always remember that there is a potential for injury as well. Your value as a salon professional depends on your ability to stay informed about new developments and products and how to use them effectively and safely.

REVIEW **QUESTIONS**

1. What is chemistry?

2. Why is a basic understanding of chemistry important?

3. What is the difference between organic and inorganic chemistry?

4. What are atoms?

5. What are elements?

6. What are the physical and chemical properties of matter? Give examples.

7. What is the difference between physical and chemical changes? Give examples.

8. Describe the three states of matter.

9. Explain elemental molecules, compound molecules, pure substances and physical mixtures.

10. What is the difference between solutions, suspensions, and emulsions? Give examples.

11. Define pH and the pH scale.

12. Explain the difference between oxidation and reduction reactions.

CHAPTER **GLOSSARY**

acid	A solution that has a pH below 7.0, and turns litmus paper from blue to red.
alkali	A solution that has a pH above 7.0, and turns litmus paper from red to blue.
alkanolamines	Substances used to neutralize acids or raise the pH of many hair products; often used in place of ammonium hydroxide.
ammonia	A colorless gas with a pungent odor, composed of hydrogen and nitrogen; Not used in the salon in a gaseous form, but instead is mixed with water to create ammonium hydroxide.
atom	The smallest particle of an element that still retains the properties of that element.
chemical change	A change in the chemical and physical properties of a substance by a chemical reaction that creates a new substance or substances.
chemical properties	Those characteristics that can only be determined by a chemical reaction and a chemical change in the substance.
chemistry	Science that deals with the composition, structures, and properties of matter, and how matter changes under different conditions.
combustion	Rapid oxidation of a substance, accompanied by the production of heat and light.
compound molecules	Combinations of two or more atoms of different elements united together chemically.
element	The simplest form of matter, which cannot be broken down into a simpler substance without a loss of identity.

elemental molecules	Chemical combinations of atoms of the same element.
emulsion	A mixture of two or more immiscible substances united with the aid of a binder or emulsifier.
exothermic	Chemical reactions which produce heat.
glycerin	Sweet, colorless, oily substance used as a moisturizing ingredient in cosmetic products.
hydrophilic	Water loving.
immiscible	Not capable of being mixed.
inorganic chemistry	The study of substances that do not contain carbon.
ion	An atom or molecule that carries an electrical charge.
ionization	The separation of an atom or molecule into positive and negative ions.
lipophilic	Oil loving.
matter	Any substance that occupies space and has mass (weight).
miscible	Capable of being mixed with another liquid in any proportion without separating.
molecule	Two or more atoms joined chemically.
oil-in-water (O/W) emulsion)	Oil droplets emulsified in water.
organic chemistry	The study of substances that contain carbon.
oxidation	The addition of oxygen to, or the subtraction of hydrogen from, a substance.
oxidizing agent	A substance that releases oxygen.
pH	A measure of the acidity or alkalinity of a substance.
physical change	A change in the form or physical properties of a substance without the formation of a new substance.
physical mixture	A physical combination of matter, in any proportions.
physical properties	Those characteristics that can be determined without a chemical reaction and that do not cause a chemical change in the substance.
pure substance	A chemical combination of matter, in definite proportions.
redox	Contraction for reduction-oxidation; chemical reaction in which the oxidizing agent is reduced and the reducing agent is oxidized.
reduction	The subtraction of oxygen from, or the addition of hydrogen to, a substance.
silicones	Special types of ingredients used in hair conditioners and as water-resistant lubricants for the skin.
solute	The substance that is dissolved in a solution.

solution	A stable mixture of two or more mixable substances.
solvent	The substance that dissolves the solute to form a solution.
surfactants	Surface active agents; substances that act as a bridge to allow oil and water to mix, or emulsify.
suspension	An unstable mixture of undissolved particles in a liquid.
volatile	easily evaporating.
volatile organic compounds (VOCs)	substances containing carbon which evaporate quickly and easily.
water-in-oil (W/O) emulsion	water droplets are emulsified in oil.

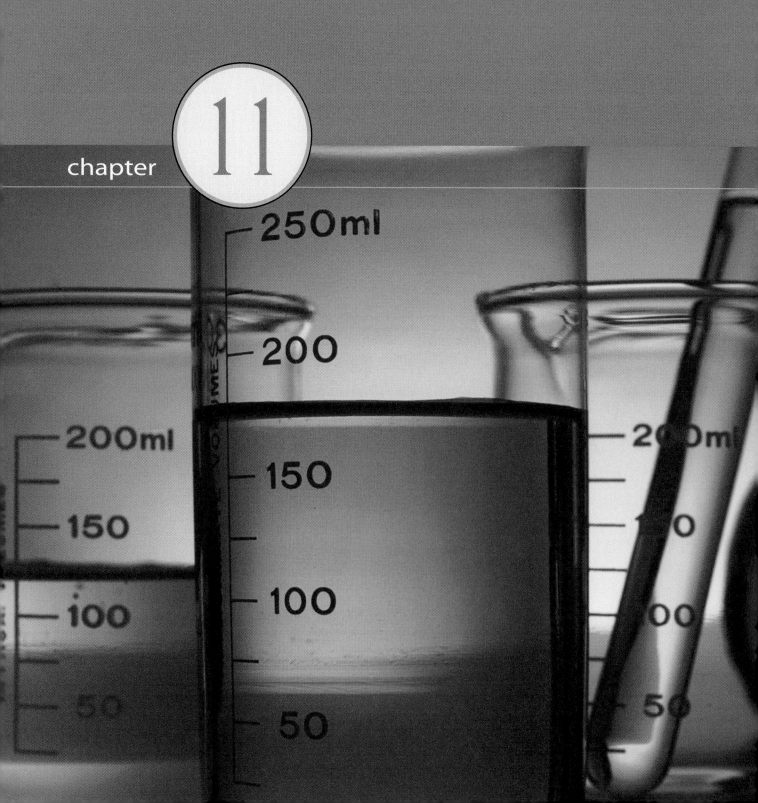

Nail Product
Chemistry Simplified

LEARNING OBJECTIVES

After completing this chapter, you will be able to:

1. Understand the basic chemistry of salon products.

2. Explain adhesion and how adhesives work.

3. Identify the two main categories of nail coatings.

4. Describe the basic chemistry of all artificial nail enhancements.

5. Describe the overexposure principle and its application to nail care products.

KEY **TERMS**

Page number indicates where in the chapter the term is used.

adhesion
pg. 177

cross-linker
pg. 181

oligomer
pg. 181

primer
pg. 177

adhesive
pg. 177

evaporate
pg. 176

overexposure
pg. 183

simple polymer chain
pg. 181

coatings
pg. 179

gas
pg. 176

polymerization
pg. 180

vapor
pg. 176

corrosive
pg. 177

monomers
pg. 180

polymer
pg. 180

A lmost everything you do depends on chemistry, and with a little chemical product knowledge you can troubleshoot and solve common salon problems that may cause service breakdown and problem nails for your clients. Chemical knowledge is the key to becoming a great nail professional. Even if you just want to "do nails," your success depends on having an understanding of chemicals and chemistry.

UNDERSTANDING CHEMICALS

It is incorrect to think all chemicals are dangerous or toxic substances. Most chemicals are completely safe. Everything around you is made of chemicals. The walls, this book, food, vitamins, even oxygen is a chemical. In fact, everything you can see or touch, except light and electricity, is a **chemical**. Chemical molecules are like tiny tinker toys. They can be arranged and rearranged into an unlimited number of combinations. Petroleum oil can be chemically converted into vitamin C. Acetone can be changed into water or oxygen. Paper can be made into sugar. The possibilities are endless. In medieval times, alchemists searched in vain for ways to turn lead into gold. Today, it is possible to do so, but the process costs more than the value of the gold.

Fumes and Vapors

Most people are very familiar with the definitions of solid and liquid. It is easy to see that something liquid is not a solid. However, since people cannot easily see the differences between **gas** and **vapor**, these terms are often confused. There is a very important difference between these two terms. Gases are very different from vapors. Vapors are formed when liquids **evaporate** into the air. Any substance that is liquid at room temperature will form vapors. The higher the temperature, the faster vapors will form. Also, vapors will turn back into liquids if they are cooled again. Water, alcohol, and acetone form vapors. All types of nail enhancement systems will form vapors. Monomer liquids (even odorless monomer), UV gels, wrap resins, and adhesives all form vapors, not gases or fumes.

Fumes are a mixture of soot-like particles and vapors. They usually result from burning substances, such as candles, incense, cigarettes, and gasoline in a car engine. They must not be confused with vapors, which are described below.

ADHESION AND ADHESIVES

Adhesion is a force of nature that makes two surfaces stick together.

Adhesion results when the molecules on one surface are attracted to the molecules on another surface. Paste sticks to paper because its molecules are attracted to paper molecules. Oils, waxes, and soil will contaminate a surface and block adhesion. This is why a clean, dry surface will provide better adhesion.

Adhesives

An **adhesive** is a chemical that causes two surfaces to stick together. Adhesives allow incompatible surfaces to be joined. Scotch® tape is a plastic that is coated with a sticky adhesive. Without the adhesive, the plastic film would not stick to paper. The sticky adhesive layer acts as a "go-between," and holds the tape to the paper. Adhesives are like a ship's anchor. One end of the anchor holds the ship, and the other end attaches to the ground.

There are many types of adhesives. Different adhesives are compatible with different surfaces. Glue is actually a very old term for any adhesive made by boiling animal hides, hooves, and bones. Your childhood paste and glue may have been of this sort. Today, the word "glue" is used for many types of adhesives, ranging from epoxy resins to the high-tech cyanoacrylate adhesives used by nail professionals. Even though they are called glue, adhesive is the more accurate term.

Primers

Primers are substances that improve adhesion. Nail polish base coats are primers. Why? Because the base coats make nail polish adhere better. Base coats act as the "go-between" or "anchor." They improve adhesion.

Other types of primers are sometimes required with artificial nail enhancements. There are three basic types: acid based, nonacid, and acid free. These are especially useful if the client has oily skin. Most types of primers act like double-sided sticky tape (Figure 11–1). One side sticks well to the nail enhancement and the other side holds tightly to the nail plate. A common misconception is that nail primers "eat" the nail. This is completely false.

Nail clippings can soak for many years in any primer without dissolving. Still, nail primers must be used with caution. Some are very corrosive to soft tissue. A **corrosive** is a substance that can cause visible and possibly

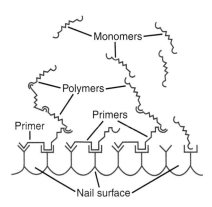

Figure 11–1 Many primers act as "double-sided sticky tape" to anchor monomers firmly to the surface of the natural nail plate.

permanent skin damage. Nail primers, like most professional nail products, must never touch the skin! Acid-based primers are corrosive (very acidic) and can cause painful burns and scars to soft tissue. This is why corrosive primers must be kept in containers with child-resistant caps.

Even though primers will not damage the nail plate, corrosive acid-based primers can burn the nail bed tissue. Over-filing the natural nail will excessively thin the nail, making it more porous. If too much primer is used, the nail plate can become overly saturated with it. Tiny amounts may reach the nail bed causing sensitivity and painful burns. It may also lead to separation of the nail plate from the bed. Use primer sparingly! One very thin coat is enough for most clients. If you find that you rely on two or more coats to prevent lifting, something is wrong! Check your nail preparation and application procedure for problems. Primer can become a crutch, covering up improper application or inadequate nail plate preparation. In the long run, it is better to get to the root of the problem and improve your technique rather than rely on excessive amounts of primer.

Not all primers are corrosive to skin. Noncorrosive primers, sometimes called **nonacid** or **acid-free** primers, do not contain methacrylic acid, the acid-base primer ingredient. Nonacid primers may actually contain other acids, while acid-free primers contain no acids and have a neutral pH. Both types are noncorrosive to skin and, therefore, will prevent burning of the soft tissue. They must be used with caution and skin contact must be avoided (Figure 11–2). Prolonged and repeated skin contact is caused by improper application. Over time, repeated contacts with the product may lead to an allergic reaction. If you never bring the product into contact with the skin, it is extremely unlikely the client will become allergic to the product. Product vapors do not cause skin allergies. These types of allergies are caused by repeated product skin contact. Thus, it is best to avoid all contact between nail enhancement products such as primers and soft tissues.

A Clean Start

Good adhesion depends on proper technique and high-quality products.

The best way to ensure success is to start with a clean, dry surface. Washing the hands and scrubbing the nail plate removes surface oils and contaminants that interfere with proper adhesion. Scrubbing also gets rid of the bacteria that cause most fingernail infections. Skipping this important step is a major contributor to fingernail infections and can lead to product lifting, mainly in the cuticle area. Improper nail preparation is a leading cause of most types of nail enhancement product lifting.

A nail dehydrator temporarily removes surface moisture from the nail plate. Moisture on the surface of the plate can interfere with product adhesion, just as surface oils can. Some dehydrators remove both moisture and oil. But, within 30 minutes, the normal natural oils and moisture will begin to return to the nail plate. How is that information useful? It should suggest that for problem lifters, it might help to dehydrate only one hand at a time, very thoroughly, and after a good scrubbing.

It is a myth that nail enhancements and tips do not stick unless you "rough up the nail." This is absolutely false and very harmful to clients. Ad-

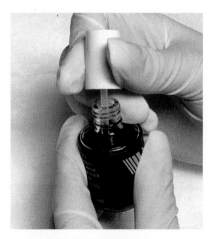

Figure 11–2 Wear gloves when using primers, adhesives, wrap and acrylic monomers, and ultraviolet gels.

hesion is best when the nail plate is clean and dry. Use only a medium/fine (240 grit) abrasive or buffer to remove only the surface shine. Avoid using heavy-grit abrasives, heavy-handed filing (too much downward pressure), and improper use of electric files. All of these can strip away layers of the natural nail plate. The thinner the nail plate, the weaker it will be. This is not what your clients pay for when they come to you for service. Thinner nail plates create a weaker foundation for artificial nail enhancements. The thicker the nail plate, the better the foundation will be for these type of services. In other words, your clients will have better success wearing artificial nails if you do not over-file the nail plate! This is extremely important to remember. How you to treat the natural nail when applying artificial nails can make or break your professional nail career. So, read the section below very carefully. Keeping the nail plate thick, strong, and healthy is the nail professional's first duty!

When artificial nails are removed, clients can see the damage caused by heavy filing. They mistakenly blame primers and nail enhancements for what they see. Rough filing damages both the nail plate and underlying sensitive tissues of the nail bed. Do not be a nail professional who does this to customers or you might not be a nail professional for very long! Also, heavy abrasives and over-filing may cause the nail plate to lift and separate from the nail bed. Once this occurs, clients often develop infections under the nail plate.

Over-filing the nail plate causes more problems for nail professionals than you might realize. Over-filing is one of the leading causes of artificial nail enhancement service breakdown. It can lead to lifting, breaking, free-edge chipping, and free-edge product separation or "curling." It also can promote allergic reactions and may cause painful friction burns to the soft tissue of the nail bed. Roughing up the plate causes potentially dangerous, excessive thinning of the nail plate. It must be avoided at all costs.

If you feel that you need to rough up the nail plate to get good adhesion, then something is wrong! Many nail professionals have great success without roughing up the nail plate. Why? The answer is simple: They properly spend more time and attention preparing the nail plates by removing all dead tissue from the side walls and cuticle area, as well as bacteria, oil, and moisture from the nail plate. They use correct application techniques and high-quality professional products. Lifting problems can usually be traced back to one of those key areas and usually most of these problems are caused by improper nail preparation.

FINGERNAIL COATINGS

As a nail professional, you must perform many tasks. The most important of these is to apply coatings to the nail plate. **Coatings** are products that cover the nail plate with a hardened film. Examples of typical coatings are nail polish, top coats, artificial nail enhancements, and adhesives. The two main types of coatings include:

○ Coatings that cure or polymerize (chemical reaction)

○ Coatings that harden upon evaporation (physical reaction).

Nail polish and top coats are examples of coatings created by evaporation. Artificial nail enhancements are examples of coatings created by chemical reactions.

Monomers and Polymers

Creating a nail enhancement is a good example of a chemical reaction. Trillions of molecules must react to make just one sculptured nail. Durable and long-lasting coatings or nail enhancements are all created by chemical reactions. All monomer liquid and powder, UV gels, no-light gels, wraps, and adhesives work in this fashion.

The molecules in the product join together in extremely long chains, each chain containing millions of molecules. These gigantic chains of molecules are called **polymers** (POL-uh-murs). Polymers can be liquids, but they are usually solid. Chemical reactions that make polymers are called **polymerizations** (puh-lim-uh-ruh-ZAY-shuns). Sometimes the terms **cure**, **curing**, or **hardening** are used, but they all have the same meaning.

There are many different types of polymers. Teflon®, nylon, hair, and wood are polymers. Proteins are also polymers. Nail plates are made of a protein called keratin. So, nail plates are also polymers.

The individual molecules that join to make the polymer are called **monomers** (MON-uh-murs). In other words, monomers are the molecules that make up polymers. For example, amino acids are monomers that join together to make the polymer we call keratin (Figure 11–3).

Understanding Polymerizations

If you understand the simple basics of polymerizations, you will be able to prevent many common salon problems. Liquid and powder systems, gels or no-light gels, and wraps—they each seem very different, but they are actually quite similar. Each type of product is made from a different, but closely related monomer. Monomers are like track runners mingling around the starting line, patiently waiting for the race to begin. The race starts when the proper signal is given. Once given, the runners do not stop until they reach the finish line.

The same is true for monomer molecules. They are like the runners, waiting for something to trigger the polymerization. This is done by a special ingredient called an **initiator**. Initiator molecules energize! They carry extra energy. Each time an initiator touches a monomer, the initiator excites it with a boost of energy. But, the monomer molecules do not like the extra energy and try to get rid of it. They do this by attaching themselves to the tail end of another monomer and passing the energy along. The second monomer uses the same trick to get rid of the energy.

As this game of tag continues, the chain of monomers gets longer and longer. A billion monomers can join in less than a second!

Soon, the many growing monomer chains begin to get in each other's way. They become tangled and knotted, which explains why the product starts to thicken. Eventually, the chains are much too long and crowded to freely move around. The product has become a teeming mass of

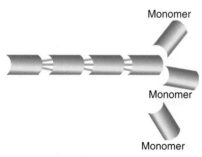

Monomer

Monomer

Monomer

Figure 11–3 A simple polymer chain grows by adding monomers in a head-to-tail fashion.

microscopic-sized strings. When this occurs, the surface is hard enough to file, but it will be several days before the chains reach their ultimate lengths. This explains why all artificial nail enhancements become stronger during the first 48 hours.

Oligomers are short chains of monomers that have had the growth of their chains halted before they became polymers. Oligomers are useful, because they can be joined quickly and easily into long chains to create polymers. In a sense, oligomers are like microwave dinners that are partially cooked so that they finish cooking more quickly in your kitchen. Oligomers are important ingredients in UV gels, and are what give them their sticky consistency. Without oligomers, UV gel products might take 2 or 3 hours to harden into artificial nails, instead of 2 or 3 minutes.

Simple Versus Cross-Linking Polymer Chains

Normally, the head of one monomer reacts with the tail of another, and so on. The result is a long chain of monomers attached head to tail. These are called **simple polymer chains**. Wraps and tip adhesives form this type of polymer. In these polymers, the tangled chains are easily unraveled by solvents, which explains why they are easily removed. Polymer chains can also be unraveled by force. Products with simple polymer chains are easily damaged by sharp impacts or heavy stresses. Dyes and stains can also get lodged between the tangled chains. Nail polishes, marker ink, foods, and many other things may cause unsightly stains on the surface.

To overcome these problems, UV gels and liquid and powder systems use small amounts of special monomers called cross-linkers. A **cross-linker** is a monomer that joins different polymer chains together. These cross-links are like rungs on a ladder. Cross-links create strong net-like polymers. The result is a three-dimensional structure of great strength and flexibility, which we call artificial nail enhancements.

The nail plate and hair also contain cross-links, which make them tough, durable, and resilient. Besides increasing the strength of both natural and artificial nails, cross-links make them more resistant to staining. Cross-links are also more resistant to solvents. This explains why cross-linked artificial nails take longer to remove in acetone than uncross-linked products such as wraps and tip adhesives.

Evaporation Coatings

Nail polishes, top coats, and base coats also form coatings. However, these products are entirely different. They do not polymerize. No chemical reactions occur and they contain no monomers or oligomers. These products all work strictly by evaporation. The majority of the ingredients are volatile or quickly evaporating solvents. Special polymers are dissolved in these solvents. These polymers are not cross-linked polymers, so they dissolve easily. As the solvents evaporate, they leave behind a smooth polymer film. This film can hold pigments, which give it color. Artist paints and hair sprays work in the same fashion. Of course, the strength of non–cross-linked polymers is much lower than cross-linked nail enhancement polymers. This is why polishes are prone to chipping and are so easily dissolved by removers. Now you can see for yourself the great difference between coatings that cure or polymerize and those that harden upon evaporation.

"Better for the Nail" Claims

Some believe that certain types of artificial nail enhancement products are "better" for the natural nail. This is absolutely false! No one type of nail enhancement product is better for the nail plate than another. What is better for the nail? That is easy to answer. The best thing for the natural nail is highly skilled, educated, and conscientious nail professionals. They are the natural nail's best friend. Good nail professionals protect the health of the nail plate and prevent natural nail damage and infection. The job of every nail professional is to nurture the nail plate and surrounding skin. When problems occur, they are usually caused by improper nail plate preparation, improper application or maintenance, or improper removal. It is wise to educate yourself about the products you are using and their proper application. Any artificial nail product can be applied, worn, and removed safely. It is up to you to use your knowledge and skill to see that it happens. Educate your clients to routinely maintain their nail enhancements, so that they can help ensure that their nails will always be in perfect condition. For example, suggest professional products designed to penetrate the natural and artificial to keep it flexible, that is, penetrating nail oils.

Protect Yourself

Take extreme care to keep brush handles, containers, and table tops clean and free from product dusts and residues. Repeatedly handling these items will cause overexposure if the items are not kept clean. Artificial nail enhancement products are not designed for skin contact! If you avoid contact, neither you nor your client will ever develop an allergic reaction. Many serious problems can be related to contact dermatitis. Do not fall into the trap of developing bad habits.

THE OVEREXPOSURE PRINCIPLE

We usually think of toxic substances as dangerous poisons. We hear the term "toxic" often, but should nail professionals try to avoid products that are toxic? The answer to this question may surprise you.

Paracelsus, a famous sixteenth-century physician, was the first to talk about poisons and toxins in a scientific way. What he said was so profound that scientists to this day quote him regularly. He said, "All substances are poisons; there is none that is not a poison. Only the dose differentiates a poison and a remedy." Paracelsus was right, and he was the first to recognize that everything on Earth is toxic to some degree. There is nothing in the world that is completely non-toxic. In fact, the word "non-toxic" is a made-up marketing term that has no precise scientific meaning.

safety caution!

During the removal process of some artificial nail products, your client's fingertips must soak in acetone. Place a clean terrycloth towel over the container. This helps to minimize the acetone vapors. For more information on the safety of acetone, see the "Is Acetone Safe?" section in *Nail Structure and Product Chemistry*, second edition, by Douglas Schoon (Delmar/Thomson Learning, 2005).

($) business TIP

RETAIL AS YOU WORK

All services that you perform provide the perfect opportunity to sell nail care products to your clients. For example, during a hand massage, if the client comments that the lotion you are using feels good, selling it should be easy—just explain the lotion's important features and benefits, and then ask if they would like some for home use. Even if the client seems uninterested in the products that you are using, you can still sell other items.

Talk to your clients about the product you are using while applying it to their nails, hands, or feet, saying something like:"This is our latest high-shine top coat," or "This oil would be very beneficial for your dry nail plates" (or whatever else you think that they could benefit from). Feature the products you use while performing the service. At the end of the manicure, place the item in the client's hand and ask if you can add it to her or his ticket. This last step is crucial to close the sale. If you make a recommendation early in the appointment, but do not pursue it at the end, the client often forgets about it.

The **overexposure principle** is the modern-day expression of what Paracelsus learned. This important principle says that **overexposure** determines toxicity.

The next time someone tells you that a product is "nontoxic," think about what you have learned. Salt water is very toxic to drink. Still, we can safely swim in the ocean without fear of poisoning. Rubbing alcohol is also quite toxic. A tablespoonful could poison and kill a small child, but we manage to use it quite easily, and safety will be maintained if kept out of reach of children. Toxicity does not make a substance automatically unsafe; instead it means that we must learn how to use it in a safe manner.

REVIEW **QUESTIONS**

1. True or false? Primers can eat the nail plate. Explain your answer.

2. Define monomers.

3. What are the two main differences between irritations and allergic reactions?

4. What six things can you avoid or do to ensure that clients never suffer from a product allergy?

5. ___ and/or ____ skin contact can cause a client to become allergic to products.

6. In your own words, explain what Paracelsus discovered about toxic substances. How can you use this knowledge to work safely?

CHAPTER **GLOSSARY**

adhesion	Chemical reaction resulting in two surfaces sticking together.
adhesive	Agent that causes two surfaces to stick together.
coatings	Products, including nail polish, top coats, artificial nail enhancements, and adhesives, that cover the nail plate with a hard film.
corrosive	A substance capable of seriously damaging skin, eyes, or other soft tissues on contact. Some corrosives have delayed action (minutes); others affect the skin almost instantly.
cross-linker	Monomer that joins together different polymer chains.
evaporate	Change from liquid to vapor form.
gas	A state of matter different from a liquid or solid. Gases are not formed by evaporation of liquids, as are vapors. Gases must not be confused with vapors or fumes.
monomer	Individual molecule that joins others of its kind to make a polymer.

oligomer	Short monomer chain that has had its chain growth halted before it became a polymer.
overexposure	Dangerously prolonged, repeated or long-term contact with certain chemicals.
polymerization	Chemical reaction that creates polymers; also called curing or hardening.
polymer	Substance formed by combining many small molecules (monomers) or oligomers, usually in extremely long, chain-like structure.
primer	Substance that improves adhesion.
simple polymer chain	Result of long chain of monomers that are attached from head to tail.
vapor	What is formed when liquids evapororate into the air.

Basics of Electricity

LEARNING OBJECTIVES

After completing this chapter, you will be able to:

1. Define the nature of electricity and the two types of electric current.

2. Define electrical measurements.

3. Understand the principles of electrical equipment safety.

KEY **TERMS**

Page number indicates where in the chapter the term is used.

alternating current (AC)
pg. 189

converter
pg. 189

fuse
pg. 191

rectifier
pg. 189

amp
pg. 189

direct current (DC)
pg. 189

insulator or nonconductor
pg. 188

ultraviolet (UV) rays
pg. 190

circuit breaker
pg. 191

electric current
pg. 188

kilowatt
pg. 190

volt
pg. 189

complete circuit
pg. 189

electricity
pg. 188

ohm
pg. 190

watt
pg. 190

conductor
pg. 188

E ven if you have decided to join the professional cosmetology field because you love to do nails, your career will heavily rely on the use of electricity. To use their products and electricity effectively and safely, all professionals within the cosmetology field need to have a basic working knowledge of their respective tools and how they are maintained.

ELECTRICITY

Just as we have provided you with a very general overview of chemistry, we will do the same with electricity since it, too, will play an important role in your work. If you look out at lightning on a stormy night, what you are seeing is the effects of electricity. If you plug a poorly wired appliance into a socket and sparks fly out, you are also seeing the effects of electricity. You are not really "seeing" electricity, but instead its effects on the surrounding air. Electricity does not occupy space or have physical or chemical properties; therefore, it is not matter. If it is not matter, then what is it? **Electricity** is a form of energy. It is a flow of electrons, which are negatively charged particles that swirl around atoms like a swarm of bees.

An **electric current** is the flow of electricity along a conductor. All substances can be classified as conductors or insulators, depending on the ease with which an electric current can be transmitted through them.

A **conductor** is any substance that conducts electricity. Most metals are good conductors. Copper is a particularly good conductor, and is used in electric wiring and electric motors. The ions in ordinary water make it a good conductor. This explains why you should not swim in a lake during an electrical storm.

An **insulator** (IN-suh-layt-ur) or **nonconductor** is a substance that does not easily transmit electricity. Rubber, silk, wood, glass, and cement are

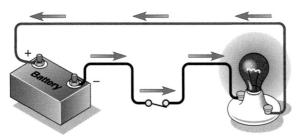

Figure 12–1 A complete electrical circuit.

good insulators. Electric wires are composed of twisted metal threads (conductor) covered with rubber (insulator). A **complete circuit** (SUR-kit) is the path of an electric current from the generating source through conductors and back to its original source (Figure 12–1).

Types of Electric Current

There are two kinds of electric current.

> **Direct current (DC)** is a constant, even-flowing current that travels in one direction only. Flashlights, cellular telephones, and cordless electric drills use the direct current produced by batteries. The battery in your car stores electrical energy. Without it, your car would not start in the morning. A **converter** is an apparatus that changes direct current to alternating current. Some cars have converters that allow you to use appliances that would normally be plugged into an electrical wall outlet.

> **Alternating current (AC)** is a rapid and interrupted current, flowing first in one direction and then in the opposite direction. This change in direction happens 60 times per second. Hair dryers and curling irons that plug into a wall outlet use alternating current. A **rectifier** is an apparatus that changes alternating current to direct current. Cordless electric clippers and battery chargers use a rectifier to convert the AC current from an electrical wall outlet to DC current needed to recharge their DC batteries.

Electrical Measurements

The flow of an electric current can be compared to water flowing through a garden hose. Individual electrons flow through a wire in the same way that individual water molecules flow through a hose.

A **volt** (V), or voltage, is the unit that measures the pressure or force that pushes the flow of electrons forward through a conductor, much like the water pressure that pushes the water molecules through the hose (Figure 12–2). Without pressure, neither water nor electrons would flow. Car batteries are 12 volts, normal wall sockets that power your hair dryer and curling iron are 121 volts, and most air conditioners and clothes dryers run on 220 volts. A higher voltage indicates more power.

An **amp** (A), or ampere (AM-peer), is the unit that measures the strength of an electric current (the number of electrons flowing through a

Figure 12–2 Volts measure the pressure or force that pushes electrons forward.

wire). Just as a water hose must be able to expand as the amount of water flowing through it increases, so a wire must expand with an increase in the amount of electrons (amps). A hair dryer rated at 12 amps must have a cord that is twice as thick as one rated at 5 amps; otherwise, the cord might overheat and start a fire. A higher amp rating indicates a greater number of electrons and a stronger current (Figure 12–3).

A **milliampere** (mil-ee-AM-peer) is one-thousandth of an ampere. The current for facial and scalp treatments is measured in milliamperes; an ampere current would be much too strong and would damage the skin or body.

An **ohm** (O) is a unit that measures the resistance of an electric current. Current will not flow through a conductor unless the force (volts) is stronger than the resistance (ohms).

A **watt** (W) is a measurement of how much electric energy is being used in 1 second. A 40-watt light bulb uses 40 watts of energy per second.

A **kilowatt** (K) is 1,000 watts. The electricity in your house is measured in kilowatts per hour (kwh). A 1,000-watt (1-kilowatt) hair dryer uses 1,000 watts of energy per second.

Light and Heat Energy

Catalysts are used to make reactions happen more quickly. Some catalysts use heat as an energy source while others use light. Whatever the source, catalysts absorb energy like a battery. At the appropriate time, they pass this energy to the initiator and the reaction begins. For example, light-cured nail enhancements use ultraviolet (UV) light. **Ultraviolet rays** are invisible and have short wavelengths, are the least-penetrating light rays, produce chemical effects, and kill germs. All other nail enhancement products use heat energy.

You can see why it is important to protect UV curing products from light. Sunlight and even artificial room lights can start polymerization in the container. The same can happen when heat-curing monomers are put in a hot car trunk, a store window, or other warm area. The high heat may also cause polymerization in the container. Products that require normal "incandescent" light bulbs are *not* light-curing monomers. They are using the extra heat released from the light bulb to speed evaporation of solvents.

Figure 12–3 Amps measure the number of electrons flowing through the wire.

Figure 12–4   Fuse box.

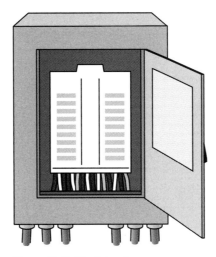

Figure 12–5   Circuit breakers.

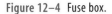

ELECTRICAL EQUIPMENT SAFETY

When working with electricity, you must always be concerned with your own safety, as well as the safety of your clients. All electrical equipment should be inspected regularly to determine whether it is in safe working order. Careless electrical connections and overloaded circuits can result in an electrical shock, a burn, or even a serious fire.

Safety Devices

A **fuse** (FYOOZ) is a special device that prevents excessive current from passing through a circuit. It is designed to blow out or melt when the wire becomes too hot from overloading the circuit with too much current, such as when too many appliances or faulty equipment are connected to an electricity source. To re-establish the circuit, disconnect the appliance, check all connections and insulation, and insert a new fuse (Figure 12–4).

A **circuit breaker** is a switch that automatically interrupts or shuts off an electric circuit at the first indication of overload. Circuit breakers have replaced fuses in modern electric circuits. They have all the safety features of fuses but do not require replacement, and can simply be reset. Your hair dryer has a circuit breaker located in the electric plug designed to protect you and your client in case of an overload or short circuit. When a circuit breaker shuts off, you should disconnect the appliance and check all connections and insulation before resetting (Figure 12–5).

Guidelines for Safe Use of Electrical Equipment

Careful attention to electrical safety helps to eliminate accidents and to ensure greater client satisfaction. The following reminders will help ensure the safe use of electricity.

o All the electrical appliances you use should be UL certified (Figure 12–7).

safety caution!

Underwriter's Laboratory (UL) certifies the safety of electrical appliances. Curling irons, hair dryers, and electric drills that are UL approved are certified to be safe when used according to the manufacturer's directions. Always look for the UL symbol on electrical appliances and take the time to read and follow the manufacturer's directions.

The principle of "grounding" is another important way of promoting electrical safety. All electrical appliances must have at least two electrical connections. The "live" connection supplies current to the circuit. The ground connection completes the circuit and carries the current safely away to the ground. If you look closely at electrical plugs with two rectangular prongs, you will see that one is slightly larger than the other. This guarantees that the plug can only be inserted one way, and protects you and your client from electrical shock in the event of a short circuit.

For added protection, some appliances have a third circular, electrical connection that provides an additional ground. This extra ground is designed to guarantee a safe path of electricity if the first ground fails, or is improperly connected. Appliances with a third circular ground offer the most protection for you and your client (Figure 12–6).

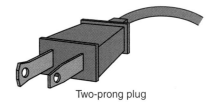

Two-prong plug

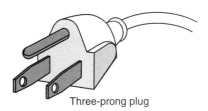

Three-prong plug

Figure 12–6   Two-prong and three-prong plugs.

Figure 12–7 UL symbol as it appears on electrical devices.

safety caution!

Never tamper with wiring or electrical plugs to get them to fit into a receptacle that they were not designed for.

○ Read all instructions carefully before using any piece of electrical equipment.

○ Disconnect all appliances when not in use.

○ Inspect all electrical equipment regularly.

○ Keep all wires, plugs, and electrical equipment in good repair.

○ Use only one plug to each outlet; overloading may cause the circuit breaker to pop (Figure 12–8).

○ You and your client should avoid contact with water and metal surfaces when using electricity, and do not handle electrical equipment with wet hands.

○ Do not leave your client unattended while connected to an electrical device.

○ Keep electrical cords off the floor and away from people's feet; getting tangled in a cord could cause you or your client to trip.

○ Do not attempt to clean around electric outlets while equipment is plugged in.

○ Do not touch two metal objects at the same time if either is connected to an electric current.

○ Do not step on or place objects on electrical cords.

○ Do not allow electrical cords to become twisted; this can cause a short circuit.

○ Disconnect appliances by pulling on the plug, not the cord.

○ Do not attempt to repair electrical appliances unless you are qualified.

YOU HAVE THE POWER

There are many benefits for the client who takes advantage of the various salon services that use electricity. In the course of your career, developments in technology will undoubtedly introduce new, innovative salon services

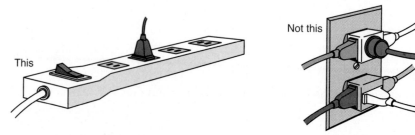

Figure 12–8 One plug per outlet.

that were not available when this book was written. Your value as a salon professional depends on your ability to stay informed about these new developments.

While the use of electricity has great benefits, always remember that there is a potential for injury as well. You need to learn as much as you can about the workings of electricity in the salon and view your education as a lifelong learning experience.

REVIEW QUESTIONS

1. Define electric current .

2. Explain the difference between a conductor and a nonconductor or insulator.

3. Describe the two types of electric current and give examples of each.

4. Explain the difference between a volt and an amp.

5. Define ohm.

6. Define watt and kilowatt.

7. Explain the function of a fuse.

8. What is the purpose of a circuit breaker?

9. What is the purpose of grounding, and how is it accomplished?

10. List at least five steps for electrical safety.

CHAPTER GLOSSARY

alternating current (AC)	Rapid and interrupted current, flowing first in one direction and then in the opposite direction, changing directions 60 times per second.
amp	Unit that measures the strength of an electric current (the number of electrons flowing through a wire).
circuit breaker	Switch that automatically interrupts or shuts off an electric circuit at the first indication of overload.
complete circuit	The path of an electric current from the generating source through conductors and back to its original source.
conductor	Any substance that conducts electricity.
converter	Apparatus that changes direct current to alternating current.
direct current (DC)	Current that travels in one direction..
electric current	Flow of electricity along a conductor.

electricity	Form of energy created by a flow of electrons.
fuse	Special device that prevents excessive current from passing through a circuit.
insulator or nonconductor	Substance that does not easily transmit electricity; not a conductor.
kilowatt	1,000 watts.
ohm	Unit that measures the resistance of an electric current.
rectifier	Apparatus that changes alternating current to direct current.
ultraviolet (UV) rays	Invisible rays that have short wavelengths, are the least penetrating rays, produce chemical effects, and kill germs; also called cold rays or actinic rays.
volt	Unit that measures the flow of electrons forward through a conductor.
watt (W)	Unit that measures how much electric energy is being used in 1 second.

NAIL CARE

Manicuring

LEARNING OBJECTIVES

After you have completed this chapter, you will be able to:

1. Identify the four types of nail implements and/or tools required to perform a manicure.

2. Demonstrate the safe and correct handling of nail implements and tools.

3. Exhibit a proper setup of a manicuring table.

4. Demonstrate the necessary three-part procedure requirements for nail services.

5. Identify the five basic nail shapes.

6. Perform a basic and conditioning oil manicure incorporating all safety, sanitation, and disinfection requirements.

7. Demonstrate the correct technique for the application of nail polish.

8. Perform the five basic nail polish applications.

9. Perform the hand and arm massage movements associated with manicuring.

10. Perform a paraffin-wax hand treatment.

11. Display all sanitation, disinfection, and safety requirements essential to nail and hand care services.

12. Define and understand aromatherapy.

13. Identify carrier oils and understand their use.

14. Understand how aromatherapy can be incorporated into a service.

KEY **TERMS**

Page number indicates where in the chapter the term is used.

aromatherapy
pg. 231

bevel
pg. 201

carrier oil
pg. 232

chamois buffer
pg. 202

effleurage
pg. 228

essential oil
pg. 231

mild abrasive
pg. 206

oval nail
pg. 214

petrissage kneading movement
pg. 230

pledget
pg. 204

pointed nail
pg. 214

pumice powder
pg. 206

round nail
pg. 214

square nail
pg. 214

squoval nail
pg. 214

T he importance of having well-manicured nails and hands has become a significant part of our culture for both men and women. It is one of the fastest-growing services requested in a salon. Once you have learned the basic knowledge and mastered the fundamental techniques in this chapter, you will be on your way to becoming a professional and providing these much-requested services. As a professional, it is imperative that you learn to work with the tools required for your trade, and incorporate all safety, sanitation, and disinfection specifications during any procedure. The four types of nail technology tools that you will incorporate into your services include:

1. Equipment

2. Implements

3. Materials

4. Professional nail cosmetic products

NAIL TECHNOLOGY TOOLS

Equipment

Equipment includes all permanent tools used to perform nail services that are not implements.

Manicure Table with Adjustable Lamp

Most standard manicuring tables include a drawer (for storing properly sanitized and disinfected implements and professional products), and an attached adjustable lamp. The lamp should have a 40- to 60-watt incandescent bulb or a true-color fluorescent bulb. The heat from a higher-wattage incandescent or halogen bulb can interfere with the proper curing of artificial nail enhancement products. Do not rely on your light source to warm your client's hands. Warm client's hands by placing them on a warming pad or adjusting the temperature of the salon.

Figure 13–1 Fingerbowl filled with warm water and liquid soap, with nail brush.

Nail Professional's Chair and Client's Chair

The nail professional's chair should be selected for ergonomics, comfort, durability, and easy cleaning (sanitizing). The client's chair must be durable, comfortable, and easy to clean. For the comfort of all clients, select a client chair that can be raised and lowered, does not have arms on the sides, and supports the back so that their arms can rest on the nail table without stretching.

Fingerbowl

A fingerbowl is specifically designed for soaking the client's fingers in warm water with liquid soap or moisturizing soak product added. A fingerbowl can be made from materials such as plastic, metal, or glass, and should be durable and easy to sanitize after use on each client (Figure 13–1).

Disinfection Container

A disinfection container is a receptacle with a cover that is large enough to hold a liquid disinfectant solution in which the implements requiring disinfection can be completely immersed. Complete immersion is an important requirement. Even the handles of all the implements must be completely submerged. Containers that do not allow the entire implement, including handles, to be submerged are not adequate or acceptable for professional salons. Total immersion of the implements during disinfection is a requirement of the federal Environmental Protection Agency (EPA). Disinfectant containers come in a number of shapes, sizes, and materials. They must have a lid, which is used to keep the disinfectant solution from becoming contaminated when not in use. Some containers are equipped with a tray—lifting the tray by a handle removes implements from the solution, without contamination of the solution or implements. After removing the implements from the disinfectant container, they should be rinsed and/or air dried in accordance with the manufacturer's instructions. It is important to remember that disinfectants must never be allowed to come in contact with the skin. If your disinfectant container does not have a lift tray, always remove the implements using tongs or tweezers. Never allow your fingers to come in contact with disinfectant solution, as this contaminates the solution and damages the skin. Never place any used implements into the disinfectant container until they have been properly cleaned. Implements cannot be disinfected unless they are first properly sanitized. Remember, cleaning is the most important step, and it must occur before disinfection begins (Figure 13–2).

Client's Arm Cushion

An 8" × 12" cushion for this purpose, specially made for manicuring, can be used. A towel that is folded to cushion size may also be used. Of course, a fresh clean towel must be used for each appointment.

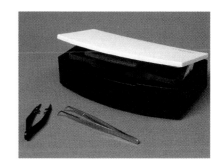

Figure 13–2 Disinfection container.

Wipe Container

This container holds clean absorbent cotton or lint-free wipes.

Supply Tray

The tray holds cosmetics such as polishes, polish removers, and creams. It should be durable, balanced, and easy to clean.

Ultraviolet or Electric Nail Polish Dryer

A nail polish dryer is an optional item designed to shorten the time necessary for the client's nail polish to dry. Electric dryers have heaters that blow warm air onto the nail plates to speed evaporation of solvents from nail polishes, causing them to harden more quickly. Ultraviolet or other light bulb–type nail polish dryers also create warm air to speed drying and work in the same fashion as electric dryers.

Implements

Implements are tools used to perform your services. In general, all implements must be properly cleaned and disinfected prior to use on another client. Some are considered disposable, and must be thrown away after a single use.

Figure 13–3 Wooden pusher.

Wooden Pusher

Use the wooden pusher to remove cuticle tissue from the nail plate or to clean under the free edge. Hold the stick as you would a pencil. *If you drop a wooden pusher on the floor, it must be discarded.* It is a disposable implement, and not intended for reuse. You may also use a wooden pusher to apply cosmetics by wrapping a small piece of cotton around the end (Figure 13–3). *The cotton on your wooden pusher must be changed after each use.*

Metal Pusher

The metal pusher, incorrectly called a cuticle pusher, is actually used to push back the eponychium, but can also be used to gently scrape cuticle tissue from the natural nail plate. Hold the metal pusher the way you hold a pencil. The spoon end is used to loosen and push back the eponychium. If you have rough or sharp edges on your pusher, use an abrasive file to dull them. This prevents digging into the nail plate or damaging the protective barrier created by the eponychium and cuticle. These devices must be properly sanitized and disinfected before use on a client. Also, use them with great care. If used improperly, they can damage the nail unit and lead to infections of the matrix or tissue surrounding the nail plate (Figure 13–4).

Figure 13–4 Metal pusher.

Abrasive Nail Files and Buffers

Abrasive nail files and buffers are available in many different types and grits, such as firm, rigid supporting cores to padded and very flexible cores, and grit ranging from less than 180 to over 240 per centimeter. A rule of thumb is the lower the grit, the larger the abrasive particles on the board and the more aggressive its action. Therefore, lower-grit boards (less than 180 grit) are relatively aggressive and will quickly reduce the thickness of any surface. Lower-grit boards also produce deeper and more visible scratches on the surface than do higher-grit boards. Therefore, lower-grit boards must be used with greater care, since they can cause more damage. Medium-grit abrasives (180 to -240 grit or higher) are used to smooth and refine surfaces. Fine-grit abrasives are in the category of 240 and higher grits. They are designed for buffing, polishing, and removing very fine scratches. Abrasive boards and buffers typically have one, two, or three different grit surfaces, depending on type and style. Coarse grit should not be used directly on the surface of the natural nail since it can create excessive thinning and damage. Coarse-grit abrasives must be used with great care, since they may create serious damage to the nail unit, if not used correctly. It is best to stick with medium- or fine-grit abrasives while performing a manicure.

To **bevel** the nail, hold the board at a 45-degree angle and file, using gentle pressure, on the top or underside of the nail.

Many abrasive boards and buffers can be sanitized and disinfected. Check with the manufacturer to see if the abrasive of your choice can be disinfected. All abrasives must be cleaned and disinfected before reuse on another client. Abrasives that cannot survive the sanitizing and disinfection process without being damaged or rendered ineffective are considered disposable and must be discarded after use on a single client.

It is never a good idea to store abrasives or other implements in a plastic bag or other sealed container. Airtight storage containers can promote bacterial growth. These containers create the perfect environment for pathogens to grow and multiply before your client's next appointment. Always store your clean and disinfected abrasives in a clean, unsealed container that will protect them from contamination by dust and other debris, while still allowing air to circulate freely (Figures 13–5 and 13–6).

Nipper

A nipper is used to carefully trim away tags of dead skin. Never use the nipper to cut, rip, or tear any living tissue. Never use the nipper to trim or cut away the proximal nail fold (eponychium). To use the nippers, hold them in the palm of your hand with the blades facing the eponychium. Place your

Figure 13–5 Abrasive nail file.

Figure 13–6 Four-way abrasive block.

here's a tip...

Cutting the proximal nail fold is what creates the hardened tissue that clients do not like. When this living tissue is cut, the body reacts by creating hardened skin. To help soften this hardened tissue, recommend that the client use daily applications of a penetrating nail oil and perform weekly conditioning oil treatments as a part of your regular services. After about a month, clients will see that this hardened tissue disappears, revealing the healthy pink tissue underneath.

Figure 13–7 Nippers.

Figure 13–8 Holding a nail buffer.

Figure 13–9 Alternative way to hold a nail buffer.

thumb on one handle and three fingers on the other handle, with your index finger on the screw to help guide the blade. They are multi-use tools that must be properly cleaned and disinfected before use on every client. It is wise to have several sets available so that you have a clean and disinfected pair ready for clients while the others are being processed (Figure 13–7).

Tweezers

Tweezers can be used for a wide range of uses, including lifting small bits of debris from the nail plate or removing implements from disinfectant solutions. Tweezers are multi-use tools that must be properly cleaned and disinfected since they may come in contact with a client's skin or nails.

Nail Brush

A nail brush is used to clean fingernails and to remove dust and debris with warm soapy water. Hold the nail brush with the bristles turned down and away from you. Place your thumb on the handle side of the brush that is facing you, and place your fingers on the other side. These brushes must be properly sanitized and disinfected before use on a client. Used nail brushes can be kept in a disinfectant container in the bathroom after clients scrub their nails. The safest way to do this is to have a basket or container of nail brushes that are clean and disinfected near the sink. After each client uses a clean nail brush to scrub their nails, it must be placed in a separate storage container. At the end of the day, remove all of the brushes and clean and disinfect them correctly. Allow the nail brushes to air dry on a clean towel.

Chamois Buffer

The **chamois** (SHAM-ee) **buffer** is used to add shine to the nail and to smooth out wavy ridges on nails. Be guided by your instructor on how to hold the chamois buffer. Check with your instructor to determine whether chamois buffers are allowed by your state regulations (Figures 13–8 and 13–9).

Three-Way Buffer

A new abrasive technology is a buffer that replaces the chamois and creates a beautiful shine on actual nail plates or artificial nails. These buffers do not require the use of dry buffing powders and produce an equally high shine with much less effort and mess.

Nail Clippers

Nail clippers are used to shorten the nail plate. If your client's nail plates extend very far past the free edge, clipping them short will save filing time. They are multi-use, so they must be properly sanitized and disinfected before use on every client.

Sanitation and Disinfection for Implements and Tools

It is a good idea to have at least two complete sets of implements and abrasives ready and waiting, so that you will always have a completely clean and disinfected set for each client, with no waiting between appointments. If you have only one set of implements, remember that it takes approximately 20 minutes to properly clean and disinfect implements after each use. An overview of sanitation and disinfection or implements and tools follows. (For a more complete discussion, see Chapter 5.)

1. **Wash with warm water.** Thoroughly wash all implements/tools by scrubbing with liquid soap and warm water, and then rinse away all traces of soap with warm running water. All visible debris must be removed before proceeding to the next step.

2. **Fully immerse.** All non-disposable multi-use tools or implements must be completely and fully immersed in a disinfection container that is filled with an appropriate disinfectant solution that is approved by your state board regulations and properly prepared according to the manufacturer's instructions. Follow the disinfectant manufacturer's instructions for the required disinfection time.

3. **Rinse and dry.** Rinse the implements (if required), and then air dry or dry with a clean towel when you remove them from the disinfection container.

4. **Store properly.** Store clean and disinfected tools or implements in a clean container and sanitary manner. Never store them in sealed containers or plastic bags. One appropriate method is to wrap them in a clean dry towel that has been taped or tied closed to prevent re-contamination of the implements via dust or other debris. Your instructor may be able to provide you with other valuable ideas and suggestions for storing implements that meet these guidelines. Remember, never allow your fingers to come into contact with a disinfectant solution.

Materials

Some materials and supplies that are used during a manicure are designed to be disposable and must be replaced for each client. These items are considered to be "non-disinfectable."

Disposable Towels or Terrycloth Towels

A fresh, clean terrycloth towel or a disposable towel is used to cover the client's armrest cushion before each manicure. Another fresh towel must be used to dry the client's hands after soaking in the fingerbowl. Other terrycloth or lint-free disposable towels are used to wipe spills that may occur around the fingerbowl. Fresh towels are an example of materials that can be properly cleaned, but do not require the disinfection procedures necessary to ensure the safety of implements or abrasives.

Brushes and Applicators

Any brush or applicator that comes into contact with client's nails or skin, must be properly sanitized and disinfected before use on another client. If they cannot be properly cleaned and disinfected, they must be disposed of after a single use. Check with the manufacturer if you are unsure whether a brush or applicator can be properly sanitized and disinfected. One exception to this rule would be brushes used in products that are not capable of becoming contaminated with bacteria, such as alcohol, nail polish, artificial nail monomers or ultraviolet gels, nail primers, dehydrators, and bleaches, among others. Since these products cannot harbor pathogen growth, and are therefore considered to be "self-disinfecting," these brushes do not need to be sanitized and disinfected between each use. However, a brush used to apply penetrating nail oil to the nail plate would be considered unsanitary, since these products can become contaminated with bacteria if the brush is placed back into the product.

Cotton Balls, Pads, or Pledgets

Lint-free, plastic-back fiber or cotton pads are often used to remove nail polish. These are preferred over cotton balls, since the plastic backing protects nail professionals' fingertips from overexposure to drying solvents and other chemicals.

Cotton can be wrapped around the end of a wooden pusher to remove nail polish from areas that are hard to reach. It can also be used for applying other nail cosmetics, such as cuticle removers. Small fiber-free squares known as **pledgets** can also be used.

Plastic or Metal Spatulas

A plastic or metal spatula must be used for removing nail cosmetics from their respective containers. If a spatula comes into contact with your skin or the client's skin, it must be properly cleaned and disinfected before being used again. This will prevent contamination of your products. Never use the same spatula to remove unlike products from different containers. Never use your fingers to remove cosmetics from a container, as they can contaminate cosmetics and may help to spread infections. A closed contaminated container of nail cosmetics is a perfect place for bacteria from fingers to grow. Cosmetic products that contain water can provide perfect growth opportunities for pathogens. All containers should be closed when not in use to avoid contamination.

Trash Containers

A metal trash container with a self-closing lid that is operated by a foot pedal should be located next to your workstation. This type of container is one of the best ways to prevent excessive odors and vapors in the salon. The trash container should be lined, and should be closed when not in use. It must be emptied at the end of each workday before you leave.

Professional Nail Cosmetic Products

As a nail professional, you need to know how to properly use each nail cosmetic and what ingredients it contains. You must know how to properly apply each cosmetic and how to avoid causing or aggravating a client's skin allergies or sensitivities. This section provides a basic understanding of several professional tools. For more detailed information on products and ingredients, see *Nail Structure & Product Chemistry*, Second Edition, by Doug Schoon (Thomson Delmar Learning, 2005).

Soap

Soap is used to clean the nail professional's and client's hands before a service begins. It is also mixed with warm water and used in the finger bowl as a manicure soak. Liquid soaps are recommended and preferred because bar soap harbors bacteria and can become a breeding place for pathogens.

Polish Remover

Removers are used to dissolve and remove nail polish. These products contain solvents such as acetone or ethyl acetate. Oil is sometimes added to offset the drying effect of these products. Products claiming to be "non-acetone" generally contain either ethyl acetate or methyl ethyl ketone. Like acetone, both are safe for this application. Acetone works more quickly and is a better solvent than the other types of removers. Non-acetone removers will not dissolve wrap resins as quickly as acetone, so they are preferred when removing nail polish from wrap -types of nail enhancements. Both acetone and non-acetone polish removers can be used safely. As with all products, be sure to read and follow the manufacturer's instructions for use.

Nail Creams and Penetrating Nail Oils

These products are designed to soften dry skin around the nail plate and to increase the flexibility of natural nails. They are especially effective on nails that appear to be brittle or dry. Nail creams contain ingredients designed to seal the surface and hold in the moisture found in the skin. Penetrating nail oils are designed to absorb into the nail plate (or surrounding skin) and increase flexibility. These oils will also help seal in valuable moisture. Typically, oils that can penetrate the nail plate or skin will have longer-lasting effects than creams, but both can be highly effective and useful for clients, especially as daily-use homecare products.

Cuticle Removers

Cuticle removers are designed to loosen and dissolve dead tissue from the nail plate so that it can be more easily and thoroughly removed from the nail plate. These products typically contain 2- to 5-percent sodium or potassium hydroxide plus glycerin or other moisturizing ingredients to counteract the skin-drying effects of the remover. Since these products typically contain a significant amount of alkaline ingredients, they can be very drying/damaging to living tissue in the absence of proper care. Thus, removers must be used in strict accordance with the manufacturer's directions, and skin contact must be an avoided where possible. Excessive exposure of the eponychium can cause skin dryness, splitting, and hang nails.

Nail Bleach

Apply nail bleach to the nail plate and under the free edge to remove yellow surface discoloration or stains (e.g., tobacco stains). Usually these products contain hydrogen peroxide or some other keratin-bleaching agent.

Always use these products exactly as directed by the manufacturer to avoid damaging the natural nail plate or surrounding skin. Since these products can be corrosive to soft tissue, take care to limit skin contact.

Pumice Powder

Pumice powder (PUM-iss) is used with the chamois buffer to create additional shine on the surface of the nail plate. Pumice powder is a **mild abrasive** (ah-BRAY-sihv), which polishes fine scratches from the surface of the plate.

Colored Polish, Enamel, Lacquer, or Varnish

Colored coatings applied to the natural nail plate are variously known as polish, enamel, lacquer, or varnish. These are different marketing terms used to describe the same types of products containing similar ingredients. "Polish" is a generic term describing any type of solvent-based colored film applied to the nail plate for the purpose of adding color or special visual effects (e.g., sparkles). It is usually applied in two coats, but sheer colors may require only one coat. Colored polish contains a solution of nitrocellulose in a mixture of volatile solvents, such as toluene or ethyl acetate. Once the solvents evaporate, a solid film is left behind to secure the color to the nail plate. The "drying time" is largely determined by the amount and type of solvents used, as well as the temperature of the salon and the client's hands. In general, products with a thicker viscosity will contain fewer solvents and appear to dry more quickly. Thinner viscosity products contain more solvents and are slower drying. However, products that dry more quickly will often harden in the container more quickly as well. To avoid wasting products and prevent this from occurring, always keep the caps of nail polish bottles tightly sealed. This is your best defense against preventing premature evaporation of solvents.

Care must be taken not to get nail bleach on skin because it can cause skin dryness and irritation.

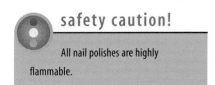

safety caution!

All nail polishes are highly flammable.

Base Coat

The base coat creates a colorless layer on the natural nail that improves adhesion of polish. Base coat also prevents polish from imparting a yellowish staining or other discoloration to the natural nail plate, some people's nail plates are especially susceptible to stains from red or dark colors. These products usually rely on resins which act as an anchor for polish. Like nail polishes, base coats contain solvents designed to evaporate. After evaporation a sticky, adhesion promoting film is left behind on the surface of the nail plate. Base coats are also important to use on artificial nails, since they will help prevent surface staining from polishes.

Nail Hardener

Nail hardeners are used to either improve the surface hardness or durability of weak or thin nail plates. They can also prevent splitting or peeling of the nail plate. There are several basic types of nail hardeners:

> **Protein hardener** is a combination of clear polish and protein, such as collagen. These provide a clear hard coating on the surface of the nail,

but do not change or affect the natural nail plate itself. Collagen and protein are very large molecules and cannot absorb into the nail plate.

Other types contain reinforcing fibers such as nylon, but also cannot absorb into the nail plate. Therefore, the protection they provide comes from the coating itself. These products can be used on any type of natural nail.

Formaldehyde hardeners Formaldehyde containing nail hardeners **can** contain up to 5 percent formaldehyde. But typically they are between ¾ and 1% formaldehyde. Formaldehyde creates bridges or cross-links between the keratin strands that make up the natural nail, thereby making the plate much stiffer and more resistant to bending. These products are useful for thin and weak nail plates, but should never be applied to plates that are already very hard, rigid and/or brittle. Formaldehyde hardeners can make brittle nails become so rigid that they may split and shatter. Also, formaldehyde hardeners must be kept off the skin because they can cause adverse skin reactions. If signs of excessive brittleness or splitting, discoloration of the nail bed, development of ventral pterygium or other signs of adverse skin reactions occur, discontinue use. Once clients have achieved the desired effects with this type of hardener, they should discontinue use until the nails begin to grow out again. In other words, use as needed until clients reach the desired goal and then discontinue use until the product is needed again.

Dimethyl urea hardeners use dimethyl urea (DMU) to also add cross-links the natural nail plate, but unlike those containing formaldehyde do not cause adverse skin reactions. These hardeners do not work as quickly as formaldehyde containing hardeners, but they will not over harden in nails and are much less likely to cause skin sensitivity.

Top Coat

Top coats are applied over colored polish to prevent chipping and to add a shine to the finished nail. These contain ingredients that create hard shiny films after the solvent has evaporated. Typically the main ingredients are acrylic or cellulose-type film formers.

Nail Polish Dryers

These products are designed to hasten the drying of nail polishes are typically either applied with a dropper, brush or sprayed on to the surface of the polish. These promote rapid drying by pulling solvents from the nail polish, causing the colored film to form more quickly. These products can dramatically shorten the dry time and will reduce the risk of smudging.

Hand Cream and Lotion

Hand lotion or cream adds a finishing touch to a manicure. Since they soften and smooth the hands, they make the skin and finished manicure look as beautiful as possible. Hand cream helps the skin retain moisture, so hands are less prone to becoming dry, or cracked. Hand creams or lotions can be used in conjunction with warming mitts or paraffin dips to speed penetration into the skin.

PROCEDURE 13-1

BASIC TABLE SETUP

It is important that your manicure table is sanitary and properly equipped with implements, materials, and the cosmetic products needed to perform the service. Everything you need during a service should be at your fingertips. Having an orderly table will save you time and give your client more confidence in your abilities. Suggested placement of supplies on the manicuring table appears below. Since regulations regarding table set-up vary from state to state, be guided by your instructor. To set up your table, use the following procedure.

1. *Clean table.* Clean manicure table and drawer with an appropriate or approved disinfectant cleaner.

2. *Prepare arm cushion.* Wrap your client's arm cushion with a clean terrycloth or disposable towel. Place these in the middle of the table so that the cushion extends toward the client and the end of the towel extends in your direction.

3. *Fill disinfectant container.* Ensure that your disinfection container is filled with clean disinfectant solution at least 20 minutes before your first manicure of the day. Use any disinfectant solution approved by your state board regulations, but make sure that you use it *exactly* as directed by the manufacturer. Also make sure that you change the disinfectant every day or whenever it becomes cloudy or visibly contaminated with debris. Nothing bothers a client or inspector more than seeing implements taken from a disinfectant jar filled with a cloudy, "dirty-looking" liquid. Put yourself in your client's shoes and put your best foot forward. If you are going to practice sanitation and disinfection, do it right. Do not just go through the motions!

   Put all disinfectable implements into the disinfection container, but only after they have been thoroughly washed and all visible debris has been removed. Place the disinfection container to your right if you are right-handed, or to your left if you are left-handed.

4. *Place products.* Place the professional products that you will use during the service (except polish) on the right side of the table behind your disinfection container (if left-handed, place on left).

5. *Place abrasives.* Place the abrasives and buffers of your choice on the table to your right (if left-handed, to the left).

6. *Place fingerbowl.* Place the fingerbowl and brush in the middle or to the left of the table, toward the client. The fingerbowl should not be

moved from side to side of the manicure table. It should stay where you place it for the duration of your manicure.

7. **Prepare for waste disposal.** Tape or clip a plastic bag to the right side of table (if left-handed, tape to left side), if a metal trash receptacle with a self-closing lid is not available. This is used for depositing used materials during your manicure. These bags *must* be emptied after each client departs to prevent product vapors from escaping into the salon air.

8. **Place polishes.** Place polishes to the left (if left-handed, place on right).

9. **Prepare drawer.** The drawer can be used to store the following items for immediate use: extra cotton or cotton balls in their original container or in a fresh plastic bag, abrasives, buffers, nail polish dryer, and other supplies. Never place used materials in your drawer. Only completely sanitized and disinfected implements stored in an unsealed container (to protect them from dust and re-contamination) and extra materials or professional product should be placed in the drawer. Your drawer should always be organized and clean (Figure 13–10).

Figure 13–10 Basic table setup. Your instructor's table set-up may vary, and is equally correct.

Nail Conditioners

Nail conditioners contain ingredients to reduce brittleness of the nail plate and moisturize the surrounding skin. They should be applied as directed by the manufacturer, but they are especially useful when applied at night before bedtime.

safety caution!

All base coats and top coats, as well as nail polishes, are highly flammable.

CHOOSING A NAIL SHAPE

After the client consultation, you will discuss the shape and color of nails that your client prefers. Keep the following considerations in mind: shape of the hands, length of fingers, shape of the cuticle area, hobbies, recreational activities, and type of work. The length and shape of the nail plate should reflect all of these considerations. Generally it is recommended that the shape of the nail plate enhance the overall shape of the fingertip (Figure 13–11).

Regulatory Agency ALERT!

Material safety data sheets, commonly referred to as MSDSs, provide valuable safe-handling information about the products, as well as first aid and proper storage information. Salons must carry an MSDS sheet for every professional product in use. They must be kept on file or in a notebook with easy access for staff to use as a reference. The company or distributor from which you order professional products is required by law to provide you with appropriate MSDSs. Your instructor can explain the importance of MSDSs and how to read them.

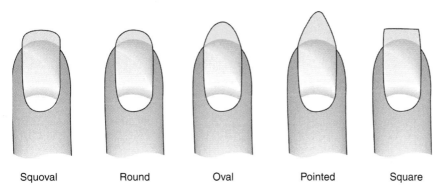

| Squoval | Round | Oval | Pointed | Square |

Figure 13–11 The five basic nail shapes: squoval, round, oval, pointed, and square.

PROCEDURE 13-2
HANDLING BLOOD DURING A MANICURE

On occasion, a client will be cut and blood is drawn. It could happen from careless use of a nipper or abrasive file. When this occurs, the first thing you must consider is your own safety and that of your clients. Using proper sanitation and disinfection techniques is a sure way to guarantee safety. Should you accidentally cut a client, do not panic. Instead, take the following steps.

1 *Put on gloves.* Immediately put on gloves and inform your client of what has occurred. Apologize and proceed.

2 *Apply pressure.* Apply slight pressure to the area with cotton and then clean with an antiseptic.

3 *Stanch bleeding.* If the bleeding does not stop, have the client hold the cotton to the wound or use a bandage to secure it in place for a few more minutes until the bleeding stops .

4 *Complete service.* If appropriate, continue and complete the service, avoiding the area where the injury occurred.

5 *Discard used materials.* Properly dispose of any blood-contaminated absorbent materials and abrasive files used during the service by sealing them inside a plastic bag and place this bag in the trash can. Blood contaminated materials must be "double-bagged"; this step fulfills that requirement. Your instructor will inform you of proper disposal methods or techniques required by your state regulations.

6 *Clean table and disinfect implements.* Properly clean and disinfect all implements in accordance with your regulatory oversight agency.

7 *Remove gloves and wash hands.* Once you have removed your gloves, wash your hands for at least 30 seconds using a liquid soap and warm running water.

   Always remember to use the "universal precautions" established by the Occupational Safety and Health Administration when handling items exposed to blood or bodily fluids (see Chapter 5). Be guided by your instructor for your state's mandatory requirements and procedures for disinfecting any implements that have come into contact with blood or bodily fluids.

PROCEDURE 13-3

PRE-SERVICE SANITATION

NOTE: The following applies to both salon implements and multi-use tools. Before your service begins you must perform the following steps.

1. ***Wash implements (sanitize).*** Rinse all implements with cool or warm running water, and then thoroughly wash them with soap and warm water. Brush grooved items if necessary, and open hinges (Figure 13–12).

2. ***Rinse implements in water.*** Rinse away all traces of soap with cool or warm running water. The presence of soap in most disinfectants can cause them to become inactive. Soap is most easily rinsed off in warm, but not hot, water. Hotter water will not work any better and can be damaging to hands. Dry thoroughly with a clean or disposable towel. Your implements are now properly sanitized and ready for disinfection (Figure 13–13).

3. ***Immerse implements.*** It is extremely important that your implements be completely clean before placing them into the disinfectant solution. If you do not, your disinfectant may become contaminated and rendered ineffective. Immerse implements in an appropriate disinfection container holding an EPA-registered disinfectant for the required time (usually 10 minutes). If it is cloudy, the solution has been contaminated and must be replaced. Make sure to avoid skin contact with all disinfectants by using tongs or rubber gloves (Figure 13–14).

4. ***Wash hands with liquid soap.*** Thoroughly wash your hands with liquid soap, rinse, and dry with a clean fabric or disposable towel. Liquid soaps are far more sanitary than bar soaps and are required by law in most states. A soap dish can also breed bacteria (Figure 13–15).

5. ***Rinse and dry implements.*** Remove implements from disinfectant solution with tongs or while wearing rubber gloves, rinse well in water, and wipe dry with a clean fabric or disposable towel to prevent rust (Figure 13–16).

Figure 13–12 Wash implements.

Figure 13–13 Rinse implements in clear water.

Figure 13–14 Immerse implements in disinfectant.

Figure 13–15 Wash hands with a liquid soap.

Figure 13–16 Remove implements with tongs or wearing rubber gloves and then rinse.

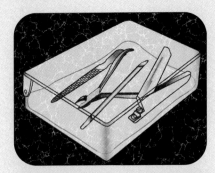

Figure 13–17   Store sanitized implements in a covered container.

Figure 13–18   Sanitize table.

Figure 13–19   Disinfect the surface of your table.

6   *Follow approved storage procedure.* Follow your regulatory oversight agency's requirements for storage of properly sanitized and disinfected manicuring implements. The regulations will tell you to store sanitized and disinfected implements in unsealed containers, or to keep them in a cabinet sanitizer until ready for use (Figure 13–17). Never store your implements in airtight containers. This will prevent them from properly drying and can create an environment that will foster bacterial growth.

7   *Sanitize table.* To sanitize, wipe manicuring table with cleaning solution (Figure 13–18).

8   *Disinfect surface.* To disinfect a surface that comes in contact with the client's skin, spray surface with any EPA-registered disinfectant or equivalent that is allowed by your state regulations for use in disinfecting large surfaces.

Allow the surface to remain wet for 10 minutes and wipe dry, and then spray again and let air dry (Figure 13–19).

9   *Prepare the client's cushion.* Put a clean towel over your manicuring cushion. Be sure to use a clean towel for each client (Figure 13–20).

10   *Refill disposable materials.* Put a new wooden pusher stick, cotton balls, and other disposable materials on your manicuring table. These materials are discarded after use on *one* client (Figure 13–21).

11   *Use hand sanitizers.* Clients like to see that you practice sanitation. Make a ceremony of this and they will trust you. After your clients have thoroughly washed their hands, you can offer them a waterless hand sanitizer gel or wipe for their hands. You can do so as well. Be sure to make an effort to regularly rehydrate your hands, as repeated use of hand sanitizers can cause skin dryness (Figure 13–22). It is very important to remember that these products cannot and do not replace proper hand washing. Proper hand washing is a vital part of the service and it cannot be skipped or ignored. Clients must properly wash their hands before and after the service, and you must properly wash your hands between each customer.

Now you are ready to begin your service.

Figure 13–20   Wrap cushion in a clean towel.

Figure 13–21   Replenish disposable materials.

Figure 13–22   Use sanitizing hand wash.

PROCEDURE 13-4

POST-SERVICE PROCEDURE

1. **Schedule next appointment.** Set up date, time, and services for your client's next appointment. Write the information on your business card and give it to the client.

2. **Advise client.** Advise client about proper home maintenance for their service. For example, if they have long nails or nail extensions, advise them to take care when opening doors or file cabinet drawers. If the service was a pedicure, advise them of the importance of wearing properly fitted and comfortable shoes.

3. **Promote product sales.** Depending on the service provided, there may be a number of retail products that you should recommend for the client to take home. This is the time to do so.

4. **Clean work area.** Clean your work area and properly dispose of all used materials.

5. **Disinfect implements.**

6. **Record service information.** Record service information, observations, and product recommendations on the client service form.

The five basic shapes that customers prefer are discussed in the following.

The **square nail** is completely straight across with no rounding at the edges. You should recommend a length for nails based on your consultation.

The **squoval nail** has a free edge that is rounded off and should extend only slightly past the fingertip. This shape is sturdy because the width of the nail is not altered and there is no square edge to break off. Clients who work with their hands—on a typewriter, computer, or assembly line—will need shorter, squoval nails.

The **round nail** should be slightly tapered and extend just a bit past the tip of the finger. Round nails are the most common choice for male clients because of their natural shape.

The **oval nail** is an attractive and more conservative nail shape that fits most women's hands. The oval shape is a squoval nail with even more rounded corners. Professional clients who have their hands on display (e.g., businesspeople, teachers, or salespeople) may want longer oval nails.

The **pointed nail** is suited to thin hands with narrow nail beds. The nail is tapered somewhat longer than usual to emphasize and enhance the slender appearance of the hand; however, these nails are weaker, break more easily, and are more difficult to maintain. They should be recommended to fashion-conscious people who do not need the strongest, most durable shape of nail enhancements.

BASIC MANICURE

Three-Part Procedure

It is easy to keep track of what you are doing if you break your procedures down into three individual parts. These three parts are pre-service, actual service performed, and post-service/recommendations.

1. Pre-service
   - Complete pre-service sanitation according to Procedure 13–3.
   - Greet your client with a smile (Figure 13–23).
   - Have client remove jewelry and place it in a safe, secure place.
   - Have your client wash and dry her or his hands using a liquid soap and clean terrycloth or disposable towel.
   - The client should already have filled out the information on their consultation form. At this stage, you can use this information to perform a client consultation and fill out the client service form. These forms are used to record responses from clients and record your observations before and after the service. Before beginning, always check the nails and skin area to make sure that they are healthy and that the service you are providing is appropriate. If there is a reason that the service cannot be performed, explain the reason to the client, and when appropriate suggest that he or she seek medical attention. All of this information should then be recorded on the client service form. If there are no potential issues observed, continue with the service.

Figure 13–23 Greet your client with a smile.

PROCEDURE 13-5

PERFORMING A BASIC MANICURE

Begin working with the hand that is *not* the client's favored hand. The favored hand will need to soak longer, because it is used more often. In brief, if the client is left-handed, begin with the right hand; if the client is right-handed, begin with the left hand.

During the manicure, talk with your client about the products and procedures you are using. Suggest additional products that the client will need to maintain the manicure between salon visits. These products might include nail or skin treatments, polish, lotion, top coats, and so on. **NOTE:** This procedure is written for a right-handed client.

1. *Remove polish.* Begin with your client's left hand, little finger. Saturate cotton ball or plastic-backed cotton pad with polish remover. Hold saturated cotton on nail while you silently count to 10. The old polish will now remove easily from the nail plate with a stroking motion toward the free edge. If all polish is not removed, repeat this step until all traces of polish are gone. It may be necessary to put cotton around the tip of a wooden pusher and use it to clean polish away from the nail fold area. Repeat this procedure on each finger (Figure 13–24).

2. *Shape the nails.* Using your abrasive board, shape the nails as you and the client have agreed. Start with the left hand, little finger, holding it between your thumb and index finger. Do not use less than a medium-grit (180) abrasive file to shape the natural nail. File from the right side to the center of the free edge and from the left side to the center of the free edge (Figure 13–25). To lessen the chance of developing ingrown nails, do not file into the corners of the nails (Figure 13–26). File each hand from the little finger to the thumb. Never use a sawing back and forth motion when filing the natural nail, as this can disrupt the nail plate layers and cause splitting and peeling.

   Never file nails that have been soaking in water. Water will absorb into the nail plate and make it softer and more easily broken or split during filing. If the nails need to be shortened, they can be cut with nail clippers. This will save time during the filing process.

3. *Soften the eponychium and cuticles.* After filing the nails on the left hand, place the fingertips in the fingerbowl to soak and soften the eponychium (living skin) and cuticle (dead tissue on the nail plate) while you file the nails on the right hand.

Figure 13–24 Remove polish.

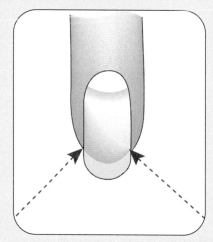
Figure 13–25 Shape nails.

Figure 13–26 Do not file into the corners of the nail.

here's a tip...

Roll a piece of cotton between your hands before you use it. This keeps loose cotton fibers from sticking to the nail or finger. An alternative way to remove nail polish is to moisten small pieces of cotton, called **pledgets** (PLEJ-ets), with nail polish remover and put them on all the nails at the same time.

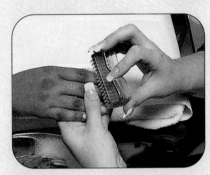

Figure 13–27 Clean nails.

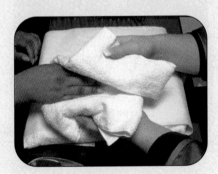

Figure 13–28 Dry hand.

4 *Clean nails.* Brushing the nails and hands with a nail brush cleans fingers and helps remove pieces of debris from the nails. Remove the left hand from the fingerbowl and brush the fingers with your nail brush. Use downward strokes, starting at the first knuckle and brushing toward the free edge (Figure 13–27).

5 *Dry hand.* Dry the hand with the end of a fresh towel. Make sure you dry between the fingers. As you dry, gently push back the eponychium (Figure 13–28).

6 *Apply cuticle remover.* Use a cotton-tipped wooden or metal pusher or cotton swab to apply cuticle remover to the cuticle on each nail plate of the left hand (Figure 13–29). Take care to avoid getting this type of product on living skin, since it can cause dryness or irritation. Spread evenly, and avoid using so much that it runs into the soft tissue. Cuticle removers soften skin by dissolving it, so that they are inappropriate for regular skin contact, especially with your own skin. Typically, these products have a pH of 12 or higher and are corrosive. After leaving the product on for the manufacturer's recommended length of time, the cuticle will be easily removed from the nail plate with a wooden pusher or other implement designed for such purposes.

7 *Loosen and remove cuticles.* Use your wooden pusher or the spoon end of your metal pusher to gently push and lift cuticle tissue off each nail plate of the left hand (Figure 13–30). Use a circular movement to help lift dead tightly adhering tissue. Now place the right hand into the fingerbowl to soak while you continue to work on your client's left hand (Figure 13–31).

8 *Clip away dead tags of skin.* Use nippers to remove any loosely hanging tags of skin (hangnails). Never rip or tear the living skin, since this can damage skin and may lead to infection (Figure 13–32).

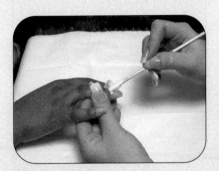

Figure 13–29 Apply cuticle remover.

Figure 13–30 Loosen and remove the cuticle from the nail plate.

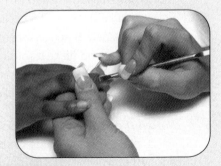

Figure 13–31 Soak hand.

9 **Clean under free edge.** Carefully clean under the free edge using a cotton swab or cotton-tipped wooden pusher. Cleaning too aggressively in this area can break the hyponychium seal under the free edge and cause onycholysis. Remove right hand from the fingerbowl. Hold the left hand over the fingerbowl and brush one last time to remove bits of debris and traces of cuticle remover. It is important to make sure that all traces of cuticle remover are washed from the skin, as remnants can lead to dryness and/or irritation. Then, let the client rest the left hand on the towel (Figure 13–33).

10 **Repeat steps 5 to 9 on the right hand.**

11 **Bleach nails (optional).** If the client's nails are yellow, you can bleach them with a nail bleach designed specifically for this purpose. Apply the bleaching agent to the yellowed nail with a cotton-tipped orangewood stick. Be careful not to brush bleach on your client's skin, because it may cause irritation.

　　Repeat application if nails are extremely yellow. You may need to bleach certain clients' nails several times, as all of the yellow stain or discoloration may not fade after a single service. You should plan to repeat the procedure when the client receives the next manicure. Surface stains are removed more easily than those that travel deep into the nail plate. Yellow discoloration that goes deep into the nail plate will never be completely removed by nail bleaches. These products work best for surface stains (e.g., tobacco).

12 **Buff with a high-shine buffer.** Use a high-shine buffer to smooth out surface scratches and give the natural nail a brilliant shine (Figures 13–34 and 13–35).

Figure 13–32 Clip away dead tags of skin.

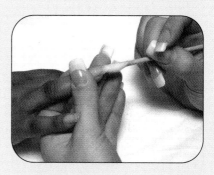

Figure 13–33 Clean under free edge.

safety caution!

　　When pushing back the eponychium, take care not to use too much force or pressure since damage to this area could harm the nail matrix.

Regulatory Agency ALERT!

　　State or province regulations do not permit nail professionals to cut or nip living skin. This practice can lead to serious skin infections and injury.

here's a tip...

　　Excessive downward pressure or low-grit abrasives can generate excessive heat on the nail bed. This can lead to a friction burn that could result in onycholysis and possible infection. If your client is feeling heat or a sharp burning sensation as you file, you should lighten the downward pressure and/or use a less aggressive (higher-grit) abrasive. The client should not feel burning sensations on their nail beds as you file.

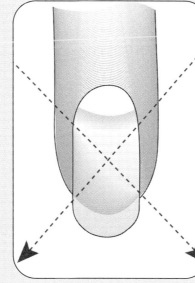

Figure 13–35 Buff nail in an "X" pattern with downward strokes.

Figure 13–34 Buff nails.

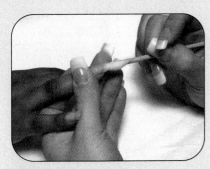

Figure 13–36 Apply cuticle oil.

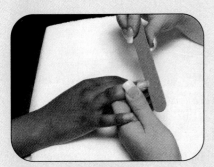

Figure 13–37 Bevel nail.

13 *Apply nail oil.* Use a cotton-tipped wooden pusher, cotton swab, or an eyedropper to apply nail oil to each nail plate. Start with the little finger, left hand, and massage oil into the nail plate and surrounding skin using a circular motion (Figure 13–36).

14 *Bevel nails.* To bevel (BEH-vel) the underside of the free edge, hold a medium-grit abrasive board at a 45-degree angle, and file with an upward stroke. This removes any rough edges or cuticle particles. A fine-grit abrasive board or buffer may also be used (Figure 13–37).

15 *Apply lotion and massage.* Applying hand lotion is the finishing touch for any manicure, but should be done before you apply the polish, since it may interfere with proper adhesion. You can use the lotion to massage your client's hands and arms. (Follow the procedure for hand and arm massage on pages •••.)

16 *Remove traces of oil.* You must remove all traces of lotion or oil from the nail plate before proceeding, or the polish will not adhere as well. Use a small piece of cotton saturated with alcohol or polish remover, and scrub the nail plate clean as if you were removing a stubborn red nail polish. Do not forget to clean under the free edge of the nail plate to remove any remaining massage lotion. The cleaner you get the nail plate, the better the polish will adhere to the nail plate.

17 *Choose a color.* If your client is undecided about the color of the nail polish, help the client to choose one. Suggest a shade that complements the skin tone. If the manicure and polish are for a special occasion, pick a color that matches the client's clothing or the holiday season. Generally, darker shades are appropriate for fall and winter and lighter shades are better for spring and summer.

Always have a wide variety of nail polish colors available. Before applying polish, you may ask your client to pay for the service, put on any jewelry, sweater, or jacket, and get out car keys. This will avoid smudges to the freshly applied polish.

18 *Apply polish.* The greatest success in applying nail polish is best achieved by using four coats. The first, the base coat, is followed by two coats of polish color and one application of top coat to give a protective seal. The techniques are the same for all applying polishes, base coats, or topcoats. Never shake your polish bottles. Shaking will cause air bubbles to form and make the polish application rough and appear irregular. Gently roll the polish bottles between your palms to thoroughly mix.

When applying, remove the brush from the bottle and wipe it on the inside of the neck of the bottle to remove excess polish. You should have a bead of polish on the end of the brush. There should be enough polish on the brush to add one layer of polish to the nail plate without having to dip the brush back into the polish bottle, unless the nail plate is unusually long. Hold the brush at approximately a 30- to 35-degree angle. Place it 1/16″ away from the cuticle area, starting in the center of the nail. Brush toward the free edge of the nail. Use the same technique for the entire nail. If you go back and dab at any spots that you missed, the polish might appear uneven on the nail.

When applying the colored polish, if you miss a small area on your client's nail you can cover this area before you apply the second coat, but definitely practice covering the entire nail each time especially near the cuticle area to avoid a shadow of the polish. In addition to the finished nail appearance, the purpose of using multiple layers of product when applying polish is to provide the best longevity and durability of the service. By building layer upon layer, you will improve adhesion and staying power. It is not necessary to apply fix or heavy coatings. Instead, use thin even coats. This will create maximum smoothness and minimum drying time. On completion of the polish application the polish should appear smooth and even on the nails.

> **here's a tip...**
>
> When applying an iridescent or frosted polish, it is imperative to make sure that the strokes are parallel to the sidewalls of the nail.

2. Actual service performed
   - *During* the actual manicure, talk with your clients about the products that you are using, and suggest the products that they need to purchase to maintain their nails and skin care between appointments.
   - *Before* the polish application, ask your client to replace jewelry, locate necessary keys, pay for the service and retail products, and put on any outer clothing such as a sweater or jacket. By suggesting that your client complete these steps ahead of the polish application, chances of smudging the polish once the application is completed are decreased.

3. Post-service
   - Complete post-service procedure according to Procedure 13–4.

Finishing the Nails

The following points provide guidelines for the proper application of nail finishes.

Nail strengthener/hardener (optional). Apply this before the base coat if the client requests this service, and if her nail plates are thin and weak.

> **here's a tip...**
>
> A flat nylon bristle brush, size 6 or 8, can be used to remove polish around the cuticle area and the sidewalls surrounding the nail plate. Dip the brush into acetone, touch it to the towel to release excess acetone, and clean around the perimeter of the nail. Never leave this brush sitting in the acetone, as it will loosen the bristles from the ferrule.

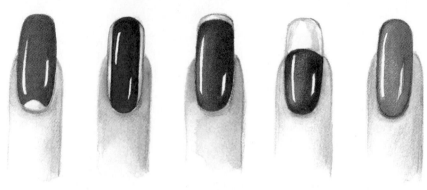

Figure 13–38 Five polish options: half moon or lunula, slimline or free walls, hairline tip, free edge, or full coverage.

Figure 13–39 Finished manicure.

Base coat. Always apply a base coat to keep polish from staining the artificial or natural nails, and to help colored polish adhere to the nail plate.

Colored polish. Apply two coats of colored polish. Complete your first color coat on both hands before starting the second coat. If you get polish on the skin surrounding the nail plate, use a cotton-tipped wooden pusher saturated with polish remover to clean it off. Never use a polish corrector pen because they are unsanitary.

Top coat. Apply one coat of top coat to prevent chipping and to give nails a glossy, finished appearance.

Five Types of Polish Application

Once you have mastered the techniques necessary to apply polish correctly and expertly, you can now focus on creating the following five types of polish applications (Figure 13–38).

Full coverage. Entire nail plate is polished.

Free edge. The free edge of the nail is unpolished. This helps to prevent polish from chipping.

Hairline tip. The nail plate is polished and 1/16" is removed from the free edge. This prevents polish from chipping.

Slimline or free walls. Leave 1/16" margin on each side of nail plate. This makes a wide nail appear narrow.

Half-moon or lunula. A half-moon shape, the lunula, at the base of the nail is unpolished.

Polishing is very important. It is the last step in a perfect manicure and the last thing your client sees between visits. When your client looks at their nails polished perfectly, they will admire them, and you for doing a great job (Figure 13–39).

PROCEDURE 13-6

FRENCH AND AMERICAN MANICURES

French polish applications, as well as American polish applications, are both very popular and are often requested in the salon. These polish techniques create nails that appear clean and can have a natural appearance; they provide a good base for endless service designs that can be enhanced with the use of hand-painted art, air-brushing, rhinestones, pearls, or stripping tape. The French manicure usually has a dramatic white on the free edge of the nail, where the American manicure calls for a more subtle white. Perform the basic manicuring procedures up to the polish application.

1 *Apply base coat.* Apply a base coat to the nail. The base coat can be applied under the free edge as well. If the nail has pitting, striations, or ridges, use a ridge-filling base coat to mask these imperfections and provide a smooth surface for the polish. Ridge filling base coats contain an opacifying colorant that fills in and hides these minor surface defects.

2 *Apply white polish.* Apply white polish to the free edge by starting at one side (usually left side of nail) and sweeping across toward the center of the free edge on a diagonal line. Repeat this on the right side of the nail. This will form a "V" shape. Some clients like this look. If not, fill the open top of the "V," so that you have an even line across the free edge. White may be applied under the free edge. Allow the white polish to dry (Figures 13–40 to 13–42).

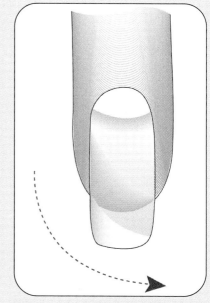

Figure 13–40 Apply white polish on free edge from the left side of the nail to the center.

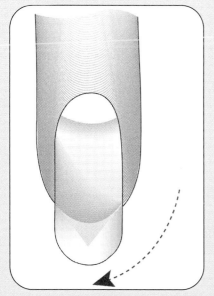

Figure 13–41 Apply white polish on free edge from the right side of the nail to the center.

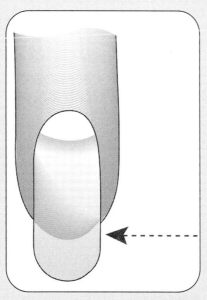

Figure 13–42 Fill in "V" with white polish.

Figure 13–43 Finished French manicure

→ here's a tip...

Buy an artist color wheel and learn about the theory of color. You can use what you learn to help clients select complementary colors that match their skin tone. Color theory is fun and easy to learn, and this knowledge will benefit you in many ways, including with cosmetics and fashions.

3 **Apply translucent polish.** Apply a sheer white, pink, natural, or peach color polish from the base to the free edge. Be careful not to get any on the eponychium. Most clients will prefer a pink shade, but choose the color according to skin tone and client preference. This is an important and valuable service that you can provide to your clients and they will love you for it.

4 **Apply top coat.** Apply a top coat over the entire nail plate and under the free edge (if applicable to situation) (Figure 13–43). (For more information, see Chapter 19.)

PROCEDURE 13-7
CONDITIONING OIL MANICURE

A conditioning oil manicure is recommended for clients who have ridged and brittle nails or dry skin around the nail plate. It improves the hand and nail plate condition and leaves the skin soft. Warm oil treatments are extremely beneficial to clients who are hard on their nails, such as nail biting and or activities resulting in plates that split, shatter, become brittle, or become overly rigid.

1 **Perform pre-service sanitation and table setup.**

2 **Begin manicure.** Begin working with the hand that is not the client's favored hand. It is important to remember that during the procedure you should talk with your client about the professional products you recommend for them to use between salon visits.

3 **Remove old polish.**

4 **Shape nails.** Shape the nails on the hand that is not the client's favored hand.

5. ***Apply oil.*** Apply a penetrating, conditioning nail oil with a cotton swab or eye dropper, and massage it into nail plate and surrounding skin. Explain the benefits of this step to your clients and tell them that daily use of the professional product that you recommend will be greatly beneficial and will preserve the manicure until the next salon visit.

6. ***Apply lotion.*** Apply hand lotion to your hand and spread it over the client's hand, arm, and elbow. This will give you enough lotion for the massage.

7. ***Proceed with hand and arm massage.*** Follow the procedure for hand and arm massage described on pages 227–30.

8. ***Remove cuticle tissue from nail plate.*** Use a wooden pusher covered with cotton or a metal pusher to gently push back the eponychium.

9. ***Remove tags of dead skin.*** Use nippers to trim away any tags and dead skin. Take great care not to rip or tear living tissue as this could increase the risk of infection. Let the client rest the hand on a clean terrycloth or disposable towel.

10. ***Repeat on other hand.*** Proceed with steps 7 through 9, and distribute lotion on each hand after these steps.

11. ***Remove excess lotion.*** If necessary, take a warm terrycloth towel and wipe off excess lotion, or have client wash hands.

12. ***Remove oil.*** Remove all traces of oil and lotion from the surface of the nail plate. Saturate cotton in alcohol or polish remover and vigorously wipe off oil and lotion from nail plates. This is an important step, so perform it well. This step removes only oils remaining on the surface; beneficial oils that absorbed into the nail plate during your treatment are not removed.

13. ***Apply polish.***

14. ***Complete manicure post-service.*** Make recommendations to client for take-home products.

here's a tip…

If the client needs a deep nail conditioning treatment, the following add-on service may be performed. First, saturate a cotton ball with a penetrating and conditioning nail oil and press it against the nail plate. Second, wrap the entire finger and cotton ball with a piece of tinfoil large enough to seal the bottom just below the first finger joint. The foil will secure the oil-saturated cotton against the nail plate. This technique utilizes the body's own heat to warm the oil to a toasty 98°F. Oil this warm will penetrate more quickly than oil at room temperature and will condition the nail plate more deeply (Figures 13–44 and 13–45).

Figure 13–44 Apply nail oil with cotton swab or eye dropper, and then massage into skin.

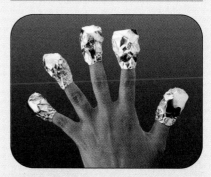

Figure 13–45 Deep nail conditioning treatment.

Figure 13–46 Greet client with a handshake.

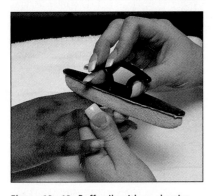

Figure 13–47 Evaluate client's nails.

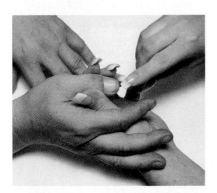

Figure 13–48 Buff nails with an abrasive buffer.

PERFORMING A MAN'S MANICURE

Men are becoming increasingly aware of the importance of having well-groomed nails and hands. Consequently, there are many people seeking services offered by a nail professional. A man's manicure is executed using the same procedures as described previously for the basic manicure or the conditioning oil treatment. Follow each of the steps but *omit the colored polish*, replace this step instead with either clear polish or with buffing the nails with a high-shine abrasive buffer. Upon arrival, greet the client with a handshake and escort him to your station (Figure 13–46). Next, consult with the client to determine the type of service that he is requesting, and then complete the client information form. Evaluate the client's current nail condition to determine what products are needed (Figure 13–47).

Begin the service by removing old polish if present from a previous manicure, and shaping the nails. The most common and requested shape for men's nails is round, but always ask whether he has a preference. Next, wash and dry the nails and hands, and carefully apply cuticle remover, following standard procedure. Most men will need a little more work done on their cuticle areas and eponychium than women. If the client prefers, the manicure procedure can be shortened at this point by buffing the nails with an abrasive buffer to add shine (Figure 13–48).

After cleansing and shaping nails, apply hand lotion, and massage the hands and lower arms (Figure 13–49). A citrus- or spice-scented hand cream is recommended over a flowery scent for the male client. If a polish application is requested, apply a base coat and a clear satin topcoat, followed with nail polish drier (Figure 13–50).

The man's manicure is complete (Figure 13–51).

PARAFFIN WAX TREATMENT

Paraffin wax treatments work by trapping moisture in the skin while the heat causes skin pores to open. Besides opening the pores, heat from the warm paraffin increases blood circulation. This is considered to be a luxurious add-on service and can be safely performed on most clients.

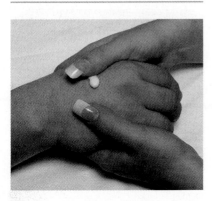

Figure 13–49 Apply hand lotion.

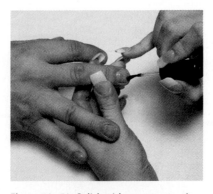

Figure 13–50 Polish with a matte or satin polish, if preferred.

Figure 13–51 Finished man's manicure.

PROCEDURE 13-8

PARAFFIN WAX TREATMENT BEFORE MANICURE

This paraffin wax treatment is performed before a basic manicure (Figure 13–52).

1. Perform pre-service sanitation and table setup.

2. Check to ensure that client's hands are free from open wounds, diseases, or disorders. If it is safe to perform the procedures, continue with the service. Assure clients that they are receiving a sanitary service. Never use this option as a way of avoiding hand washing (Figure 13–53).

3. Apply moisturizing lotion or penetrating oil to client's hands and gently massage into the skin.

4. Test the temperature of the wax.

5. Position the hand for the dipping procedure (Figure 13–54). The palm should be flat with the wrist slightly bent and the fingers slightly apart.

6. Aid the client in dipping one hand into the wax up to the wrist for about 3 seconds. Remove. Allow the wax to solidify before dipping again (Figure 13–55).

7. Repeat this process three to five times.

Figure 13–52 Client consultation.

here's a tip...

Several other procedures for applying paraffin wax include partially filling a plastic bag with the wax and inserting the client's hand into the warming mitt or glove, or wrapping the hand with cheesecloth before dipping in the paraffin wax. In both cases, covering a hand with a plastic bag and inserting it into a warming mitt can dramatically enhance the service.

Figure 13–53 As an extra precaution, you may use a liquid or spray-on hand sanitizer after hands have been cleansed by washing.

Figure 13–54 Position the hand for the dipping procedure.

Figure 13–55 Aid the client in dipping one hand into the wax.

Figure 13–56 Wrap the hands in plastic wrap and cover with warming mitts.

Figure 13–57 To remove the paraffin, start at the wrist, massage lightly to loosen wax, and peel paraffin or unwrap gauze from hand.

8   Wrap the hands in plastic wrap or insert them into plastic gloves before inserting them into a warming mitt (Figure 13–56).

9   Repeat this procedure on the other hand.

10 Allow the paraffin to remain on the hands for approximately 5 to 10 minutes.

11 To remove the paraffin, with plastic gloves still on the client's hand, start at the wrist, massage the client's hands gently to loosen the wax, and peel the paraffin from the hands (Figure 13–57).

12 Properly dispose of the used paraffin. It is unsanitary to reuse paraffin.

13 Begin the manicuring procedure.

PROCEDURE 13-9

PARAFFIN WAX TREATMENT DURING A MANICURE

1   Perform pre-service sanitation and table setup.

2   Remove old polish and shape the nails to the desired shape. If any repairs are needed, complete the procedures for necessary repairs before proceeding with the manicure.

3   Apply moisturizer to client's hands and gently massage into skin.

4   Complete steps 4 to 12 in Procedure 13–8.

5   Proceed with the manicuring procedure.

Be guided by your instructor for the amount of time the hands should be left in the paraffin wax, and state or province regulations.

Paraffin is a petroleum by-product that has excellent sealing properties to hold in moisture. Special units are utilized to melt solid wax into a liquid and then maintained at a temperature generally between 125 and 130°F. When using this treatment only use the equipment that is designed specifically for this use. Never try to heat the wax in anything other than the proper equipment. This can be very dangerous and may result in painful skin burns or a fire.

If proper procedures are followed, paraffin will not adversely affect artificial nail enhancements or natural nails. Be guided by your instructor and your state regulations because some states require the service to be performed before the manicure.

HAND AND ARM MASSAGE

A hand and arm massage is a service that can be offered with all types of manicures. They are included in all spa manicures, and can be performed on most clients.

A massage is one of the client's high priorities during the manicure, as most clients look forward to the soothing and relaxing effects. The massage manipulations should be executed with rhythmic and smooth movements, never leaving the client's arm or hand untouched during the procedure.

During the manicure it is suggested that the massage be performed after the basic manicure procedure, just before the polish application. After performing a massage, it is essential that the nail plate be thoroughly cleansed to ensure that it is free from any residue such as oil, cream, wax, or lotion. You can use alcohol or nail polish remover to cleanse the nail plate.

Hand and arm massages are optional during a basic manicure, but it will be to the advantage of the nail professional to incorporate this special, relaxing service to the client. This will show the client that you are giving them 100 percent of your time, knowledge, and service.

here's a tip...

Never file nails that have been soaking in warm water. Nail plates absorb water quickly and become soft. Filing with an abrasive may make them break or split.

safety caution!

Read and follow all operating instructions that come with your paraffin heating unit. Generally, you should avoid giving paraffin treatments to anyone who has impaired circulation or skin irritations such as cuts, burns, rashes, warts, or eczema. Senior citizen clients may be more sensitive to heat, because of medications or age-related thinning of the skin. Place a small patch of wax on the client's skin to see if the temperatures can be tolerated by these individuals.

PROCEDURE 13-10

HAND AND ARM MASSAGE

Hand Massage Techniques

Figure 13–58 Relaxer movement.

1 **Relaxer movement.** This is a form of massage known as "joint movement." At the beginning of the hand massage, the client has already received hand lotion or cream. Place the client's elbow on a cushion covered with a clean towel. With one hand, brace the client's arm.

With your other hand, hold the client's wrist and bend it back and forth slowly, 5 to 10 times, until you feel that the client has relaxed (Figure 13–58).

2 **Joint movement on fingers.** Bring the client's arm down, brace the arm with the left hand, and with your right hand start with the little finger, holding it at the base of the nail. Gently rotate fingers to form circles. Work toward the thumb, about three to five times on each finger (Figure 13–59).

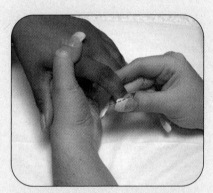

Figure 13–59 Joint movement on fingers.

3 **Circular movement in palm.** This is **effleurage** (EF-loo-rahzh)—light stroking that relaxes and soothes. Place the client's elbow on the cushion and, with your thumbs in the client's palm, rotate in a circular movement in opposite directions (Figure 13–60).

4 **Circular movement on wrist.** Hold the client's hand with both of your hands, placing your thumbs on top of client's hand, and your fingers below the hand. Move your thumbs in a circular movement in opposite directions from the client's wrist to the knuckle on back of the client's hand. Move up and down, three to five times. The last time that you rotate up, wring the client's wrist by bracing your hands around the wrist and gently twisting in opposite directions. This is a form of friction massage movement that is a deep rubbing action and very stimulating (Figure 13–61).

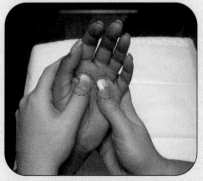

Figure 13–60 Circular movement—effleurage.

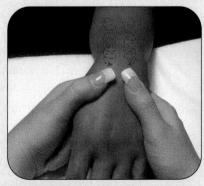

Figure 13–61 Circular movement on wrist.

5   *Circular movement on back of hand and fingers.* Now rotate down the back of the client's hand using your thumbs. Rotate down the little finger and the client's thumb, and gently squeeze off at the tips of client's fingers. Go back and rotate down the ring finger and index finger, gently squeezing off. Now do the middle finger and squeeze off at the tip.

safety caution!

Do not massage if client has high blood pressure, a heart condition, or has had a stroke. Massage increases circulation and may be harmful to such a client. Have client consult a physician first. Be very careful to avoid vigorous massage of joints if your client has arthritis or joint injury. Talk with your client throughout the massage, and adjust your touch to the client's needs.

here's a tip...

Before performing the following massage techniques, make sure that you are sitting in a comfortable position and not stretching or leaning forward toward your customer. While giving the customer a massage, you must take care to ensure that your posture is correct and relaxed. Sitting or working in an uncomfortable or strained position can cause back, neck, and shoulder injuries. If this is done repeatedly, it could lead to cumulative trauma disorders (CTDs) and possibly permanent injury.

Arm Massage Techniques

1. **Distribute lotion or cream.** Apply a small amount of lotion or cream to the client's arm and work it in. Work from the client's wrist toward the elbow, except on the last movement; work from the elbow to wrist, and then squeeze off at fingertips as you did at the end of the hand massage. Apply more lotion if necessary (Figure 13–62).

2. **Effleurage on arms.** Put the client's arm on the table, bracing the arm with your hands. Hold your client's hand palm up in your hand. Your fingers should be under the client's hand, and your thumb side by side in your client's palm. Rotate your thumbs in opposite directions, starting at the client's wrist and working toward the elbow. When you reach the elbow, slide your hand down the client's arm to the wrist and rotate back up to the elbow three to five times. Turn the client's arm over and repeat three to five times on the top side of arm (Figure 13–63).

3. **Wringing/friction movement.** A friction massage involves deep rubbing to the muscles. Bend the client's elbow so the arm is horizontal in front of you, with the back of the hand facing up. Place your hands around the arm with your fingers facing the same direction as the arm, and gently twist in opposite directions as you would wring out a washcloth from wrist to el-

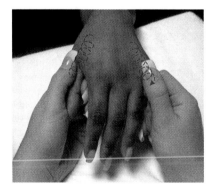

Figure 13–62 Circular movement on back of hand and fingers.

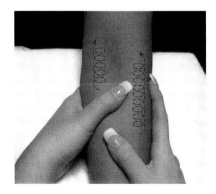

Figure 13–63 Effleurage on arms.

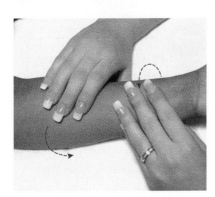

Figure 13–64 Wringing movement on arm–friction massage.

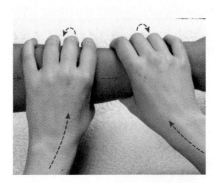

Figure 13–65 Kneading movement on arm.

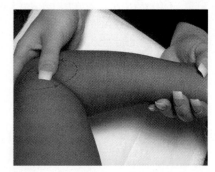

Figure 13–66 Rotation of elbow.

bow. Do this up and down the forearm three to five times (Figure 13–64).

4. **Kneading movement.** This technique is called the **petrissage** (PE-tre-sahza) **kneading movement**. It is very stimulating and increases blood flow. Place your thumb on the top side of the client's arm so that they are horizontal. Move them in opposite directions, from wrist to elbow and back down to the wrist. This squeezing motion moves flesh over bone and stimulates the arm tissue. Do this three to five times. (Figure 13–65).

5. **Rotation of elbow—friction massage movement**. Brace the client's arm with your left hand and, apply lotion to the elbow. Cup elbow with your right hand and rotate your hand over the client's elbow. Do this three to five times. To finish the elbow massage, move your left arm to the top of the client's forearm. Gently slide both hands down the forearm from the elbow to the fingertips as if climbing down a rope. Repeat this three to five times (Figure 13–66).

SPA MANICURE

Spa manicures are fast becoming a much-requested and desired salon service, but they are more advanced than basic manicures. Nail professionals who advance their education and knowledge necessary for implementing this service may find this area to be very lucrative, as well as more beneficial to your clients. Spa manicures encompass not only extensive knowledge of nail care but skin care as well. They are known for their pampering, distinctive results, and skin-care-based methods. All spa manicures should include a relaxing massage and some form of exfoliation for not only polishing and smoothing, but also for enhancing penetration of your professional products.

Spa manicures usually come with unique and distinctive names that describe the treatment with imagination and flair. For example, "The Rose

Garden Rejuvenation Manicure" incorporates the use of rose oils and rose petals for ambience. The "Alpha Hydroxy Acid Manicure" incorporates the use of an alpha hydroxy acid–based product for exfoliation and skin rejuvenation.

Additional techniques that may be incorporated into a spa manicure consist of aromatic paraffin dips; aromatherapy; aromatic hand and arm massages with specifically recommended oils and lotions; hand masks; and warm, moist towel applications. When performing any advanced procedures, which include any oils or cosmetics, always check with your client regarding preferences and allergies.

AROMATHERAPY

The practice of **aromatherapy** involves the use of **essential oils** that are extracted via various forms of distillation from seeds, bark, roots, leaves, wood, and/or resin. Each part produces a different aroma. For instance, Scotch pine needles, resin, and wood each yield a different aroma. The time of day that the plant was harvested also changes the aroma. The use of essential oils is limitless. Tables 13–1 to 13–4 are provided to assist you in the use of essential oils as a cosmetology practitioner.

During your time in school it is imperative that you learn the basic procedures, as well as sanitation, disinfection, and other safety requirements necessary for ensuring the safety of your clientele. Passing a state board examination does not automatically mean that you will be a successful nail professional. State board examinations are the first hurdle. Once you get out into the "real world," you will be required to perform at a very high level and expected to have a great deal of professional knowledge, if you are to be truly successful.

A license coupled with basic knowledge of professional manicuring procedures is the necessary foundation for building advanced techniques, but it is only the beginning of your career. You must continue to learn and grow as a professional, if you want to keep competitive in today's marketplace.

Advanced techniques may be learned from your instructor, through attending advanced nail care seminars, or studying *Spa Manicuring for Salons and Spas* by Janet McCormick, published by Milady, an imprint of Thomson Delmar Learning. For an in-depth understanding of natural nail anatomy, disorders, and so forth, see *Nail Structure & Product Chemistry*, second edition, by Douglas Schoon, also published by Milady.

TABLE 13-1 ● TEN BASIC ESSENTIAL OILS

Lavender	Herbaceous (having the characteristics of an herb), overall first-aid oil, antiviral and antibacterial, boosts immunity, antidepressant, anti-inflammatory, relaxant, balance, and antispasmodic
Chamomile	Fruity, anti-inflammatory, digestive, relaxant, PMS, soothes frayed nerves, migraine, stamina, and antidepressant
Marjoram	Herbaceous, antispasmodic, anti-inflammatory, headaches, comfort, menstrual cramps, and antiseptic
Rosemary	Camphoraceous (from the wood or bark of the camphor tree), stimulating to circulation, relieves pain, and decongestant
Tea tree	Camphoraceous, antifungal, and antibacterial
Cypress	Coniferous (mostly from evergreen trees with cones, such as pine) astringent, stimulating to circulation, and antiseptic
Peppermint	Minty, digestive, clears sinuses, antiseptic, energy, decongestant, and stimulant
Eucalyptus	Camphoraceous, decongestant, antiviral, antibacterial, and stimulant
Bergamot	Citrus aroma, antidepressant, antiviral, antibacterial, water retention, and anti-inflammatory
Geranium	Floral, balancing to mind and body, tranquility, antifungal, and anti-inflammatory

TABLE 13-2 ● CARRIER OILS

Sweet almond oil	This is an excellent lubricant and is softening to the skin. It is a medium- to light-weight multipurpose massage or skin oil.
Sunflower seed oil	Highly lubricating and softening, medium- to light-weight oil, and highly resistant to degradation from oxygen and light.
Apricot oil	Especially for prematurely aged, dry skin; a light-weight massage oil.
Avocado oil	Recommended for dull and dehydrated skin, a medium- to heavy-weight oil.
Grapeseed oil	A very popular, light-weight massage oil with a fine texture and little odor.
Jojoba oil	A natural oil that resembles the structure of skin's sebum, giving it excellent penetration and moisturizing properties. Also an excellent carrier oil.
Olive oil	An excellent natural oil that contains squalene, a component of skin sebum.

NOTE: A carrier oil is a base oil with an essential oil added for easier use and less concentration that can cause skin irritations.

TABLE 13-3 ● CHOOSING AN AROMA

Desired Result	Useful Oils
Calming	Lavender, rosemary, sandalwood, ylang ylang, vetiver
Ambience	Vanilla, cinnamon, orange, pine, jasmine, lavender, bayberry, rose, cherry, lemon
Energy	Eucalyptus, orange, peppermint, geranium, spearmint, jasmine, lemon, fennel
Invigorating	Spearmint, peppermint, lemon, rosemary
Stress relief	Lavender, chamomile, vetivert
Clear minds	Rosemary, cypress
Romance	Ylang ylang, sandalwood, jasmine
Foot odor	Sage, baking powder
Bactericide	Cinnamon, clove, lemon, eucalyptus, lavender, pine, grapefruit, lime
Cuts and scrapes	Tea tree, lavender, eucalyptus
Barber's rash	Lemongrass, peppermint, geranium
Nail infection	Tea tree
Oily skin	Bergamot, geranium, clary sage, petigrain, cedarwood

TABLE 13-4 ● RECIPES FOR MANICURES AND PEDICURES

Desired Result	Recipe
Nail strengthening	20 drops lemon, 15 drops carrot oil, 13 drops grapeseed oil, 13 drops rosemary, 13 drops avocado oil. Blend together and keep in light-sensitive bottle. Use on client after nails have been polished by adding one drop around cuticle and allowing it to absorb into the matrix.
Cuticle softener	15 drops carrot oil, 12 drops peppermint, 12 drops eucalyptus, 2 oz jojoba oil. Blend together and keep in light-sensitive bottle. Use one drop on each nail and massage well into the cuticle.
Age deterrent (spot reduction)	15 drops lemon, 10 drops lime, 5 drops rosemary, 5 drops lavender, 1 drop spearmint, 1 oz grapeseed oil. Blend together and keep in light-sensitive bottle. Use 2 to 3 drops on back of hands, not on nails. Gently massage back of hand for 3 to 4 minutes to see fading of discoloration within 4 to 5 treatments.
Decadent manicure	$^1/_4$ cup heavy cream, 10 drops of pure or blended essential oil of your choice, 1 bowl of fragrant salts for aroma only, a few candles, spa music in background. Light candles and prepare aromatics. Place hands in heavy cream and essential oils and let soak for 5 to 10 minutes. Proceed with normal manicure. Wipe off nails before applying polish.
Dry and cracked heels on feet	10 drops rose, 5 drops chamomile, 5 drops geranium, 5 drops pettigraine oil. Blend ingredients and keep in light-sensitive bottle. Add 8 to 10 drops to the pedicure water before adding anything else. Soak feet for 10 minutes. Proceed with pedicure. Before massage, add 3 to 4 drops on each heel and massage until completely penetrated.
Swollen feet	15 drops lavender, 15 drops chamomile, 15 drops rosemary, 15 drops fennel, 4 oz jojoba oil. Blend ingredients and keep in light-sensitive bottle. Use about 25 to 30 drops as a massage oil for a thorough massage. Have client elevate feet for 10 to 15 minutes above the heart.
Decadent pedicure	1 to 2 cups heavy cream, 25 drops of pure or blended essential oil of your choice or 3 fragrant salt crystals in the pedicure bath, 1 bowl of fragrant salts for aroma only (or candle if permitted), spa background music. Light candles and/or prepare aromatics. Place feet in heavy cream mixture and let soak for 5 to 50 minutes. Proceed with normal pedicure. Wipe off toes before applying polish.

REVIEW **QUESTIONS**

1. List the four types of nail implements or tools used in manicuring.

2. Describe the procedures for sanitizing and disinfecting implements.

3. Briefly describe the procedures for handling blood in a salon.

4. Describe the procedure for a basic manicure table setup.

5. List two types of polish remover.

6. Why is having a material safety data sheet for all the products used in a salon important?

7. List the five basic nail shapes.

8. What special factors should be considered when selecting the nail shape?

9. List and discuss the three-part procedure sequence required in manicuring.

10. Describe the correct procedures for polish application.

11. What is the purpose of a conditioning oil treatment?

12. Discuss the basic differences between a female manicure and a male manicure.

13. What are the benefits of a paraffin wax treatment?

14. List the suggested procedures for performing a paraffin wax treatment.

15. Name five hand and arm massage techniques.

16. What is aromatherapy?

17. How are essential oils used?

18. List five basic essential oils and their uses.

19. Why is a carrier oil sometimes necessary?

CHAPTER **GLOSSARY**

aromatherapy	The use of aromatic fragrances to induce relaxation; therapy through aroma.
bevel	To slope the free edge of the nail surface to smooth any rough edges.
carrier oil	A base oil used in aromatherapy that is added to an essential oil to dilute the concentration of the essential oil. The carrier oil adds slippage and makes the massage easier to perform.
chamois buffer	An implement that holds a disposable chamois cloth, used to add shine to the nail and to smooth out wavy ridges on nails.
effleurage	A light, continuous-stroking massage movement applied with fingers and palms in a slow and rhythmic manner.
essential oil	Oils used in aromatherapy that are extracted via diverse forms of distillation from seeds, bark, roots, leaves, woods, and resin.
mild abrasive	Substances used for smoothing nails and skin (e.g., pumice).

oval nail	A nail shape that is square with slightly rounded corners. This shape is attractive for most women's hands.
petrissage kneading movement	A kneading movement in massage performed by lifting, squeezing, and pressing the tissue.
pledget	Small, fiber-free square often used by nail professionals to remove polish because the cotton fibers from the squares do not adhere to the nails, which can interfere with the polish application.
pointed nail	A nail shape suited to thin hands with narrow nail beds. The shape is tapered and somewhat longer; however, these nails are often weak and may break easily.
pumice powder	A white or grayish powdered abrasive derived from volcanic rock, used for smoothing and polishing.
round nail	A nail shape that is slightly tapered and extends just a bit past the tip of the finger. This natural looking shape is common for male clients.
square nail	A nail shape that is completely straight across with no rounding at the edges. The length of the nail can vary.
squoval nail	A nail shape that extends slightly past the tip of the finger with a rounded free edge.

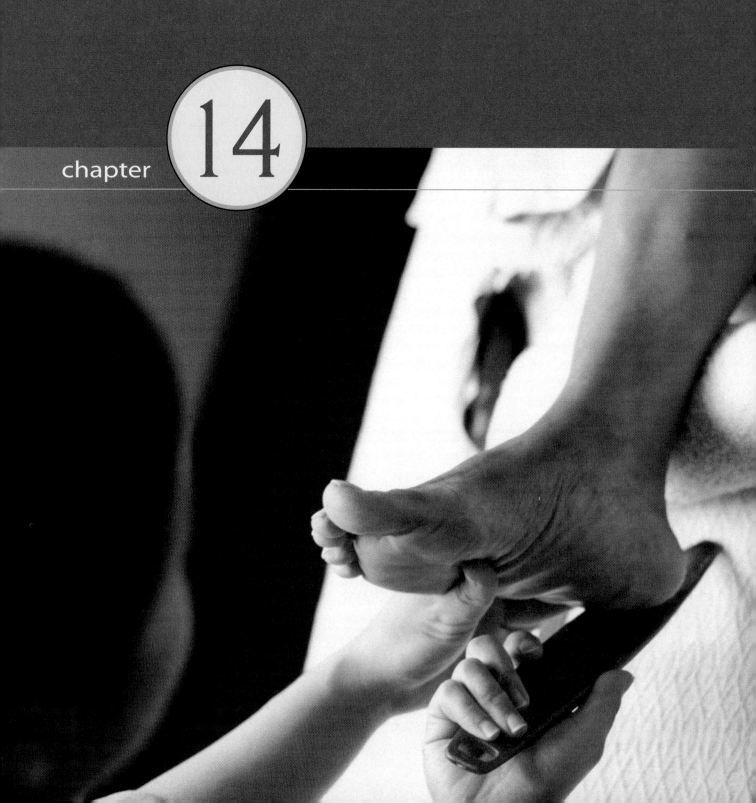

Pedicuring

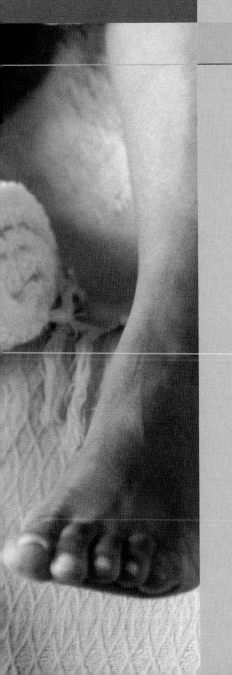

chapter 14

CHAPTER OUTLINE

- Pedicure Supplies
- Pedicures
- Foot Massage
- More about Pedicuring
- Pedicure Implements

LEARNING OBJECTIVES

After you have completed this chapter, you will be able to:

1. Identify the equipment and materials needed for a pedicure and explain.
2. List the steps in the pedicure pre-service procedure.
3. Demonstrate the proper procedures and precautions for a pedicure.
4. Describe the proper technique to use in filing toenails.
5. Describe the proper technique for trimming the nails.
6. Demonstrate your ability to perform foot massage properly.
7. Understand proper cleaning and disinfecting of pedicure equipment.

KEY TERMS

Page number indicates where in the chapter the term is used.

abrasive scrub
pg. 249

callus softener
pg. 250

curette
pg. 251

effleurage
pg. 245

exfoliating scrub
pg. 257

foot file (paddle)
pg. 252

foot soak
pg. 248

friction movement
pg. 247

hand movement
pg. 245

masque
pg. 250

massage
pg. 245

massage oil
pg. 249

nail rasp
pg. 252

nippers
pg. 252

paraffin bath
pg. 250

pedicure
pg. 238

petrissage
pg. 245

tapotement
pg. 245

toenail clippers
pg. 251

T he information in this chapter will show you the pedicuring skills you need to care for clients' feet, toes, and toenails. A **pedicure** includes trimming, shaping, exfoliating skin and polishing toenails as well as foot massage. Pedicures are a standard service performed by nail professionals. They are a basic part of good foot care and hygiene. They are particularly important for clients who are joggers, dancers, cosmetologists or anyone who spends a lot of time standing on their feet. Once the client experiences the comfort, relaxation and value of a good pedicure they will return for more. In short, pedicure services are for just about everyone, but different clients will have different needs. For example, not all clients will want or need a full pedicure service.

Some clients only need a professional nail trimming. Do not limit yourself. Tailor your pedicure service to meet the needs of your entire clientele. Talk to your clients about getting monthly pedicures to ensure healthy, happy feet, as they are in constant use and need routine maintenance. Proper foot care, through pedicuring, improves both personal appearance and basic foot comfort.

here's a tip...

When making an appointment for a pedicure, suggest that your client wear open-toe shoes or sandals so that polish will not smear and caution clients not to shave their legs within 24 hours before the pedicure. In the pedicure area, post a sign cautioning clients about shaving their legs. Tiny microscopic abrasions from shaving increase the risk of stinging, irritation or infection. So, this is an important consideration to heed.

PEDICURE SUPPLIES

You will need the following supplies in addition to your standard manicure set-up to perform pedicures (Figures 14–1 and 14–2).

Pedicuring station. A station includes a comfortable chair with armrests for the client, a footrest for the client, and an ergonomic chair for the nail professional. Pedicure stations that combine all these items into one piece of furniture are available.

Pedicuring stool and footrest. A pedicuring stool is a low stool that will make it easier for you to work on your client's feet. Some pedicuring stools come with a footrest for the client, or a separate footrest can be used. Make sure the chair is comfortable and will allow you to sit in an ergonomically correct position.

Pedicure basin or bath. The pedicure bath is filled with warm water and liquid soap to soak the client's feet. The bath must be large enough to completely immerse both of the client's feet.

Toe separators. Foam rubber toe separators or cotton used to keep toes apart while polishing the nails.

Foot file or paddle Used to exfoliate dry skin or smooth calluses.

Toenail clippers Any type of toenail clippers specifically designed for professional use will be acceptable for a professional pedicure.

Liquid soap Liquid soap for pedicuring contains a mild detergent for cleansing the feet.

Foot lotion, oil or cream Lotions, oils and creams are an important part of the service and are used to condition and moisturize feet. They are also used for performing a foot massage.

Pedicure slippers Disposable paper or foam slippers are needed for those clients who have not worn open-toe shoes and want to avoid smudging toenail polish.

Figure 14–1 Pedicure station including client's chair, footrest, and pedicuring stool.

PEDICURES

As with other procedures, a pedicure involves three parts: the pre-service, the pedicure procedure, and the post-service. In the pre-service you will clean and disinfect your implements, greet your client, and do a client consultation. Next you will perform the steps involved in the actual procedure.

Then, in the post-service, you will schedule another appointment for your client, make recommendations and sell the beneficial retail products you discussed during the service, clean your area then sanitize and disinfect all disinfectable implements and abrasives.

Figure 14–2 Supplies needed for pedicure.

Pedicure Pre-service

Your pedicure area should be close to a sink so it is convenient when you fill the pedicure baths with water.

1. Complete pre-service sanitation. Complete your pre-service sanitation and disinfection procedure. (This procedure is described in Chapter 13 on pages 211–212.)

2. Station set up. Your station should be set up to include a comfortable and ergonomically correct pedicuring stool/chair, client's chair, and a footrest for your client.

3. Arrange towels. Spread one terry cloth towel on the floor in front of client's chair to put feet on during the pedicure. Put another towel over the footrest. This will be used to dry the feet.

4. Set up standard manicure table. Set up your standard manicuring table for use while doing pedicures. You'll also need to add

Figure 14–3 Portable pedicure supply cart containing all the implements and supplies for a pedicure.

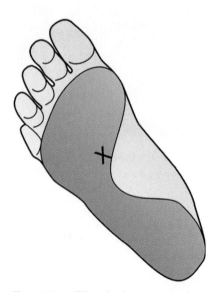

Figure 14–4 "X" marks the spot.—Applying pressure to this area will often have a calming effect on ticklish or apprehensive clients.

toe separators, an **abrasive foot file/paddle**), toenail clippers, liquid soap, foot lotion, oil or cream, a rapid nail dryer and pedicure slippers.

5. Fill basin with warm water. Add a measured amount of liquid soap to the bath (follow manufacturer's directions).

6. Greet your client with a smile.

7. Complete the client consultation. Check for nail disorders and decide if it is safe and appropriate to perform a service on your client. Determine if the client is diabetic, has psoriasis or other signs of a medical condition that would warrant taking extra precautions. If infection or inflammation is present, refer your client to their physician. If any signs of infection are present, you must not perform a pedicure-you are risking your professional license if you do! Record the client's responses and your observations.

Pedicure Service

When using a manufacturer's product line, it is recommended that you follow their recommendations and suggested procedures. They have been tested and found to enhance the effectiveness of their product line. You should time the individual steps of the pedicure based on the time suggested by the manufacturer to complete the entire service economically and efficiently. Do not give the client the feeling of being rushed, but develop your procedures so there are no wasted motions. Have your implements and products within easy reach (Figure 14–3). There should be no distractions for you or the client during the pedicure. You should always understand and keep in mind your client's goals and expectations for the service. Make the client feel that you have nothing more to do than to take care of their needs. Talk to them if they wish to talk, but if they want to drift off, allow them the peace and tranquility they are seeking.

Be gentle, but firm, when handling the foot. A gentle, light touch can produce a tickling sensation, which is not at all relaxing. In fact, this may cause the client to become tense and pull away from the pedicurist during the service. Many people normally cannot stand having their feet touched, but will accept and tolerate a firm, comfortable grip on the foot (Figure 14–4).

In most instances, when working on the foot, it should be grasped between the thumb and fingers at the mid-tarsal area. This accomplishes two things:

1. It locks the foot, making it rigid instead of being flexible and loose. It also allows the placing of the thumb or index finger at that point on the bottom of the foot where the two skin creases meet on the ball. This spot is usually located at the beginning of the longitudinal arch.

2. Applying a firm grip at this point has a calming effect on the client and overcomes any apprehension about someone touching their feet.

PROCEDURE 14-1

PERFORMING A PEDICURE

During the procedure, talk with your client about the products that are needed to maintain the service between salon visits. You might recommend polish, top coat, foot lotion or cream.

1 *Remove shoes and socks.* Ask your client to remove shoes, socks, and hose and roll pant legs to the knees.

2 *Soak feet.* Put client's feet in soap bath for 5 minutes to soften and clean the feet before you begin the pedicure (Figure 14–5).

3 *Dry feet thoroughly.* Make sure you dry between the toes. Ask client to place both feet on the towel you have placed on the floor (Figure 14–6).

4 *Remove existing polish.* Remove polish from little toe on left foot working towards big toe. Repeat with the right foot (Figure 14–7).

5 *Clip nails.* Carefully clip the toenails of the left foot so that they are even with the end of the toe (Figure 14–8). Don't Clip nails too short. Take care not to break the hyponychium, which is an important part of the seal that protects the toe nail unit from infection.

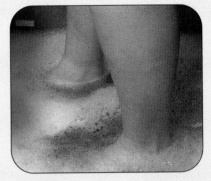

Figure 14–5   Soak feet for 5 minutes to soften and cleanse skin.

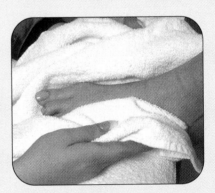

Figure 14–6   Dry feet thouroughly.

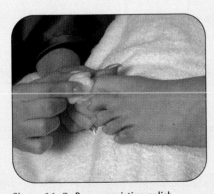

Figure 14–7   Remove existing polish.

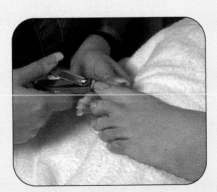

Figure 14–8   Carefully clip toenails.

here's a tip...

Add a few drops of aromatherapy oil to the foot bath to excite the client's senses and enhance the overall experience.

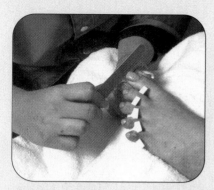

Figure 14–9 File nails.

Figure 14–10 Use foot file.

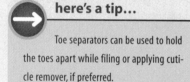

here's a tip...

Toe separators can be used to hold the toes apart while filing or applying cuticle remover, if preferred.

6 *File nails.* Carefully file the nails of the left foot with an appropriate abrasive file.

File them straight across, rounding them slightly at the corners to conform to the shape of the toes. Smooth rough edges with the fine side of an abrasive file (Figure 14–9). Repeat this step on the other foot.

7 *Use foot file.* Use foot file on ball and heel of foot to smooth dry skin and calluses. Do not try to completely remove a client's calluses. Removing this protective layer can lead to blisters, irritation or infections (Figure 14–10).

8 *Rinse foot.* Place left foot in foot bath.

9 *Repeat steps 7 and 8 on right foot.*

10 *Brush nails.* While the left foot is in the foot bath, brush nails with nail brush. Remove the foot and dry thoroughly (Figure 14–11).

11 *Apply cuticle remover.* Use a new cotton-tipped wooden push or eye dropper to apply cuticle remover to left foot. Begin with the little toe and work toward the big toe (Figure 14–12).

12 *Removing cuticle tissue.* When performing a pedicure, do not push back the eponychium. Feet are more susceptible to infections and pushing back the eponychium (or cutting) can increase the risk of serious infections on feet. This is especially important for clients with diabetes or psoriasis. Carefully remove the cuticle tissue using a wooden or metal pusher taking care not to break the important seal it creates between the nail plate and eponychium. Use a nipper to carefully remove any loose tags of dead skin, but don't cut, rip or tear the living skin, since this could lead to serious infections, as well (Figure 14–13).

13 *Brush foot.* Ask your client to dip left foot into foot bath. With the left foot over the foot bath, brush with nail brush to remove bits of debris and cuticle remover. Dry the foot thoroughly and place foot on towel.

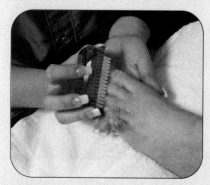

Figure 14–11 Brush nails.

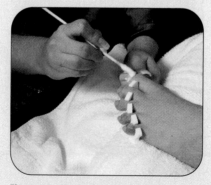

Figure 14–12 Apply cuticle remover.

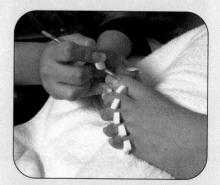

Figure 14–13 Carefully remove the dead cuticle tissue from the nail plate.

14 *Apply lotion, cream or oil.* Apply lotion, cream or oil to foot for skin conditioning and massage. Use a firm touch to avoid tickling your client's feet (Figure 14-14).

15 *Massage foot.* Perform foot massage on the left foot. Then place foot on a clean towel on the floor. (See foot massage techniques on pages 246–247.)

16 *Proceed with steps 10-15 on the right foot.*

17 *Remove traces of lotion.* Remove traces of lotion, cream or oil from toenails of both feet with a small piece of cotton or plastic back cotton pad that has been saturated with polish remover.

18 *Apply polish.* Insert the toe separators. Apply base coat, two coats of color, and top coat to toenails. Spray with rapid polish dryer to prevent smudging of the polish. Place feet on a towel to dry (Figure 14—15).

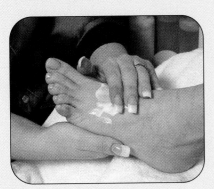

Figure 14–14 Apply lotion.

Figure 14–15 Finished pedicure.

> ⚠ **Regulatory Agency ALERT!**
>
> Never use a razor or other sharp device to cut calluses from the feet. These are potentially dangerous devices which must never be used by nail professionals, especially for diabetic clients. It is not legal in any state for a nail professional to perform medical procedures - using a razor is prohibited and can cause you to lose your license.

The actual pedicure procedure can be divided into five basic steps: the soak, nail care, skin care, massage, and polishing of the nails (optional). Each of these steps is distinct from the other. Depending on client needs, some steps may not be necessary. For example, some clients may only need nail care. This will take less time than a more complete treatment. If you have a great massage technique, clients may want only the soak and a massage to relieve tension and stress after a day's work. Or many may want the full treatment, since they are there to be pampered. Remember; be innovative and creative when it comes to your pedicure services.

> **safety caution!**
>
> Be sure the floor around the pedicure area is dry because wet floors are slippery. You or your clients can fall. When water is spilled, wipe it up immediately. The same holds true for slippery oils, lotions or creams. You must always be on guard to ensure your client's safety. That's your job as a salon professional!

Pedicure Post-Service

Your pedicure is not complete until you have performed the following:

1. **Make another appointment.** Schedule another pedicure appointment for your client.

2. **Advise client.** Advise client about proper foot care. For example, remind the client that wearing tight shoes and very high heels can cause problems with the feet.

here's a tip...

Think that you don't have 10 minutes between pedicures to disinfect? Before reaching for the massage lotion, clean the basin and fill with water and disinfectant solution. The disinfectant can remain in the basin while you complete the pedicure. This keeps you on schedule and shows the client that you are providing safe services.

3. **Recommend take home products.** Suggest that your client purchase and use the professional products that you have discussed during the pedicure or recommend at the end of the service. Products such as polish, foot lotions or creams, skin moisturizers, softeners, cooling gels, powders and top coat help to maintain the pedicure until their next service.

4. **Clean and disinfect pedicure basin.** After every pedicure, disinfect the pedicure basin as instructed in the following procedure.

5. **Clean your table.** Then clean and disinfect implements and multi-use tools, i.e. abrasives. In most areas this procedure calls for 20 minutes of proper cleaning and disinfection before implements or pedicure basin can be used on the next client. Return your table to its basic set-up.

5. **Disinfect foot spa.** Using procedure 5-2 on page 77, disinfect the foot spa after each client.

FOOT MASSAGE

Massage is defined in the medical dictionary as "a method of manipulation of the body by rubbing, pinching, kneading, tapping, etc." The art of massage has probably been around since the beginning of time. Most of us enjoy being touched and the art of massage takes touching to a higher, even therapeutic level. Foot massage during a pedicure stimulates blood flow and is relaxing to the client.

There are three basic forms of **hand movements** utilized in therapeutic massage. These consist of:

○ —light or hard stroking movements called **effleurage**.

○ —compression movements called **petrissage**, which includes kneading, squeezing, and friction.

$ business TIP

PUSHING PEDICURES DURING COLD WEATHER

It's relatively easy to sell pedicures during the summer. The weather is warm and clients want their bare or sandal-clad feet in tip-top shape. But in the winter, feet are bundled up in layers of socks and shoes or boots. Many clients forget about foot care, because they don't see their feet as much. Pedicures should be promoted as a healthy service for the feet. They are an important part of good grooming and a preventative health aid. Pedicures are not just for summer. Monthly pedicures keep feet healthy and happy. Like other parts of the body, feet can suffer from extreme dryness, and cracking. Remind clients that feet are in daily use and they need routine maintenance, for both men and women, especially during the winter months.

o —percussion or **tapotement**, in which the sides of the hands are used to strike the skin in rapid succession.

Effleurage relaxes muscles, and improves circulation to the small, surface blood vessels.

Petrissage helps to increase movement by stretching muscles and tendons. Tapotement is also a technique for improving circulation.

There are a number of massage styles and techniques. No matter what technique you use, perfect it so that it becomes second nature to you.

Study and practice different methods to individualize the massage for different clients. During this part of the pedicure, be keenly aware of your client's needs and meet those requirements by giving a massage that fulfills them. They will probably be back for more!

The amount of pressure applied during the massage should be only as deep as is comfortable for you and your client. Ask the client whether they would like more or less pressure. Be aware of what parts of the massage the client needs or enjoys most and put a greater emphasis in these areas. Sit in a comfortable and unstrained position and keep your wrists straight in order to reduce the risk of injury to your back, shoulders, arms, wrists and hands. Do not favor your dominant or strongest hand; always remembering to use both hands equally. Pay attention to your own body's positioning and make sure you are working ergonomically. For example, avoid leaning toward or stretching to reach your client's feet. Sit in a comfortable and relaxed position. Although it is important to give your client the best possible service, it's more important to keep yourself healthy during the process and avoid injuries caused by strain or repeated motion. Take a minute to stretch before and after a pedicure, to keep your body limber and more resistant to injury. Stretching isn't just for athletes; it can help us all if done regularly.

Attention to these finer details will always make your massage stand out from others and will keep your body healthy at the same time.

Foot Massage Techniques

These techniques and illustrations provide directions for massage of the left foot.

1. **Relaxer movement to the joints of the foot.** Rest client's foot on foot rest or stool. Grasp the leg just above the ankle with your left hand. This will brace the client's leg and foot. Use your right hand to hold left foot just beneath toes and rotate foot in a circular motion (Figure 14–16).

2. **Effleurage on top of foot.** Place both thumbs on top of foot at the instep.

    Move your thumbs in circular movements in opposite directions down the center of the top of the foot. Continue this movement to the toes. Keep one hand in contact with foot or leg, slide one hand at a time back firmly to instep and rotate back down to toes. This is a relaxing movement. Repeat 3-5 times (Figure 14–17).

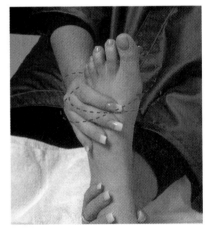

Figure 14–16 Relaxer movement to the joints of the foot.

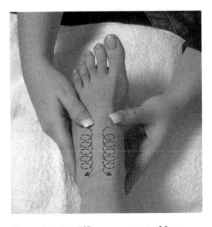

Figure 14–17 Effleurage on top of foot.

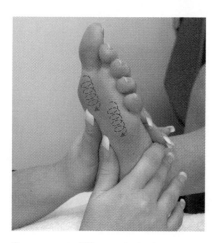

Figure 14–18 Effleurage on heel.

3. **Effleurage on heel (bottom of foot).** Use the same thumb movement that you did in the previous massage technique. Start at the base of the toes and move from the ball of the foot to the heel, rotating your thumbs in opposite directions. Slide hands back to the top of the foot.

     This is a relaxing movement. Repeat 3-5 times (Figure 14–18).

4. **Effleurage movement on toes.** Start with the little toe, using thumb on top and index finger on bottom of foot. Hold each toe and rotate with thumb. Start at base of toe and work toward the end of the toes.

     This is relaxing and soothing. Repeat 3-5 times (Figure 14–19).

5. **Joint movement for toes.** Start with the little toe and make a figure eight with each toe. Repeat 3-5 times (Figure 14–20).

6. **Thumb compression**-friction movement.. Make a fist with your fingers, keeping your thumb out. Apply firm pressure with your thumb and move your fist up the heel toward the ball of the foot. Work from the left side of foot and back down the right side toward the heel. As you massage over the bottom of the foot, check for any nodules or bumps. If you find one, be very gentle because the area may be tender. This movement stimulates the blood flow and increases circulation (Figure 14–21).

7. **Metatarsal scissors (a petrissage massage movement, kneading).** Place your fingers on top of foot along the metatarsal bones with your thumb underneath the foot. Knead up and down along each bone by raising your thumb and lower fingers to apply pressure. This promotes flexibility and stimulates blood flow. Repeat 3-5 times (Figure 14–22).

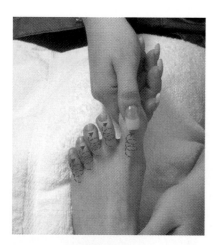

Figure 14–19 Effleurage on toe.

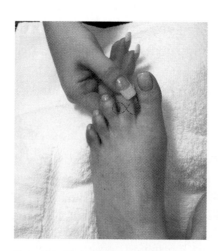

Figure 14–20 Joint movement for toes.

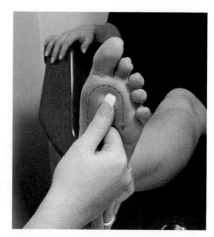

Figure 14–21 Thumb compression— "friction movement."

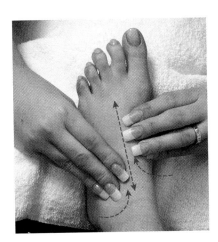

Figure 14–22 Metatarsal scissors.

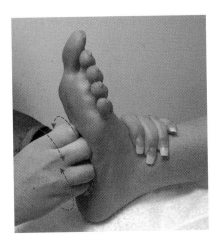

Figure 14–23 Fist twist compression.

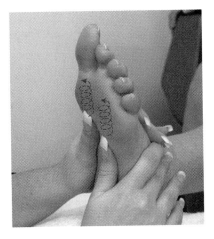

Figure 14–24 Effleurage on instep.

8. **Fist twist compression (a friction movement, deep rubbing).** Place left hand on top of foot and make a fist with your right hand. Your left hand will apply pressure while your right hand twists around the bottom of the foot. This helps stimulate blood flow. Repeat 3-5 times up and around foot (Figure 14–23).

9. **Effleurage on instep.** Place fingers at ball of foot. Move fingers in circular movements in opposite directions. Massage to end of each toe, gently squeezing the tip of each toe (Figure 14–24).

10. **Percussion or tapotement movement.** Use fingertips to perform percussion or tapotement (tah–POT–mynt) movements to lightly tap over the entire foot to complete massage.

MORE ABOUT PEDICURING

The basic step-by-step pedicure procedure is a necessary learning tool to help you master a warranted and valuable service. There is, however, additional information needed to enable you to go beyond the basics. The products, implements, and equipment you will need to perform a pedicure are an important part of the service. The basic pedicure procedure is just the beginning. There is much more to come. When you become more proficient and begin to customize a pedicure, the following information will be indispensable in helping you accomplish that end.

Just as there are "systems" for nail enhancement products, so are there pedicure systems or lines available from many manufacturers of professional nail products. These manufacturers produce a complete line of products for the professional pedicure. It is recommended that you check out all of these lines. Compare them with each other and decide for yourself which is best for your clients. The educational support and commitment of the company is important in making this decision.

There are basic types of products necessary for the pedicure service. The basic product types are;

o Soaks

o Abrasives

o Massage preparations

o Cuticle removers.

Foot soaks. Soaks are products used in the pedicure bath to soften the skin. A good soak must contain a gentle, but effective soap to thoroughly clean and deodorize the feet. Antibacterial soaps are no more effective than other soaps that do not make anti-bacterial claims. Therefore, don't choose a product simply because it's "antibacterial". Like all soaps, their main function is to make bacteria so slippery that they slide off the skin. Therefore, you can see that all soaps are anti-bacterial, whether they make this claim or not.

Dead Sea salts are one of the ingredients often found in foot soaking products. These contain many types of salt including; sodium, calcium and magnesium salts. All of these are thought to be highly beneficial to skin. It's better to use professionally formulated products because they are designed to properly cleanse the foot without being overly harsh to the skin. Other ingredients may include natural oils used for their moisturizing and/or aromatherapy qualities. The soak does set the stage for the rest of the pedicure, so be sure to use a high quality soak and start your pedicure service on a good note.

Beware of misleading product claims. - There is no additive or soak that is added to the water during a pedicure that kills pathogens and replaces your obligation to clean and disinfect after the pedicure. Any chemical that is strong enough to kill pathogens is not safe for contact with skin. Disinfectants must **never, NEVER** be placed in the foot bath with the client's feet. This is a dangerous practice which must be avoided.

Abrasive scrubs are used to help in the removal and smoothing of the dry, flaky skin and calluses. They are usually either creams or lotions which contain an abrasive powder as the exfoliating agent. These are used to remove dry, flaky skin and leave it feeling smoother and moisturized. Avoid excessive abrasive scrubs since they can damage clients' skin. Abrasive scrubs can also remove the living skin from the hands of the pedicurist, if the product is used very often in a short period of time. If hands become sore from doing many repeated services, it would be wise to wear gloves while using the abrasive scrub or find a product that is gentler.

Sea sand, ground apricot kernels, pumice, quartz crystals, and plastic beads are all exfoliating agents found in pedicure scrubs. Essential aroma oils, beneficial extracts and other moisturizers, which help to condition the skin, may also be found in various scrub preparations.

Massage preparations consist of oils, creams and lotions used to lubricate, moisturize, and invigorate the skin. They allow the hands of the pedicurist to glide soothingly over the skin during the massage part of the pedicure. They also help to promote a general feeling of relaxation and well-being in the client. Most quality **massage oils** are a blend of therapeutic oils, which help promote skin health.

Aromatherapy oils may also be incorporated for their relaxing and calming effects. Tea tree oil is often included for its antiseptic properties, as well as its medicinal fragrance. The pedicurist, like some massage therapists, may want to formulate their own massage oil. Some massage therapy supply stores have base massage oils to which different essential oils can be added. A number of massage oils can be formulated in this manner to match individual client needs. This will give a customized quality to the pedicure. It is better to prepare only small quantities of these blends, i.e. the amount required for the service. Formulating larger amounts of these oils must be done under very clean (hygienic) conditions or the blends could become contaminated with bacteria and spoil within a short period of time.

Cuticle removers are products designed to soften cuticles for removal fromr the nail plate. These products are highly alkaline and corrosive substances capable of dissolving cuticles or other tissues within a very short period of time. Since these products are so fast acting, they must not be left on the nail plate for any longer than recommended by the product manufacturer, usually one to two minutes. If left on longer than recommended, serious damage can occur to the nail plate and/or surrounding skin. Improper use can also result in dry, splitting eponychium and sidewalls. Cuticle removers must only be applied to the nail plate and contact with living skin must be avoided. Cuticle removers must be completely rinsed off after use or skin irritation may develop. If not thoroughly removed, residues on the nail plate can also cause lifting. Nail professionals should avoid prolonged or repeated skin contact with these products and safety eyewear should be worn to prevent accidental eye exposure. Any highly alkaline substances can be potentially dangerous if accidentally splashed in the eye or used incorrectly, so read the directions and follow them exactly.

Add-on Products

These products are used to enhance and expedite the pedicure experience.

Professional strength **callus softeners** are offered to help soften and smooth calluses, especially, heels and over pressure points. These products are applied directly to the callus and allowed to soak in for a short period of time to soften the hard tissue, making them easier to remove with abrasive boards, blocks or paddles. These products usually contain either sodium hydroxide or lactic acid, both are powerful callus softening ingredients. Sodium hydroxide is highly alkaline, usually pH 12 or higher. Lactic acid is an alpha hydroxy acid and products formulated with these types of ingredients are usually pH 4 or less. In both cases, it is very important to read and understand manufacturer's instructions and use exactly as directed. Both should be considered potentially hazardous to eyes and safety glasses should be worn whenever using or pouring them. Be sure to wash your hands before touching your face or eye area. Used improperly, these types of products can cause severe burns to client's skin and may cause irritation to nail professional's hands with repeated exposure. Used correctly, they can be very safe and effective.

Masques are usually composed of mineral clays, moisturizing agents, skin softeners, aromatherapy oils and beneficial extracts. They are applied to the skin and left in place for five minutes. These are beneficial skin treatments that are highly valued by clients.

Hot **paraffin baths** for the feet are an excellent addition to the pedicure. The paraffin bath stimulates circulation and the deep heat helps to reduce inflammation and promote circulation to the affected joints. Apply moisturizing lotions, creams or oils to the skin and use the paraffin to seal them in allowing the heat to speed penetration of beneficial ingredients.

Aromatherapy oils can also be incorporated into the paraffin bath. Clients feel pampered and the hot paraffin wax service adds to the relaxation of the pedicure experience. **Do not** give this service to clients with impaired foot circulation, loss of feeling, or other diabetic-related problems. The hot wax may cause burns or skin breakdown in these situations.

Other items necessary for the best-ever pedicure could include:

- **Pedicure slippers**. Disposable paper or foam slippers are needed for those clients who have not worn open toe shoes.

- **Pedicure sandals**. Sandals, with toe separators incorporated in their design, can be purchased by the client and brought in with them every time they have a pedicure.

> **here's a tip...**
>
> Be sure to wipe excess oil or lotion from the bottom of the client's foot before putting on slippers to prevent them from slipping and falling.

PEDICURE IMPLEMENTS

The use of high quality, professional implements and equipment by the nail professional is very important. A high quality professional implement will last the user many years and make the job easy. This is particularly true when it comes to working on the foot. Improper implements can easily cause injury to toenails and the soft tissues of the foot. For your client's safety, only use implements and equipment made specifically for performing professional pedicures.

In addition, appropriate implements and equipment will make foot services easier and quicker.

Here are some basic implements that you will need:

Toenail Clippers. Use only professional implements made for cutting toenails. Toenail clippers are not just larger than fingernail clippers; they are specifically designed for toenails.

These come with either curved or straight jaws (Figures 14–25 and 14–26). The best clippers have jaws which come to a fairly fine point. Those with blunt points are difficult to use in the small corners of highly curved nail plates.

Curettes. A curette is a small, "ice cream scooper" shaped implement that, if carefully used, allows for more efficient removal of debris from the nail folds and cuticle area (Figures 14-27 and 14-28). Properly used,

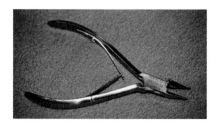

Figure 14–25 5-½"- nail nippers with straight jaws.

Figure 14–26 Close-up of jaws of nail nipper.

the curette is the ideal implement for pedicures, especially around the edges of the great toe nail plate. A double-ended curette, which has a 0.06 inch (1.5 mm) diameter on one end and a 0.1 inch (2.5 mm) diameter on the other, is recommended. Some are made with a small hole making the curette easier to clean after it has been used. The curette must never be used to" cut out" any tissue or debris that is strongly adhering to the living tissues. The nail professional must never use curettes with sharp edges. These can seriously injure clients. Only those with dull edges are safe and appropriate. Sharp edged curettes may seriously injure the client, so they must be avoided.

Nail rasp. This rasp is a metal file designed to be used in a specific fashion. Rasp are designed to file in one direction. The filing surface of the implement is about ⅛-inch wide and about ¾-inch long (Figure 14–29). It is attached to a straight or angled metal handle. The angled file is recommended because it is easier to use along the nail groove, where the nail plate meets the living sidewall tissue. This implement smoothes the edges of the nail plate along the nail groove. It should be placed in the nail groove against the free edge of the nail plate.

The file is then gently pulled along the edge of the nail toward the end of the toe. This will smooth any rough edges of the nail plate, which may have been produced during the trimming or curetting procedures. This process may be repeated a number of times to make sure there are no rough edges remaining along the nail margin.

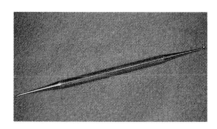

Figure 14–27 Double-ended curette.

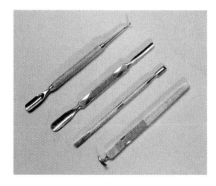

Figure 14–28 Close-up of curette.

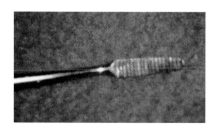

Figure 14–29 Close-up of nail rasp.

The nail rasp, like the curette, is mainly used along the side wall of the nail plate on the great toenail. The lesser toenails do not usually require filing along their sidewalls. Removing sharp edges along the nail plate edge reduces the possibility of the nail plate digging into the soft tissues and creating an ingrown nail. As you become proficient in the use of this file you will find it to be an invaluable and time-saving implement. Properly used, it will add the professional finishing touch required in the care of toenails.

Abrasive Nail and Foot Files. To file the free edge of the toenails and, in some cases, to thin them, an abrasive nail file is an excellent implement (Figure 14–30). For some toenails, coarse grit abrasives are needed, but for most, a medium grit will work best. Abrasive files are made of many types of abrasive materials including, aluminum oxide, diamond chips or nickel. Nickel and diamond abrasive files do not fill up with nail debris as quickly during use.

Foot files or paddles are larger than those designed for finger and toe nails. These large sanding files are designed to reduce dry, flaky skin and smooth foot calluses. They come in many different grits and shapes (Figure 14–31). These must be properly cleaned and disinfected between each use or disposed of after a single use, if the manufacturer has not designed them to be disinfectable. In general, if an abrasive file cannot survive proper cleaning and disinfection procedures without being rendered unusable, it must be considered disposable.

Foot paddles with disposable and replaceable abrasive surfaces are also available.

Nippers can be used to remove dead tags of skin, but take great care to avoid cutting, tearing or ripping living tissue. Avoid using nippers on clients who are diabetic since the risk of infection from accidental injury is great. Also, avoid using nippers on clients with psoriasis since injury to the toenail unit can create new psoriasis lesions where the damage occurs.

Pedicure Equipment

This section will discuss various large equipment items necessary to provide a pedicure service. As with implements, high quality, comfortable, easy to use equipment will be cost effective and also will help to promote your

Figure 14–30 Close-up of an abrasive nail file.

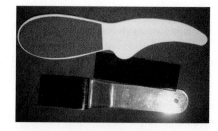

Figure 14–31 Abrasive foot paddle.

foot care services. If you are uncomfortable and awkward while performing your services, you may end up injuring your back, neck, arms, wrists or shoulders. Also, if you're relaxed, then your client will relax and enjoy the pedicure.

Pedicure Carts

These carts are a useful way to keep your supplies organized (Figure 14-32). There are many different designs and manufacturers of such carts. These carts have drawers and shelves for organized storage of implements and pedicure products. Some of these units even include a space for the footbath. Most units are designed to be compact, so they will take a very little space.

Water Baths

These useful and transportable devices can be purchased in a wide variety of sizes, shapes and costs. They must be manually filled and emptied after each client service.

If you use the portable type, be sure to have a comfortable chair or lounge in a private or semi-private area for the client to sit in while receiving the pedicure. Also, your chair should be adjustable, so that you can work at a comfortable height and reduce the risk of back strain. A step above the portable water bath is a more customized pedicure unit, which has a removable foot bath built into the unit (Figures 14-33 and 14-34). These are constructed with both the client and the nail professional in mind. They add to the service and are more ergonomically designed, making it much easier for the nail professional to perform the pedicure. A portable pedicure cart has a place for the foot bath, and storage area for supplies.

There are also portable foot basins with built-in, motorized whirlpool action that can be filled from the sink (Figure 14–35). After the

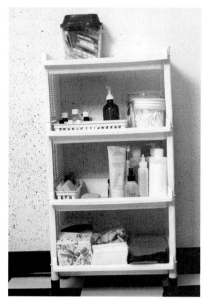

Figure 14-32 A portable pedicure cart has a place for the foot bath, storage area for supplies, and an adjustable footrest.

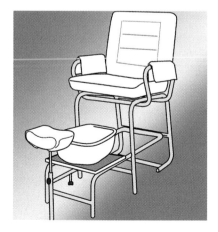

Figure 14–33 A customized type of pedicure station, well-built and affordable. It has an adjustable footrest and a place for the water bath.

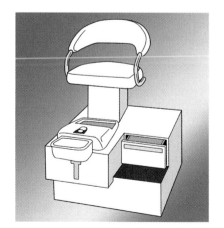

Figure 14–34 A pedicure center should be well constructed. Many have a removable foot bath, storage drawer, and adjustable footrest.

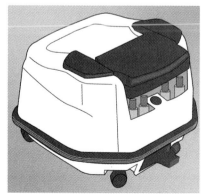

Figure 14–35 A fully self-contained portable foot basin.

Figure 14–36 A fully-plumbed throne-type pedicure unit comes with many options including a massage unit built into the client chair.

service, they are drained by pumping the water back into the sink drain. They have built-in foot rests and areas for storage of the pedicure materials. They add an extra touch to the service by the gentle massaging action of the whirlpool.

The ultimate pedicure foot bath is the fully plumbed pedicure basin chair or "throne" (Figure 14–36). These units are not portable. The unit is attached to both hot and cold water as well as to a drain. If a floor drain is not available a pump option can be purchased to pump the water to an available sink.

Some units may also have a built-in massage feature as well as a warmer in the client chair, which adds to the relaxation of the pedicure.

No matter which water bath unit you have, be sure your seat fits both you and the unit. Look for a stool or chair that is adjustable for height and gives good lower back support. These are more ergonomic and will help prevent back pain or injury.

Once the client has left, sanitize (wash with soap and water) the equipment and implements that were used for the pedicure and then completely immerse the clean implement and abrasives into the disinfectant solution. If you are doing many pedicures, you may need two sets of implements One set can be disinfecting while you use the other set on your client. Properly clean and disinfect your pedicure tub as directed by your state regulations. Your instructor will provide you with specific details on these requirements. This is an extremely important step that must not be forgotten. Although wise, you will put your clients at risk of developing skin infections. Take this responsibility seriously and be sure to properly clean and disinfect all pedicure equipment, implements, etc.

$ business TIP

SERVICE FOR THE ELDERLY

The elderly also need care and maintenance for their feet on a year-round basis. There is a large segment of the elderly population who cannot reach their feet and need help in their foot care maintenance. It is estimated that 40 million Americans suffer from some form of arthritis. Many of them cannot reach their feet or cannot squeeze the nail nippers. They need proper foot care that a good pedicurist can provide. The nail professional who offers pedicure services for this segment of the population will be doing these individuals a great favor and will find plenty of willing clients in need of their services.

PROCEDURE 14-2
THE FULL SERVICE PEDICURE

1   ***The soak.*** This service starts the procedure. It is important to soften and prepare the skin for what is to follow. The water must not exceed 104°F. You should use a thermometer to ensure that it is that the proper temperature. Place the soaking product into the water according to manufacturer's recommendation. Allow the client to soak for approximately five minutes to clean the foot and soften the skin. You have time during this part of the service to make sure everything you will need for the rest of the pedicure is in its proper place. Then you won't have to look for some needed item in the middle of the pedicure process, which looks very unprofessional to your clients.

2   ***Nail care.*** Remove one foot from the bath and dry it with a towel.

(a) Remove polish. Remove any existing nail polish from the toenails.

(b) Apply cuticle remover. At this point apply cuticle remover and/or callus softeners where needed. This will give the product time to work while you care for the nails.

(c) Use curette. Next, the curette is used to gently push the soft tissue folds away from the walls of the lateral nail plate (Figure 14–37). This allows you to visually inspect the nail plate so that it can be trimmed without injuring the client. If there is extra build up of debris between the nail plate and surrounding tissue it should be gently removed with the curette. To use this implement, place the rounded side of the spoon toward the wall of living skin. A gentle scooping motion is then used along the nail plate to remove any loose debris. A gentle pressure is all that is necessary to accomplish the removal of the built-up debris. The pressure of this debris is quite uncomfortable if left in place. You may need to repeat this scooping motion a number of times to adequately remove enough of the loose debris. Take care not to overdo it. **Do not** use this implement to dig into the soft tissues along the nail fold. These living tissues are delicate and may be easily injured. Any debris attached to the soft tissue that is not easily removed in the manner described, must be removed by a medical doctor or podiatrist. If the tissue is inflamed, i.e. ingrown toenail, this must also be referred to a qualified medical doctor or podiatrist.

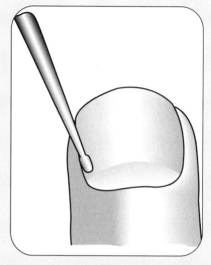

Figure 14–37 The curette is used to gently push the soft tissue away from the nail plate.

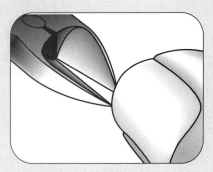

Figure 14–38 The nail nippers are used like a pair of scissors.

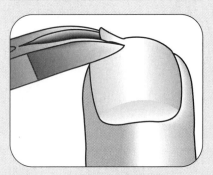

Figure 14–39 Trim the nail at a 45-degree angle. Notice the tilt of the nipper to reduce the possibility of injury to the underlying soft tissue.

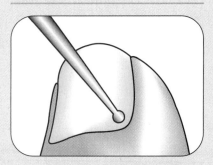

Figure 14–40 The curette is also used to remove the cuticle tissue from the surface of the nail plate.

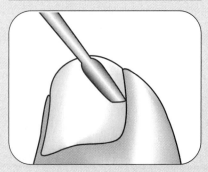

Figure 14–41 The small nail file or rasp is used to gently smooth and remove any rough edges or hooks left behind after the trimming process.

(d) Trim toenails. The nails should now be carefully trimmed using the toenail clippers. The clippers are used like a pair of scissors (Figure 14–38). The nail is trimmed in a number of small cuts to avoid flattening it out and injuring the hyponychium during the process. Place the clipper over the free nail edge and slightly tilt the top of the clipper back toward the nail plate. This reduces the possibility of cutting the soft tissues of the hyponychium under the free edge (Figure 14–39). Give the clipper a slight squeeze before actually cutting the nail. The reaction of the client to this squeeze will tell you if you are cutting too deep and are against living tissue. If you get a reaction, reposition the clipper on the nail and start the process over.

Trim the lesser toenails straight across. The big toenail is usually the most challenging to trim. The nail groove can often contain debris, lint, soap and other material that has built up over time. Trim the great toenail just as described for the lesser toes but pay particular attention to the sidewall area. Do not leave any rough edges or "hooks" that can catch on soft tissue. These can create an opportunity for infections. Remove these rough edges with a nail rasp.

After the nails have been trimmed with the clipper, go back with the curette and gently remove any debris left along the side walls. This is done, as previously described, by placing the cupped part of the curette against the lateral nail wall and edge of the nail. Gently draw the curette along the nail plate. This process may have to be repeated a number of times. In most instances this will remove an adequate amount of the debris thus relieving the pressure and making the client comfortable. During this process also recheck the nail plate along the sidewall areas for rough edges or "hooks" left behind after trimming.

(e) Remove cuticle tissue. The curette is also used to remove cuticle tissue from the top of the nail plate (Figure 14–40). The eponychium should not be pushed back on toenails. Any small break in the seal created by the cuticle and eponychium may increase the chance of infections. To remove the cuticle tissue very carefully draw the curette over the plate away from the eponychium in a sweeping "C" type motion from the nail fold toward the center of the nail plate.

This motion is then repeated from the opposite side of the nail plate. You may need to repeat these motions a number of times to remove all of the cuticle tissue from the top of the nail plate.

Be careful not to cut or injure the eponychium during this process.

(f) Smooth edges of nail plate. The small nail rasp is then used to smooth the edges of the nail plate along the nail grooves (Figure 14– 41). The rasp is made for this purpose. It is narrow and will only file the nail in one direction. It can be used to remove, smooth, and round off any sharp points or edges. Do not probe with the rasp, but instead gently draw it along the edge of that portion of the nail plate that you have just trimmed. Small, short strokes with the file, from back to front will accomplish the task.

(g) Smooth remainder of nail. The abrasive file should then be used to finally shape and smooth the rest of the nail. If the nail is very thick, a file can be used to slightly thin the nail plate.

(h) Repeat process on other foot. After completing the nail service on one foot place it back in the foot bath and repeat the process described above on the other foot. The entire nail trimming process should take approximately 15 minutes.

3 *Skin care.* Care of the skin is the next step in the full service pedicure. The skin has been softened by the solution in which it is soaking. The thicker areas of callus have been softened with the professional strength callus softeners during the nail trimming procedure.

(a) Exfoliate. **Exfoliating scrubs** can now be used to remove the dry or scaly skin. One foot is again removed from the bath and the scrub is liberally applied. Using a massaging motion, the pedicurist scrubs the dry skin off the foot. Use extra pressure (which creates more friction) on the heels and other areas where more callus and dry skin builds up.

(b) Smooth calluses. During this process, the abrasive foot paddle is used to smooth and reduce the thicker areas of callus. Remember that callus protects the underlying skin from irritation and is there for a purpose. Remove only enough to make the client comfortable. *Calluses should be softened and smoothed-not excessively thinned or removed.* You may need to educate your client about callus formation and the protective function it provides. Also discuss products for home use to help soften and condition calluses between salon appointments.

(c) Rinse. The foot is then rinsed in the bath. Do not forget to clean between the toes. These areas are often missed.

(d) Apply masque. If a skin masque product is to be used, this is a good time to apply it.

    After rinsing and cleaning the foot, apply the masque according to manufacturer's recommendations. Afterwards, wrap the foot in a clean towel and place it on the foot rest.

(e) Scrub and treat calluse on other foot. The abrasive scrubbing and callus smoothing process is then completed on the other foot. The entire process should take approximately 10 minutes. At this point approximately thirty-five minutes have been used for the pedicure. You may wish to allow the client to relax with the mask product (if used) for another five minutes. This will leave twenty minutes for the massage and polish.

    A hot wax service may also be added instead of a skin masque as a separate add-on part of the pedicure. The wax must be applied in accordance with manufacturer's instructions. Lotions, creams or oils can be applied to the foot before application of the paraffin wax. The heat will increase penetration of the ingredients into the skin. After the

Figure 14–42 Apply nail polish after thoroughly cleaning the nail plate.

paraffin is removed, the residual product left on the skin can be used for a relaxing massage. After applying the wax, a plastic bag is placed over the foot and the foot is placed into a terry cloth boot or wrapped in a towel. The process is repeated on the other foot, and then the client should be allowed to relax for five minutes. Remember like all add-on services, they take more time, require special equipment and provide more value of benefit to the client. Therefore, you should charge extra for these services. Your time and services are very valuable, so don't be afraid or hesitant to charge for them.

4 **The massage** is a part of the professional pedicure where the nail professional can excel. This is what the client has been looking forward to and often enjoys the most. A good massage will make the client come back again for another pedicure. The nail professional who perfects a good massage technique will build a good reputation. Massage aids relaxation, which is one of the most important reasons for giving a massage. Massage will give the client a sense of well being and has a tremendous calming effect which reduces stress. The massage also promotes increased circulation and muscle relaxation within the lower extremities. (See the massage section of this chapter.)

5 *Apply nail polish (optional).* After the massage, if the client desires, nail polish should be applied according to manufacturer's recommendations. Insert toe separators during this procedure. Is very important to remove all traces of massage products from the toenails with polish remover or polish will not adhere very well. Apply base coat, two coats of polish, and a topcoat (Figure 14–42). Place feet on a towel and allow the polish to dry. A rapid nail polish dryer can speed up this process.

6 **Post-pedicure procedures.** Follow the post-service procedure found on pages 243–244.

REVIEW **QUESTIONS**

1. Name five pedicure supplies.

2. List the steps in the pedicure pre-service.

3. Describe the proper technique to use when filing toenails.

4. Describe the proper technique for trimming toenails.

5. List the steps in the pedicure post-service.

6. Name and describe six foot massage techniques.

7. Explain why calluses should never be removed.

8. Why must you be especially careful when giving a pedicure to a diabetic client?

CHAPTER **GLOSSARY**

abrasive scrub	Slightly abrasive product containing softening agents or oils to penetrate dry, flaky skin and callus that need to be smoothed during a pedicure.
callus softener	Helps soften and smooth calluses, especially on heels and over pressure points.
curette	Small, spoon-shaped implement used for cleaning debris from the edges of nail plate.
effleurage	A light, continuous-stroking massage movement applied with fingers and palms in a slow and rhythmic manner.
exfoliating scrub	Is used to remove dry or scaly skin.
foot file (paddle)	Large abrasive file used to remove dry, flaky skin and smooth calluses.
foot soak	Product containing gentle soaps, moisturizers, and so on, that are used in a pedicure bath to cleanse and soften the skin.
friction movement	Firm pressure applied to the bottom of the foot using thumb compression to work from side to side and toward the heel.
hand movement	Process of skillfully treating, working, or operating with the hands.
masque	Usually composed of mineral clays, moisturizing agents, skin softeners, aromatherapy oils, and beneficial extracts.
massage	Method of therapeutic manipulation of the body by rubbing, pinching, kneading, and tapping.
massage oil	Blend of oils used to lubricate, moisturize, and invigorate the skin during a massage.
nail rasp	Metal file with an edge that can file the nail plate in only one direction.
nippers	Implement used for manicures and pedicures to trim tags of dead skin.
paraffin bath	Used to stimulate circulation and to reduce inflammation and promote circulation to the affected joints.
pedicure	Standard service performed by nail professionals that includes care and massage of feet and trimming, shaping, and polishing toenails.
petrissage	Kneading movement in massage performed by lifting, squeezing, and pressing the tissue.
tapotement	Massage movement using a short, quick hacking, slapping, or tapping technique.
toenail clippers	Professional implements with curved or straight jaws used for cutting toenails.

Electric Filing

CHAPTER OUTLINE

LEARNING OBJECTIVES

After completing this chapter, you will be able to:

1. Understand how to use an electric file safely for basic procedures.
2. Identify the types of electric files and choose the best machine for you.
3. Understand power and speed.
4. Understand the most frequently used types of bits.
5. Understand basic filing techniques used to ensure safety.

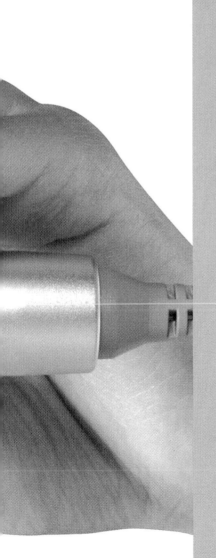
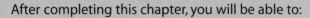

KEY TERMS

Page number indicates where in the chapter the term is used.

bit	**flute**	**revolutions per minute**	**rings of fire**
pg. 266	pg. 265	**(RPM)**	pg. 268
concentric	**grit**	pg. 264	**torque**
pg. 265	pg. 265		pg. 264

The information contained in this chapter comes from the Association of Electric File Manufacturers (AEFM™). The AEFM is a product-neutral training organization that sets the industry standard for safe electric file use. The AEFM offers standardized courses internationally, and these courses are approved for continuing education units and advanced training worldwide. In many states, nail professionals must take an AEFM safety course before using an electric file in the salon. For more information, visit *www.aefm.org*.

ARE ELECTRIC FILES SAFE?

Yes! Electric files are as safe as the nail professional using them. Electric files are not the reason that nail damage or injury occurs—improperly trained or careless nail professionals are the true cause. You should never use an electric file until you have received proper training. Education can be obtained from the AEFM (*www.aefm.org*), books and videos, and manufacturers' classes and industry trade shows.

Types of Machines

There are several types of machines available to nail professionals today, and knowing the proper use and care of each is important to the overall success of the service.

Belt Driven

These are dental machines and have long belts on pullies that attach to the motor. They are cumbersome, and not suitable for the professional nail industry.

Micromotor Machines

All professional nail machines are called micromotor machines. Why micromotors? Because the motor is in the handpiece. The base is a transformer that converts the electricity in the wall plug to the type of electricity that the motor needs to work. Handheld micromotor machines have a small box on the end of the cord where it plugs in to the wall socket. These machines are usually less powerful and less expensive than traditional micromotor machines, but can still accomplish all of the same procedures.

Craft and Hobby Tools

These are not suitable for use in the professional salon industry because they are manufactured for use on glass, wood, and ceramics. The only way that these tools can be used with professional nail bits is to modify them from the original factory condition by changing the collet or adding a flex-shaft adaptor. The vibration of these machines can damage the natural nail, interfere with the curing of enhancement products, and cause damage to the wrist and arm of the professional. The bottom line then is that craft and hobby tools should never be used in salons (Figure 15–1).

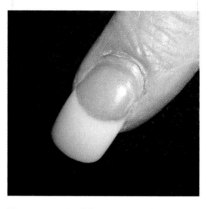

Figure 15–1 Nail damage caused by improper use of electric files.

CHOOSING AN ELECTRIC FILE

When choosing an electric file, evaluate your wants, needs, and budget. Budget will be the determining factor, so make sure that you look for the best machine in your price range.

Consider features of machines when looking to purchase. Features that you should consider are summarized below.

- Forward and reverse. The only time that reverse is needed is for left-handed techs, but remember that some bits do not cut when turning in reverse.

- Keyless chuck for ease in changing bits. Most machines have twist-lock chucks for ease in changing bits.

- Foot pedal. Not all machines offer a foot pedal option, so be sure that the one you are looking at has this feature available if you decide you want one. There are two types of foot pedal, so be sure that you know what you are buying: on and off—the foot pedal turns the machine on or off when you press and release it, and you must adjust the speed of the machine with your hand on the box; and variable speed—this pedal works like the accelerator of a car, that is, the more you press the faster the bit turns, and when you reduce pressure, the bit slows down.

- Closed casings on handpiece. Some machines have slots or openings in the handpiece. These openings allow dust and debris to get inside the handpiece that can cause damage to the motor. Closed casings can prolong the life of your machine.

- Variable speed (high, medium, low) versus range of speed (from lowest to highest, and whether it can be stopped at any speed in between).

- RPM and torque (highest and lowest range of machine).

- Comfortable handpiece (weight, size, shape). You have to like it.

- Low vibration. This will be quieter, will not interfere with the curing of enhancement products, and will reduce the risk of develop-

Figure 15–2 Selection of electric files with bits.

ing cumulative trauma disorders such as carpal tunnel syndrome, and will prolong your working life behind the table.

The information provided in this chapter will help you make a well-informed decision about *how, when, and why to use an electric file* (Figure 15–2). This book shows the basics that you need to get started, but your education should not stop here. You should seek additional education from the AEFM educational programs and/or other professional resources.

Power and Speed

Speed is defined in **revolutions per minute**, or RPM. This means the number of times the bit turns in a complete circle in 1 minute. Machines vary in RPM capacity, between 2,000 and 35,000. Think of RPM as a speedometer in a car—the motor works in the middle of the range from zero to the highest number (you do not drive your car at the highest number on the speedometer). Working in the middle range of its capacity prolongs the working life of the motor.

Torque is understood as power. Machines vary in torque and RPM, so know your machine's capacity. More powerful machines have larger motors and heavier handpieces. This means higher torque, so you should work at lower speeds because these machines are stronger and can accomplish more at a lower speed.

Less powerful machines have smaller motors and lighter handpieces, so you will work at higher speeds. These lightweight, less powerful machines can do all of the same procedures as more powerful machines, but need to work at higher speeds to compensate. These machines are wonderful for techs who have been working for many years and have begun to experience the effects of cumulative trauma to their hand and arm.

Life Expectancy

How long should an electric file last? That depends on two things:

o **Usage.** The more you use your electric file, the greater the wear and tear on the device.

$ business TIP

PRACTICE MAKES PERFECT

Before you ever use an electric file on a client, it is extremely important to get proper education, and practice, practice, practice. Glue a tip on a dowel or round clothespin and hold the dowel as you would a client's finger. Apply nail enhancement product to the tip and practice until you have gained confidence in your abilities. Then practice on a classmate or salon mate who can tell you about your technique and give you honest feedback. It is important that you are comfortable holding the hand piece, and that you learn to use the correct speed so that you do not injure the client. The more you work with your electric file, the more comfortable and skilled you will become.

○ **Maintenance.** If you regularly maintain and care for your electric file, it will be in good working order for many years. Regular maintenance is important. Check with the manufacturer for recommended cleaning, service, and replacement of cords.

Maintenance and Warranties

When you purchase your electric file, make sure to ask about the warranty. Do not purchase an electric file that does not have a warranty. Terms and conditions of the warranty will vary, but most manufacturers will fix or replace a malfunctioning electric file within 1 year of purchase at no cost.

Machines vary in cost from $25 for battery-operated models to over $1,500 for high-end machines. Keep in mind that all machines can perform the same procedures, but some do it easier than others do. Purchase the best machine that you can afford—it is the most valuable tool you will use in professional nail services.

CHOOSING BITS

Chacteristics to consider and questions to ask about **bits** are discussed in this section.

Wobble and vibration. Concentric is a term used to describe bits that are balanced while spinning. A bent bit will wobble while spinning, while concentric bits do not wobble or cause vibration. Using a bit that is not concentric is unsafe; if you drop the handpiece with a bit in it and the bit is bent, throw it away.

Even filing surface. Is the filing surface even? Distorted or uneven surfaces can leave scratches in the surface of the nail.

Surface smoothness. Are the particles evenly distributed? If the particles on the bit are larger in some areas, it will scratch the surface as you file instead of refining it.

Sharp edges. Bits are cut with finished edges so that they are not too sharp. Feel the edges of the bit before using it. If these are sharp, dull the edges with a file with the bit spinning at a slow speed.

Grits. Grit is measured by particle of abrasive per square inch. In higher grits, there are even more, smaller particles crammed into the same space. Lower grit abrasives use larger and more of aggressive abrasive particles while higher grit abrasive use a smaller, finer grit particles. This holds true for all abrasive boards, blocks, buffers, and bits. One exception to the rule is carbide bits. Carbide bits are measured by the number of **flutes** (grooves) in each bit. The larger and deeper the grooves, the coarser the bit. Shallower and closer spaced grooves create a finer bit. Never use coarser than medium grit bits on enhancement products.

Shank. The standard-size shank for nail machines is 3/32" (craft bits are larger at 1/8") (Figure 15–3).

here's a tip...

A great time for maintenance is while you are on vacation, since most manufacturers can service and return your machine to you within a week.

here's a tip...

An electric file should run smoothly without excessive vibration. Wobbling bits can cause vibration that can harm the electric file, cause damage to the client's nails, and may cause the nail professional to develop a cumulative trauma disorder (CTD). Handpieces or bits that vibrate excessively increase the risk of injury to your hand and/or wrist. If your handpiece creates excessive vibration, it should be immediately serviced. Remember, repetitive motions of any type, including motions used while electric filing, can cause repetitive trauma disorders such as CTDs. If you develop symptoms related to any type of repetitive trauma disorder, you should consult with a physician for diagnosis and treatment.

Figure 15–3 Bits are as important as the type of electric file you choose.

Figure 15–4 Sanding bits.

Figure 15–5 Diamond bits.

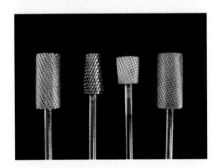

Figure 15–6 Carbide bits.

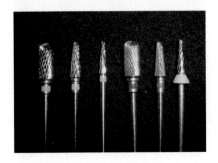

Figure 15–7 Swiss carbide bits.

Types of Bits

There are hundreds of different **bits** available, but there are four types of bits that are most frequently used in salons. These are **sanders** (sleeves), **diamond**, **carbide**, and **Swiss carbide** bits.

Sanders or sleeves are made of paper and fit onto a noncutting bit called a **mandrel**. Sanders or sleeves chip the surface of the product, come in varying grits, and can be used in a back-and-forth motion with the machine in either forward or reverse. Sanders cause the most heat and generate the smallest dust particles of any bit. You should only use medium- and fine-grit sanders and sleeves. These are single-use items and must be thrown away after one use. *Never save or try to disinfect sleeves or sanders* (Figure 15–4).

Diamond bits are made from either natural or synthetic diamond particles attached to the surface of metal bits. Diamond bits come in various grits, chip the surface of the product, and can be use in a back-and-forth motion with the machine in either forward or reverse. Diamond bits vary significantly in quality and price, but are all capable of accomplishing the same procedures. Lower-quality bits cost less, but leave scratches in the surface of the product. If you use these because of budgetary constraints, simply follow with another grit to smooth out the surface of the product. Higher-quality diamond bits have more consistency in construction because each particle on every bit is cut the same size and shape and then adhered to medical stainless steel. These are more desirable, but are much more expensive. In compensation, they also last longer and give much better results than less expensive ones. You should never need to use coarser than medium-grit diamond bits on enhancement products (Figure 15–5).

Carbide bits are available in varying types of metals, shapes, sizes, and grits. These bits have various coatings to enhance filing results. A notable feature about carbide bits is that they have surface cuts called "flutes," which are cut at an angle. These flutes *shave the surface* of the product as they file, instead of chipping like diamond bits. There is less airborne dust when using carbide bits.

There are two types of carbide bits: **traditional** and **cross-cut**. Traditional carbides must be used from right to left with the machine in forward rotation. If used in a back-and-forth motion, traditional carbides will skip on the return stroke, leaving scratches on the surface of the enhancement. With cross-cut carbides, the grooves are cut at the same angle and shave evenly when filing back and forth. Cross-cut carbides can be used to file both directions, and can be used in a back-and-forth filing motion (Figure 15–6).

Like regular carbide bits, Swiss carbide bits have flutes and shave the surface as they file. The difference between the two types of bits is that Swiss carbide bits have rounded ends for safety in filing the cuticle area and sides of the nail. These bits are made of high-quality medical stainless steel, are crosscut and can be used in a back-and-forth motion when filing.

Swiss carbide bits are excellent for beginners because if used near the side walls and eponychium there is little risk of cutting the skin. This allows the nail professional to focus on building filing techniques without being afraid of cutting the client (Figure 15–7).

Never use carbide or Swiss carbide bits on the natural nail!

Buffing Bits

These bits are made from soft, natural materials such as chamois, leather, goat's hair, or cotton rag. All are effective in applying buffing cream and bringing nails to a high-gloss shine. These bits can be reused just like towels, and should be cleaned by washing with soap and water or in a washing machine at the end of each day (Figure 15–8).

Figure 15–8 Buffing bits.

Pedicure Bits

These are made of diamond, sapphire, and ruby particles, and are used to smooth calluses. Some bits can be used with callus reduction products on thick areas of the heel.

Jewelry Bits

A long, slender carbide has been made for drilling a hole into the free edge of an artificial nail to attach nail jewelry (Figure 15–9). Only use jewelry bits on the extended free edge of the nail, and never over the nail bed.

Figure 15–9 Pedicure and jewelry bits.

Cleaning and Disinfecting Bits

Cleaning and disinfecting bits is the same for other disinfectable multiuse tools and implements. Never use a bit on a client that has not been properly sanitized and disinfected. Before disinfecting, clean the bit to remove all visible debris with a brush, an ultrasonic unit, or soaking the bit in acetone. After cleaning, completely immerse metal bits in a disinfectant solution that is correctly diluted for 10 minutes. Rinse and dry the bits and then store them in a sanitary manner. A bit holder on top of the table is fine (does not need to be covered) as long as there is no dust or debris on the bits.

Rusting

Two things can cause bits to rust: poor quality metals and leaving the bits in a disinfecting solution for more than 10 minutes.

here's a tip...

Never reach into a disinfectant solution to remove bits. Use a pair of tweezers or tongs if a lift tray is not available. Disinfectants can irritate or damage fingers with repeated exposure.

HOW TO USE AN ELECTRIC FILE

Use a balance finger for better control during filing. Start by balancing your arms on the table. Do not work holding your hand suspended above the table (Figure 15–10). Brace your hands together much as you do when applying nail polish. This keeps the client's finger secure and avoids movement during filing. Balance the pinky finger of your filing hand on the tip of the pinky that you extend. This may seem awkward at first, but will give you better stability as you work. By balancing your hands this way, it takes the downward pressure off the tip of the bit and gives you better control. Hold the handpiece as you would hold a pencil.

Important Things to Remember

1. Use the **correct bit angle.** When using an electric file, it is important to always keep the bit flat and parallel with the table to avoid causing damage to the nail.

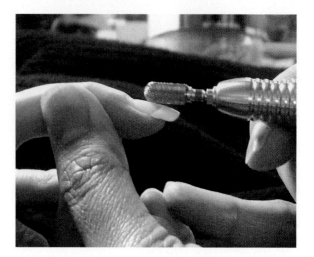

Figure 15–10   Use the balance finger to achieve proper balance and control.

2. Avoid **rings of fire**. Rings of fire are caused by holding bits at the wrong angle, which allows the edge of the bit to dig into the surface of the nail. This can cause damage to the natural nail (Figure 15–11).

3. Choose the **correct speed.** Be sure to use a safe working speed. Higher speeds allow you to use less pressure. If the bit grabs and wraps around the finger, this is an indication that your filing hand is tense. If the speed of the electric file "bogs down," the speed is too low.

Artificial Product Maintenance

To prep artificial nails for rebalancing, use a medium-grit bit to smooth old product in the growth area of the nail. Keep the bit parallel to the table and reduce the product down to the natural nail without touching the nail itself.

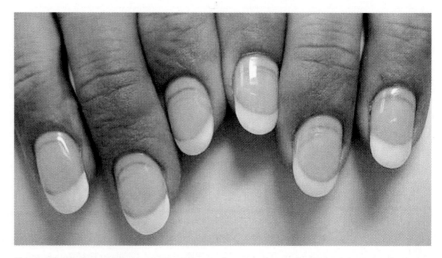

Figure 15–11   Rings of fire.

Removing Lifted Product

Never nip loose nail enhancement product. Many bits can be used to remove the lifted areas and loose product. This is an advanced technique; take a course before you attempt this.

Cracks

Use a slender barrel or bullet bit and place it sideways into the crack. Slowly bevel a trench with the body of the bit, exposing the crack so that new product can fill in the groove and reinforce that area.

Shaping C-Curves

Barrel-shaped or tapered Swiss carbide bits are best to use under the free edge to refine C-curves.

Rebalances

A rebalance can be performed in a variety of ways. Some techs prefer to reduce the entire nail and apply a new layer of product, and some prefer to simply thin the product at the growth area. Either can be done with any shaped medium-grit bit. Use care not to touch the natural nail when filing.

Finishing

Graduating grits is the key to finishing nails without leaving scratches. Graduate bits from coarser to finer as with hand-held abrasives. Remember that the coarsest grit needed for electric files is medium. Removing the dust each time bits are changed will make the final results smoother.

Buffing Oils

The use of buffing oils can enhance your finish work by reducing heat and holding dust on the surface of the bit. Never use buffing oil before applying UV gel sealers—this can cause the product to lift or discolor.

High-Shine Buffing

After filing to a smooth finish, artificial nails can be shined with a buffing bit and buffing cream. Lift the bit frequently and do not to apply too much pressure; these bits can heat up quickly and burn your client.

Buffing Creams

The use of buffing creams enhances the shine with buffing bits. Most creams come with pumice and can be used with any buffer bit.

TROUBLESHOOTING

Reducing Dust

Because of the way that bits cut, different types of bits cause different sizes of dust particles. The smallest particles are caused by sanders or sleeves. The dust is finer and flies higher into the air and can enter your breathing zone. If you use sanders, wear an appropriate dust mask when filing.

Diamond bits create slightly heavier particles that do not fly as high into the air and are not as likely to enter the breathing zone.

Carbide and Swiss carbide bits shave the surface of the product, create heavier particles that are directed down toward the table. There is very little airborne dust when using carbide or Swiss carbide bits.

Heat

Improper filing techniques can cause heat to build up on the nail. Heat is caused by pressing down too hard toward the nail when filing. Heat can cause the client discomfort and can damage the natural nail. If a client says, "ouch, that's hot," what do you do with your machine speed? Your first instinct is to turn it down (reduce speed). But if you reduce the speed, you have to press harder and that will cause more heat! The proper course of action is to turn the speed of the machine *up* (increase speed slightly) and *reduce* the pressure down! Always lift the bit frequently during filing.

Causes of Heat

- Applying too much down pressure during filing
- Incorrect speed (RPM)
- Leaving the bit in the same place for too long while filing
- Using sanders or sleeves—these generate more heat than metal bits

Solutions to Reduce Heat

- Adjust the speed of machine (RPM)
- Apply less pressure during filing
- Lift the bit frequently during filing
- Use quality metal bits

Grabbing

Grabbing occurs when the bit "grabs" the skin around the nail during filing. Grabbing can be avoided by using the bit at the proper angle when working around sidewalls and the cuticle area. It is important to remember that bits have two sides; we tend to look at the side toward the center of the nail while filing. It is the other side that is on or near the skin that can grab and cut the skin. Bits turn clockwise so it is a given that the bit will dig into the skin if it gets too close to the sides of the nail.

Potential Causes of Grabbing

- Bit too close to the skin
- Improper angle of the bit

Solutions to Grabbing

- Keep the bit parallel to table.
- Angle the finger, not the bit, to file the sides of the nail and the cuticle area.
- Use bits with rounded ends (Swiss carbides or safety bits).

Rings of Fire

Causes of Rings of Fire

- Wrong angle of the bit
- Too much pressure on front of the bit

Solutions to Rings of Fire

- Keep the bit parallel to the table.
- Increase the speed of your machine.
- Reduce the amount of pressure applied down during filing.

Product Breakdown

Artificial enhancement products are like a jungle of vines that are densely packed. Trauma, heat, and vibration can cause the vines to snap. Trauma, vibration, or damage to the product can break down the product and weaken the enhancement, especially with older product. **Free edge separation** can be caused by rebalancing incorrectly. This can cause from loss of adhesion of the product to the nail.

After several weeks, especially into the fourth or fifth week after original application, products can become brittle. **Microshattering** is most likely to occur after the second fill or maintenance appointment.

Potential Causes of Microshattering

- Improper speed of the machine during filing
- Poor quality or bent bits
- Using bits that are too coarse
- Using low-quality and brittle nail enhancement products
- Holding the handpiece at the wrong angle
- Poor skills in application of products
- Working too aggressively with the machine

Solutions to Microshattering

- Use a slower speed.
- Use proper filing techniques.

○ Keep the bit parallel to the table during filing.

○ Use correct application techniques.

○ Make sure the bit is not bent.

○ Use a finer grit bit.

○ Use quality products according to manufacturer's instructions.

○ Receive more education on how to properly use these devices.

Vibration

High vibration is something to avoid when using an electric file. Vibration can create problems with enhancement products, and can be harmful to the nail professional's hand, wrist. and arm as well, and may lead to cumulative trauma disorders such as carpal tunnel syndrome. Choose a machine with the least vibration possible.

The best way to test the vibration of a machine is to hold the handpiece, turn on the power, and feel the vibration. If the vibration is high and it is uncomfortable just holding it for a minute or so, it will be a problem when you use the machine in the salon.

Safety Tips for Electric Filing

Keep the bit parallel to the table.

Angle the client's hand, not the handpiece.

Compensate for pressure with speed. If you feel that you need to press harder, increase the speed of the machine and *reduce* the pressure you apply to the nail.

Lift the bit frequently when filing to avoid causing heat build-up. Avoid using bits in a heavy-handed or aggressive way.

Keep bit straight up and down when shortening the free edge to avoid skipping, which can cause the product to weaken and break down.

Turn the client's hand, not the bit, to file around the side walls and cuticle area.

Keep long hair tied back or put up so that that it is not caught in the handpiece.

Wear a dust mask during filing to avoid inhaling dust particles.

Get proper education before using any machine or product.

Be sure to pay attention to what you are doing, and use care while working with any product or machine on a client.

Wear eye protection when filing to avoid dust particles from getting into the eyes.

Avoid repetitive motions that cause pain, swelling or injury to the wrist, elbow, shoulder arms or back.

YOU HAVE THE VALUE

A true nail professional will recognize the value of seeking advanced training on correctly and safely using an electric file before using one on a client. An electric file is a safe tool in the hands of a skilled and knowledgeable user. Remember to practice proper sanitation and disinfection, and always use electric files safely. You will find that this will enhance your work as well as save you time and money.

safety caution!

Remember that electric filing should never hurt or injure the client, nor should this tool cause nail plate damage. If it does, re-evaluate the way you are using the electric file and seek additional education. Never use an electric file on the natural nail until you have received advanced education.

REVIEW QUESTIONS

1. Can electric files be used safely?
2. What types of electric file are most often used by nail professionals?
3. Define torque.
4. Define RPM.
5. Which type of bits have grits?
6. How are carbide bits different from those with grits?
7. What causes clients to feel excessive heat?
8. How do you clean and disinfect bits?
9. Why should bits be concentric?
10. Which shank sizes cannot be used in professional electric files?

CHAPTER GLOSSARY

bit	Attachment to the machine that actually does the filing.
concentric	Balanced bits that do not wobble or vibrate.
flute	Long, slender cut or groove found on carbide and Swiss carbide bits.
grit	Number of abrasive particles per square inch.
revolutions per minute (RPM)	Number of times a bit rotates in 1 minute.
rings of fire	Grooves carved into the nail caused by filing with bits at the incorrect angle.
torque	Power of machine or its ability to keep turning when applying pressure during filing.

Nail Tips, Wraps, and No-Light Gels

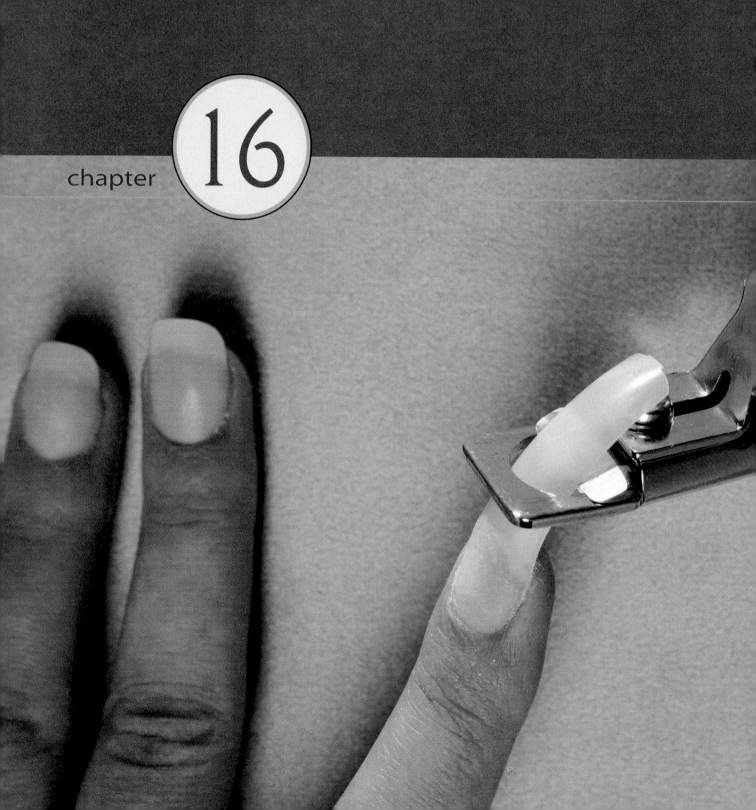

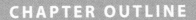

CHAPTER OUTLINE

- Nail Tips
- Nail Wraps
- No-Light Gels

LEARNING OBJECTIVES

After completing this chapter, you will be able to:

1. Identify the supplies needed for nail tips and explain why they are needed.

2. Identify the three types of nail tips.

3. Demonstrate the proper procedure and precautions to use in applying nail tips.

4. Demonstrate the proper removal of tips.

5. List four kinds of nail wraps and what they are used for.

6. Explain benefits of using silk, linen, fiberglass, and paper wraps.

7. Demonstrate the proper procedures and precautions used in fabric wrap application.

8. Describe the maintenance of fabric wrap. Include a description of the 2-week and 4-week rebalance.

9. Explain how to use fabric wrap for crack repairs.

10. Demonstrate the proper procedure and precautions for fabric wrap removal.

11. Define no-light gels.

12. Demonstrate the proper procedures for applying no-light gels.

KEY TERMS

Page number indicates where in the chapter the term is used.

abrasive board pg. 277	**fiberglass** pg. 281	**nail wrap** pg. 281	**silk** pg. 281
ABS pg. 276	**linen** pg. 281	**no-light gel** pg. 291	**stress strip** pg. 289
buffer block pg. 277	**nail tip** pg. 276	**paper wrap** pg. 282	**tip cutter** pg. 279
fabric wrap pg. 281	**nail tip adhesive** pg. 277	**repair patch** pg. 289	

O ne of the most popular services that a nail professional can offer clients is the opportunity to wear beautifully cared for nails in almost an endless variety of length and strength. In many cases, this is accomplished by the use of a **nail tip**, a plastic, pre-molded nail shaped from a tough polymer made from **ABS** or tenite acetate. Nail tips are adhered to the natural nail to add extra length and to serve as a support for nail enhancement product. Tips are combined with another service, such as a fabric wrap, overlay, or sculptured nail extensions. Nail tips are not long-wearing and can break easily without reinforcement called an **overlay**. Overlays are acrylic (methacrylate) liquid and powder, wraps or UV gels applied over a tip for added strength. These tips serve as a support for nail enhancement products. Sculpting a nail requires more technical skill, so nail tips were created to serve as a "canvas" to create a beautiful nail. In this chapter, you will learn the correct way to apply nail tips.

NAIL TIPS

This section begins with a list of supplies required for nail tip application. Procedures for nail tip application pre-service, nail tip application, post-service nail tip application, and removing nail tips follow.

Supplies for Nail Tips

In addition to the materials on your basic manicuring table, you will need the following supplies for nail tip application (Figure 16–1).

> **Abrasive board.** Rough surface that is used to shape or smooth the nail and remove surface shine They come in many shapes, sizes, and colors.

Nail Tip Application Post-Service

1. **Make another appointment.** Schedule another appointment with your client to return in 2 or 3 weeks to have the nails manicured and rebalanced, and possibly for a pedicure as well.

2. **Take-home product recommendations.** Suggest professional products that you believe your client would benefit from, such as polish, top coat, and hand lotions, among others. These are valuable maintenance tools for clients to have at home and they will appreciate your professional recommendation.

3. **Clean up around your table.** Take the time to restore the basic setup of your table, re-stock supplies, and make sure that all caps are tight.

4. **Discard used materials.** Place all used materials into the trash receptacle.

5. **Clean your table, and then sanitize and disinfect implements and multiuse tools, such as abrasives implements.** Perform complete pre-service sanitation and disinfection procedures. Implements need to be cleaned and disinfected before they can be used on the next client, and this procedure will take about 20 minutes.

NAIL WRAPS

Nail wraps are types of nail enhancements made by using a nail-size piece of cloth or paper bonded to the top of the nail plate with **wrap resin**. It is the heart of a nail wrap system and what gives these systems their unique properties. These systems can be used to lengthen the natural nail, but are most often used as coatings or "overlays" on the natural nail plate and on nail tips. Wrap resins are made from cyanoacrylate monomers, and are closely related to those used to create other types of artificial nail enhancements. Nail wraps are used to repair or strengthen natural nails or to create nail extensions. Wraps can be cut from a swatch of cloth, rolls of fabric, or a piece of paper to fit a client's nail size and shape, or they can be purchased pre-cut. Pre-cut overlays have an adhesive backing.

Fabric wraps are made from silk, linen, or fiberglass. **Silk** is a thin natural material with a tight weave that becomes transparent when wrap resin is applied. A silk wrap is lightweight and has a smooth appearance when applied to the nail. **Linen** is a closely woven, heavy material. It is much thicker and bulkier than other types of wrap fabrics. Wrap resins do not penetrate linen as easily as silk or fiberglass. Because it is opaque, even after adhesive is applied, a colored polish must be used to cover it completely. Linen is used because it is considered to the strongest wrap fabric. A **fiberglass** wrap is a very thin synthetic mesh with a loose weave. The loose weave makes it easy to use and for adhesive to penetrate, which improves adhesion. Even though fiberglass is not as strong as linen or silk, it can create a durable nail enhancement. **Paper wraps** are made of very thin paper. Paper was one of the very first materials used to create wraps. They are quite simple to use, but do not have the strength and durability of fabric wraps. For this reason, paper wraps are considered a temporary service.

Fabric Wraps

Supplies

In addition to the materials on your basic manicuring table, you will need the items in the following list (Figure 16–12).

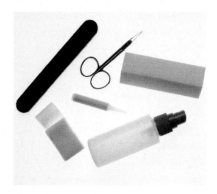

Figure 16–12 Materials necessary for fabric wrap application.

> **Fabric.** Small swatches of linen, silk, or fiberglass material can be cut to fit a client's nail size and shape. You may also find pre-cut wrap material with an adhesive backing.
>
> **Nail tip adhesive.** Adhesives are used to secure the nail tip or fabric to the natural nail. The adhesive usually comes in a tube with a pointed applicator tip called an **extender tip** or in brush-on form. When working with wrap resins, be sure to protect your eyes with protective eyewear and offer them to your client as well.
>
> **Wrap resin and activator.** Resin and its hardening activator for application to the fabric. The manufacturer's instructions for using these products may differ slightly from the general guidelines presented below. Activators speed up the curing process of resins and adhesives. When used incorrectly, they may cause a heat spike that can be uncomfortable to the client and could even cause nail bed damage. You must always use products in accordance with the manufacturer's instructions. Also, your instructor may teach slightly different techniques that are equally correct.
>
> **Small scissors.** Use small and sharp scissors for cutting fabric.
>
> **Nail buffer or adhesive.**
>
> **Small piece of plastic or tweezers.**

Nail Wrap Pre-Service

Use the following preparation for all nail wrap procedures.

1. Perform the pre-service sanitation and disinfection procedure. (This procedure is described in chapter 13.)

2. Set up a standard manicuring table. Add fabric, wrap resin and activator, small scissors, nail buffer, and a small square of thin plastic sheeting to your table.

3. Greet your client and ask him to wash his hands with liquid soap and to rinse thoroughly with warm running water. Dry hands and nails thoroughly with a clean fabric or disposable towel.

CHAPTER **GLOSSARY**

abrasive board	Thin, elongated board with a rough surface.
ABS	Acrylonitrile butadiene styrene.
buffer block	Lightweight, rectangular abrasive block.
fabric wrap	Nail wrap made of silk, linen, or fiberglass.
fiberglass	Very thin synthetic mesh with a loose weave.
linen	Closely woven, heavy material used for nail wraps.
nail tip	Artificial nail made of ABS or tenite acetate polymer that is adhered to the natural nail to add length.
nail tip adhesive	Liquid or gel-like product made from cyanoacrylate monomer, and used to secure a nail tip to the natural nail.
nail wrap	Nail-size pieces of cloth or paper that are bonded to the top of the nail plate with nail adhesive; often used to repair or strengthen natural nails or nail tips.
no-light gel	Thickened cyanoacrylate monomers.
paper wrap	Temporary nail wrap made of very thin paper. Not nearly as strong as fabric wraps.
repair patch	Piece of fabric cut to completely cover a crack or break in the nail during a 4-week fabric wrap maintenance procedure.
silk	Thin, natural material with a tight weave that becomes transparent when adhesive is applied.
stress strip	Strip of fabric, $1/8$" long, applied during a 4-week fabric wrap rebalance to repair or strengthen a weak point in a nail enhancement.
tip cutter	Implement similar to a nail clipper, designed especially for use on nail tips.

Acrylic (Methacrylate)
Nail Enhancements

chapter **17**

LEARNING OBJECTIVES

After completing this chapter, you will be able to:

1. Explain acrylic (methacrylate) nail enhancement chemistry and how it works.

2. List the supplies needed for acrylic (methacrylate) nail enhancements application.

3. Demonstrate the proper procedures for applying acrylic (methacrylate) nail enhancements, using forms, over tips, and on natural nails.

4. Practice safety precautions involving the application of nail primers.

5. Describe the proper procedure for maintaining healthy acrylic (methacrylate) nail enhancements.

6. Perform regular rebalance procedures and repairs.

7. Implement the proper procedure for removal of acrylic (methacrylate) nail enhancements.

8. Explain how the application of odorless acrylic (methacrylate) products differs from the application of traditional acrylic (methacrylate) products.

KEY **TERMS**

Page number indicates where in the chapter the term is used.

EDITOR'S NOTE: Nail enhancements based on mixing together liquids and powders are commonly referred to as "acrylic" (a-KRYL-yk) nails. It might surprise you to discover the real definition of "acrylic," since for many years this word has actually been used incorrectly by the nail enhancement industry. The term "acrylic" actually refers to an entire family of thousands of different substances, but all share important, closely related features. Acrylics are used to make a wide range of things including contact lenses, cements for mending broken bones, Plexiglas windows, and even makeup and other cosmetics. Surprisingly, all artificial nail enhancement products are based almost entirely on ingredients that come from the acrylic family. For example, the ingredients in two-part liquid and powder enhancement systems belong to a sub-branch of the acrylic family called "methacrylates." In other words, "acrylic" is a very general term for a large group of ingredients. Liquid and powder artificial nail enhancement products are based on the **methacrylates** *(METH-ah-cry-latz) subcategory. You can see some similarity in the spelling of the terms, which indicates that they are from the same chemical family or group. To avoid further confusion, you will find that the two-part liquid and powder enhancement system in this book will be referred to as acrylic (methacrylate) nails.*

Acrylic (methacrylate) nail enhancements are created by combining monomer (MON-oh-mehr) liquid and **polymer** (POL-i-mehr) powder; thus the name liquid and powder. "Mono" means "one" and "mer" stands for "units," so a monomer is one unit called a "molecule." "Poly" means "many," so polymer means "many units" or many molecules. This is important to remember, since you will hear these terms many times throughout your career.

Liquid and powder products can be applied in three basic ways:

1. Applied to the natural nail as a protective overlay

2. Over a nail tip

3. Sculpted to extend the natural nail using a flexible form

A natural hair brush is the best device to use in applying these products. The brush is immersed in the monomer liquid. The natural hair bristles absorb and hold the monomer like a reservoir. The tip of the brush is then touched to the surface of the dry polymer powder, and as the monomer liquid absorbs the polymer powder, a small bead of product forms. This small bead is then carefully placed on the nail surface and molded into shape with the brush. The liquid portion is usually based on **ethyl methacrylate** monomer, but often contains other monomers used as customizing additives.

It may seem strange to learn that polymer powder is also made mostly from ethyl methacrylate monomer. The polymer powder is made using a special chemical reaction called **polymerization** (POL-i-mehr-eh-za-shun). In this process, trillions of monomers are linked together to create long chains. These long chains create the tiny round beads of polymer powder used to create certain types of artificial nails.

During the production of the polymer, the powder forms into tiny round beads of slightly varying sizes. These are poured through a series of special screens that sort the beads by size. The ones that are the right size are separated and then mixed with other special additives and colorants. The final mixture is packaged and sold as acrylic (methacrylate) polymer powder. It is a surprisingly high-tech process that requires very special manufacturing equipment, lots of quality control, and scientific know-how to do it right.

Special additives are actually blended into both the liquid and powder. These additives ensure complete set or cure, maximum durability, color stability, and shelf-life, among other attributes. It is these special "custom" additives that make different products work and behave differently. The polymer powders are usually blended with pigments and colorants to create a wide range of shades, including pinks, whites, and milky translucents, as well as reds, blues, greens, purples, yellows, oranges, browns, and even jet black.

When liquid is picked up by a brush and mixed with the powder, the bead that forms on the end of the brush quickly begins to harden. It is then put into place with other beads and shaped into place as they harden. In order for this process to begin, the monomers and polymers require special additives called **catalysts** (KAT-a-list) and **initiators.** A catalyst is an additive designed to speed up chemical reactions. Catalysts are added to the monomer liquid and used to control the set or curing time. In other words, when the monomer liquid and polymer powder are combined, the catalyst (in the liquid) helps control the set-up or hardening time. How? The catalyst energizes and activates the initiators. The initiators start a **chain reaction** that leads to the creation of fantastically long polymer chains. It is actually the initiators found in the powder that (once activated) will spring into action and start causing monomer molecules to permanently link together into these long polymer chains. This is another example of the polymerization process discussed above, except this time, its actually occurring on the fingernail. The polymerization process begins the second the liquid in the brush picks up powder from the container and forms a bead. Creating polymers can be thought of as a chain reaction, much like many dominos lined up and set on their edges—tap the first domino, it hits the next, and so on. This is how polymers form. Once the monomers join together to create a polymer, they do not detach from each other easily. The initiator that is added to the polymer powder is called benzoyl peroxide (BPO). It is the same ingredient used in over-the-counter acne medicine, except that it has a different purpose in nail enhancement products. BPO is used to start the chain reaction that leads to curing (hardening) of the nail enhancement. There is much less BPO in nail powders than in acne treatments. Diverse nail enhancement products often use different amounts of BPO, since the polymer powders are designed to work specifically with a certain monomer liquid. Some monomer liquids require more BPO to properly cure than others. This is why it is very important to use the polymer powder that was designed for use with the monomer liquid that you are using. Using the wrong powder can create nail enhancements that are not properly cured and may lead to service breakdown or could increase the risk of your clients developing a skin irritation or sensitivity. To learn more about how products work and how to troubleshoot problems, see *Nail Structure and Product Chemistry*, second edition, by Douglas Schoon (Thomson Delmar Learning, 2005).

ACRYLIC (METHACRYLATE) NAIL ENHANCEMENTS USING FORMS

Today's acrylic (methacrylate) polymer powders come in many colors, including variations of basic pink, white, clear, and natural. These colors can be used alone or blended to create everything from customized shades of pink to match or enhance the color of your client's nail beds, to bold primaries or pastels that can be used to create a wide range of designs and patterns. With these powders you can create unique colors or designs that can be locked permanently in the artificial nail. They offer a wonderful way to customize your services or to express your artistry and creativity. Acrylic (methacrylate) overlays and nail enhancements can be created with a single color powder, if the client wears nail polish all the time. Or they can be created by using a pink or natural colored powder over the nail bed or a natural or soft white powder to replicate a natural nail free edge. A stark white powder can be use to create the French manicure look. The finished nail enhancement can be polished with nail polish or buffed to a high-glossy shine for a more natural look. These types of services are extremely versatile and highly durable, which partially explains their great popularity.

Supplies for Acrylic (Methacrylate) Nail Enhancements

In addition to the supplies in your basic manicuring setup, you will need the items listed below (Figure 17–1).

Acrylic (methacrylate) monomer liquid. The monomer liquid will be combined with acrylic (methacrylate) polymer powder to form the sculptured nail. The amount of monomer liquid and polymer powder used to create a bead is called the **mix ratio**. A bead mix ratio can be best described as "dry," "medium," or "wet." If equal amounts of liquid and powder are used to create the bead, it is called a "dry bead." If twice as much liquid as powder is found in the bead, it is called a "wet bead." Halfway between these two is a "medium" bead, which consist of 50 percent more liquid than powder. In general, medium beads are the ideal mix ratio for working with monomer liquids and polymer powders. Mix ratio typically ensures proper set and maximum durability of the nail enhancement. For instance, if too much or too little flour is added when making cookies, the cookies will be dry and crumbly (too much flour) or too soft and gooey (too little flour). The same holds true for monomer liquids and polymer powders. If too much powder is picked up in the bead, the enhancement will cure incorrectly and may lead to brittleness and/or discoloration. If too little powder is used, the nail enhancement can become weak, and the risk of clients developing skin irritation and sensitivity may increase.

Acrylic (methacrylate) polymer powder. Polymer powder in white, clear, natural, pink, and many other colors is available. The color(s) you choose will depend on the nail enhancement method you are using.

Nail dehydrator. Apply liberally to natural nail plate only and avoid skin contact. Nail dehydrators remove surface moisture and tiny amounts of oil left on the natural nail plate, both of which can block ad-

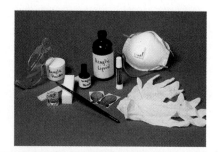

Figure 17–1 Materials needed for application of acrylic (methacrylate) nail enhancements.

hesion. This step is a great way to help prevent lifting of the artificial nail enhancements.

Nail primer. Many kinds of nail primers are available today. Acid-based primer (methacrylic acid) was once widely used to enhance the adhesion of enhancements to the natural nail. Since this type of nail primer is corrosive to the skin and potentially dangerous to eyes, "acid free" and "nonacid primers" were developed and are in wide use today. These alternatives work as well as or better than acid-based nail primers. Since they are not corrosive to skin or eyes, they have an added advantage. Even so, all nail primer product must be used with caution, and skin contact must be avoided. Read the manufacturer's instructions and refer to the respective MSDS sheet for safe handling recommendations and instructions. Acid-based nail primers must be used with caution and strictly in accordance with the manufacturer's instructions.

For acid-based nail primers: Using a tiny applicator brush, insert the brush tip into the nail primer. Touch the brush tip to the edge of the bottle's neck to release the excess primer back into the bottle. With a relatively dry brush, using a light dotting action, carefully dab the brush tip to the center of the properly prepared natural nail. The acid-based primer will spread out and cover the nail plate. Do not use too much product to avoid running into the skin and causing burns or injury. *Be sure to read the label for the manufacturer's suggested use and precautions.*

For nonacid and acid-free nail primers: Using the applicator brush, insert brush into the nail primer. Wipe off excess from the brush and using a slightly damp brush, ensure that the nail plate is completely covered. Avoid using too much product to avoid running into the skin and causing skin irritation or sensitivity. The brush should hold enough product to treat two or three nails before dipping back into the container. Be sure the entire nail plate is covered. Also, read the label for the manufacturer's suggested application procedures and precautions.

Abrasives. Select a medium grit (180 to 240) for natural nail preparation and initial shaping. Choose a medium grit for smoothing and a fine buffer (350 grit or higher) for final buffing. A three-way buffer is used to create a high shine on the enhancement when no polish is worn. If you avoid putting the product on too thickly, a 180 grit is usually enough to shape the nail enhancement. Avoid using coarser (lower-grit) abrasives on freshly applied enhancement product, since they can create damage to the freshly created nail enhancement. **Acrylic (methacrylate) nail enhancements** take 24 to 48 hours to reach peak strength. Using overly coarse abrasives or aggressive techniques on freshly applied enhancement products of any type must be avoided.

Nail forms. These are placed under the free edge and used to extend the nail enhancements beyond the fingertip for additional length.

here's a tip...

Manufacturer's instructions for using these products may differ slightly from the general guidelines presented below. You should always use products in accordance with the manufacturer's instructions.

here's a tip...

Hand sanitizers do not clean the hands. They cannot remove dirt or debris from hands. They only kill some of the bacteria on skin, not all of it. But, they do give clients peace of mind. Clients like to see nail professionals using hand sanitizers and many clients prefer to use them as well. Keep a high-quality, professional hand sanitizer at your station and offer some to your clients. Let them see you using it, and they will have a greater degree of confidence in the cleanliness of your services. But do not let them replace hand washing—there is no replacement for that.

here's a tip...

The best way to dispose of small amounts of liquid monomer is to mix them with small amounts of the corresponding powder design to cure them. (This is safe for volumes less than a half-ounce of monomer liquid, as well as ounces, quarts, or gallons.) They should never be disposed of in the trash or down the drain. Tiny amounts left in a dappen dish can be wiped out with a paper towel and disposed of in a metal trash can with a self-closing lid, as long as skin contact is avoided during the process and the trash is disposed of several times during the day so that vapors do not just evaporate and escape into the salon air.

These nail forms are often made of paper/mylar coated with adhesive backs, or pre-shaped plastic or aluminum. Each of these forms is disposable, excepting aluminum forms, which can be properly cleaned and disinfected.

Nail tips. These are pre-formed nail extensions made from ABS or tenite acetate plastic, and are available in a wide variety of shapes, styles, and colors, such as natural, white, and clear. (See Chapter 16 for more information and instructions.)

Nail adhesive. There are many types of nail adhesives used for securing nail tips to the natural nails, but they are all based on cyanoacrylate monomers. Each type uses different, customized additives to enhance set times, strength, and other properties. It is chiefly the special additives that a manufacturer chooses that make these adhesives different from each another.

Choose a small size (4 to 6 grams maximum) because these adhesives have a short shelf life and can expire within 6 months after the date of purchase, depending on usage and storage conditions. To obtain the maximum shelf life, be sure to close the cap securely, set upright, and store out of direct sunlight and at room temperature between 60° to 85°F. If you do not, the nail adhesive may harden in the tube and will have to be discarded.

Dappen dish. The monomer liquid and polymer powder are each poured into a special holder called a dappen dish. These dishes must have narrow openings to minimize evaporation of the monomer into the air. Do not use open-mouth jars or other containers with large openings. These will dramatically increase evaporation of your liquid and can allow the product to be contaminated with dust and other debris. Your dappen dish must be covered with a tightly fitting lid when not in use. Each time the brush is dipped into the dappen dish, the remaining monomer is contaminated with small amounts of polymer powder. So *never* pour the unused portion of monomer back into the original container. Empty the monomer from your dappen dish after the service and wipe it clean with a disposable towel. Avoid skin contact with monomer during this process to avoid skin irritation or sensitivity. Wipe clean with acetone, if necessary, before storing in a dust-free location.

Nail brush. The best brush for use with these types of procedures is composed of sable hair. Synthetic and less expensive brushes do not pick up enough monomer liquid or do not release the liquid properly. Choose the brush shape and size with which you feel the most comfortable. Avoid overly large brushes, since they can hold excessive amounts of liquid that may dilute the enhancement product and lead to service breakdown. They also increase the risk of accidentally touching the client's skin with liquid monomer and may increase the risk of developing skin irritation or sensitivities.

Safety eyewear. Safety eyewear should be used to protect eyes from flying objects or accidental slashes. There are many types and styles to

COLORED ACRYLIC (METHACRYLATE) POWDERS

Polymer powders are now available in a wide range of colors that mimic almost every shade available in nail polish. Nail artistry with acrylic (methacrylate) nails is limited only by your imagination. Some nail professionals use colors to go beyond the traditional pink and white French manicure combinations and offer custom blended colors to their clients. They maintain recipe cards so that they can reproduce these custom blends on demand. This new technique allows nail professionals to create customized nail enhancements that your clients cannot get from anyone else. As with all customized techniques, clients are willing to pay a few dollars more for the special service.

Also, don't forget to offer gift certificates in all denominations.

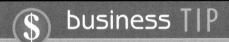

CELEBRATE THE HOLIDAYS

Take advantage of gift-giving holidays such as Christmas, Chanukah, St. Valentine's Day, Secretary's Day, and Mother's Day to provide your customers with professional products that were designed for you to retail. It's easy to make lots of extra money during the holidays. Decorate festively to encourage clients to consider shopping for presents, and offer a wide range of gifts that customers can conveniently buy while they are at their appointments. Try creating two or three festive packages with different product combinations and sizes, priced from $5.00 to $15.00. People buy these for stocking stuffers or to give them as office or church/synagogue gifts. They will thank you for making their shopping easier and for your professional product recommendations.

REVIEW **QUESTIONS**

1. Describe the origin of acrylic nail chemistry and what makes it work.

2. List the supplies needed for nail enhancement application.

3. Describe the procedures for application of nail enhancements using forms and using tips, and as an overlay on natural nails.

4. Describe precautions that must be taken to safely apply acid-based nail primers. What must be avoided?

5. Describe how catalysts work and explain where they are found in acrylic (methacrylate) nail enhancement systems.

6. Describe how accelerators work and explain where they are found in acrylic (methacrylate) nail enhancement systems.

7. Describe how to perform a rebalance on nail enhancements using monomer liquid and polymer powder.

8. Describe the proper procedure for removing the nail enhancements.

9. Explain how the application of odorless enhancement products differs from the application of traditional acrylic (methacrylate) nail products based on ethyl acrylic (methacrylate).

10. Explain why it is important to use the powder that was designed for the liquid monomer that you are using.

CHAPTER **GLOSSARY**

acrylic (methacrylate) nail enhancements	A nail enhancement created by combining acrylic (methacrylate) monomer liquid with polymer powder.
catalyst	Substance that speeds up chemical reactions between monomer liquid and polymer powder.
chain reaction	Process that joins together monomers to create very long polymer chains; also called "polymerization reaction."
ethyl acrylic (methacrylate)	Monomer used in most acrylic (methacrylate) monomer and polymer powder systems.
odorless acrylic (methacrylate) product	Nail enhancement product that is slightly different from acrylic (methacrylate) products. These systems use monomers that have a very low odor and do not have the strong smell of products based on ethyl acrylic (methacrylate). If others in the salon cannot smell the monomer liquid when in use, it is considered odorless.
polymer	Substance formed by combining many small molecules (monomers), into very long chain-like structures.
polymerization	Chemical reaction that creates polymers; also called curing or hardening.
rebalancing	Method for maintaining the beauty, durability, and longevity of the nail enhancement.

UV Gels

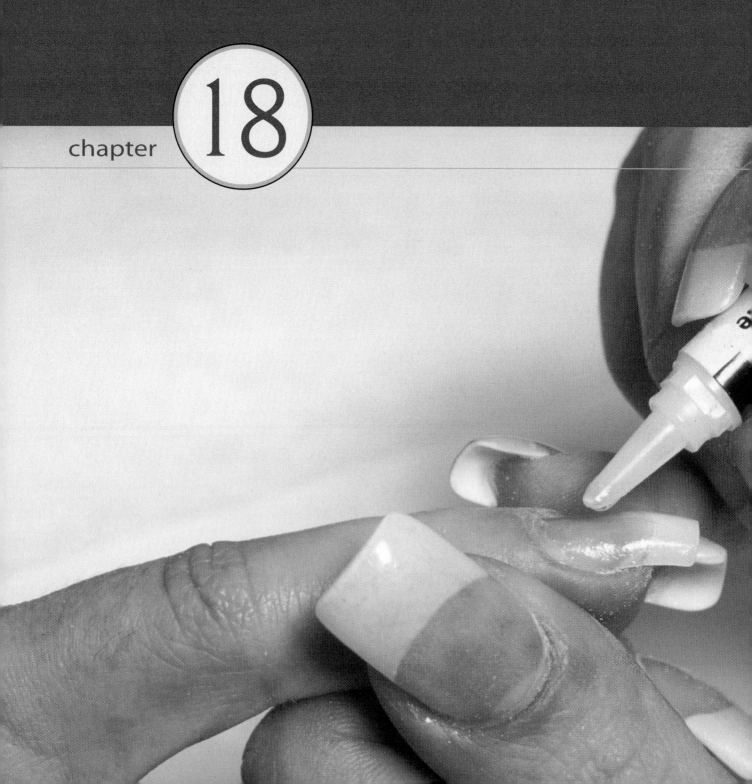

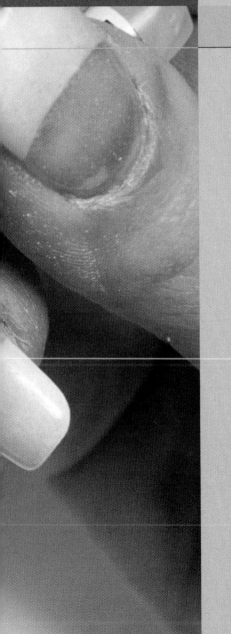

LEARNING OBJECTIVES

After completing this chapter, you will be able to:

1. Describe the chemistry and main ingredients of UV gels.

2. Identify the supplies needed for UV gel application.

3. Demonstrate the proper procedures for maintaining UV gel services using forms over tips and on natural nails.

4. Describe the one-color and two-color methods for applying UV gels.

5. Explain how to safely and correctly remove UV gels.

KEY **TERMS**

Page number indicates where in the chapter the term is used.

inhibition layer
pg. 324

oligomer
pg. 320

one-color method and two-color method
pg. 324

urethane acrylate or urethane methacrylate oligomer
pg. 320

UV gel
pg. 320

UV lamp
pg. 320

UV lightbulb
pg. 321

wattage
pg. 321

T his chapter introduces **UV gels** as an alternative method for an artificial nail enhancement service. Nail enhancements based on UV curing chemistry are not traditionally thought of as being "acrylics," but they are. Like wrap resins, adhesives, and methacrylate nail enhancements, UV gel enhancements rely on ingredients from the acrylic family. Their ingredients are part of a subcategory of this family and are called "acrylates," whereas wrap resins are from the subcategory called "cyanoacrylates," and monomer liquid/polymer powder nail enhancements are from the same category called "methacrylates."

Although most UV gels are made from "acrylates," new UV gel technologies have been recently developed that use their cousins, the "methacrylates." Like wraps and methacrylate nail enhancements, UV gels can also contain monomers, but they rely mostly on a related form called an **oligomer**. Remember the terms "mono" meaning "one" and "poly" meaning "many" in Chapter 16? Now we will add a new term, "oligo," which means "few." An oligomer is a short chain of monomers that is not long enough to be considered a polymer. Since nail enhancement monomers are liquids, while polymers are solids, it is not surprising that oligomers are in between. Oligomers are often thick, gel-like, and sticky. Traditionally, UV gels rely on a special type of acrylate called a **urethane acrylate**, while newer UV gel systems use **urethane methacrylates**.

UV gels can be easy to apply, file, and maintain. They also have the advantage of having very little odor. Although they are not as durable as methacrylate nail enhancements, UV gels can create beautiful, long-lasting nail enhancements. The application process differs from other types of nail enhancements. After the nail plate is properly prepared, each layer of product applied to the natural nail, nail tip, or form requires exposure to UV light to cure or harden. The UV light required for curing comes from a special lamp designed to emit the proper type of UV light.

UV GEL ON TIPS OR NATURAL NAILS

In addition to the materials in your basic manicuring setup, you will need the following items:

○ **UV gel lamps.** UV gel lamps are designed to produce the correct amount of UV light needed to properly cure UV gel nail enhancement products. UV gels are usually packaged in small opaque pots or squeeze tubes to protect them from UV light. Even though UV light is invisible to the eye, it is found in sunlight and tanning lamps.

Also, both "true-color" and "full-spectrum" bulbs emit a significant amount of UV light. If the UV gel product is exposed to these types of ceiling or table lamps, the products shelf life may be shortened, causing the product to harden in its container.

It is important to know that wattage does not indicate how much UV light a **UV lamp** will emit. **Wattage** is a measure of how much electricity the bulb consumes, much like miles per gallon tell you how much gasoline it will take to drive your car a certain distance. Miles per gallon will not tell you how fast the car can go, just like wattage does not indicate how much UV light a lamp will produce. Depending on their circuitry, different lamps and bulbs produce greatly differing amounts of UV light. For these reasons, it is important to use the UV lamp that was designed for the selected UV gel product. Use the lamp that was specifically designed for that UV gel product and you will have a much greater chance of success and fewer problems.

UV light bulbs will stay blue for years, but after a few months of use they may produce too little UV light to properly cure the enhancement. Typically, UV bulbs must be changed two or three times per year, depending on use of the UV lamp. If bulbs are not changed regularly, service breakdown, skin irritation, and sensitivity become more likely to occur.

For more interesting and useful information about UV gel enhancement products, see *Nail Structure and Product Chemistry*, second edition, by Douglas Schoon (Thomson Delmar Learning, 2005).

o **Brush.** Synthetic brushes with small, flat, square bristles to hold and spread the UV gel.

o **UV gel primer.** Primers are designed specifically to improve adhesion of UV gels to the natural nail plate. Use UV gel primers as instructed by the manufacturer of the UV gel product that you are using and heed all recommendations and precautions.

o **Nail tips.** Use nail tips recommended for use with UV gel nail enhancement systems.

o **Nail dehydrator.** Removes surface moisture and tiny amounts of oil left on the natural nail plate, both of which can block adhesion. This step is a great way to help prevent lifting of the nail enhancements.

o **Nail adhesive.** There are many types of nail adhesives for securing pre-formed nail tips to natural nails. Select a type best suited for the work that you are doing. For example, do not purchase large-size containers, unless you can use them up fairly quickly. Even though you can usually save money by purchasing your professional products in bulk amounts, nail adhesives only have a shelf life of 6 months or less, depending on your usage. One way to improve shelf life is to close the cap securely, and store at 60° to 85° Fahrenheit.

o **Abrasive files and buffers.** Select a medium abrasive (180 to 240 grit) for natural nail preparation. Choose a medium/fine abrasive

(240 grit) for smoothing, and a fine buffer (350 grit or higher) for finishing. A high-shine buffer can also be used if desired, and nail polish is not to be worn.

UV Gel Application Pre-Service

1. **Complete the pre-service sanitation and disinfection procedure in Chapter 13.**

2. **Prepare your workstation with everything you need at your fingertips.** Set up your standard manicuring table. Add the additional supplies needed to perform the services to your table. Always have enough supplies to prevent running out while performing the service.

3. **Greet your client with a smile.** Then ask the client to wash hands with liquid soap and rinse with warm running water. You must also wash your hands. Both you and the client must dry hands thoroughly with a clean disposable towel.

4. **If this is your client's first appointment, a client consultation form should be prepared.** Mark the date of the service. This is important in the scheduling of future appointments. Record any skin or nail disorders and allergies, and determine if it is safe and appropriate to perform this service on the client. If the client is a nail biter or does heavy work as a daily routine, write a brief notation. Record any specific information about the service you will perform, such as UV gel overlay without polish, and if polish is preferred, record the client's color preference. This will help keep you in touch with your client's needs.

5. **If this is a return visit, perform client consultation, using the consultation form to record responses and observations.** Check for nail disorders and decide whether it is safe and appropriate to perform a service on this client. If the client cannot receive a service, explain your reasons and refer the client to a doctor, if appropriate.

UV Gel Application Post-Service

Your UV gel service is complete. Follow the post-service procedure described below.

1. **Make another appointment.** Schedule another appointment with the client to maintain nail enhancements. A rebalance will be necessary in 2 or 3 weeks, depending on how quickly the nails grow. Encourage your client to return for a basic manicure between rebalance appointments if the UV gel enhancements are polished.

2. **Recommend take-home products.** Suggest professional products that you believe your client would benefit by using,

PROCEDURE 18-1

LIGHT CURED GEL APPLICATION

1. **Clean nails and remove existing polish.** Begin with your client's little finger on the left hand, and work toward the thumb. Then repeat on the right hand. Ask the client to place nails into a finger bowl with liquid soap. Then use a nail brush to clean nails over the fingerbowl. Thoroughly rinse with clean water to remove soap residues that can cause lifting.

2. **Push back eponychium and carefully remove cuticle from the nail plate.** Use a cotton-tipped wooden or metal pusher to gently push back eponychium, and then apply cuticle remover to the nail plate. Use as directed by the manufacturer and carefully remove cuticle tissue from the nail plate.

3. **Remove oily shine from natural nail surface.** Lightly buff nail plate with medium/fine (240 grit) abrasive to remove the natural oils that cause the shine on the surface of the nail plate.

4. **Apply nail dehydrator.** Apply nail dehydrator to nails with cotton-tipped wooden pusher, cotton pad with a plastic backing, brush, or spray. Begin with the little finger on the left hand and work toward the thumb (Figures 18–1 and 18–2).

5. **Apply nail tips if desired.** If your client requires nail tips, apply them according to the procedure described in Chapter 14. Be sure to shorten and shape tip prior to application of the UV gel. During the procedure, the UV gel overlaps the tip's edge to prevent lifting. During the filing process, the seal can be broken, allowing the UV gel to peel or lift. Be careful not to break this seal (Figure 18–3).

6. **Natural nail preparation.** Follow the manufacturer's instructions for natural nail preparation. Your success as a nail professional depends on your ability to properly prepare the nail plate for services. This is a very important step, so do it well. Using the applicator brush, insert brush into the nail primer. Wipe off excess from brush, and using a slightly damp brush, ensure that the nail plate is completely covered. Avoid using too much product to prevent running into the skin, which can increase the risks of developing skin irritation or sensitivity (Figure 18–4).

7. **Apply first UV gel (base coat gel).** Firmly brush UV gel onto entire nail surface including free edge. Keep UV gel from touching the eponychium or side walls. Leave a tiny free margin between the UV gel enhancement

Figure 18–1 Apply nail plate dehydrator.

Figure 18–2 Remove oily shine from natural nail using vertical strokes.

here's a tip...

The procedure recommended for applying and curing UV gel varies from one manufacturer to another. Some systems recommend applying UV gel to four nails on one hand and curing, and then repeating this procedure on the other hand before applying and curing UV gel on the thumbnails. Be sure to follow the instructions recommended by the manufacturer of the system that you are using.

Figure 18–3 Select nail tip for proper fit, and then trim and shape prior to UV gel application.

Figure 18–4 Carefully apply nail primer to the natural nail and avoid skin contact.

Figure 18–5 Apply first UV gel (base coat UV gel).

product and the skin to reduce the risk of the client developing skin irritation or sensitivity. Apply to client's left hand from pinky to pointer (Figure 18–5). If performing a **one-color method**—that is, nail polish will be worn—you may use a clear, or natural color UV gel. If performing a **two-color method**, you should use a pink or natural color UV gel at this stage.

8 ***Cure first UV gel (base coat gel).*** Properly position the hand in the UV lamp for the required cure time as defined by the manufacturer (Figure 18–6). Always cure each layer of the UV gel for the time required by the manufacturer's instructions. Curing for too little time can result in service breakdown, skin irritation, and/or sensitivity. Improper positioning of the hands inside the lamp can also cause improper curing.

9 ***Repeat steps 8 and 9 on the right hand.*** Then repeat the same steps for both thumbs.

10 ***Apply second UV gel (building UV gel).*** Apply a small amount of UV gel over the properly cured first layer. Carefully pull the UV gel across the first layer, and smooth it into place. Avoid patting the brush or pressing too hard. Brush the UV gel over and around the free edge to create a seal. Avoid touching the skin under the free edge to prevent skin irritation and sensitivity. Repeat this application process for the other four nails on the client's left hand from pinky to pointer. If performing a one-color method, you will use the same colored UV gel as before. If performing a two-color method, use white gels to create a smile line at the free edge. Then apply pink UV gel over remainder of the nail plate, leaving a tiny free margin between the UV gel and skin.

11 ***Cure second UV gel (builder UV gel).*** Properly position the hand in the UV lamp for the manufacturer's required cure time.

12 ***Repeat steps 11 and 12 on the right hand, and then repeat the same steps for both thumbs.***

13 If required, another layer of the second UV gel (builder UV gel) may be applied. Repeat steps 11 and 12 for both hands (Figures 18–7 and 18–8).

14 ***Remove inhibition layer.*** UV gels cure with a tacky surface called an **inhibition layer**. This layer can be removed by filing with a medium abrasive (180 to 240 grit) or with alcohol, acetone, or other suitable re-

Figure 18–6 Cure in UV lamp for the required time.

Figure 18–7 Apply second UV gel (building UV gel).

Figure 18–8 Dispense a smaller amount of UV gel.

mover on a plastic-backed cotton pad to avoid skin contact. Prolonged or repeated skin contact with the inhibition layer may cause skin irritation or sensitivity. Avoid placing your arm in fresh filings from UV gel enhancements (Figure 18–9).

15 ***Check nail contours.*** UV gel nails are softer, so they file very easily. Using a medium abrasive (180 to 240 grit), refine the surface contour. File carefully near the side walls and eponychium to avoid injuring the client's skin (Figure 18–10). Bevel down, stroking the file at a 45-degree angle from the top center dome to free edge. Check the free edge thickness and even out imperfections with gentle strokes with the abrasive.

16 ***Remove dust.*** Remove dust and filings with a disinfectable nylon brush. Be sure to properly clean and disinfect these brushes between each client, as required by your state regulations. Your instructor will advise you about these requirements (Figure 18–11).

17 ***Apply third UV gel (sealer or finisher UV gel).*** Apply a small amount of the third UV gel (sealer or finisher UV gel). Starting from base of the nail plate, stroke toward the free edge, using polish-style strokes and covering the entire nail surface. Be sure to wrap this final layer under the natural nail's free edge to seal the coating and provide additional protection. Avoid touching the client's skin.

18 ***Repeat steps 12 and 16.***

19 ***Remove the inhibition layer.*** Remove this layer if required. Avoid skin contact.

20 ***Apply nail oil.*** Rub nail oil into surrounding skin and nail surface (Figure 18–12).

21 ***Apply hand lotion and massage hand and arm.***

22 **Clean nail enhancements.** Ask the client to dip nail enhancements into a fingerbowl filled with liquid soap. Then use nail brush to clean enhancements over fingerbowl. Thoroughly rinse with water to remove soap residues that can cause polish to lift. Dry thoroughly with a clean disposable towel.

23 ***Apply nail polish*** (Figure 18–13).

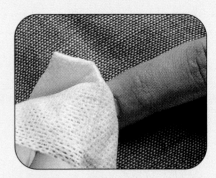
Figure 18–9 Remove inhibition layer with plastic-back cotton pad.

Figure 18–10 File, shape, and contour entire surface.

here's a tip...

During the procedure, keep the brush and UV gel away from sunlight, UV gel lamps, and full-spectrum table lamps to prevent them from hardening.

Figure 18–11 Remove dust and filings with a disinfectable nylon brush.

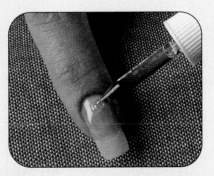
Figure 18–12 Apply nail oil and massaged into speed penetration.

Figure 18–13 Apply polish.

PROCEDURE (18-2)

UV GEL OVER FORMS

Some clients wish to lengthen nail enhancements beyond the free edge. The following demonstrates the technique for achieving longer nail enhancements with UV gels.

Figure 18–14 Apply UV gel to natural nail and form.

Figure 18–15 Cure UV gel as specified.

Figure 18–16 Apply UV gel to entire nail without nail form.

1 ***Complete UV gel application pre-service.*** Place UV gel supplies, including nail forms, on your manicuring table.

2 ***Apply nail forms.*** Fit forms onto all ten fingers just as described in Chapter 17. Remember to clean and disinfect multiuse forms, if disposable forms are not used. Clear plastic forms are sometimes used to allow UV light to penetrate from the underside for more complete curing of the free edge (Figure 18–14).

3 ***Apply first UV gel (base coat UV gel).*** Brush UV gel onto free edge of the form and create a free edge. Add more UV gel to cover the remainder of the natural nail. Keep UV gel from touching eponychium or sidewalls. Use the same color gel that was previously used in this step.

4 ***Cure first UV gel (base coat gel).*** Properly position the hand in the UV lamp for the cure time required by the manufacturer (Figure 18–15). Always cure each layer of the UV gel for the time required by the manufacturer's instructions.

5 ***Repeat steps 3 and 4 on the right hand.*** Then repeat same steps for both thumbs.

6 ***Apply second UV gel (building UV gel).*** Apply a small amount of UV gel over the properly cured first layer. Pull it across the first layer and smooth. Avoid touching the skin. Repeat this application process for the other four nails on the client's left hand from pinky to pointer. If performing a one-color method, you may use a clear, pink or natural color UV gel. If performing a two-color method, you should use a pink or natural color UV gel over the nail bed area and a white UV gel to create a smile line.

7 ***Properly position hand and cure UV gel for the required time.***

8 ***Carefully remove nail forms.***

9 ***Shape free edge.*** Use a medium abrasive (180 to 240 grit) to shape the free edge of the enhancement.

10 ***Apply second UV gel (building UV gel).*** If required, apply second UV gel over the entire nail enhancement and cure properly (Figure 18–16).

11 *Remove inhibition layer.* This layer can be removed by filing with a medium of abrasive (180 and 240 grit) or with alcohol, acetone, or other suitable remover on a plastic-backed cotton pad to avoid skin contact. Avoid skin contact with the inhibition layer.

12 *Check nail contours.* Using a medium abrasive (180 to 240 grit), refine the surface contour.

13 *Remove dust.* Remove dust and filing with a disinfectable nylon brush.

14 *Apply third UV gel (sealer or finisher).* Apply a small amount of third UV gel (sealer or finisher UV gel). Starting from the base of the nail plate, stroke toward the free edge using polish-style strokes, covering the entire nail surface. Be sure to wrap this final layer under the natural nail's free edge to seal the coating and provide additional protection. Avoid touching the client's skin underneath the free edge with UV gel.

15 *Cure UV nail.* Properly cure UV nail enhancement as recommended.

16 *Repeat steps 11 and 12.*

17 *Apply nail oil.* Rub nail oil into surrounding skin and nail surface.

18 *Apply hand lotion and massage hand and arm.*

19 *Clean nail enhancements.* Ask client to dip nails into a fingerbowl filled with liquid soap. Then use a nail brush to clean nails over the fingerbowl. Thoroughly rinse with water and dry thoroughly with a clean disposable towel.

20 *Apply nail polish if desired.*

21 *Complete UV gel application post-service.*

such as polish, nail oil, topcoat, and hand lotions, among others. These are valuable maintenance tools and they will appreciate your professional recommendation.

3. **Clean up around your table.** Take the time to restore the basic setup of your table, restock supplies, and make sure that all caps are tight.

4. **Clean brush.** Clean brush according to manufacturer's instructions. Keeping it away from UV light sources will make cleaning much easier and will prevent you from ruining your brush.

5. **Discard used materials.** Dispose of waste materials. After all used materials have been collected, seal them in a plastic bag and discard it in a metal, self-closing waste receptacle. It is important to remove items soiled with enhancement product from

your manicuring station after each client. This will help maintain the quality of your salon's air. Dispose of these items according to your local rules and regulations.

6. **Clean your table, and then clean and disinfect implements and multiuse tools, such as abrasives.** Perform your complete pre-service sanitation and disinfection procedures. Implements need to be cleaned and disinfected before they can be used on the next client, and this procedure will take about 20 minutes.

UV GEL MAINTENANCE AND REMOVAL

UV gel enhancements must be rebalanced every 2 to 3 weeks as described previously in this chapter, depending on how fast the client's nails grow. Use a medium abrasive file (180 to 240 grit) to thin and shape the enhancement. Be careful not to damage the natural nail plate with the abrasive.

UV Gel Removal

Read and follow manufacturer's recommended procedure to remove UV gel nails. UV gel enhancements can be more quickly removed by carefully reducing the thickness with a medium coarse abrasive (120 to 180 grit) before soaking in acetone or product remover. Once the enhancement begins to soften, gently scrape it from the nail plate with a wooden pusher stick.

Follow up with a gentle buffing of the natural nail using a fine buffer (350 grit or higher). This will remove product residues and smooth the nail plate. Condition surrounding skin with nail oil and lotion or follow with a manicure.

$ business TIP

TEEN TIME

Take advantage of teenagers' interests in good grooming by introducing them to professional nail care. Some great promotion suggestions include a 20-percent discount on all prom and graduation nail services. Contact local schools to see when these events take place, and then spread the word by advertising the promotion in high school newspapers 6 to 8 weeks ahead of time.

Another option is to hold a "back-to-school night." Decorate the salon in fun colors, provide refreshments, and invite teens to pay a $10.00 registration fee for a night of nail education and fashion manicures, plus a take-home bag of trial-sized products. Many professionals report success with discounted nail extensions offered to the cheerleading squad, sports manicures to the volleyball team, or even a "good grade" discount for any teen earning a 3.0 or higher grade point average.

REVIEW **QUESTIONS**

1. Describe the chemistry of UV gel nail enhancements, and how they differ from other types of enhancements. How are their major ingredients different and how are they the same?

2. Identify the supplies needed for UV gel nail enhancement application.

3. Demonstrate the proper procedures for applying UV gel nail enhancements using forms.

4. Why is it important to use the proper UV lamp with the UV gel of your choice?

5. Explain how UV gels are safely and correctly removed.

6. What does wattage mean in terms of UV gel lights?

7. What is the tacky layer called on the surface of UV gel nails?

8. What precaution must be taken when removing a tacky layer from a UV gel nail?

9. What are oligomers and why are they important to UV gel nail enhancements?

10. What types of oligomers are used in UV gels?

CHAPTER **GLOSSARY**

inhibition layer	Tacky surface left on the nail once a UV gel has cured.
oligomer	Short chain of monomers that is not long enough to be considered a polymer.
one-color method	Gel is applied over the entire surface of the nail.
two-color method	Two different colors of gel are applied to the surface of the nail, in different places, as in a French manicure.
urethane acrylate oligomer or urethane methacrylate oligomer	Main ingredient used to create UV gel nail enhancements.
UV gel	Type of nail enhancement product that hardens when exposed to a UV light.
UV lamp	Specialized electronic device that powers and controls UV lights to cure UV gel nail enhancements.
UV lightbulb	Special bulb that emits UV light to cure UV gel nail enhancements.
wattage	Measure of how much electricity a lightbulb consumes.

The Creative Touch

chapter 19

CHAPTER OUTLINE

- The Basics and Foundation of Nail Art
- Creating Nail Art
- Gold Leafing
- Freehand Painting
- Using an Airbrush for Nail Color and Nail Art
- Getting Started and Finished
- Traditional French Manicure (With Optional Lunula)

LEARNING OBJECTIVES

After completing this chapter, you will be able to:

1. Describe three different nail art supplies.

2. Describe techniques for using these supplies.

3. Demonstrate one nail art application.

4. Describe the use of the color wheel.

5. Describe the basic nail art brushes and their uses.

6. Describe airbrush equipment.

7. Demonstrate proper airbrush techniques.

8. Describe the two-color fade.

9. Describe how the French manicure is achieved using airbrushing.

KEY TERMS

Page number indicates where in the chapter the term is used.

air hose
pg. 344

belly
pg. 339

color fade (color blend)
pg. 343

color wheel
pg. 334

complementary color
pg. 335

double loading
pg. 341

floating the bead
pg. 334

fluid nozzle (tip)
pg. 344

foil adhesive
pg. 336

foiling
pg. 336

freehand painting (flat nail art)
pg. 339

French manicure
pg. 343

gem
pg. 335

gravity-fed
pg. 344

heel
pg. 339

leafing (gold leafing)
pg. 337

marbleizer (stylus)
pg. 346

mask knife
pg. 343

mask paper
pg. 343

nail art
pg. 332

needle
pg. 344

position
pg. 341

pressure
pg. 340

primary color
pg. 335

pull
pg. 341

secondary color
pg. 335

stencil
pg. 343

stripette or short striper
pg. 340

striping tape
pg. 337

tertiary colors
pg. 335

tip
pg. 339

well (small color cup or reservoir)
pg. 344

N ail art offers endless opportunities to express your creativity and your client's unique personality. There are numerous tools and supplies with which you can custom design, along with an endless palette of artistic creations. Your imagination and your client's preferences are your only limitations. This has fast become one of the most popular add-on services that salons are offering. Nail art gives you and your client the flexibility of originating designs ranging from conservative, office-appropriate art forms to the more flamboyant holiday and expressive specialty art forms. This is one of those perks that you get from being a nail professional, where you can really have fun with your job (Figure 19–1).

THE BASICS AND FOUNDATION OF NAIL ART

The Rules

With so many forms of **nail art** to choose from, even the most artistically challenged can produce impressive works of art. There are only a few basic rules to follow to achieve success in nail art.

1. The first rule is to be open-minded. Never look at a piece of nail art and think that you could never possibly do that, because you can! Anyone can create beautiful pieces of nail art, if they have patience and practice. You will be surprised how easy it is.

Figure 19–1 Nail art is the most creative part of a nail technician's job.

2. The second rule is to expose yourself to all avenues of art services. At first, select art subjects or designs that you are most comfortable with. Then, as you become more confident, add to your repertoire.

3. The third rule is to always listen to your client. As outstanding as your artwork may be, if it does not fit the client's lifestyle or comfort zone, the client will not be satisfied.

4. The final rule is to always remember that there is no such thing as an art mistake, only creative opportunities. Ralph Waldo Emerson once wrote, "Every artist was first an amateur." To be successful and proficient, you must practice, practice more, and practice again. You will find that with patience and perseverance, nail art is very rewarding.

The Basics

There are a few things to know about nail art.

1. Ample time must be scheduled for these services. When you introduce your client to your services, be sure to explain the time requirements. Some art services are relatively quick, while others can be time consuming. This keeps you on schedule and gives the client a realistic idea of the time and work required.

2. Have a display of your nail art designs, tastefully suited to your clientele and salon atmosphere. Seeing your work in advance removes clients' apprehension, and gives them a clear idea of what they can expect. A display will also generate interest in your art services.

3. Be competitively priced. Be sure that you are priced appropriately for your area and clientele. Always base your prices on the cost of materials, time investment, and general availability, but be sure that a service common to your area is priced competitively. For more specialized art service, such as freehand designs,

price your work based on the time investment, cost of materials, and your level of expertise. You are a professional. Be sure to price your services reflectively, and be prepared to render artwork deserving of the fee.

4. Invest in good-quality tools that will need replacement far less often if properly maintained, and the results will be of a higher quality. High-quality air compressors are examples of tools worth the investment. This will be discussed later in the air-brushing section of this chapter.

5. Dedicate a pair of small scissors, such as stork shears, to be used solely for nail art purposes. This will help you avoid ruining or contaminating your silk and fiberglass wrap fabrics. It will make everything much easier on you all the way around.

6. Let a polished nail dry completely before applying some types of nail art, unless specifically directed to do otherwise. When certain forms of multi-layered art are applied too quickly, the final product will take longer to dry and harden, and it quite likely will yield an undesired result.

   Additionally, always allow nail art to dry completely before sealing it. When sealing nail art, be very careful not to touch the brush of the sealer to the surface of the nail, as it too can damage your art. Take the brush, load it with a generous bead of sealer, and drop the bead on the nail surface. With the brush, gently guide the bead over the entire surface of the nail until it is completely covered. This is referred to as **floating the bead**, as the brush basically floats on the surface of the sealer, directing its flow, but never coming in contact with the nail surface itself. Mastering this technique will save you a great deal of time and frustration.

Nail art is an exciting and creative part of a nail professional's job. It turns enhancements and natural nails into small canvases on which you can paint pictures; create designs; make collages with gems, foils, leafing, and tapes; or express your client's creative side. In this chapter, you will gain a basic working knowledge of the most common forms of nail art products, tools, supplies, and procedures. However, there is always more to learn. Exploration of these options and continuing education are strongly encouraged, especially in freehand art and airbrushing. Also, if you watch a more experienced person work, you are sure to learn something new.

Color Theory

Before you can expect to successfully produce appealing nail art, it is imperative that you have a working knowledge of colors and how they relate, blend, clash, and complement one another. In many art supply stores, you can easily obtain laminated color guides called **color wheels**.

The color wheel illustrates and identifies the **primary colors**, **secondary colors**, **tertiary colors**, and **complementary colors**. The light we see reflected from a surface is called **color**. Red nail polish appears that way because red light is reflecting off of its surface (Figure 19–2). Knowing the classifications of color will aid you in selecting both a polish and paint palette for your artwork that are pleasing to the eye and professional looking. It is must-know information when selecting paints for freehand nail art and airbrushing.

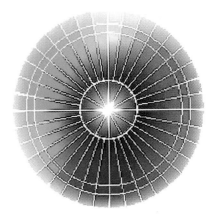

Figure 19–2 Color wheel.

1. **Primary colors** are pure pigment colors that cannot be obtained from mixing any other colors together. They are the pure colors from which all other colors are made, and are often modified by adding varying amounts of black and white. Primary colors are red, yellow, and blue.

2. **Secondary colors** are the colors resulting from mixing equal parts of two primary colors together. They also sit opposite the primary colors on the color wheel, and are the complementary colors of the primary colors. Secondary colors are orange (1:1 red and yellow), green (1:1 yellow and blue), and violet (1:1 blue and red).

3. **Tertiary colors** are the colors directly resulting from mixing equal parts of one primary color and one of its nearest secondary colors. Tertiary colors are red-orange, red-violet, blue-violet, blue-green, yellow-green, and yellow-orange. Some also refer to tertiary colors as intermediate colors.

4. **Complementary colors** are those colors located directly opposite each other on the color wheel. When complementary colors are mixed together in equal parts they produce a neutral, muddy brown, and when mixed in unequal parts they produce a neutral color dominated by the color of the greatest amount. When these colors are applied side by side, they enhance each other, and thus make each other stand out. We see "black" when no color is reflecting from a surface. Black nail polish absorbs light that hits its surface and none is reflected back to our eyes. Nail polish looks "white" when all colors are reflected. The color that we actually see depends on which colors are reflected, and which are absorbed. Colors located beside each other on the color wheel (analogous colors) blend well together, and are beautiful when airbrushing a fade.

CREATING NAIL ART

Gems

Tiny rhinestones are popular nail art accents. They come in different sizes, colors, and shapes. **Gems** add sparkle, dimension, and texture to any design. To apply the gem, apply a dab of top coat or nail art sealer on the nail where the gem is to be adhered. Dampening the end of a wooden pusher with nail art sealer, pick up the gem by touching the dampened stick to the colorful, shiny side of the gem and placing it on the nail in the prepared

Figure 19–3 Polished nail that is ready for foiling.

part of the nail. Tweezers also work well when handling larger gems. You may need to apply a small amount of pressure on the gem when placing it on the nail to imbed it for better adhesion. Once the gem is applied, finish it with a generous coat of nail art sealer.

If you remove the gem using acetone, moderate pressure, and a little patience, you may be able to reuse the gem. If the shiny, reflective backing separates from the gem during the removal process, the gem is no longer usable, as it will no longer brightly reflect color.

Foiling

Foiling is one of the easiest and most cost-effective nail art techniques, yet it renders stunning results. It also affords almost endless creative opportunities (Figure 19–3). Foil is available in a wide variety of colors and patterns, with gold, silver, and snakeskin among the most popular. It is most often sold in rolls, ranging from a few inches to several feet in length, but may also be found as pre-cut pieces. While pre-cuts are easy to handle and can be more convenient, they are usually more costly. To apply foil, you must first polish the nail and allow it to completely dry. The polish color will show through in spots, so it should be selected to enhance the color scheme and/or design.

Once the nail is dry, apply a very thin and even coat of **foil adhesive**. This is a special adhesive, just for foiling, that is generally tinted white or pink and appears cloudy when it is wet. When the adhesive becomes transparent, it will act as double-sided sticky tape, sticking to the nail surface and pulling the foil from the cellophane. (Do not let the adhesive over-dry, or the foil will not stick to it.) If the adhesive is not allowed to become clear, it will be too wet, and the foil will not stick to it, and the nail polish will lift off the nail. This can be the trickiest part of the entire service. While the adhesive is drying, select the foil to be used and take small cuttings of each color that you wish to use. Usually, one-to-three colors are used per nail, and each strip is cut to a length of between 1" and 2", depending on the number of colors being used. If a patterned piece is selected or only one color is desired, the cuttings must be large enough for each nail.

Once the adhesive is ready, carefully hold the foil with your fingers, with the shiny, colored side facing up, and the dull, matted side (usually gold or gray) facing toward the nail surface.

Foiling Method 1

Quickly touch the matte back side of the foil to the surface of the nail, pulling the back away immediately. Continue doing the quick touch-and-pull (up-and-down) motion over the nail surface until the desired amount of color has been deposited on the nail surface. Keep in mind that the foil is actually being removed from a clear sheet of cellophane; where color has been deposited, the foil will now appear clear where color is removed. Use a new piece of the foil, because the clear cellophane will remove the nail polish.

Foiling Method 2

This method provides a more complete coverage of color. The cut foil is gently laid on the surface of the nail, and lightly burnished with a wooden pusher. When the desired amount of color coverage has been achieved, slowly peel the cellophane from the nail. This method is very effective with pre-patterned foil, such as animal skin, floral, and holographic designs. Afterwards, you must seal the nail with the nail art sealer. As with all nail art, always **float the bead** or the foil color may smear or be damaged. As the nail art sealer dries, you will see an eye-catching crinkling effect. This service takes very little time and is very popular, as well as lucrative.

Striping Tape

Striping tape comes in rolls or pages of various colors, widths, and lengths. Although the color selection is generous, gold, silver, and black have been the most popular colors for years. The tape has a tacky backing, and is only applied to a thoroughly dry nail polish. If applying the nail tape over another design, the design must also be dry.

GOLD LEAFING

Leafing material is very fragile and extremely thin with a foil-like consistency. It is usually available in sheets, although it is occasionally found in smaller, loose pieces of the material. Leafing comes in a variety of colors, including gold and silver. The sheets of leafing are packaged in quantities ranging from 10 to 100 sheets per unit. It is most commonly known as leafing or gold leafing, but is also known as **nuggets** or **nugget sheets**. Because leafing is very fragile, you must handle it with great care. The sheets are packaged in bags or containers with sheets of thin tissue paper layered between the pages of leafing. When removing the sheets from the packaging, use tweezers or the paper that separates the sheets. Leafing is very lightweight, easily torn, and blown away by the slightest air current, so keep the packages closed at all times and away from drafts or fans.

The application of leafing is quick and easy. With the nail prepared as usual, polished, and completely dry, apply a thin, even coat of foil adhesive. Once the adhesive has reached the tacky stage by turning clear, apply the desired color(s) in small pieces or by the sheet. For this, use tweezers, or for the smaller pieces, a slightly dampened wooden pusher. Rub gently with your finger, using a slight amount of pressure. If using a sheet, you will get a more thin and even coverage. If using smaller pieces, you will get a more textured appearance, giving the effect of nuggets. Once the application is completed, seal the finished nail art by floating a bead of sealer over the entire nail. Leafing makes a great artform on its own, or acts as a complementary accent to other types of art. For example, if you were to paint half of the nail red and the other half black, you could highlight the meeting point of the two colors with gold or silver leafing.

here's a tip...

As with all other forms of nail art, you must recommend that your client reapply top coat every 3 to 4 days to maintain a good seal and a high-gloss finish.

PROCEDURE 19-1

GOLD LEAF APPLICATION

1 *Polish nails and let dry.*

2 *Apply adhesive on area that you want to cover with gold* (Figure 19–4).

3 *Using tweezers or a wooden pusher, place bits of gold leafing on nail and gently press on tacky adhesive.* Continue doing this until the design is complete (Figures 19–5 and 19–6).

4 *Use a wooden pusher to press gold leaf flat onto nail* (Figure 19–7).

5 *Apply sealer over gold leaf to finish.* Let dry. If you are going to add striping tape or a gemstone, do it before applying the final coat of clear polish (Figure 19–8).

6 *A second or third coat of clear polish may be applied if needed to cover the nail design.* Let each layer dry slightly before applying the next (Figure 19–9).

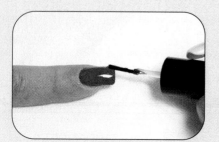

Figure 19–4 Apply adhesive.

Figure 19–5 Apply gold leaf.

Figure 19–6 Complete design.

Figure 19–7 Press gold leaf flat.

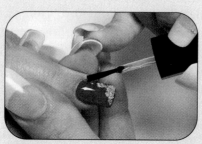

Figure 19–8 Apply clear polish.

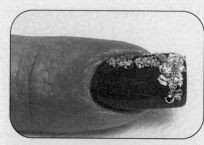

Figure 19–9 Finished nail with gold leaf.

FREEHAND PAINTING

Freehand painting, also referred to as **flat nail art**, is a very expressive form of nail art, with few limitations. With imagination, education, knowledge, practice, and the right tools, you can create amazing nail art.

A working understanding of the theory of color is imperative, as well as having tools that work for you. Brushes and paints are the most critical tools for freehand art, and proper selection of both is important. Quality and familiarity are necessary for the production of a satisfying, high-quality piece of finished art.

Figure 19–10 Selection of brushes.

Brushes

Brushes come in many sizes, shapes, and qualities. There are a variety of natural bristle types, resulting in a range of brushes from very soft to very firm. Synthetic bristles are best used for water-based paints (Figure 19–10). Smaller-size brushes are usually a better choice for painting nails.

Bristles can be made of any one or a combination of many types of natural fibers. The fibers, which comprise the bristles, or the actual brush itself, are bundled together and inserted into the ferrule. The very end of the bristles, farthest away from the handle, is referred to as either the **tip** or **chisel edge**, depending on the style of the brush. Round brushes, for example, would have pointed tips, while flat brushes have a chiseled edge. The midsection of the bristles is called the **belly** of the brush. This is the area of the brush that retains the most paint. The ferrule is the metal band around the brush that helps to hold the bristles in place. The area in which the bristles meet the ferrule is called the **heel** of the brush. The more common brushes for flat nail art are discussed below.

Round Brush

This is the most common and versatile style of brush. It has a tapered, pointed tip and large belly. It has a very good capacity for holding paint.

Round brushes made of the softer hairs have a pointed tip and stiffer bristles, and do not form a point at the tip. They are flexible and allow intricate details if they have a fine point at the tip. This is a good brush for accomplishing many different stroke patterns.

Liner Brush

This is a very versatile brush and possibly more common than round brushes. It is a very good detail brush, and is preferred for line work, outlining, and even lettering.

Flat Brush

This brush has a square tip with long bristles, which gives it added flexibility. It is also referred to as a shader brush. A flat brush holds a large amount of paint and is very versatile. When used flat on the painting surface, it will result in long, fluid strokes. The flat tip edge or chiseled edge can render a fine line. This brush is useful for techniques such as **double loading**, blending, and shading.

Bright Brush

This is a short, flat brush. The shortness of the bristles results in more texture and control.

Fan Brush

This brush is another version of a flat brush. The bristles or hairs are spread out like a fan. This brush is most commonly used for blending and special effects. When used in a dry brush technique, the brush can be slightly loaded with paint at the tips and floated across the painting surface for an airbrush-like effect.

Spotter Brush

This brush is also called a **detailer**. It is a short, round brush, having little belly and a very fine point at the tip. This brush offers maximum control for intricate detailed work.

Striper Brush

This brush comes in various lengths. The striper brush is an extremely long, flat brush, having only a few fibers. It is incredibly efficient when creating long lines, striping effects, and animal prints. The shorter version of this brush, called the **stripette** or **short striper**, yields a similar effect. For the beginner, this brush is challenging to control, but with relatively little practice it can be easily mastered.

There are other brush styles, all having their own special effect to offer an artist. However, it is better to begin with a limited palette of colors and supply of brushes. This better enables the novice artist to master the basics before becoming overwhelmed with extra tools.

As your artistic abilities increase, add to your tool supply and expand your portfolio of designs. Having a good liner, striper, round, fan, flat, and detailer is more than enough to get started. Another useful tool for the free-hand artist, is a **marbleizer**, also known as a **stylus**. These come in a variety of sizes. They have wooden handles with a rounded tip and metal extension. The rounded ball tips range in size and are excellent for dotting small circles of color on a nail, creating polka dots, eyes, bubbles, and much more. Additionally, they can be used to swirl drops of different colored paints or polish across the nail surface, giving a marbleized finish.

Strokes

Brush strokes are accomplished in a variety of ways, but there are three basic techniques to master: pressure, pull, and position. The **pressure** refers to the amount of force that an artist applies to the brush while stroking. The more pressure applied, the larger the coverage area and the wider the stroke. As the amount of pressure is decreased, the width of the stroke decreases. Lightening the pressure gradually while pulling the brush across the paint surface, will taper the stripe and create a point where the brush tip lifts from the surface.

The second basic technique is the **pull**. The nail professional must learn to pull the brush, not push it. Pulling the brush across the paint surface creates a more fluid stroke. Pushing it will give a rough and spattered stroke that is more difficult to control.

The third basic technique is **position**. Position refers to how you hold the brush on the nail. For instance, the brush could be held in a straight up-and-down manner, with only the tip touching the paint surface, or it could be held flat and pulled across the surface. The first position is for detailed work such as lettering, intricate details, and outlining. The latter would be done when striping. When you combine the pressure, pull, and position, you will be amazed at how many different design strokes you can create with only a few brushes.

Some of the most versatile strokes include the comma (pollywog) "C," leaf, "S," ribbon, and teardrop (Figure 19–11).

Design Techniques

Animal Stripes

To create a zebra, paint or polish the entire nail in white and then paint the stripes with black paint (Figure 19–12). To create a tiger stripe, paint or polish the nail gold, bronze, or copper, and then paint stripes with black paint.

Examples of other color variations that are popular and work well are black on purple, blue, or pink. Using your liner or short striper brush, load the lower three-quarters of the brush with paint. Touch the tip of the brush to one side of the nail and lay the belly of the brush on the nail.

Your stopping point should be near the center of the nail. Pull the brush across the nail toward the center in a slightly wavy motion, lifting it away from the nail near the stopping point. Continue this down one entire side, leaving ample room between strokes for an opposing stroke from the other side to meet at the center.

Starting with more paint on the very tip of the brush adds to the width at the beginning point.

Hearts

Hearts are much easier to create than you might think (Figure 19–13). Simply place three dots on the prepared painting surface in the outline of an inverted triangle. Then connect the dots with a detailer as though you are drawing with a pencil, positioning the brush straight up and down. In the middle of the two upper dots, bring the design down into a "v" shape, taking a rounded edge from the top dots down to the lower dot, joining all together in a "v" at the bottom.

Flower Petals

Create these petals by loading a #2 flat brush or smaller with a darker color on one side and a lighter color on the other. This is called **double loading**. Place the tip of the brush on the properly prepared nail. Lay the brush down

Figure 19–11 The most versatile strokes include the comma (pollywog), "C," leaf, "S," ribbon, and teardrop.

Figure 19–12 Animal stripes are quite popular.

Figure 19–13 Hearts are easier than they look.

Figure 19–14 Flower petals.

to about half of its length on the nail. Pivot one side of the brush a quarter turn, applying increased pressure in the beginning and less toward the end of the movement. Then pull the brush to the end of the petal, which is actually toward the center on some flowers, lifting up and away as you approach the ending point. This stroke will give you a wide teardrop, creating a flower petal. By double loading, you automatically get a shaded/highlighted effect.

One important detail of the double load is that highlights look more natural if they are all on the same side of the flower. To achieve this, the brush must begin from the same position so that the colors will be in the same location for each petal. Another type of flower petal is accomplished by using a 10/0 liner brush, laying the tip on the prepared painting surface, applying pressure, and pulling. As you pull up and away, move the brush in a slight "C" shape, narrowing the stroke at the end. This is called a **comma stroke**. Both of these strokes can yield several designs when placed singularly or grouped together (Figure 19–14).

Leaves

A leaf is made the same way as a flower petal, with the narrower part of the stroke being the outermost part of the leaf. To add width and dimension to the leaf, double load a small, flat brush with two shades of green. Start with the flat brush on its chiseled edge, perpendicular to the nail. Press, pivot a quarter turn left or right, lift, and pull up. Look at nature and duplicate it.

Stems and Branches

These are easily and quickly incorporated into a design with a striper brush, liner brush, or flat brush. With a striper or liner, simply pull the brush, applying more pressure where width is desired and less where it is not. With a flat brush, lay in the stem or branch by using the chiseled edge of the brush only, pulling it into place. Experiment with combinations of lines accented with flowers, dots, and hearts. You will be surprised at how many designs you can create. As always, continuing education and hands-on training are strongly recommended, especially in the beginning.

Good luck and ENJOY.

Colored Acrylic (Methacrylate) Powder Designs

The range of colored acrylic (methacrylate) nail powders or clear powders with glitter or sparkle have opened a new door for the nail artist. Mastering nail enhancement product application, color knowledge, and brush strokes put you at the threshold of design magic. Creating permanent designs with colored acrylic (methacrylate) powders can be as rewarding as any of the previously mentioned art forms. Experiment with your own designs, or seek out manufacturers who make colored and/or sparkle powders. There are also continuing education classes and videos available to help you reach your full creative potential.

USING AN AIRBRUSH FOR NAIL COLOR AND NAIL ART

Airbrushing nails has become a popular salon service. Many nail professionals are offering their clients an alternative to traditional nail color by airbrushing the nail color for their clients. Subtle color combinations may be achieved by airbrushing two or more colors on the nails at the same time. This technique is called a **color fade** or **color blend** (Figure 19–15).

By airbrushing the nail color, the nail professional may charge an additional price for the special nail color technique.

One of the most popular techniques used in airbrushing is the **French manicure** (Figure 19–16). This technique creates a smooth white tip with perfect shape every time. The airbrushed French manicure is accomplished quickly. To achieve this you must use a **design tool**, such as a **stencil** or **mask paper** (Figure 19–17). There are pre-cut stencils and mask paper on the market that have designs already in them. You may custom-cut your own designs by using a **mask knife** on uncut stencil or mask paper (Figure 19–18). Using the founded edge of a nail form used for nail extensions works equally well. Place the material to be cut on a glass plate or self-healing mat, and carefully cut your design out with the mask knife. Use the full edge of the knife, not just the point of the blade, or you will have an uneven and jagged cut.

Airbrush Equipment and Operation

An airbrush looks like a small spray paint gun. It uses compressed air to force paint out of its tip, creating a fine mist of paint. There are many types of airbrushes available that are suitable for airbrushing fingernails. Some airbrushes are made with metal parts. Other airbrushes made of solvent resistant plastic are now available (Figure 19–19). All airbrushes work on the same principle: They combine air and paint to form an atomized spray (extremely tiny droplets) for painting. Airbrushes differ in the (1) type of trigger action, (2) location of air and paint mixing, and (3) ease of use and maintenance.

Figure 19–15 Two-color fade.

Figure 19–16 French manicure.

Figure 19–17 Stencils are made of plastic, paper, or fabric.

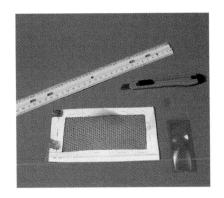

Figure 19–18 Customized mask stencil with paper and knife.

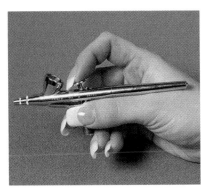

Figure 19–19 Double-action airbrush.

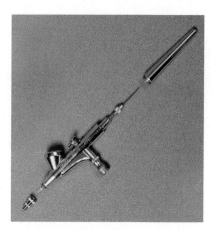

Figure 19–20 Parts of the airbrush: handle, shell/body, nozzle/tip, cap, and needle.

Each airbrush has a small cone-shaped **fluid nozzle**, also called a **tip**, that a tapered **needle** fits into (Figure 19–20). When the needle fits snugly in the fluid nozzle, no paint is released when the trigger is depressed. When the needle is drawn back, the airbrush begins to release paint. The farther the needle is drawn back, the more paint is allowed to come through the opening.

There are many different makes of airbrush systems available on the market today. Avoid those that are designed to deliver large volumes of paint; they are not economical or practical choices for airbrushing nails. Some airbrush systems are designed for **gravity-fed** paint (gravity pulls the paint into the airbrush). This type of airbrush usually has a **well** or **small color cup** for holding the paint. A well (also called a **reservoir**) is a hole in the top of the airbrush, where drops of paint are placed. If the airbrush has a color cup, it may be located on top of the airbrush or it may be attached to the side of the airbrush for the paint.

When you purchase an airbrush, retain the manufacturer's airbrush diagram that comes with it for future reference. This diagram outlines the correct type of air source, which is a small compressor. The compressor takes air from the room you are working in and compresses it. You may require an air pressure regulator attached to the compressor in order to control the air pressure being released into your **air hose**. Most airbrush nail professionals work at a pressure between 25 and 35 lb per square inch (psi). You will require a moisture trap or separator for your airbrush system since the moisture in the air will condense into liquid when an error is compressed. When the compressed air from the compressor reaches the air hose, the moisture begins to accumulate in the air hose. The moisture will form water droplets that will eventually be spit out from the airbrush. A moisture trap will prevent this from happening.

You will need airbrush paint, airbrush cleaner, and appropriate top coat or sealer to protect the airbrush paint on the nail. Check that the literature and product labeling clearly state that the products you are using are recommended for use on nails. Always use the airbrush and related products according to the manufacturer's instructions and heed all precautions. Consult your professional beauty or nail distributor to learn more about the many different types of airbrush and related items available. Many manufacturers offer complete systems for airbrushing nails that include everything you need to get started. Your school may have different types or brands of equipment available for you to experiment with.

GETTING STARTED AND FINISHED

Setup and Practice

When you begin practicing, you will need a table, good lighting, a comfortable chair, your airbrush equipment, and supplies. Prepare a number of nail tips to be airbrushed by mounting them to wooden sticks and apply a base coat recommended by the paint manufacturer. Assemble your airbrush, hose, and compressor per the manufacturer's directions. Place your airbrush paints and airbrush polishes in an accessible tray, roll cart, drawer, or polish rack. Have your design and cleaning tools in a tray, drawer, or roll cart ready for use. Put your airbrush cleaner in a squirt bottle.

Set up a cleaning area for the airbrush off to the side of the work area. Either side is fine as long as it is comfortable for you. One recommended setup is to have a separate roll cart for all of your airbrushing equipment and supplies. You could also use one of the drawers that is at a comfortable height when you sit at your work table. Pull out the drawer and line it with terry or paper toweling. Inside the drawer, place your plastic tray or jar that you will spray your airbrush into when cleaning it. Regardless of what you are using—an open tray, bowl, or jar—generously line the inside with absorbent material to prevent your overspray from spattering all over. Place your cleaning brushes, airbrush cleaner bottle, and other cleaning items in the open drawer. Avoid spraying into your wastebasket—it looks unsanitary and unprofessional.

Begin practicing on absorbent paper. Some manufacturers suggest that before you start airbrushing, place a few drops of cleaner into your airbrush and spray it out into your cleaning station. To become familiar with how your airbrush operates, start spraying onto the paper approximately 2" to 3" from the surface of the paper. The first thing most people notice, if you are spraying properly, is that you will not see the airbrush paint leave your airbrush. It will seem to appear magically on the paper in front of you.

To airbrush properly, you need to move your whole arm up and down, diagonally, or side to side in order to move the airbrush spray around on your surface. Do not move from the wrist! Your wrist must remain straight and relaxed. If you move from the wrist, you will find that the airbrush color will be inconsistent in coverage and intensity. This will occur because the airbrush starts out far from the surface, moves closer as your wrist straightens out and then farther away as your wrist completes the movement. If you find that you are moving your wrist, grasp your wrist with your other hand while practicing and consciously move your whole arm. After a while, your movements will correct themselves and you will be fine.

Practice spraying a consistent row of dots. When the dot appears where you expect it to, you have learned how to properly aim your airbrush. The next practice step is to draw lines. To draw crisp lines, you must have the airbrush nozzle very close to the paper. The farther you pull the airbrush away from the paper, the wider and softer the line will become. After experimenting with dots and lines, draw a grid on your paper by drawing horizontal and vertical lines overlapping each other. This will create rows of boxes. Place a dot in each of the boxes. You are now ready to practice the technique used for airbrushing nails.

When airbrushing nails, the distance from the nail will vary according to the type of airbrush you are using. Most people will use the airbrush 2" to 3" from the nail surface. On your paper, spray a smooth, even box of color by moving your arm back and forth slowly.

Develop even color with no lines by moving back and forth over the same area a few times. If you are seeing streaks or lines on the paper and not a smooth even box of color, the airbrush is either too close to the paper or you are releasing too much paint at a time. Practice this technique until you can achieve an even coating of color on the paper with no streaks (Figure 19–21).

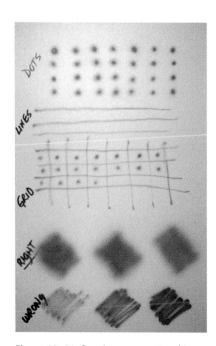

Figure 19–21 Practice on paper to achieve an even coating of color.

PROCEDURE 19-2
AIRBRUSHING

One of the benefits of adding airbrushing to your services is that you do not require live models to practice your skills. You must become proficient at airbrushing nail tips before working on clients. When you are skilled at airbrushing on nail tips, you are ready to practice on a few close friends or relatives to become comfortable holding the client's hand and cleaning up the over-spray when finished.

1 *After completing your nail service, ask clients to pay for the service prior to the airbrush nail color service.* This will prevent them from damaging your work before it had a chance to completely dry by digging in their purse.

2 *Ask the client to use a nail brush and cleanse their hands and nails of any oils or other contaminants left after the nail service.* Dry the nail plate, eponychium, and lateral side walls thoroughly, checking for droplets of water or missed oils and debris that would interfere with the airbrush nail color application.

3 *Apply base coat to the clean and properly prepared natural nails.*

4 *Airbrush your client's nails just as you practiced on the nail tips.* Hold the client's hand in yours. Your hand should encircle each of your client's fingers as you spray it. Your hand catches the overspray as you work so that it does not fall onto the other nails on your client's hand. Place your thumb on the finger just above the cuticle area. Most of the over-spray lands on your thumb and a bit may land on the client's finger. This reduces cleanup on your client. Use a similar procedure when airbrushing toenails. The paint washes off your hands when you wash them before your next client, but it is better to wear a disposable nitrile glove to prevent prolonged and repeated skin exposure to the paint that could lead to skin dryness or irritation.

5 *Apply sealer or top coat to the dry airbrushed surface.* Keep your polish brush parallel to the nail, guiding the sealer down the length of the nail. Float the brush across the surface; do not touch the nail with the bristles of the brush or it may scratch or smear the paint.

Be sure to have enough bonder on the polish brush; a dry brush may also damage your work. Apply sealer to all ten nails. Be sure to cover the entire surface, as well as the free edge and underside. Avoid skin contact, and leave a tiny free margin between the product and the skin to avoid potential irritation.

6 *Paint that is not properly sealed to the nail may be washed away later.* Sealer on the surrounding skin will also seal paint over-spray to the skin, making it difficult to remove. For these reasons, use extreme care when applying the sealer. Allow the top coats and sealer to dry 3 minutes or as recommended by the manufacturer of the product. Clean your airbrush and put it away at this time.

7 *Apply sealer.* Allow the client's nails to dry for 10 minutes.

8 *Remove over-spray from client's skin.* This may be accomplished at the nail table, pedicure station, or, with some airbrush skin cleaner products, at a sink. Have the client pat hands or feet on a towel to dry the skin, but avoid pressure on nails for another 10 minutes. Use a wooden pusher or cotton-wrapped implement saturated with alcohol, nail oil, or polish remover to remove any paint accidentally sealed to skin.

9 *Apply a quick-dry product if desired.* Use spray-on instead of brush-on quick-dry polishes for less risk of damaging the airbrushed nail. These services will require at least 4 hours before they are completely dry, but they will be sufficiently hardened to be protected after 30 minutes.

<table><tr><td>

⟶ here's a tip...

Airbrushed nail color **lasts as long as traditional nail polish services**. If you do not get these results, first check to be sure that you are using the product properly. Evaluate your airbrush nail paint and polishes. You may need to experiment with various brands or combinations of products for maximum durability.

</td></tr></table>

Now you are ready to practice on nail tips. Apply the recommended base coat to nail tips, and place them 2" to 3" apart on your practice surface area. Lightly coat the nail with your selected airbrush color. Repeated passes over the nail will build up the airbrush nail color. When first learning, most people are impatient and want to see the color right away. If you are too close to the nail tip or release paint too quickly on the nail surface, the paint will puddle and begin to run off the nail. Figure 19–22 shows an example of a nail tip sprayed too quickly and/or too closely. The second nail tip has the correct appearance. When correctly applied, airbrush paint appear dulls on the nail tip and has a powdery look. If the airbrush paint is shiny or appears as droplets, wipe the nail tip off with a water-dampened wipe or cotton pad and try again. A great way to practice is by airbrushing nail color on five nail tips at a time, just as if you were working on a client's hand. Apply one dry, powdery layer of color to each nail tip. Usually three passes of the airbrush across the nail tip will create a light color coating. Move to the next nail tip and repeat the procedure until you have airbrushed each nail tip with one coating of paint. Start with the first nail tip and repeat the procedure on each nail tip until you have reached your desired airbrushed nail color. When you have successfully completed applying the airbrushed nail color to the five nail tips, you are ready to move on to practicing a color fade or French manicure.

Airbrushed nail color is removed with nail polish remover. In order to offer airbrushed nail color successfully to every client you service, it is necessary to have your airbrush equipment and supplies ready to use at all times. Many people have airbrush systems that are in a box collecting dust. When an opportunity arises for them to use their airbrush equipment, they are not prepared and usually do not have the time in their schedule to set up their airbrush system. Having your airbrush system in a roll-cart by your side or set up at a nail table/pedicure station provides you with the ability to airbrush at a moment's notice, simply by plugging in or turning on your compressor.

Figure 19–22 Nail tip at left shows what happens when paint is sprayed too close to the nail tip or too much paint is released on the surface. The paint will puddle and run off the nail. The nail on the right has the correct appearance, achieved by light passes of the airbrush to build up color.

PROCEDURE 19-3
TWO-COLOR FADE APPLICATION

Figure 19–23 Apply base coat.

TWO-COLOR FADE

The nail color fade or color blend is another highly preferred airbrushed nail color service. It will appeal to every client. In this technique, the colors you choose are the key to success. A conservative client might prefer subtle, soft hues of similar colors, while an outgoing client might choose bold colors that strongly contrast. This multicolor airbrush nail service justifies an additional charge. This technique may be used as the background for another design or stand on its own as a unique, customized service.

1 Complete the pre-service procedure and **apply your base coat to the nail**. Nail base coats may be opaque white or crystal clear, or may have special effects such as glimmers or sparkles (Figure 19–23).

2 *Load airbrush with paint.* Place your paint color into your gun and start spraying onto the surface next to your nails. When the airbrush paint is spraying correctly, you are ready to apply paint to the nail. Apply a thin even coat, going back and forth diagonally over the top two-thirds of the nail, moving your whole arm. If you are working on more than one nail, apply this light thin coat diagonally to all the nails. Apply more coats of the airbrush paint at the base of the nail, with fewer coats toward the center of the nail to create a soft edge for the second color to overlap (Figure 19–24).

3 *Continue applying light, thin coats of paint diagonally until you have reached the desired color or opacity at the base of the nail plate* (Figure 19–25).

Figure 19–24 Create a soft edge for the second color to overlap.

Figure 19–25 Continue applying paint until your desired color is released.

4 ***Clean your airbrush to remove the first color paint.*** Choose a color that is appropriate for your client—one that contrasts and creates a transition color. Use the color wheel to help you decide. When airbrushing the second color, start at the bottom of the nail tip and move up two-thirds of the nail (Figure 19–26). Apply more coats or passes of the airbrush over the free edge or nail tip, with fewer passes or coats of paint through the center of the nail. The two colors must, when overlapped, begin to form a beautiful transition zone between them.

5 ***Continue to apply a light, even coat, moving back and forth diagonally over the bottom two-thirds of the nail.*** Continue until you have achieved the desired color at the free edge of the nail (Figure 19–26). Remember that when working on your client, the airbrushed color fade on the right hand should be a mirror image of the color fade on the left hand. Many nail professionals prefer to have the colors travel from the outer corner of the nail (toward the pinkie finger) to the inner corner of the cuticle area (toward the thumb), but each airbrush artist has her or his own style.

6 ***Apply a top coat or sealer and let it dry for 3 minutes.*** If you are not going to continue airbrushing, clean your airbrush at this time. You may also apply a second layer of top coat or sealer for maximum durability. Instruct your client on home maintenance of the airbrushed nail color. The color-fade technique is unique to the airbrush, since it is the only tool capable of giving a smooth transition zone. The photo (Figure 19–27) shows a few possible variations of this design. The nail tip on the left is a subtle blend for the conservative client. It is a cognac nail color with a transparent gold shimmer splashed at the free edge. The center nail is a bit more daring: pearl red at the base of the nail fading into a true pink nail tip. The nail tip on the right is the final result of this procedure. This nail color selection is for a bold client who wants people to notice her nails!

Figure 19–26 For the second color, start at the bottom of the nail tip and move up two-thirds of the nail.

Figure 19–27 Three variations of the design.

here's a tip...

Many metallic and pearlescent paints will not be visible until they are covered with a top coat or sealer, and most paints look very different afterward as well.

PROCEDURE 19-4
TRADITIONAL FRENCH MANICURE APPLICATION

Figure 19–28 Apply base coat.

1 *Apply a clear base coat to the nail(s).* You may use a French manicure polish over the nail bed area, if desired. Allow plenty of time for the nail polish to dry. (If you choose not to airbrush the nail bed area, go to step 4.) You can use a crystalline base coat to neutralize the color of the nail tip (Figure 19–28).

2 *Choose your French manicure airbrush paint.* Mist the French manicure color over the nail lightly. If you want the color to be opaque, continue the passes of your airbrush over the nail until the desired color or opacity is achieved. If your client desires a transparent French manicure color, mist the opaque color lightly. Most airbrush paint colors may be made slightly transparent by adding a couple drops of distilled water, if recommended by the paint manufacturer.

3 *Optional shimmer.* Add a shimmer to your French manicure paint by misting a gold highlight or shimmer evenly over the French beige (Figure 19–29).

Figure 19–29 Add a shimmer to your French manicure by using a gold highlight.

4 *French tip application with a stencil.* You will use a curved edge to cover the nail bed area and expose the nail tip so that it can be sprayed white. This is an excellent method for a soft-edged French nail tip. You can cut a curved piece of paper into the proper shape, but there are many ready-made stencils on the market, including the rounded edge of a nail form used for nail extensions. Hold the stencil as close to the nail as possible, exposing the area to be sprayed. Keep the stencil parallel to the nail to avoid scratching the paint on the nail. Self-adhesive masks are available, and can be more user-friendly for this service. When you have the stencil lined up, mist the nail tip white. Build the color slowly, to avoid getting the paint wet and runny.

here's a tip...

Watch the edge of your stencil if it is plastic. The paint easily accumulates and may run down onto the nail.

Dry the stencil with air from your airbrush without moving it, as it is difficult to line up the stencil in precisely the same position. When working with stencils, mist paint and then blow air to dry the nail tip and stencil. Repeat the process until the nail tip is the desired color (Figure 19–30).

5 *If the nails that you are working on have a deep C-curve, you may have to touch up the stenciled nails.* Using the stencil, roll the finger sideways and carefully line up the stencil with the white tip that has been sprayed previously. Lightly mist the sides of the nail to match and complete the white tip. This problem is resolved with the use of self-adhesive masks.

6 *Optional.* Adding a lunula or moon with a stencil creates the "real" look. Mist the lunula slightly lighter than nail tip color.

7 *Apply nail sealer or top coat.* After you have completed all nails, apply your nail sealer or top coat, and let it dry for 3 minutes.

8 *This procedure is easily accomplished on toes.* Use your preferred method to apply the French manicure to the toes.

9 *Cleanse the fingers or toes with airbrush paint cleanser as previously described* (Figure 19–31).

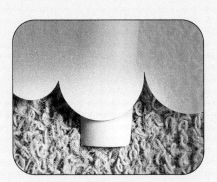

Figure 19–30 Mist paint over the stencil.

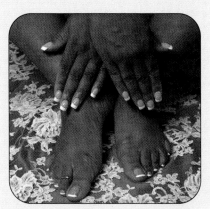

Figure 19–31 Finished French manicure.

TRADITIONAL FRENCH MANICURE (WITH OPTIONAL LUNULA)

The French manicure look is the single best reason for nail professionals to use an airbrush. No other technique can compare! The airbrushed French manicure is easier, quicker, and more attractive. It has a clean, sophisticated look, yet retains a neutral color application that matches all clothing. There are three popular methods, and to each of these you may add a white lunula or moon to the cuticle area if desired (for a slight additional charge).

REVIEW **QUESTIONS**

1. Why should you develop nail art skills?

2. List the three basics of nail art.

3. What is the technique called for airbrushing two or more colors on the nail at the same time?

4. List four nail art services.

5. List four of the classifications of color on the color wheel.

6. How does the finished airbrushed French manicure differ from the traditional application?

7. Describe the parts of the airbrush and how they work together to release the paint.

8. Describe the best airbrush to use for nails.

9. What is the most common choice for an air source for airbrushing nails?

10. What is the most common air pressure used by nail professionals when airbrushing?

11. Describe the procedure for an airbrushed version of a French manicure.

CHAPTER **GLOSSARY**

air hose	Hose that connects an airbrush compressor (the air source) to the airbrush itself.
belly	Midsection of the brush bristles; the area of the brush that retains the most paint.
color fade (color blend)	Airbrushing technique applying subtle color combinations across the same nail at the same time.
color wheel	Color guide that illustrates and identifies the primary, secondary, tertiary, and complementary colors.
complementary colors	Colors located directly opposite each other on the color wheel.
double loading	Placing two different colors of paint on either side of the brush—usually a darker color on one side and a lighter color on the other.
floating the bead	Technique used to seal nail art where a bead of sealer is dropped onto the nail surface, and the brush floats across the surface and completely covers it with sealer.
fluid nozzle (tip)	Small cone-shaped nozzle at the end of an airbrush that holds the needle that releases the paint.
foil adhesive	Special adhesive just for foiling that is generally tinted white or pink and appears cloudy when it is wet.
foiling	One of the easiest and most cost-effective nail art techniques, it is applied after polish with a foil adhesive to create colors and patterns not available with standard polishing techniques.
freehand painting	Also referred to as flat nail art; a very expensive form of nail art using brushes and paint to create designs.
French manicure	Airbrushing technique that creates a natural-looking nail with a smooth white tip at the free edge.

gem	Tiny jewel that adds sparkle, dimension, and texture to any nail art.
gravity-fed	Airbrush system designed to pull the paint into the airbrush using gravity.
heel	Point at which the bristles of the brush meet the ferrule.
leafing (gold leafing)	Also known as nuggets or nugget sheets. Thin, fragile foil-like material, available in gold, silver, and a variety of other colors used to create a quick and easy form of nail art.
marbleizer (stylus)	Tool with wooden handles and a rounded ball tip that can range in size, and are excellent for dotting small circles of color on a nail.
mask knife	One-sided knife used to cut designs out of mask paper or plastic to create nail art stencils.
mask paper	Paper used to create nail-art design stencils.
nail art	Add-on service offered at many salons that applies creative and unique custom designs to the finished nail.
needle	Piece that fits into the fluid nozzle of an airbrush and controls the amount of paint released when the trigger is depressed.
position	Way that a brush is held to create nail art; the brush can be positioned straight up -and -down or laid down with the bristles pulled across the paint surface.
pressure	Amount of force that an artist applies to a brush while in the stroke motion when applying nail art.
primary colors	Colors that cannot be obtained from mixing together other colors.
pull	Flow of a brush across a painted nail surface, giving it a fluid movement and avoiding a rough spattered look.
secondary colors	Colors resulting from mixing equal parts of two primary colors; the positions opposite to the primary colors on a color wheel.
stencil	Precut designs made of plastic, paper, or fabric, used to create nail art.
stripette or short striper	Shorter version of the stripe brush.
striping tape	Tacky-backed tape available in an assortment of colors that is applied over nail polish or other nail art to create bolder designs.
tertiary colors	Colors resulting from mixing equal parts of one primary color and one of its nearest secondary colors.
tip	Very end of the bristles, farthest away from the handle.
well (small color cup or reservoir)	Hole in the top of the airbrush where drips of paint are placed and stored.

BUSINESS SKILLS

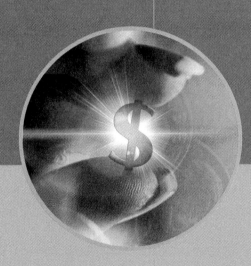

Seeking Employment

LEARNING OBJECTIVES

After completing this chapter, you will be able to:

1. Discuss the essentials of becoming test-wise.

2. Explain the steps involved in preparing for employment.

3. List and describe the different types of salon businesses.

4. Write an achievement-oriented resume and prepare an employment portfolio.

5. Explain how to explore the job market and research potential employers.

6. Be prepared to complete an effective employment interview.

KEY **TERMS**

Page number indicates where in the chapter the term is used.

deductive reasoning
pg. 361

resume
pg. 368

transferable skills
pg. 370

work ethic
pg. 366

employment portfolio
pg. 372

test-wise
pg. 358

T here are plenty of great jobs out there for energetic, hardworking, talented people. If you look at the top professionals in the field, you will find they were not born successful; they achieved success through self-motivation, energy, and persistence. Like you, these practitioners began their careers by enrolling in cosmetology school. They were the ones who used their time wisely, planned for the future, went the extra mile, and drew on a reservoir of self-confidence to meet any challenge. They owe their success to no one but themselves, because they created it. If you want to enjoy this same success, you must prepare for the opportunities that await you.

No matter what changes occur in the economy, there are often more jobs available for entry-level cosmetology professionals than there are people to fill them. This is a tremendous advantage for you. It does not mean, however, that you do not have to thoroughly research the job market in your chosen area before committing to your first job (Figure 20–1). If you make the right choice, your career will be on the road to success. If you make the wrong choice, it will not be a tragedy, but it will cause unnecessary delay.

PREPARING FOR LICENSURE

Before you can obtain the career position you are hoping for, you must first pass your state licensing examination and secure the required credentials. Many factors will affect how well you perform during that licensing examination and on tests in general. They include your physical and psychological state; your memory; time management; and the skills you have developed in reading, writing, note taking, test taking, and general learning.

Of all the factors that will affect your test performance, the most important is your mastery of course content. Even if you feel that you have truly learned the material, though, it is still very beneficial to have strong test-taking skills. Being test-wise means understanding the strategies for successfully taking tests.

Preparing for the Test

A **test-wise** student begins to prepare for taking a test by practicing good study habits and time management that are such an important part of effective studying. These habits include the following:

○ Having a planned, realistic study schedule

Figure 20–1 Job listings are often posted on the school bulletin board.

- Reading content carefully and becoming an active studier

- Keeping a well-organized notebook

- Developing a detailed vocabulary list

- Taking effective notes during class

- Organizing and reviewing handouts

- Reviewing past quizzes and tests

- Listening carefully in class for cues and clues about what could be expected on the test

In addition, there are other, more holistic (having to do with the "whole you") hints to keep in mind.

- Make yourself mentally ready and develop a positive attitude toward taking the test.

- Get plenty of rest the night before the test.

- Dress comfortably.

- Anticipate some anxiety (feeling concerned about the test results may actually help you do better).

- Avoid cramming the night before an examination.

On Test Day

After you have taken all the necessary steps to prepare for your test, there are a number of strategies you can adopt on the day of the actual exam that may be helpful (Figure 20–2).

1. Relax and try to slow down physically.

Figure 20–2 Candidates taking the licensing examination.

2. If possible, review the material lightly the day of the exam.

3. Arrive early with a self-confident attitude; be alert, calm, and ready for the challenge.

4. Read all written directions, and listen carefully to all verbal directions before beginning.

5. If there are things you do not understand, do not hesitate to ask the examiner questions.

6. Skim the entire test before beginning.

7. Budget your time to ensure that you have plenty of opportunity to complete the test; do not spend too much time on any one question.

8. Wear a watch so that you can monitor the time.

9. Begin work as soon as possible and mark the answers in the test booklet carefully, but quickly.

10. Answer the easiest questions first in order to save time for the more difficult ones. Quickly scanning all the questions first may clue you in to the more difficult questions.

11. Mark the questions you skip so that you can find them again later.

12. Read each question carefully to make sure that you know exactly what the question is asking, and that you understand all parts of the question.

13. Answer as many questions as possible. For questions that you are unsure of, guess or estimate.

14. Look over the test when you are done to be ensure that you have read all questions correctly, and have answered as many as possible.

15. Make changes to answers only if there is a good reason to do so.

16. Check the test booklet carefully before turning it in (for instance, you might have forgotten to put your name on it!).

Deductive Reasoning

Another technique that students should learn to use for better test results is called **deductive reasoning**. Deductive reasoning is the process of reaching logical conclusions by employing logical reasoning.

Some strategies associated with deductive reasoning follow.

Eliminate options known to be incorrect. The more answers you can eliminate as incorrect, the better your chances of identifying the correct one.

Watch for key words or terms. Look for any qualifying conditions or statements. Keep an eye out for such words and phrases as: **usually, commonly, in most instances, never, always**, and the like.

Study the stem (the basic question or problem). It will often provide a clue to the correct answer. Look for a match between the stem and one of the choices.

Watch for grammatical clues. For instance, if the last word in a stem is "an," the answer must begin with a vowel rather than a consonant.

Looking at similar or related questions. They may provide clues.

In answering essay questions, watch for words such as **compare, contrast, discuss, evaluate, analyze, define**, or **describe** and develop your answer accordingly.

In reading-type tests that contain long paragraphs followed by several questions, read the questions first. This will help identify the important elements in the paragraph.

Understanding Test Formats

There are a few additional tips that all test-wise learners should know, especially with respect to the state licensing examination. Keep in mind, of course, that the most important strategy of test taking is to **know your material**. With that said, however, consider the following tips on the various types of question formats.

True/False

○ Watch for qualifying words (**all, most, some, none, always, usually, sometimes, never, little, no, equal, less, good, bad**). Absolutes (**all, none, always, never**) are generally **not** true.

○ For a statement to be true, the **entire** statement must be true.

○ Long statements are more likely to be true than short statements. It takes more detail to provide truthful, factual information.

Multiple Choice

o Read the entire question carefully, including all the choices.

o Look for the best answer; more than one choice may be true.

o Eliminate incorrect answers by crossing them out (if taking the test on the test form).

o When two choices are close or similar, one of them is probably right.

o When two choices are identical, both must be wrong.

o When two choices are opposites, one is probably wrong, and one is probably correct, depending on the number of other choices.

o "All of the above" types of responses are often the correct response.

o Pay special attention to words such as **not**, **except**, **but**.

o Guess if you do not know the answer (providing there is no penalty).

o The answer to one question may be in the stem of another (Figure 20–3).

FINAL EXAM

1. The study of the hair is called:
   - a. hairology
   - b. dermatology
   - c. trichology
   - d. biology

2. Hair is not found on the palms of the hands, soles of the feet, lips, and:
   - a. neck
   - b. eyelids
   - c. ankles
   - d. wrists

3. The technical term for eyelash hair is:
   - a. cilia
   - b. barba
   - c. capilli
   - d. supercilia

4. Hair is composed chiefly of:
   - a. oxygen
   - b. keratin
   - c. melanin
   - d. sulfur

5. The two main divisions of the hair are the hair root and:
   - a. hair shaft
   - b. follicle
   - c. papilla
   - d. bulb

6. The hair root is located:
   - a. above the skin surface
   - b. below the skin surface
   - c. under the cuticle
   - d. within the cortex

7. The hair root is encased by a tubelike depression in the skin known as the:
   - a. bulb
   - b. arrector pili
   - c. papilla
   - d. follicle

8. The club-shaped structure that forms the lower part of the hair root is the:
   - a. arrector pili
   - b. bulb
   - c. papilla
   - d. hair shaft

Figure 20–3 Sample of a multiple-choice test.

Matching

○ Read all items in each list before beginning.

○ Check off items from the brief response list to eliminate choices.

Essays

○ Organize your answer according to the cue words in the question.

○ Think carefully and outline your answer before you begin writing.

○ Make sure that what you write is complete, accurate, relevant to the question, well organized, and clear.

Remember that even though you may understand test formats and effective test-taking strategies, this does not take the place of having a complete understanding of the material on which you are being tested. In order to be successful at taking tests, you must follow the rules of effective studying and be thoroughly knowledgeable of the exam content for both the written and the practical examination.

In order to be better prepared for the practical portion of the examination, the new graduate should follow these tips:

○ Practice the correct skills required in the test as often as you can.

○ Participate in "mock" licensing examinations, including the timing of applicable examination criteria.

○ Familiarize yourself with the content contained in the examination bulletins sent by the licensing agency.   .

○ Make certain that all equipment and implements are clean, sanitary, and in good working order prior to the exam.

○ If allowed by the regulatory or licensing agency, observe other practical examinations prior to taking yours.

○ If possible, locate the examination site the day before the exam to ensure that you are on time for the actual exam.

○ As with any exam, listen carefully to the examiner's instructions and follow them explicitly.

○ Focus on your own knowledge, and do not allow yourself to be concerned with what other test candidates are doing.

○ Follow all sanitation and safety procedures throughout the entire examination.

PREPARING FOR EMPLOYMENT

When you chose to enter the field of cosmetology, your primary goal was to find a good job after being licensed. Now you need to reaffirm that goal by reviewing a number of important questions.

○ What do you really want out of a career in cosmetology?

○ What particular areas within the beauty industry are the most interesting to you?

INVENTORY OF PERSONAL CHARACTERISTICS

PERSONAL CHARACTERISTIC	Exc.	Good	Avg.	Poor	Plan for Improvement
Posture, Deportment, Poise					
Grooming, Personal Hygiene					
Manners, Courtesy					
Communications Skills					
Attitude					
Self-Motivation					
Personal Habits					
Responsibility					
Self-esteem, Self Confidence					
Honesty, Integrity					
Dependability					

INVENTORY OF TECHNICAL SKILLS

TECHNICAL SKILLS	Exc.	Good	Avg.	Poor	Plan for Improvement
Hair shaping/cutting					
Hairstyling					
Hair Coloring					
Texture Services, Perming					
Texture Services, Relaxing					
Manicuring, Pedicuring					
Artificial Nail Extensions					
Skin Care, Facials					
Facial Makeup					
Other					

After analyzing the above responses, would you hire yourself as an employee in your firm? Why or why not?

State your short-term goals that you hope to accomplish in 6 to 12 months:

State your long-term goals that you hope to accomplish in 1 to 5 years:

Ask yourself: Do you want to work in a big city or small town? Are you compatible with a sophisticated, exclusive salon or a trendy salon? Which clientele are you able to communicate with more effectively? Do you want to start out slowly and carefully or do you want to jump in and throw everything into your career from the starting gate? Will you be in this industry throughout your working career or is this just a stopover? Will you only work a 30 or 40 hour week or will you go the extra mile when opportunities are available? How ambitious are you and how many risks are you willing to take?

Figure 20–4 Inventory of personal characteristics and technical skills.

Figure 20–5 Your school counselor can help you find employment.

- What are your strongest practical skills, and in what ways do you wish to use them?

- What personal qualities will help you have a successful career?

One way that you can answer these questions is to make a copy of, and then complete the Personal Inventory of Characteristics and Skills (Figure 20–4). After you have completed this inventory and identified the areas that need further attention, you can then determine where to focus the remainder of your training. In addition, you should have a better idea of what type of establishment would best suit you for your eventual employment.

During your training, you may have the opportunity to network with various industry professionals who are invited to be guest speakers. Be prepared to ask them questions about what they like least and most in their current positions. Ask them for any tips they might have that will assist you in your search for the right establishment. In addition, be sure to take advantage of your institution's in-house placement assistance program when you begin your employment search (Figure 20–5).

Your willingness to work hard is a key ingredient to your success. The commitment you make now in terms of time and effort will pay off later in the workplace, where your energy will be appreciated and rewarded. Having enthusiasm for getting the job done can be contagious, and when everyone works hard, everyone benefits. You can begin to develop this enthusiasm by establishing good work habits as a student.

For 1 week, keep a daily record of your performance in the following areas, and ask a few of your fellow students to provide feedback as well.

- Positive attitude

- Professional appearance

- Punctuality

- Regular class and clinic attendance

- Diligent practice of newly learned techniques

- Interpersonal skills

- Teamwork

- Helping others

activity

How to Get the Job You Want

There are several key personal characteristics that will not only help you get the position you want, but will help you keep it. These characteristics include the following points.

Motivation. This means having the drive to take the necessary action to achieve a goal. Although motivation can come from external sources—parental or peer pressure, for instance—the best kind of motivation is internal.

Integrity. When you have integrity, you are committed to a strong code of moral and artistic values. Integrity is the compass that keeps you on course over the long haul of your career.

Good technical and communication skills. While you may be better in either technical or communication skills, you must develop both to reach the level of success you desire.

Strong work ethic. In the beauty business, having a strong work ethic means taking pride in your work, and committing yourself to consistently doing a good job for your clients, employer, and salon team.

Enthusiasm. Try never to lose your eagerness to learn, grow, and expand your skills and knowledge.

A Salon Survey

In the United States alone, the professional salon business numbers nearly 313,000 establishments. These salons employ more than 1,604,000 active cosmetology professionals. This year, like every year, thousands of cosmetology school graduates will find their first position in one of the types of salons described below.

Small Independent Salons

Owned by an individual or two or more partners, this kind of operation makes up the majority of professional salons. The average independent salon has three styling chairs, but many have as many as 40 styling stations. Usually, the owners are hair practitioners who maintain their own clientele while managing the business. There are nearly as many different kinds of independent salons as there are owners. Their image, decor, services, prices, and clientele all reflect the owner's experience and taste. Depending on the owner's willingness to help a newcomer learn and grow, a beginning stylist can learn a great deal in an independent salon while also earning a good living.

Independent Salon Chains

These are usually chains of five or more salons that are owned by one individual or two or more partners. Independent salon chains range from basic hair salons, to full-service salons and day spas, and offer everything from low-priced to very high-priced services.

In large high-end salons, practitioners can advance to specialized positions in color, nail care, skin care, or other chemical services. Some larger salons also employ education directors and style directors, and practitioners are often hired to manage particular locations.

Large National Salon Chains

These companies operate salons throughout the country, and even internationally. They can be budget- or value-priced, haircut only or full service, mid-price or high end. Some salon chains operate within department store chains. Management and marketing professionals at the corporate headquarters make all the decisions for each salon, such as size, decor, hours, services, prices, advertising, and profit targets. Many newly licensed cosmetology professionals seek their first jobs in national chain salons because of the secure pay and benefits, additional paid training, management opportunities, and corporate advertising. Because the chains are large and widespread, employees have the added advantage of being able to transfer from one location to another.

Franchise Salons

Another form of chain salon organization, this one has a national name and consistent image and business formula throughout the chain. Franchises are owned by individuals who pay a fee to use the name; these individuals then receive a business plan and can take advantage of national marketing campaigns. Such decisions as size, location, decor, and prices are determined in advance by the parent company. Franchises are generally not owned by practitioners, but by investors who seek a return on their investment.

Franchise salons often offer employees the same benefits as corporate-owned chain salons.

Basic Value-Priced Operations

Often located in busy, low-rent shopping center strips that are anchored by a nearby supermarket or other large business, these outlets depend on a high volume of walk-in traffic. They hire recent cosmetology graduates and generally pay them by the hour, sometimes adding commission-style bonuses if individual sales pass a certain level. Haircuts are usually priced below $15, and practitioners are trained to work fast with no frills. These types of salons rarely employ nail technicians.

Mid-Priced Full-Service Salons

These salons offer a complete menu of hair, nail, and skin services and retail products. Successful mid-priced salons promote their most profitable services and often offer "service and retail packages" to entice haircut-only clients. They also run strong marketing programs to encourage client returns and referrals. These salons train their professional styling team to be as productive and profitable as possible. If you are inclined to give more time to each client during the consultation, you may like working in a full-service salon. Here you will have the opportunity to build a relationship with clients that may extend over time.

Figure 20–6 A high-end salon.

High-End "Image" Salons or Day Spas

This type of business employs well-trained practitioners and salon assistants who offer higher-priced services to clients that are filled with luxurious extras such as a 5-minute head, neck, and shoulder massage as part of the shampoo and luxurious spa manicures and pedicures. Most high-end salons are located in trendy, upscale sections of large cities; others may be located in elegant mansions, high-rent office and retail towers, or luxury hotels and resorts. Clients expect a high level of personal service, and such salons hire practitioners whose technical expertise, personal appearance, and communication skills meet their high standards. (Figure 20–6).

Booth Rental Establishments

Booth renting (also called chair rental) is possibly the least expensive way of owning one's own business. For a detailed discussion of booth rental, see Chapter 22.

Resume Development

A **resume** is a written summary of your education and work experience. It tells potential employers at a glance what your achievements and accomplishments are. Here are some basic guidelines to follow when preparing your professional resume.

- Keep it simple. Limit to one page if possible.

- Print it on good quality bond paper that is white, buff, or gray.

- Include your name, address, phone number, and e-mail address on both the resume and your cover letter.

- List recent, relevant work experience.

- List relevant education and the name of the institution from which you graduated, as well as relevant courses attended.

- List your abilities and accomplishments.

- Focus on information that is relevant to the position you are seeking.

The average time that a potential employer will spend scanning your resume before deciding whether to grant you an interview is about 20 seconds. That means you must market yourself in such a manner that the reader will want to meet you. Never make the mistake of detailing your previous duties and responsibilities. Rather, focus on your achievements. Accomplishment statements should always enlarge on your basic duties and responsibilities.

The best way to do this is to add numbers or percentages whenever possible. You might ask yourself the following questions:

O How many regular clients do I serve?

O How many clients do I serve weekly?

O What was my service ticket average?

O What was my client retention rate?

O What percentage of my client revenue came from retailing?

O What percentage of client revenue came from color or texture services?

This type of questioning can help you develop accomplishment statements that will interest a potential employer. There is no better time for you to achieve significant accomplishments than while you are in school. Even though your experience may be minimal, you must still present evidence of your skills and accomplishments. This may seem a difficult task at this early stage in your working career, but by closely examining your training performance, extracurricular activities, and the full- or part-time jobs you have held, you should be able to create a good, attention-getting resume. For example:

O Did you receive any honors during your course of training?

O Were you ever selected "student of the month"?

O Did you receive special recognition for your attendance or academic progress?

O Did you win any cosmetology-related competitions while in school? What was your attendance average while in school?

O Did you work with the student body to organize any fundraisers? What were the results? Answers to these types of questions may indicate your people skills, personal work habits, and personal commitment to success (Figure 20–7).

Since you have not yet completed your training, you still have the opportunity to make some of the examples listed above become a reality before you graduate. Positive developments of this nature while you are still in school can do much to improve your resume.

The Do's and Don'ts of Resumes

You will save yourself a lot of problems and disappointment right from the beginning of your job search, if you keep a clear idea in your mind of what

Figure 20–7 Excelling in school can help you build a good resume.

to do and what not to do when it comes to creating a resume. Here are some of the do's:

Make it easy to read. Use concise, clear sentences and avoid "overwriting" or flowery language.

Know your audience. Use vocabulary and language that will be understood by your potential employer.

Keep it short. Make sure the overall length does not exceed two pages. One page is preferable.

Stress accomplishments. Emphasize past accomplishments and the skills you used to achieve them.

Focus on career goals. Highlight information that is relevant to your career goals and the position you are seeking.

Emphasize transferable skills. Transferable skills are the skills you have already mastered at other jobs that can be put to use in a new position.

Use action verbs. Begin accomplishment statements with action verbs such as **achieved**, **coordinated**, **developed**, **increased**, **maintained**, and **strengthened**.

Make it neat. A poorly structured, badly typed resume does not reflect well on you.

And now for the don'ts to watch out for:

Avoid salary references. Don't state your salary history or reason for leaving your former employment.

Don't stretch the truth. Misinformation or untruthful statements usually catch up with you.

Don't include personal references. Potential employers are really only interested in references that can speak about your professional ability.

Don't expect too much. Don't have unrealistic expectations of what your resume can accomplish.

Review Figure 20–8, which represents an achievement-oriented resume for a recent graduate of a cosmetology course. But keep in mind that

MARY CURL
143 Fern Circle
Anytown, USA 12345
(123) 555-1234

A cosmetologist with honors in attendance and practical skills who is creative, artistic, and works well with people of all ages.

ACCOMPLISHMENTS/ABILITIES

Academics   Achieved an "A" average in theoretical requirements and excellent ratings in practical requirements; Exceeded the number of practical skills required for graduation.

Sales   Named "Student of the Month" for best attendance, best attitude, highest retail sales, and most clients served; Increased chemical services to 30 percent of my clinic volume by graduation. Achieved a client ticket average comparable to $33.00 in the area salon market.

Increased retail sales of cosmetics by over 18 percent during part-time employment at local department store.

Client Retention   Developed and retained a personal client base of over 75 individuals of all ages, both male and female.

Image Consulting   Certified as an Image Consultant who aids in providing full salon services to all clientele.

Administration   Supervised a student "salon team" which developed a business plan for opening a twelve chair, full service salon; project earned an "A" and was recognized for thoroughness, accuracy, and creativity.

As President of the student council, organized fund raising activities including car washes, bake sales, and yard sales which generated enough funds to send 19 students to a hair show in El Paso.

Externship   Trained one day weekly at the salon for ten weeks under the state approved student externship program.

Special Projects   Reorganized school facial room for more efficiency and client comfort.

Organized the school dispensary which increased inventory control and streamlined operations within the clinic.

Catalogued the school's library of texts, books, videos and other periodicals by category and updated the library inventory list.

EXPERIENCE

Salon Etc.   Spring 2002
Student Extern in all Phases of Cosmetology
Dilberts   Summer 2002
Retail Sales, Cosmetics
Food Emporium   1999-2001
Cashier

EDUCATION

Graduate, New Alamo High School, 2000
Graduate, Milady Career Institute of Cosmetology, August 2002
Licensed as Cosmetologist, September 2002

Figure 20–8 An achievement-oriented resume.

Figure 20–9 Before and after photos in an employment portfolio.

you are much more than the sum of your parts. It just may take a while before someone recognizes that.

Employment Portfolio

As you prepare to work in the field of cosmetology, an **employment portfolio** can be extremely useful. An employment portfolio is a collection, usually bound, of photos and documents that reflect your skills, accomplishments, and abilities in your chosen career field (Figure 20–9).

While the actual contents of the portfolio will vary from graduate to graduate, there are certain items that have a place in any portfolio.

A powerful portfolio includes:

o Diplomas, including high school and cosmetology school

o Awards and achievements received while a cosmetology student

o Current resume, focusing on accomplishments

o Letters of reference from former employers

o Summary of continuing education and/or copies of training certificates

o Statement of membership in industry and other professional organizations

o Statement of relevant civic affiliations and/or community activities

o Before-and-after photographs of services that you have performed on clients or models

o Brief statement about why you have chosen a career in cosmetology

o Any other information that you regard as relevant

Once you have assembled your portfolio, ask yourself whether it accurately portrays you and your career skills. If it does not, identify what needs to be changed. If you are not sure, run it by a neutral party for feedback about how to make it more interesting and accurate. This kind of feedback is also useful when creating a resume. The portfolio, like the resume, should be prepared in a way that projects professionalism.

○ Nothing should be handwritten. All summaries and letters should be typed.

○ For ease of use, you may want to separate sections with tabs.

○ When writing about why you chose a career in cosmetology, you might include a statement that explains what you love about your new career, a description of your philosophy about the importance of teamwork and how you see yourself as a contributing team member, and a description of methods you would try in an effort to increase service and retail revenue.

Targeting the Establishment

One of the most important steps in the process of job hunting is narrowing your search. Here are some points to keep in mind about targeting potential employers:

○ **Accept that you probably will not begin in your dream job.** Few people are so lucky.

○ **Do not wait until graduation to begin your search.** If you do, you may be tempted to take the first offer you receive, instead of carefully investigating all possibilities before making a decision.

○ **Locate a salon that serves the type of clients you wish to serve.** Finding a good fit with the clients and staff is critical from the outset of your career.

○ **Make a list of area salons or establishments.** The yellow pages will be your best source for this. If you are considering relocating to another area, your local library will probably have out-of-state phone directories to help you compile your list. You may also access *www.anywho.com* on the Internet for a complete listing of businesses throughout the United States.

○ **Follow newspapers, television, and radio for salon advertising.** Get a feel for what market each salon is targeting.

Field Research

A great way to find out about jobs is to actually get out there and use your eyes, ears, and any other sense that can help you gather information. A highly effective technique that you should learn is called "networking."

Networking allows you to establish contacts that may eventually lead to a job, and helps you gain valuable information about the workings of various establishments. If possible, make contact with salons while you are still a student. You might even make contact as a salon customer yourself.

Dear Ms. (or Mr.) _____,

I appreciate the time you spent with me on the phone earlier today. I am looking forward to meeting with you and visiting your salon next Friday at 2:00 p.m. I am eager to observe your salon and staff at work. If you should need to reach me before that time for any reason, my home phone number is _____. See you on Friday.

Sincerely,
(your name)

Figure 20–10 A sample appointment confirmation note.

When you are ready to network, your first contact should be by telephone, and you should follow these guidelines:

1. Use your best telephone manner. Speak with confidence and self-assurance.

2. Ask to speak to the owner, manager, or personnel director.

3. State your name and explain that you are preparing to graduate from school in your chosen field.

4. Explain that you are researching the local salon market for potential positions, and that you need just a few minutes to ask a few questions.

5. If the person is receptive to your phone call, ask whether the salon is in need of any new practitioners, and how many the salon currently employs.

6. Ask if you can make an appointment to visit the salon to observe sometime during the next few weeks. If the salon representative is agreeable, make an appointment and confirm it with a typewritten or handwritten note on good-quality paper (Figure 20–10).

Remember that a rejection is not a poor reflection on you. Many professionals are too busy to make time for this kind of networking. The good news is that you are bound to discover many genuinely kind people who remember what it was like when they started out, and are willing to devote a bit of their time to help others who are beginning their careers.

The Salon Visit

When you visit the salon, take along a checklist to ensure that you observe all the key areas that might ultimately affect your decision making. The checklist will be similar to the one used for field trips you probably have taken to area salons while in school. Keep the checklist on file for future reference so that you can make informed comparisons between establishments (Figure 20–11).

SALON VISIT CHECKLIST

When you visit a salon, observe the following areas and rate them from 1 to 5, with 5 considered being the best.

_____ **SALON IMAGE:** Is the salon's image consistent and appropriate for your interests? Is the image pleasing and inviting? What is the decor and arrangement? If you are not comfortable or if you find it unattractiive, it is likely that clients will also.

_____ **PROFESSIONALISM:** Do the employees present the appropriate professional appearance and behavior? Do they give their clients the appropriate levels of attention and personal service or do they act as if work is their time to socialize?

_____ **MANAGEMENT:** Does the salon show signs of being well managed? Is the phone answered promptly with professional telephone skills? Is the mood of the salon positive? Does everyone appear to work as a team?

_____ **CLIENT SERVICE:** Are clients greeted promptly and warmly when they enter the salon? Are they kept informed of the status of their appointment? Are they offered a magazine or beverage while they wait? Is there a comfortable reception area? Are there changing rooms, attractive smocks, or perhaps a complimentary hand treatment while clients wait?

_____ **PRICES:** Compare price for value. Are clients getting their money's worth? Do they pay the same price in one salon but get better service and attention in another? If possible, take home salon brochures and price lists.

_____ **RETAIL:** Is there a well-stocked retail display offering clients a variety of product lines and a range of prices? Do the stylists and receptionist (if applicable) promote retail sales?

_____ **IN-SALON MARKETING:** Are there posters or promotions throughout the salon? If so, are they tasteful and of good quality?

_____ **SERVICES:** Make a list of all services offered by each salon and the product lines they carry. This will help you decide what earning potential stylists have in each salon.

SALON NAME: _____

SALON MANAGER: _____

Figure 20–11 Salon visit checklist.

After your visit, always remember to write a brief note thanking the salon representative for his or her time (Figure 20–12). Even if you did not like the salon, or would never consider working there, it is important to send a thank-you note (Figure 20–13).

Never burn your bridges. Rather, build a network of contacts who have a favorable opinion of you.

Arranging the Employment Interview

After you have graduated and completed the first two steps in the process of securing employment—targeting and observing salons—you are ready to pursue employment in earnest. The next step is to contact the establishments that you are most interested in by sending them a resume with a cover letter requesting an interview.

Dear Ms. (or Mr.) _____,

I appreciate having had the opportunity to observe your salon/spa in operation last Friday. Thank you for the time you and your staff gave me. I was impressed by the efficient and courteous manner in which your stylists served their clients. The atmosphere was pleasant and the mood was positive. Should you ever have an opening for a professional with my skills and training, I would welcome the opportunity to apply. You can contact me at the address and phone number listed below. I hope we will meet again soon.

Sincerely,

(your name, address, telephone)

Figure 20–12 Sample thank-you note.

Dear Ms. (or Mr.) _____,

I appreciate having had the opportunity to observe your salon in operation last Friday. I know how busy you and all your staff are and want to thank you for the time that you gave me. I realize that it can be somewhat disruptive to have visitors observing your activities. I hope my presence didn't interfere with the flow of your operations too much. I certainly appreciate the courtesies that were extended to me by you and your staff. I wish you and your salon continued success.

Sincerely,

(your name)

Figure 20–13 Thank-you note to a salon at which you do not expect to seek employment.

Mark your calendar for a time when it would be suitable to make a follow-up call to this letter. A week is generally sufficient. When you call, try to schedule an interview appointment. Keep in mind that some salons may not have openings, and may not be granting interviews at this time. When this is the case, be polite and ask them to keep your resume on file should an opening arise in the future. Be sure to thank them for their time and consideration.

Interview Preparation

When preparing for an interview, make sure that you have all the necessary information and materials in place (Figure 20–14), including the following items:

1. **Identification.**
   - Social Security number
   - Driver's license number

here's a tip...

When you call a salon to make an appointment for an interview, you may be told that they are not hiring at the time, but would be happy to conduct an interview for future reference. Never think that this would be a waste of time.

Take advantage of the opportunity. Not only will it give you valuable interview experience, but who knows? There is such a thing as love at first sight!

PREPARING FOR THE INTERVIEW CHECKLIST

RESUME COMPOSITION
1. Does it present your abilities and what you have accomplished in your jobs and training?
2. Does it make the reader want to ask, "How did you accomplish that?"
3. Does it highlight accomplishments rather than detailing duties and responsibilities?
4. Is it easy to read, short, and does it stress past accomplishments and skills?
5. Does it focus on information that's relevant to your own career goals?
6. Is it complete and professionally prepared?

PORTFOLIO CHECKLIST
     Diploma, secondary, and post-secondary
     Awards and achievements while in school
     Current resume focusing on accomplishments
     Letters of reference from former employers
     List of, or certificates from, trade shows attended while in training.
     Statement of professional affiliations (memberships in cosmetology organizations, etc.)
     Statement of civic affiliations and/or activities.
     Before and after photographs of technical skills services you have performed.
     Any other relevant information
Ask: Does my portfolio portray me and my career skills in the manner that I wish to be perceived? If not, what needs to be changed?

GENERAL INFORMATION
Describe specific methods or procedures you will employ in the salon to build your clientele.

Describe how you feel about retail sales in the salon and give specific methods you would use in the salon to generate sales.

State why you feel consumer protection and safety is so important in the field of cosmetology.

After careful thought, explain what you love about your new career. Describe your passion for cosmetology.

Figure 20–14 Preparing for the interview checklist.

* Names, addresses, and phone numbers of former employers
* Name and phone number of the nearest relative not living with you

2. *Interview wardrobe.* Your appearance is crucial, especially since you are applying for a position in the image and beauty industry (Figure 20–15). It is recommended that you obtain one or two "interview outfits." You may be requested to return for a second interview; hence the need for the second outfit. Consider the following points:

* Is the outfit appropriate for the position?
* Is it both fashionable and flattering to your shape and personality?
* Are your accessories both fashionable and functional (e.g., not noisy or so large that they interfere with performing services)?
* Are your nails meticulously groomed and say something about your abilities as a nail technician?
* Is your hairstyle current? Does it flatter your face and your overall style?

Figure 20–15 Dressed for an interview.

* Is your make-up current? Does it flatter your face and your overall style?
* Are you clean shaven, or is your beard properly trimmed (for men)?
* Is your perfume or cologne subtle?
* Carry a handbag or briefcase, never both.

3. **Supporting materials.**
   * Resume. Even if you have already sent one, take another copy with you.
   * Facts and figures. Have ready a list of names and dates of former employment, education, and references.
   * Employment portfolio.

4. **Answers to anticipated questions.** Certain questions are typically asked during an interview. It would be a good idea to reflect on your answers ahead of time. You might even consider role-playing an interview situation with friends, family, or fellow students. Typical questions include the following:
   * What did you like best about your training?
   * Are you punctual and regular in attendance?
   * Will your school director or instructor confirm this?
   * What skills do you feel are your strongest?
   * What areas do you consider to be less strong?
   * Are you a team player? Please explain.
   * Do you consider yourself flexible? Please explain.
   * What are your career goals?
   * What days and hours are you available for work?
   * Do you have your own transportation?
   * Are there any obstacles that would prevent you from keeping your commitment to full-time employment?
   * What assets do you believe that you would bring to this salon and this position?
   * Who is the most interesting person you have met in your work and/or education experience? Why?
   * How would you handle a problem client?
   * How do you feel about retailing?
   * Would you be willing to attend our company training program?
   * Describe ways that you provide excellent customer service.
   * Please share an example of consultation questions that you might ask a client.
   * What steps do you take to build your business, and ensure that clients return to see you?

5. **Be prepared to perform a service.** Some salons require applicants to perform a service in their chosen discipline as part of the interview. Be sure to confirm whether this is a requirement. If it is, make sure that your model is appropriately dressed and properly prepared for the experience.

The Interview

On the day of the interview, try to make sure that nothing occurs that will keep you from completing the interview successfully. There are certain behaviors you should practice in connection with the interview itself.

○ Always be on time or, better yet, early. If you are unsure of the location, find it the day before so there will be no reason for delays.

○ Project a warm, friendly smile. Smiling is the universal language.

○ Walk, sit, and stand with good posture.

○ Be polite and courteous.

○ Do not sit until asked to do so, or until it is obvious that you are expected to do so.

○ Never smoke or chew gum, even if either is offered to you. Do not come to an interview with a cup of coffee, a soft drink, snacks, or anything else to eat or drink.

○ Never lean on or touch the interviewer's desk. Some people do not like their personal space invaded without an invitation.

○ Try to project a positive first impression by appearing as confident and relaxed as you can (Figure 20–16).

○ Speak clearly. The interviewer must be able to hear and understand you.

○ Answer questions honestly. Think the question and answer through carefully. Do not speak before you are ready, and not for more than 2 minutes at a time.

Figure 20–16 Interview in progress.

FYI

Many women find it difficult to afford the two or three outfits necessary to project a confident and professional image when going out into the workplace. Fortunately, several nonprofit organizations have been formed to address this need. These organizations receive donations of clean, beautiful clothes in good repair from individuals and manufacturers. These are then passed along to women who need them. For more information, visit Wardrobe for Opportunity at *http://www.wardrobe.org*, and Dress for Success at *http://www.dressforsuccess.org*.

○ Never criticize former employers.

○ Always remember to thank the interviewer at the end of the interview.

Another critical part of the interview comes when you are invited to ask the interviewer questions of your own. You should think about those questions ahead of time and bring a list if necessary. Doing so will show that you are organized and prepared. Some questions that you might consider include the following:

○ Is there a job description? May I review it?

○ Is there a salon manual?

○ How frequently does the salon advertise?

○ How long do practitioners typically work here?

○ Are employees encouraged to grow in skills and responsibility? How so?

○ Does the salon offer continuing education opportunities?

○ Is there room for advancement?

○ If so, what are the requirements for promotion?

○ What benefits does the salon offer, such as paid vacations, personal days, and medical insurance?

○ What is the form of compensation?

○ When will the position be filled?

○ Should I follow up on your decision, or will you contact me?

Do not feel that you have to ask all of your questions. The point is to create as much of a dialogue as possible. Be aware of the interviewer's reactions and make note of when you have asked enough questions. By obtaining the answers to at least some of your questions, you can compare the information you have gathered about other salons, and then choose the one that offers the best package of income and career development.

Remember to write a thank-you note. It should simply thank the interviewer for the time he or she spent with you. Close with a positive statement that you want the job (if you do). If the interviewer's decision comes down to two or three possibilities, the one expressing the most desire may be offered the position. Also, if the interviewer suggests that you call to learn about the employment decision, then by all means do so.

 activity

Find a partner among your fellow students and role-play the employment interview. Each of you can take turns as the applicant and the employer. After each session, conduct a brief discussion regarding how it went, that is, what worked and what didn't work. Discuss how the process could be further improved. Bear in mind that a role-play activity will never predict exactly what will occur in a real interview. However, the process will assist you in being better prepared for that important event in your employment search.

Legal Aspects of the Employment Interview

Over the years, a number of issues have arisen about questions that may or may not be included in an employment application or interview, including **race/ethnicity**, **religion**, and **national origin**. Generally, there should be no questions in any of these categories.

Age or date of birth. It is permissible to ask the age of an applicant younger than 18. Age should not be relevant in most hiring decisions, so date-of-birth questions prior to employment are improper.

Disabilities or physical traits. The Americans with Disabilities Act prohibits general inquiries about health problems, disabilities, and medical conditions.

Drug use or smoking. Questions regarding drug or tobacco use are permitted. In fact, the employer may obtain the applicant's agreement to be bound by the employer's drug and smoking policies and to submit to drug testing.

Citizenship. Employers are not allowed to discriminate because an applicant is not a U.S. citizen.

It is important to recognize that not all potential employers will understand that they may be asking improper or illegal questions. If you are asked any of these questions, you may choose to answer them or not. You might simply respond that you believe the question is irrelevant to the position you are seeking, and that you would like to focus on your qualities and skills that are suited to the job and the mission of the establishment.

The Employment Application

Any time that you are applying for any position, you will be required to complete an application, even if your resume already contains much of the requested information. Your resume and the list you have prepared prior to the interview will assist you in completing the application quickly and accurately.

You may want to fill out the sample form in Figure 20–17 in preparation for your employment interviews . The form each salon uses may be different, but it will probably request similar information.

ILLEGAL QUESTIONS

How old are you?
Please describe your medical history.
Are you a U.S. citizen?
What is your native tongue?

LEGAL QUESTIONS

Are you over the age of 18?
Are you able to perform this job?

EMPLOYMENT APPLICATION

Applicants are considered for all positions, and employees are treated during employment without regard to race, color, religion, sex, national origin, age, marital or veteran status, medical condition or handicap.

PERSONAL INFORMATION

SS#_____   Phone_____   Date_____

Last name_____ First_____ Middle_____

Present street address   City   State   Zip

Permanent street address   City   State   Zip

If related to anyone employed here, state name:_____

Referred to salon by:_____

EMPLOYMENT DESIRED

Position_____

Date you can start_____ Salary Desired_____

Current Employer_____

May we contact?_____

Ever applied with this company before?_____ Where?_____ When?_____

EDUCATION

Name/location of School	Years Completed	Subjects Studied

Subject of special study or research work:

_____

What foreign languages do you speak fluently?
Read fluently:_____
Write fluently:_____

US Military Service   Rank   Present Membership

In Nat'l Guard/Reserve

Figure 20–17 Typical job application form.

Activities (other than religious) Civic, Athletic, Fraternal, etc. (Exclude organizations for which the name or character might indicate race, creed, color or national origin of its members.)

FORMER EMPLOYMENT

List below last four employers, beginning with the most recent one first.

DATE: Month/Year	Name, Address of Employer	Salary	Position	Reason For Leaving
From: To:				
From: To:				
From: To:				
From: To:				

REFERENCES

Give below the names of three persons not related to you whom you have known at least one year.

Name	Address	Business	Years Known

PHYSICAL RECORD

Please list any defects in hearing, vision, or speech that might affect your job performance.

In case of emergency, please notify:

Name   Address   Telephone

I authorize investigation of all statements contained in this application. I understand that misrepresentation or omission of facts called for is cause for dismissal if hired.

Signature_____ Date_____

Figure 20–17, cont'd.

Are you authorized to work in the United States?

In which languages are you fluent?

Employment Application

Applicants are considered for all positions, and employees are treated during employment without regard to race/ethnicity, color, religion, gender, national origin, age, marital or veteran status, and medical condition or handicap.

DOING IT RIGHT

You are ready to set out on your exciting new career as a professional nail technician. The right way to proceed is by learning important study and test-taking skills early and applying them throughout your program.

Think ahead to your employment opportunities and use your time in school to develop a record of interesting, noteworthy activities that will make your resume exciting. When you compile a history that shows how you have achieved your goals, your confidence will build and your ambitions will grow.

Always take one step at a time. Be sure to take the helpful preliminary steps that we have discussed when preparing for employment.

Develop a dynamic portfolio. Keep your materials, information, and questions organized in order to ensure a high-impact interview.

Once employed, take the necessary steps to learn all that you can about your new position and the establishment you will be serving. Read all you can about the industry. Attend trade shows and take advantage of as much continuing education as you can manage. Become an active participant in making this great industry even better. See Chapter 21 to learn some great strategies for ensuring your career success.

REVIEW **QUESTIONS**

1. What is the most important way that a learner can do well on any test?

2. Explain deductive reasoning.

3. List eight steps that learners should take prior to the actual examination to improve results.

4. List at least 12 strategies that learners can use on the day of the actual examination for improved results.

5. When considering a statement on a true/false test, why are long statements more likely to be true than shorter statements?

6. Name and describe at least five types of salon businesses.

7. List up to eight strategies that you will find helpful when writing your resume.

8. List at least six things that you should avoid when developing your resume.

9. List several items that should be included in your professional portfolio.

10. Briefly summarize the preliminary things that you should consider before beginning your salon search.

11. In your own words, explain what can be accomplished by visiting a salon prior to an employment interview.

12. Why are thank-you notes important even if you visit a salon where you do not wish to become employed?

13. List 12 important interview behaviors that you should practice.

CHAPTER **GLOSSARY**

deductive reasoning	Process of reaching logical conclusions by employing logical reasoning.
employment portfolio	Collection, usually bound, of photos and documents that reflect your skills, accomplishments, and abilities in your chosen career field.
resume	Written summary of a person's education and work experience.
test-wise	Having a complete and thorough knowledge of the subject matter, and understanding the strategies for taking tests successfully.
transferable skills	Skills mastered at other jobs that can be put to use in a new position.
work ethic	Taking pride in your work, and committing yourself to consistently doing a good job for your clients, employer and salon team.

On the Job

chapter 21

CHAPTER OUTLINE

- Moving from School to Work
- Out in the Real World
- Managing Your Money
- Discover the Selling You
- On Your Way

LEARNING OBJECTIVES

After completing this chapter, you will be able to:

1. Describe the qualities that help a new employee succeed in a service profession.
2. List the habits of a good salon team player.
3. Explain the function of a job description.
4. Describe three different ways in which salon professionals are compensated.
5. Create a personal budget.
6. List the principles of selling products and services in the salon.
7. List the most effective ways to build a client base.

KEY TERMS

Page number indicates where in the chapter the term is used.

client base pg. 398	**job description** pg. 391	**retailing** pg. 399	**ticket upgrading or upselling services** pg. 399
commission pg. 392			

Congratulations! You have worked hard in cosmetology school, passed your state's licensing exam, and have been offered your first job in the field. Now, more than ever, you need to prioritize your goals, and commit to personal rules of conduct and behavior. These goals and rules should guide you throughout your career. If you let them do so, you can always expect to have work, and enjoy all the freedom that your chosen profession can offer (Figure 21–1).

MOVING FROM SCHOOL TO WORK

Making the transition from school to work can be difficult. While you may be thrilled to have a job, working for a paycheck brings with it a number of duties and responsibilities that you may not have thought about.

Cosmetology school is a forgiving environment. You are given the chance to do a certain procedure over and over again until you get it right. Making and fixing mistakes is an accepted part of the process, and your instructors and mentors are there to help you. Schedules can be adjusted if necessary, and you are given some leeway in the matter of juggling your personal life with the demands of your schooling.

When you become the employee of a salon, however, you will be expected to put the needs of the salon and its clients ahead of your own. This means that you must always be on time for your scheduled shifts, and be prepared to perform whatever services or functions are required of you, regardless of what is happening in your personal life. If someone comes to you with tickets for a concert on Saturday, for instance, you cannot just take the day off. To do so would definitely inconvenience your clients, who might even decide not to return to the salon. It could also burden your coworkers, who, if asked to take on your appointments, might feel resentful. In short, one practitioner's selfish and immature decision can create problems for the entire salon.

Figure 21–1 Getting off to a good start.

OUT IN THE REAL WORLD

Many students believe they should be rewarded with a high-paying job, and doing only the kinds of services they wish to do, as soon as they graduate from cosmetology school. Well, welcome to the world. It does not work out that way, at least not for most people. In a job, you may be asked to do work or perform services that are not your first choice. The good news, however, is when you are really working "in the trenches," you are learning every moment, and there is no substitute for that kind of experience.

The important thing is to be honest with yourself as you evaluate your skills, in order to best determine which type of position is right for you. If you need help and direction in sorting out the different issues around the different workplaces you are considering, ask your instructor for advice.

Thriving in a Service Profession

The first thing to remember when you are in a service business is that your work revolves around serving your clients. Some people have a hard time with the idea of customer service, because they feel that it is demeaning in some way. While it is true that there will always be some clients who do not treat people with respect, the majority of people you will encounter will truly appreciate the work you do for them. They will look forward to seeing you, and will show their appreciation for your hard work with their loyalty. Never let the negativity of a few discolor your overall outlook.

Here are some points that will help guide you as you serve your clients.

Put others first. You will have to quickly get used to putting your own feelings or desires aside, and putting the needs of the salon and the client first. This means doing what is expected of you, unless you are physically unable to do so.

Be true to your word. Choose your words carefully and honestly. Be someone who can be counted on to tell the truth, and to do what you say you will do.

Be punctual. Scheduling is central to the salon business. Getting to work on time is not only respectful to your clients, but also to your coworkers who will have to handle your clients if you are late.

Be grateful. Remember that it is an honor to have a job that will provide you and your family with financial stability. If you become unhappy with your salon, look for another job and move on before you start acting out in an ungrateful, disrespectful manner.

Be a problem solver. No job or situation comes without its share of problems. Be someone who recognizes problems promptly, and finds ways to resolve them constructively.

Be respectful. Although you may not like or agree with the salon manager or her rules, you must give her the benefit of the doubt. If you find that you really cannot come to terms with the salon's rules, then it is time for you to find a new job before your anger takes over.

Be a lifelong learner. A valued employee is one who intends to keep on learning. Thinking that you will never need to learn anything more once you are out of school is immature and limiting. Your career might go in all kinds of interesting directions, depending on what new things you learn. This applies to everything in your life. Besides learning new technical skills, you should continue gaining more insight into your own behavior, and how to better deal with people, problems, and issues.

Salon Teamwork

Working in a salon requires that you practice and perfect your people skills. A salon is very much a team environment. To become a good team player, you should do the following things:

Strive to help. Be concerned not only with your own success, but also with the success of others. Stay a little later, or come in a little earlier, to help out a teammate.

Pitch in. Be willing to help with whatever needs to be done in the salon—from folding towels to making appointments—when you are not busy servicing clients (Figure 21–2).

Share your knowledge. Be willing to share what you know. This will make you a respected member of any team.

Remain positive. Given the stress of a typical salon, there will be lots of opportunities for you to become negative, or to have conflicts with your teammates. Resist all temptations to give in to maliciousness and gossip.

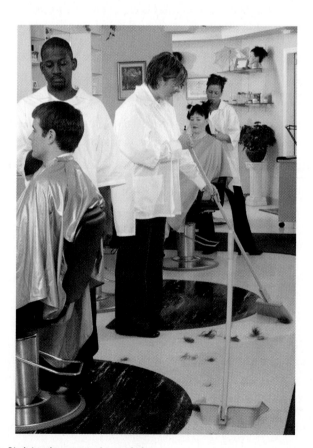

Figure 21–2 Pitch in wherever you're needed.

Become a relationship builder. Just as there are different kinds of people in the world, there are different types of relationships within the world of the salon. You do not have to be someone's best friend in order to build a good working relationship with that person.

Be willing to resolve conflicts. The most difficult part of being in a relationship is when conflict arises. A real teammate is someone who knows that conflict and tension are bad for the people who are in it, those who are around it, and the salon as a whole. Conflict is also a natural part of life. If you can work constructively toward resolving conflict, you will always be a valued member of the team.

Be willing to be subordinate. No one starts at the top. Keep in mind that beginners almost always start out lower down in the pecking order.

Be sincerely loyal. Loyalty is vital to the workings of a salon. Practitioners need to be loyal to the salon and its management. Management needs to be loyal to the staff and clients. Ideally, clients will be loyal to the practitioner and the salon. As you work on all the team-building characteristics, you will start to feel a strong sense of loyalty building up within you (Figure 21–3).

focus on...

THE GOAL

Always put the team first. While each individual may be concerned with getting ahead and being successful, a good teammate knows that no one can be successful alone. The only way you can truly be successful is for the entire salon to be successful!

The Job Description

When you take a job, you will be expected to behave appropriately, perform services asked of you, and conduct your business professionally. In order to do this to the best of your abilities, you should be given a **job description**, a document that outlines all the duties and responsibilities of a particular position in a salon or spa. Many salons have a pre-printed job description that they can give you. If you find yourself at a salon that does not use job descriptions, you may want to write one for yourself. You can then present this to your salon manager for review, to ensure that both of you have a good understanding of what is expected of you.

Once you have your job description, be sure you understand it. While reading it over, make notes and jot down any questions you may want to ask your manager. When you assume your new position, you are agreeing

Figure 21–3 Staff meetings are essential for building a loyal team.

to do everything as it is written down in the job description. If you are unclear about something, or need more information, it is your responsibility to ask.

Remember, you will be expected to fulfill all of the different functions listed in the job description. How well you do this will impact your future at the salon, as well as your financial rewards in the years to come.

In crafting a job description, the best salons cover their bases. They make sure to outline not only the duties and responsibilities of the job, but also the attitudes that they expect their employees to have, and the opportunities that are available to them. Figure 21–4 shows some highlights from a well-written job description. This is just one example. Like the salons that generate them, job descriptions come in all sizes and shapes, and feature a variety of requirements, benefits, and incentives.

Compensation Plans

When you assess a job offer, your first concern will probably be around the issue of compensation, or what you will actually get paid for your work.

Compensation varies from one salon to another. There are, however, three standard methods of compensation that you are likely to encounter: salary, **commission**, and salary plus commission.

Salary

Being paid an hourly rate is usually the best way for a new salon professional to start out, since that person will most likely not have an established clientele for a while. An hourly rate is generally offered to a new practitioner, and is usually based on the minimum wage. Some salons offer an hourly wage that is slightly higher than the minimum wage to encourage new practitioners to take the job and stick with it. In this situation, if you earn $10 per hour and you work 40 hours, you will be paid $400 that week. If you work more hours, you will get more pay. If you work less hours, you will get less pay. Regular taxes will be taken out of your earnings.

Remember: If you are offered a set salary each week, in lieu of an hourly rate, it must be equal to at least minimum wage, and you are entitled to overtime pay if you work more than 40 hours per week. The only exception would be if you were in an official salon management position.

Commission

A **commission**, a percentage of the revenue that the salon takes in, is usually offered to practitioners once they have built up a loyal clientele. A commission payment structure is very different from an hourly wage in that any money you are paid is a direct result of the total amount of service dollars you generate for the salon. Commissions are paid based on percentages of your total service dollars, and can range anywhere from 25 to 60 percent, depending on your length of time at the salon, your performance level, and the benefits that are part of your employment package. For example, at the end of the week, when you add up all the services that you have performed, your total is $1,000. If you are at the 50-percent commission level, then you would be paid $500 (before taxes). Keep in mind that until you have at least

Job Description: Assistant

Every assistant must have a cosmetology license as well as the determination to learn and grow on the job. As an assistant you must be willing to cooperate with coworkers in a team environment, which is most conductive to learning and to good morale among all employees. You must display a friendly yet professional attitude toward coworkers and clients alike.

Excellent time management is essential to the operation of a successful salon. An assistant should be aware of clients who are early and late or stylists who are running ahead or behind in their schedule. You should be prepared to assist in those situations and to change your routine if necessary. Keep the receptionist and stylists informed about clients who have entered the salon. Be prepared to stay up to an hour late when necessary. Keep in mind always that everyone needs to work together to get the job done.

The responsibilities of an assistant include:

1. Greeting clients by offering them a beverage, hanging up coats, and informing the receptionist and stylist that they have arrived.
2. Shampooing and conditioning clients.
3. Assisting stylists on the styling floor.
4. Assisting stylists in services that require extra help, such as dimensional coloring.
5. Cleaning stations and mirrors, including hand-held mirrors.
6. Keeping the styling stations and back bars well stocked with appropriate products.
7. Notifying the salon manager about items and supplies that need to be reordered.
8. Making sure the shampoo sink and drain are clean and free of hair.
9. Keeping the makeup display neat and clean.
10. Keeping the retail area neat and well stocked.
11. Keeping the bathroom and dressing room neat, clean, and stocked.
12. Performing housekeeping duties such as: emptying trash receptacles, cleaning haircolor from the floor, keeping the lunch room and dispensary neat and clean, helping with laundry, and dusting shelves.
13. Making fresh coffee when necessary.
14. Training new assistants.

Continuing Education

Your position as assistant is the first step toward becoming a successful stylist. In the beginning, your training will focus on the duties of an assistant. Once you have mastered those, your training will focus on the skills you will need as a stylist. As part of your continuing education in this salon you will be required to:

• attend all salon classes
• attend our special Sunday Seminars
• acquire all professional tools necessary for training at six weeks (shears, brushes, combs, clips, etc.)

Advancement

Upon successful completion of all required classes and seminars and your demonstration of the necessary skills and attitudes, you will have the opportunity to advance to the position of junior stylist. This advancement will always depend upon your perfomance as an assistant as well as the approval of management. Remember: how quickly you achieve your goals in this salon is up to you!

Figure 21–4 An example of a job description.

2 years of servicing clients under your belt, you may not be able to make a living on straight commission compensation.

Salary Plus Commissions

A salary-plus-commission structure is another common way to be compensated in the salon business. It basically means that you receive both a salary and a commission. This kind of structure is often used to motivate practitioners to perform more services, thereby increasing their productivity. For example, imagine that you earn an hourly wage that is equal to $300 per week, and you perform about $600 worth of services every week. Your salon manager may offer you an additional 25% commission on any services you perform over your usual $600 per week. Or perhaps you receive a straight hourly wage, but you can receive as much as a 15% commission on all the retail products you sell. You can see how this kind of structure quickly leads to significantly increased compensation (Figure 21–5).

Tips

When you receive satisfactory service at a hotel or restaurant, you are likely to leave your server a tip. It has become customary for salon clients to acknowledge beauty professionals in this way, too. Some salons have a tipping policy; others have a no-tipping policy. This is determined by what the salon feels is appropriate for its clientele.

The usual amount to tip is 15% of the total service ticket. For example, if a customer spends $50, then the tip might be 15% of that, or $7.50. Tips are income in addition to your regular compensation, and must be tracked and reported on your income tax return. Reporting tips will be beneficial to you if you wish to take out a mortgage or another type of loan and want your income to appear as strong as it really is.

In addition to your regular salary, it is customary for salon professionals to receive tips or gratuities from satisfied clients. These must also be factored into your total compensation package, and reported as income. It is important to keep good records, and to honestly report all of your earnings.

As you can see, there are a number of ways to structure compensation for a salon professional. You will probably have the opportunity to try each

Figure 21–5 Commissions on retail sales boost income.

of these methods at different points in your career. When deciding whether a certain compensation method is right for you, it is important to be aware of what your monthly expenses are, and to have a personal financial budget in place. We will address budget issues later in this chapter.

Employee Evaluation

The best way to keep tabs on your progress is to ask for feedback from your salon manager and key coworkers. Most likely, your salon will have a structure in place for evaluation purposes. Commonly, evaluations are scheduled 90 days after hiring, and then once a year after that. But you should feel free to ask for help and feedback any time you need it. This feedback can help you improve your technical abilities, as well as your customer service skills.

Ask a senior practitioner to sit in on one of your client consultations, and to make note of areas where you can improve. Ask your manager to observe your technical skills, and to point out ways you can perform your work more quickly and more efficiently. Have a trusted coworker watch and evaluate your skills when it comes to selling retail products. All of these kinds of evaluations will benefit your learning process enormously.

Find a Role Model

One of the best ways to improve your performance is to model your behavior after someone who is having the kind of success that you wish to have. Watch other practitioners in your salon. You will easily be able to identify who is really good, and who is just coasting along. Focus on the skills of the ones who are really good. What do they do? How do they treat their clients? How do they treat the salon staff and manager? How do they book their appointments? How do they handle their continuing education? What process do they use when formulating color, or deciding on product? What is their attitude toward their work? How do they handle a crisis? Conflicts?

Go to these professionals for advice. Ask for a few minutes of their time, but be willing to wait for it because in a busy salon, it may not be easy to find time to talk during the day. If you are having a problem, explain your situation, and ask if they can help you see things differently. Be prepared to listen and not argue your points. Remember that you asked for help, even when what they are saying is not what you want to hear. Thank them for their help, and reflect on the advice you have been given.

A little help and direction from skilled, experienced coworkers will go a long way toward helping you achieve your goals.

MANAGING YOUR MONEY

Although a career in the beauty industry is very artistic and creative, it is also a career that requires financial understanding and planning. Too many cosmetology professionals live for the moment, and do not plan for their futures. They may wind up feeling cheated out of the benefits that their friends and family in other careers are enjoying.

In a corporate structure, the human resources department of the corporation handles a great deal of the employee's financial planning for them. For example, health and dental insurance, retirement accounts, savings accounts, and many other items may be automatically deducted and paid out of the employee's salary. Most beauty professionals, however, must research and plan for all of those things on their own. This may seem difficult, but in fact it is a small price to pay for the kind of freedom, financial reward, and job satisfaction that a career in cosmetology can offer. And the good news is that managing money is something everyone can learn to do.

Meeting Financial Responsibilities

In addition to making money, responsible adults are also concerned with paying back their debts. Throughout your life and your career, you will undoubtedly incur debt in the form of car loans, home mortgages, or student loans. While it is easy for some people to merely ignore their responsibility in repaying these loans, it is extremely irresponsible and immature to accept a loan and then shrug off the debt. Not paying back your loans is called "defaulting," and it can have serious consequences regarding your personal and professional credit. The best way to meet all of your financial responsibilities is to know precisely what you owe, and what you earn, so that you can make informed decisions about where your money goes.

Personal Budget

It is amazing how many people work hard and earn very good salaries, but never take the time to create a personal budget. Many people are afraid of the word "budget" because they think that it will be too restrictive on their spending, or they have to be mathematical geniuses in order to work with a budget. Thankfully, neither of these fears is rooted in reality.

You can create a personal budget that ranges from being extremely simple to extremely complex. It all depends on what your needs are. At the beginning of your career, a simple budget should be sufficient. To get started, take a look at the worksheet in Figure 21–6. It lists the standard monthly expenses that most people have to budget. It also includes school loan repayment, savings, and payments into an individual retirement account (IRA).

Keeping track of where your money goes is one step toward making sure that you always have enough. It also helps you to plan ahead and save for bigger expenses such as a vacation, your own home, or even your own business. All in all, sticking to a budget is a good practice to follow faithfully for the rest of your life.

Giving Yourself a Raise

Once you have taken some time to create, use, and work with your personal budget, you may want to look at ways in which you can generate greater income for yourself. You might automatically jump to the most obvious sources, such as asking your employer for a raise, or asking for a higher percentage of commission. While these tactics are certainly valid,

Personal Budget Worksheet

A. Expenses

1. My monthly rent (or share of the rent) is $_____
2. My monthly car payment is   _____
3. My monthly car insurance payment is   _____
4. My monthly auto fuel/upkeep expenses are   _____
5. My monthly electric bill is   _____
6. My monthly gas bill is   _____
7. My monthly health insurance payment is   _____
8. My monthly entertainment expense is   _____
9. My monthly bank fees are   _____
10. My monthly grocery expense is   _____
11. My monthly dry cleaning expense is   _____
12. My monthly personal grooming expense is   _____
13. My monthly prescription/medical expense is   _____
14. My monthly telephone is   _____
15. My monthly student loan payment is   _____
16. My IRA payment is   _____
17. My savings account deposit is   _____
18. Other expenses: _____

                                        TOTAL EXPENSES $_____

B. Income

1. My monthly take-home pay is   _____
2. My monthly income from tips is   _____
3. Other income: _____

                                        TOTAL INCOME $_____

C. Balance

Total Income (B)   _____
Minus Total Expenses (A)   _____

                                        BALANCE $_____

Figure 21–6 A budget worksheet.

you will also want to think about other ways to increase your income, such as the following:

Spending less money. Although it may be difficult to reduce your spending, it is certainly one way to increase the amount of money that is left over at the end of the month. These dollars can be used to invest or save.

Increasing service prices. Although it will probably take some time before you are in a position to increase your service prices, once you have fully mastered all the services that you are performing, and you have a loyal client base, there is nothing wrong with increasing your prices every year or two, as long as you do so by a reasonable amount. Do a little research to determine what your competitors are charging for similar services, and increase your fees accordingly.

Seek Professional Advice

Just as you will want your clients to seek out your advice and services for their nail care needs, sometimes it is important for you to seek out the advice of experts, especially when it comes to your finances. You can research and interview financial planners who will be able to give you advice on reducing your credit card debt, on how to invest your money, and on retirement options. You can speak to the officers at your local bank who may be able to suggest bank accounts that offer you greater returns or flexibility with your money, depending on what you need.

When seeking out advice from other professionals, be sure not to take anyone's advice without carefully considering whether the advice makes sense for your particular situation and needs. Before you buy into anything, be an informed consumer about other people's goods and services.

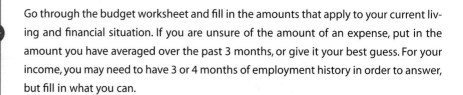

activity ▶

Go through the budget worksheet and fill in the amounts that apply to your current living and financial situation. If you are unsure of the amount of an expense, put in the amount you have averaged over the past 3 months, or give it your best guess. For your income, you may need to have 3 or 4 months of employment history in order to answer, but fill in what you can.

○ How do your expenses compare to your income?

○ What is your balance after all your expenses are paid?

○ Were there any surprises for you in this exercise?

○ Do you think that keeping a budget is a good way to manage money?

○ Do you know of any other methods people use to manage money?

DISCOVER THE SELLING YOU

Another area that touches on the issue of you and money is selling. As a salon professional, you will have enormous opportunities to sell retail products and upgrade service tickets. **Ticket upgrading**, or **upselling services**, is the practice of recommending and selling additional services to your clients that may be performed by you or other practitioners licensed in a different field (Figure 21–7). **Retailing** is the act of recommending and selling products to your clients for at-home nail care. These two activities can make all the difference in your economic picture. The following dialogue is an example of ticket upgrading. In this scene, Judy, the practitioner, suggests an additional service to Ms. King, her client, who has just had her nails done for a wedding she will be attending that evening.

Read the script yourself and change the words to make them fit your personality. Then try it the next time you feel that an additional service could help one of your clients.

Judy: I'm really glad you like your new nail color. It will be perfect with the dress you described. Don't you just love formal weddings?

Ms. King: I don't know. To tell you the truth, I don't get dressed up all that often, and putting the look together was harder than I thought it would be.

Judy: Yes, I know what you mean. Are you all set with your makeup for tonight, Ms. King? It would be a shame to have a beautiful new dress and gorgeous nails, and then have to worry about your makeup.

Ms. King: Well, actually, I was sort of wondering about that. I'm wearing this long black dress and I'm not really sure what's the best look for the occasion. Got any ideas?

Judy: Well, as you know, my specialty is nail care, but we have an excellent makeup artist right here on staff who's available for a consultation. You might want to make an appointment with her and she can do your

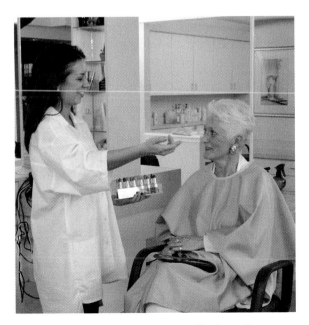

Figure 21–7   This client may wish a makeup service as well as hairstyling.

makeup for you. I don't know if you've ever had a professional do it before, but it's a real treat, and it only costs $25. Plus they throw in a small lipstick to take with you. Shall I get her for you?

Ms. King: Definitely. That sounds terrific!

Judy: You know, since this is such an important occasion, you may want to consider having Marie, one of our hairstylists do your hair as well. That will ensure that your total look is the best it can be.

Ms. King: I think that's a great idea. Thanks for the suggestion!

Principles of Selling

Some salon professionals shy away from sales. They think that it is scary, being pushy, or beneath them. A close look at how selling works can set your mind at ease. Not only can you become very good at selling once you understand the principles behind it, but also feel good about providing your clients with a valuable service.

To be successful in sales, you need ambition, determination, and a good personality. The first step in selling is to sell yourself. Clients must like and trust you before they will purchase beauty services, cosmetics, skin or nail care items, shampoos and conditioners, or other merchandise.

Remember, every client who enters the salon is a potential purchaser of additional services or merchandise. Recognizing the client's needs and preferences lays the foundation for successful selling.

To become a proficient salesperson, you must be able to apply the following principles of selling:

○ Be familiar with the merits and benefits of the various services and products that you are trying to sell, and recommend only those that the client really needs.

○ Adapt your approach and technique to meet the needs and personality of each client. Some clients may prefer a "soft sell" that involves informing them about the product, without stressing that they purchase it. Others are comfortable with a "hard-sell" approach that focuses emphatically on why a client should buy the product.

○ Be self-confident when recommending products for sale. You become confident by knowing about the products you are selling, and by believing that they are as good as you say they are.

○ Generate interest and desire in the customer by asking questions that determine a need.

○ Never misrepresent your services or products. Making unrealistic claims will only lead to your client's disappointment, and will make it unlikely that you will ever be able to sell to that client again.

○ Do not underestimate the client's intelligence, or her knowledge of her own beauty regimen or particular needs.

○ To sell a product or service, deliver your sales talk in a relaxed, friendly manner and, if possible, demonstrate use (Figure 21–8).

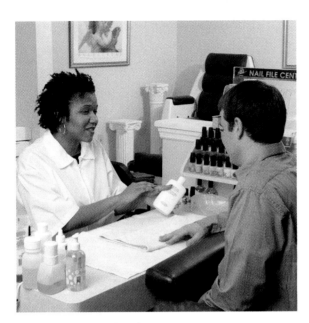

Figure 21–8 Demonstrate a product's benefits.

○ Recognize the right psychological moment to close any sale. Once the client has offered to buy, quit selling. Do not oversell, except to praise the client for the purchase and to assure him that he will be happy with it.

The Psychology of Selling

Most people have reasons for doing what they do, and when you are selling something, it is your job to figure out the reasons that might motivate a person to buy. When dealing with salon clients, you will find that their motives for buying salon products vary widely. Some may be concerned with issues of vanity (they want to look better). Some are seeking personal satisfaction (they want to feel better about themselves). Others need to solve a problem that is bothersome (they want to spend less time maintaining their nails).

Sometimes, a client may inquire about a product or service, but may still be undecided or doubtful. In this type of situation, you can help the decision along by offering honest and sincere advice. When you explain a beauty service to a client, address the results and benefits of that service. Always keep in mind that the best interests of the client should be your first consideration. You will need to know exactly what your client's needs are, and you need to have a clear idea as to how those needs can be fulfilled. Refer to the sample dialogues in this section—one involves ticket upgrading, and the other involves retailing, both of which demonstrate effective selling techniques.

Here are a few tips on how to get the conversation started on retailing products:

○ Ask every client what products they are using for home maintenance of their nails, hands and feet.

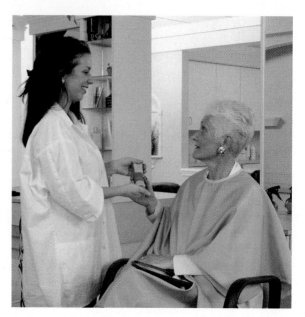

Figure 21–9 Place the product in the client's hands.

○ Place products in the client's hands whenever possible, or have them in view (Figure 21–9).

○ Advise the client about how the recommended service will benefit her (stronger nails, longer-lasting nail polish, for instance).

○ Keep retail areas clean, well lit, and appealing.

○ Inform clients of any promotions and sales that are going on in the salon.

○ Be informed about the merits of using a professional product as opposed to generic store brands.

While you realize that retailing products is a service to your clients, you may not be sure how to go about it. Imagine the following scenes and see how Lisa, the practitioner, highlights the benefits and features of a product to her client, Ms. Steiner. Note that price is not necessarily the "bottom line."

Scenario 1: Nail Client

Ms. Steiner: I just love the way you do my nails. How do you always make my cuticles and hands look like they're in such good shape ?

Lisa: I always use a penetrating cuticle oil on your cuticles, Ms. Steiner. It's a wonderful product and one you should be using on your cuticles everyday. I also use the lotion made by the same company.

Ms. Steiner: Is that the lotion you use with the great lavender scent?

Lisa: I love that light lavender scent too. It's a really great moisturizing lotion that we swear by—it's fabulous for treating dry and even chapped skin. I use it on my pedicure clients too, and it soothes that dry, rough skin that can accumulate on feet, especially in dry winter weather. Do you use any lotion at home after your shower or after having your hands in water?

Ms. Steiner: Yeah, I do, something I picked up in the grocery store one day. But it's very runny, not thick like your lotion.

Lisa: Oh, well our lotion is very rich and emollient because it has been especially formulated to stay on your hands and feet and moisturize them throughout the day.

Ms. Steiner: Yeah, well, nothing really makes much of a difference in this weather.

Lisa: Well, I can tell you that I have several clients who are using this lotion at home, and every one of them comes back in and raves about how much better their skin feels and how their dry flaky skin has gone away!

Ms. Steiner: Really?

Lisa: Yes. You may want to give it a try yourself and see how it works for you. It's available at the front when you check out. I'll grab you a bottle of lotion and the cuticle oil product, so you can look at them while I finish up your service.

Ms. Steiner: Great!

Pick a partner from class and role-play the dynamics of a sales situation. Take turns being the customer and the practitioner. Evaluate each other on how you did, with suggestions about where you can improve. Then try this exercise with someone else, as no two customers are the same.

◀ activity

How to Expand Your Client Base

Once you have mastered the basics of good service, take a look at some marketing techniques that will keep your clients coming back to you for services. These are only a few suggestions; there are many others that may work for you. The best way to decide which techniques are most effective is to try several.

Birthday cards. Ask clients for their birthday information (just the month and day, not the year) on the client consultation card, and then use it as a tool to get them into the salon again. About 1 month prior to the client's birthday, send a card with a special offer. Make it valid only the month of their birthday.

Provide consistently good service. It seems basic enough, but it is amazing how many professionals work hard to get clients, and lose them because they rush through a service and leave them feeling dissatisfied. Providing good-quality service must always be your first concern.

focus on...

RETAILING

For quick reference, keep these five points in mind when selling.

1. Establish rapport with the client.
2. Determine the client's needs.
3. Recommend products/services based on these needs.
4. Emphasize benefits.
5. Close the sale.

Be reliable. Always be courteous, thoughtful, and professional. Be at the salon when you say you will be there, and do not keep clients waiting. (Refer to Chapter 4 for tips on how to handle the unavoidable times when you are running late.) Give your clients the nail length and shape they ask for, not something else. Recommend a retail product only when you have tried it yourself, and you know what it can and cannot do.

Be respectful. When you treat others with respect, you become worthy of respect yourself. Being respectful means that you do not gossip or make fun of anyone or anything related to the salon. Negative energy brings everyone down, especially you.

Be positive. Become one of those people who always sees the glass as half full. Look for the positive in every situation. No one enjoys being around a person who is always unhappy.

Be professional. Sometimes, a client may try to make your relationship more personal than it ought to be. It is in your best interest, and your client's best interest, not to cross that line. Remember that your job is to be the client's beauty advisor, not a psychiatrist, a marriage counselor, or a buddy.

Business card referrals. Make up a special business card with your information on it, but leave room for a client to put her name on it as well. If your client is clearly pleased with your work, give her several cards. Ask her to put her name on them, and to refer her friends and associates to you. For every card you receive from a new customer with her name on it, give her 10% off her next salon service, or a complementary added service to her next appointment. This gives the client lots of motivation to recommend you to others, which in turn, helps build up your clientele (Figure 21–10).

Figure 21–10 Referral cards help build your client base.

Local business referrals. Another terrific way to build business is to work with other businesses in your area. Look for clothing stores, florists, gift shops, and other small businesses near your salon. Offer to have a card swap and commit to referring your clients to them when they are in the market for goods or services that your neighbors can provide, if they will do the same for you. This is a great way to build a feeling of community among local vendors, and to reach new clients you may not be able to otherwise.

Public speaking. Make yourself available to speak to local women's groups, the PTA, organizations for young men and women, and anywhere else that will put you in front of people in your community who are all potential clients. Put together a short program (20 to 30 minutes) in which, for example, you might discuss professional appearance with emphasis in your chosen field and other grooming tips for people looking for jobs or who are already employed.

Rebooking Clients

The best time to think about getting your client back into the salon is while she is still in your salon. It may seem a little difficult to assure your client that you are concerned with her satisfaction on this visit while you are talking about her next visit, but, in fact, the two go together. The best way to encourage your client to book another appointment before she leaves is to simply talk with her, ask questions, and listen carefully to her answers.

During the time that you are working on a client's nails, for instance, talk about the condition of her nails, her nail grooming habits at home, and the benefits of regular or special salon maintenance. You might raise these issues in a number of ways.

1. "Mrs. Rivera, when I did your fill today I noticed that your nail enhancements need to be completely replaced. Shall I book a full-set for your next visit?"

2. "Your son is getting married next month? How wonderful. Have you thought about having a deluxe pedicure service so your feet will look as beautiful as the rest of you in that new dress you told me about? I can set up an appointment for the day before the wedding."

Again, you will want to listen carefully to what your clients are telling you during their visit, because they will often give the careful listener many good clues as to what is happening in their lives. That will open the door to discussing their next appointment.

ON YOUR WAY

Your first job in the beauty industry will most likely be the most difficult. Getting started in this business means being on a big learning curve for a

focus on...

BUILDING YOUR CLIENT BASE

Some professionals believe that the more time they spend with their clients performing services, the better the service will be. Not so! Your client should be in the salon only as long as is necessary for you to adequately complete a service.

Be aware of how much time it takes you to perform your various services and then schedule accordingly. As you become more and more experienced, you should see a reduction in the amount of time it takes you to perform these services. That means clients wait less, you can increase your number of services, and the increase in services naturally increases your income.

focus on...

THE GOAL

Always remember that success does not just come to you; you make it happen. How? By being a team player, having a positive attitude, and keeping a real sense of commitment to your work foremost in your mind.

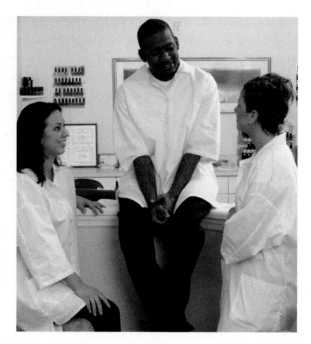

Figure 21–11 Make career satisfaction your goal.

while. Be patient with yourself as you transition from the "school you" to the "professional you." Always remember that in your work life, as in everything else you do, practice makes perfect. You will not know everything you need to know right at the start, but be confident in the fact that you are graduating from cosmetology school with a solid knowledge base. Make use of the many generous and experienced professionals you will encounter, and let them teach you the tricks of the trade. Make the commitment to perfecting your technical and customer service skills.

Above all, always be willing to learn. If you let the concepts that you have learned in this book be your guide, you will enjoy your life and reap the amazing benefits of a career in cosmetology (Figure 21–11).

REVIEW **QUESTIONS**

1. What should you look for in a salon to determine whether it is right for you?

2. List seven rules of conduct that help a new employee succeed in a service profession like cosmetology.

3. List six habits of a good team player.

4. Explain how a job description is used by the salon and by the employee.

5. What are the three most common methods of salon compensation?

6. Complete a personal budget and explain why managing your personal finances is important to your success.

7. Name at least six principles of selling retail products in the salon.

8. List the important personal characteristics that help you build a client base.

9. Explain at least three different activities that you can undertake to expand your client base.

CHAPTER **GLOSSARY**

client base	Customers who are loyal to a particular nail technician.
commission	Percentage of revenue that a salon takes in from sales earmarked for practitioner.
job description	Document that outlines all duties and responsibilities of a particular position in a salon or spa.
retailing	Act of recommending and selling products to your clients for at-home nail care.
ticket upgrading or upselling services	Practice of recommending and selling additional services to clients.

The Salon Business

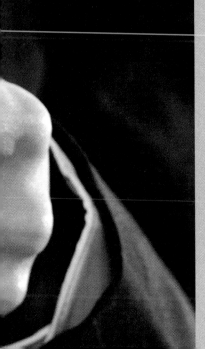

chapter 22

CHAPTER OUTLINE

- Going into Business for Yourself
- Operating a Successful Salon
- Selling in the Salon

LEARNING OBJECTIVES

After completing this chapter, you will be able to:

1. List the two ways in which you may go into business for yourself.
2. List the factors to consider when opening a salon.
3. Name and describe the types of ownership under which a salon may operate.
4. Explain the importance of keeping accurate business records.
5. Discuss the importance of the reception area to a salon's success.
6. Demonstrate good salon telephone techniques.
7. List the most effective forms of salon advertising.

KEY TERMS

Page number indicates where in the chapter the term is used.

booth rental	**consumption supplies**	**partnership**	**retail supplies**
pg. 411	pg. 418	pg. 413	pg. 418
business plan	**corporation**	**personnel**	**sole proprietor**
pg. 412	pg. 414	pg. 419	pg. 413
capital	**demographics**		
pg. 413	pg. 412		

A s you become more proficient in your craft and your ability to manage yourself and others, you may decide to become an independent booth renter, or even a salon owner. While this may seem like an easy thing to do, being a successful business person requires experience, a genuine love of people, and solid business management skills. To become a successful entrepreneur, you will need to commit to always being a student of business. You will also have to learn how to attract practitioners and clients to your business, and maintain their loyalty over long periods of time. Remember: The better prepared you are, the greater your chances of success (Figure 22–1).

Entire books have been written on each of the topics touched on in this chapter, so be prepared to read and research your business idea extensively before making any final decisions. The following information is only meant to be a general overview of the salon business.

GOING INTO BUSINESS FOR YOURSELF

If you reach a point in your life when you feel that you are ready to become your own boss, you will have two main options to consider: (1) owning your own salon, or (2) renting a booth in an existing salon. Both options have their pros and cons.

Figure 22–1 Opening your own salon or spa is a big step.

Booth Rental

Booth rental has become so popular that it is now practiced in over 50% of all salons in the United States. Currently, it is legal in every state except Pennsylvania, where there is a law prohibiting booth rental, and New Jersey where the state board does not recognize booth rental as an acceptable method of doing business. Many people see booth rental, or renting a station in a salon (also known as chair rental), as a more desirable alternative to owning a salon. In a booth rental arrangement, a practitioner generally:

o Rents a station or workspace in a salon from the salon owner

o Is solely responsible for his or her own clientele, supplies, record-keeping, and accounting

o Pays the salon owner a weekly fee for use of the booth

o Becomes his/her own boss for a very small amount of money

o Maintains expenses that are fairly low

Booth rental is a desirable situation for many practitioners who have large, steady clienteles, and do not have to rely on the salon to keep busy. Unless you are at least 70% booked all the time, however, it may not be advantageous to rent a booth.

Although it may sound like a good option, booth renting has its share of obligations, such as:

o Keeping records for income tax purposes and other legal reasons

o Paying all taxes, including higher Social Security (double that of an employee)

o Carrying adequate malpractice insurance and health insurance

o Maintaining inventory

o Managing the purchase of products and supplies

o Budgeting for advertising, or offering incentives to ensure a steady influx of new clients

o Paying for all education

o Working in an independent atmosphere where teamwork usually does not exist, and salon standards are interpreted on an individual basis

As a booth renter, you will not enjoy the same benefits as an employee of a salon would, such as paid days off or vacation time. Remember, when you are not working, you do not get paid.

Opening Your Own Salon

Like climbing Mount Everest, and all the physical and mental challenges that it entails, opening your own salon is a huge undertaking. Regardless of the type of salon you hope to open, there are some basic factors that you should consider carefully, such as:

1. **Location.** Having good visibility and accessibility are two of the most important factors in predicting the success of a business. The location that you select should reflect your target market, have access to plenty of parking, and should be far enough away from competing salons to avoid too much competition (Figure 22–2).

2. **Written agreements.** Before you open a salon, you must develop a **business plan**, a written description of your business as you see it today, and as you foresee it in the next 5 years (detailed by year). If you wish to obtain financing, it is essential that you have a business plan in place first. The plan should include a general description of the business and the services that it will provide; area **demographics** (e.g., average income in your proposed area, average cost of services, number of salons within a 5-mile radius); expected salaries and cost of related benefits; an operations plan that includes pricing structure and expenses such as equipment, supplies, repairs, advertising, taxes, and insurance; and projected income and overhead expenses for up to 5 years. A certified public accountant (CPA) can be invaluable in helping you gathering accurate financial information. The Chamber of Commerce in your proposed area typically has information on area demographics.

3. **Business regulations and laws.** When you decide to open your salon or rent a booth, you are responsible for complying with any/all local, state, and federal regulations and laws. Since the laws vary from state to state, it is important that you contact your local authorities regarding business licenses and other regulations.

4. **Insurance.** When you open your business, you will need to purchase insurance that covers malpractice, property liability, fire, burglary and theft, and business interruption. You will need

Figure 22–2 Location. Location. Location. Your salon should have good visibility, and high pedestrian traffic.

to have disability policies as well. Make sure that your policies cover you for all the monetary demands you will have to meet on your lease.

5. **Salon operation.** You must know and comply with all federal Occupational Safety and Health Administration (OSHA) guidelines, including those that require the ingredients of cosmetic preparations be available for employees. OSHA creates MSDS sheets for this purpose.

6. **Record-keeping.** You will need to keep accurate and complete records of all financial activities in your business.

7. **Salon policies.** Even small salons and booth renters should have policies that they adhere to. These ensure that all clients and associates are being treated fairly and consistently.

Types of Salon Ownership

A salon can be owned and operated by an individual, partnership, or corporation. Before deciding which type of ownership is most desirable for your situation, research each thoroughly. There are excellent reference tools available, and you can also consult a small business attorney for advice.

Individual Ownership

If you like to make your own rules, and are responsible enough to meet all the duties and obligations of running a business, individual ownership may be the best arrangement for you.

The **sole proprietor**:

o Is the owner and, most often, the manager of the business

o Determines policies, and has the last say in decision making

o Assumes expenses, receives profits, and bears all losses

Partnership

Partnerships may mean more opportunity for increased investment and growth. They can be magical if the right chemistry is struck, or they can be disastrous if you find yourself linked with someone you wish you had known better in the first place.

In a partnership two or more people:

o Share ownership in a **partnership**, although not necessarily equally. One reason for going into a partnership arrangement is to have more **capital** for investment; another is to have help running your operation.

o Pool their skills and talents, making it easier to share work, responsibilities, and decision making (Figure 22–3).

o Assume the others' unlimited liability for debts.

Figure 22–3 Partners share the work and the responsibilities.

Corporation

Incorporating is one of the best ways that a business owner can protect her or his personal assets. Most people choose to incorporate solely for this reason, but there are other advantages as well. For example, the corporate business structure saves you money in taxes, provides greater business flexibility, and makes raising capital easier. It also limits your personal financial liability if your business accrues unmanageable debts, or otherwise runs into financial trouble.

Characteristics of **corporations** follow:

○ Corporations raise capital by issuing stock certificates or shares.

○ Stockholders (people or companies that purchase shares) have an ownership interest in the company. The more stock they own, the bigger that interest becomes.

○ You can be the sole stockholder (or shareholder), or have many stockholders.

○ Corporate formalities, such as director and stockholder meetings, are required to maintain a corporate status.

○ Income tax is limited to the salary that you draw, and not the total profits of the business.

○ Corporations cost more to set up and run than a sole proprietorship or partnership. For example, there are the initial formation fees, filing fees and annual state fees.

○ A stockholder of a corporation is required to pay unemployment insurance taxes on his or her salary, whereas a sole proprietor or partner is not.

Purchasing an Established Salon

Purchasing an existing salon could be an excellent opportunity, but, as with anything else, you have to look at all sides of the picture. If you choose to buy an established salon, seek professional assistance from an accountant and a business lawyer (Figure 22–4). In general, any agreement to buy an established salon should include the following:

○ Written purchase and sale agreement to avoid any misunderstandings between the contracting parties.

○ Complete and signed statement of inventory (goods, fixtures, and the like) indicating the value of each article.

○ If there is a transfer of a note, mortgage, lease, and bill of sale, the buyer should initiate an investigation to determine whether there are defaults in the payment of debts.

○ Identity of owner.

○ Use of the salon's name and reputation for a definite period of time.

Figure 22–4 A lawyer specializing in leases and business sales is a good source of professional advice.

o Disclosure of any and all information regarding the salon's clientele, and its purchasing and service habits.

o Non-compete agreement stating that the seller will not work, or establish a new salon, within a specified distance from the present location.

Drawing Up a Lease

In most cases, owning your own business does not mean that you own the building that houses your business. When renting or leasing space, you must have an agreement between yourself and the building's owner that has been well thought out and well written. The lease should specify clearly who owns what, and who is responsible for which repairs and expenses. You should also secure the following:

o Exemption of fixtures or appliances that might be attached to the salon so that they can be removed without violating the lease.

o Agreement about necessary renovations and repairs, such as painting, plumbing, fixtures, and electrical installation.

o Option from the landlord that allows you to assign the lease to another person. In this way, obligations for the payment of rent are kept separate from the responsibilities of operating the business, should you decide to bring in another person or owner.

Protection Against Fire, Theft, and Lawsuits

o Ensure that your business has adequate locks, fire alarm system, and burglar alarm system.

o Purchase liability, fire, malpractice, and burglary insurance, and do not allow these policies to lapse while you intend to remain in business.

o Become thoroughly familiar with all laws governing cosmetology, and with the sanitary codes of your city and state.

o Keep accurate records of the number of employees, their salaries, lengths of employment, and Social Security numbers as required by various state and federal laws that monitor the social welfare of workers.

o Ignorance of the law is no excuse for violating it. Always check with your regulatory agency if you have any questions about a law or regulation.

Business Operations

Whether you are an owner or a manager, there are certain skills that you must develop in order to successfully run a salon. To run a people-oriented business, you need:

o An excellent business sense: aptitude, good judgment, and diplomacy

o Knowledge of sound business principles

Figure 22–5 Teaching a new practitioner how to cross check a haircut.

Because it takes time to develop these skills, you would be wise to establish a circle of contacts—business owners, including some salon owners—that can give you advice along the way. Consider joining a local entrepreneurs group, or your city's Chamber of Commerce, to extend the reach of your networking.

Smooth business management depends on the following factors:

○ Sufficient investment capital

○ Efficiency of management

○ Good business procedures

○ Cooperation between management and employees

○ Trained and experienced salon personnel (Figure 22–5)

○ Excellent customer service delivery

○ Proper pricing of services (Figure 22–6)

Allocation of Money

As a business operator, you must always know where your money is being spent. A good accountant and an accounting system are indispensable. The figures in Table 22–1 serve as a guideline, but may vary depending on locality.

STYLES BY DOTTI

Haircuts

Designer cuts for women	$40
Men's cut	$25
Children's cut	starting at $15
Formal updos	starting at $45

Haircolor Services

Virgin application, single-process	starting at $40
Color retouch	starting at $35
Double-process	starting at $55
Dimensional highlighting (full head)	$75
Dimensional highlighting (partial head)	$60

Texture Services

Customized perming	starting at $80
Spiral perm	starting at $100

Includes complimentary home maintenance product.

Figure 22–6 Typical salon price list.

TABLE 22-1 ● AVERAGE EXPENSES FOR SALONS IN THE UNITED STATES	
Expenses	Percent of Total Gross Income
Salaries and commissions (including payroll taxes)	53.5
Rent	13.0
Supplies	5.0
Advertising	3.0
Depreciation	3.0
Laundry	1.0
Cleaning	1.0
Light and power	1.0
Repairs	1.5
Insurance	0.75
Telephone	0.75
Miscellaneous	1.5
Total expenses	85.0
Net profit	15.0
Total	100.0

The Importance of Record-Keeping

Good business operations require a simple and efficient record system. Proper business records are necessary to meet the requirements of local, state, and federal laws regarding taxes and employees. Records are of value only if they are correct, concise, and complete. Proper bookkeeping methods include keeping an accurate record of all income and expenses. Income is usually classified as receipts from services and retail sales. Expenses include rent, utilities, insurance, salaries, advertising, equipment, and repairs. Retain check stubs, canceled checks, receipts, and invoices. A professional accountant or a full-charge bookkeeper is recommended to help keep records accurate. [Full-charge bookkeeper means someone who is trained to do everything from record sales and do payroll, to generating a profit-and-loss statement.]

Figure 22–7 Consumption supplies for each nail station.

Purchase and Inventory Records

An area that should be closely monitored is the purchase of inventory and supplies. Purchase records help maintain a perpetual inventory, which prevents overstocking or shortage of needed supplies, and also alerts you to any incidents of pilfering (petty theft by employees). These records also help establish the net worth of the business at the end of the year.

Keep a running inventory of all supplies, and classify them according to their use and retail value. Those to be used in the daily business operation are **consumption supplies** (Figure 22–7). Those to be sold to clients are **retail supplies**.

Service Records

Always keep service records or client cards that describe treatments given, and merchandise sold to each client. Either a card file system or software program will serve this purpose. All service records should include the name and address of the client, the date of each purchase or service, the amount charged, products used, and results obtained. Clients' preferences and tastes should also be noted. For more information on filling out these cards, and for examples of a client record card, see Chapter 4.

OPERATING A SUCCESSFUL SALON

The only way to guarantee that you will stay in business and have a prosperous salon is to take excellent care of your clients. Clients visiting your salon should feel they are being well taken care of, and that they always look forward to their next visit. To accomplish this, your salon must be physically attractive, well organized, smoothly run, and, above all, sparkling clean.

Planning the Salon's Layout

One of the most exciting opportunities ahead of you is planning and constructing the best physical layout for the type of salon you envision. Maximum efficiency should be the primary concern. For example, if you are opening a low-budget salon offering quick service, you will need several stations, and a small- to medium-sized reception area since clients will be moving in and out of the salon fairly quickly. Your retail area may also be on the small side, since your clients may not have a lot of disposable income to spend on retail products (Figure 22–8).

However, if you are opening a high-end salon or luxurious day spa where clients expect the quality of the service to be matched by the environment, you will want to plan for more room in the waiting area. You may, in fact, choose to have several areas in which clients can lounge between services and enjoy beverages or light snacks. Some upscale salons feature small coffee bars that lend an air of sophistication to the environment. Others offer quiet, private areas where clients can pursue business activities such as phone work or laptop activities between services. The retail area should be spacious, inviting, and well lit.

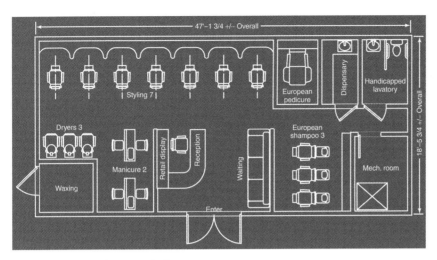

Figure 22–8 Layout for a typical salon.

Layout is crucial to the smooth operation of a salon. Once you have decided the type of salon that you wish to run, seek the advice of an architect with plenty of experience in designing salons. For renovations, a professional equipment and furniture supplier will be able to help you (Figure 22–9).

Personnel

The size of your salon will determine the size of your staff. Large salons and day spas require receptionists, hair practitioners, nail technicians, shampoo persons, colorists, massage therapists, aestheticians, and hair removal specialists.

Smaller salons have some combination of these **personnel** who perform more than one type of service. For example, the practitioner might also be the colorist and texture specialist. The success of a salon depends on the quality of the work done by the staff.

When interviewing potential employees, consider the following:

- Level of skill (What is their educational background? When was the last time they attended an educational event?)

- Personal grooming (Do they look like you would want their advice on your personal grooming?)

- Image as it relates to the salon (Are they too progressive, or too conservative for your environment?)

- Overall attitude (Do they seem more negative than positive in their responses to your questions?)

- Communication skills (Are they able to understand your questions? Can you understand their responses?)

Making good hiring decisions is crucial; undoing bad hiring decisions is painful to all involved, and can be more complicated than you might expect.

Figure 22–9 Salon dispensary.

Payroll and Employee Benefits

In order to have a successful business, one in which everyone feels appreciated and is happy to work hard and service clients, you must be willing to share your success with your staff whenever it is financially feasible to do so. You can do this in a number of ways.

- Make it your top priority to meet your payroll obligations. In the allotment of funds, this comes first.

- Whenever possible, offer hardworking and loyal employees as many benefits as possible. Either cover the cost of these benefits, or at least make them available to employees and allow them to decide if they can cover the cost themselves.

- Provide staff members with a schedule of employee evaluations. Make it clear what is expected of them if they are to receive pay increases.

- Create and stay with a tipping policy. It is a good idea both for your employees and your clients to know exactly what is expected.

- Put your entire pay plan in writing.

- Create incentives by giving your staff opportunities to earn more money, prizes, or tickets to educational events and trade shows.

Create salon policies and stick to them. Everyone in the salon should be governed by the same rules, including you!

activity ▶ What would your "dream salon" look like? Try your hand at designing a salon that would attract the kinds of clients you want, offer the services you would like to specialize in, and provide an efficient, comfortable working environment for cosmetology professionals.

Draw pictures, use word pictures, or try a combination of both. Pay attention to practical requirements, but feel free to dream a little, too. Skylights? Fountains? An employee exercise room? You name it. It's your dream (Figure 22–10)!

Managing Personnel

As a new salon owner, one of your most difficult tasks will be to manage your staff. But this can also be very rewarding. If you are good at managing others, you can make a positive impact on their lives, and their ability to earn a living. If managing people does not come naturally, do not despair. People can learn how to manage other people, just as they learn how to drive a car or do nail services. Keep in mind that managing others is a serious job. Whether it comes naturally to you or not, it takes time to become comfortable with the role.

There are many great books, both in and out of the professional salon industry that you can use as resources for managing employees and staff. Spend an afternoon online or at your local bookstore researching the topic and purchasing a variety of products that will educate and inform you. Once you have a broad base of information, you will be able to select a technique or style that best suits your personality and that of your salon.

Figure 22–10 What does your dream salon look like?

The Front Desk

Most salon owners believe that the quality and pricing of the services are the most important elements of running a successful salon. Certainly these are crucial, but too often the front desk—the "operations center"—is overlooked. The best salons employ professional receptionists to handle the job of scheduling appointments and greeting clients.

The Reception Area

First impressions count, and since the reception area is the first thing clients see, it needs to be attractive, appealing, and comfortable. This is your salon's "nerve center," where your receptionist will sit, retail merchandise will be on display, and the phone system is centered.

Make sure that the reception area is stocked with business cards, and a prominently displayed price list that shows at a glance what your clients should expect to pay for various services.

The Receptionist

Second only in importance to your practitioners is your receptionist. A well-trained receptionist is the "quarterback" of the salon, and will be the first person the client sees on arrival. The receptionist should be pleasant, greeting each client with a smile and addressing her by name. Efficient, friendly service fosters goodwill, confidence, and satisfaction.

In addition to filling the crucial role of greeter, the receptionist handles other important functions, including answering the phone, booking appointments, informing the practitioner that a client has arrived, preparing the daily appointment information for the staff, and recommending other services to the client. The receptionist should have a thorough knowledge of all retail products carried by the salon so that she or he can also serve as a salesperson and information source for clients (Figure 22–11).

During slow periods, it is customary for the receptionist to perform certain other duties and activities, such as straightening up the reception area and maintaining inventory and daily reports. The receptionist should

Figure 22–11 A good receptionist is key to a salon's success.

also reserve these slow times for making any necessary personal calls, or otherwise being away from the front desk.

Booking Appointments

One of the most important duties the receptionist has is booking appointments. This must be done with care, as services are sold in terms of time on the appointment page. Appointments must be scheduled to make the most efficient use of everyone's time. Under ideal circumstances, a client should not have to wait for a service, and a practitioner should not have to wait for the next client.

Booking appointments may be the main job of the receptionist, but when she is not available, the salon owner or manager, or any of the practitioners, can help with scheduling. Therefore, it is important for each person in the salon to understand how to book an appointment and how much time is needed for each service. Regardless of who actually makes the appointment, anyone who answers the phone or deals with clients must have a pleasing voice and personality.

In addition, the receptionist must have the following qualities:

○ Attractive appearance

○ Knowledge of the various services offered

○ Unlimited patience with both clients and salon personnel

Appointment Book

The appointment book helps practitioners arrange time to suit their clients' needs. It should accurately reflect what is taking place in the salon at any given time. In most salons, the receptionist prepares the appointment schedule for staff members; in smaller salons, each person may prepare his own schedule (Figure 22–12).

The appointment book may be an actual hardcopy book that is located on the reception desk, or it may be a computerized appointment book that is easily accessed through the salon's computer system.

Use of the Telephone in the Salon

An important part of the business is handled over the telephone. Good telephone habits and techniques make it possible for the salon owner and practitioners to increase business and improve relationships with clients and suppliers. With each call, a gracious, appropriate response will help build the salon's reputation.

Good Planning

Because it can be noisy, business calls to clients and suppliers should be made at a quiet time of the day, or from a telephone placed in a quieter area of the salon.

When using the telephone, you should:

○ Have a pleasant telephone voice, speak clearly, and use correct grammar. A "smile" in your voice counts for a lot.

Figure 22–12 Computerized appointment book.

○ Show interest and concern when talking with a client or a supplier.

○ Be polite, respectful, and courteous to all, even though some people may test the limits of your patience.

○ Be tactful. Do not say anything to irritate the person on the other end of the line.

Incoming Telephone Calls

Incoming phone calls are the lifeline of a salon. Clients usually call ahead for appointments with a preferred practitioner, or they might call to cancel or reschedule an appointment. The person answering the phone should develop the necessary telephone skills to handle these calls. In addition, some guidelines for answering the telephone are discussed below.

When you answer the phone, say, "Good morning [afternoon or evening], Milady Salon. May I help you?" or "Thank you for calling Milady Salon. This is Jane speaking. How may I help you?" Some salons require that you give your name to the caller. The first words you say tell the caller something about your personality. Let callers know that you are glad to hear from them.

Answer the phone promptly. On a system with more than one line, if a call comes in while you are talking on another line, ask to put the person on hold, answer the second call, and ask that person to hold while you complete the first call. Take calls in the order in which they are received.

If you do not have the information requested by a caller, either put the caller on hold and get the information, or offer to call the person back with the information as soon as you have it.

Do not talk with a client standing nearby while you are speaking with someone on the phone. You are doing a disservice to both clients.

Booking Appointments by Phone

When booking appointments, take down the client's first and last name, phone number, and service booked. Many salons call the client to confirm the appointment 1 or 2 days before it is scheduled.

You should be familiar with all the services and products available in the salon and their costs, as well as which cosmetology professionals perform specific services such as color correction. Be fair when making assignments. Try not to schedule six appointments for one practitioner and only two for another.

However, if someone calls to ask for an appointment with a particular cosmetology professional on a particular day and time, every effort should be made to accommodate the client's request. If the practitioner is not available when the client requests, there are several ways to handle the situation:

○ Suggest other times that the practitioner is available.

○ If the client cannot come in at any of those times, suggest another practitioner.

○ If the client is unwilling to try another practitioner, offer to call the client if there is a cancellation at the desired time.

Figure 22–13 Customer satisfaction is your best advertising.

Handling Complaints by Telephone

Handling complaints, particularly over the phone, is a difficult task. The caller is probably upset and short-tempered. Respond with self-control, tact, and courtesy, no matter how trying the circumstances. Only then will the caller be made to feel that she has been treated fairly.

The tone of your voice must be sympathetic and reassuring. Your manner of speaking should convince the caller that you are really concerned about the complaint. Do not interrupt the caller. After hearing the complaint in full, try to resolve the situation quickly and effectively.

Advertising

A new salon owner will want to get the business up and running as soon as possible to start earning some revenue, and begin to pay off debts. One of the first things the new salon owner should consider is how to advertise the salon. It is important to understand the many aspects of advertising.

Advertising includes all activities that promote the salon favorably, from a newspaper ad to radio spots, to a charity event, such as a fashion show that the salon participates in. Advertising must attract and hold the attention of readers, listeners, or viewers to create a desire for a service or product.

A satisfied client is the very best form of advertising, because she will refer your salon to friends and family. So make your clients happy (Figure 22–13)!

If you have some experience developing ads, you may decide to do your own advertising. If, however, you need help, you can hire a small local agency or ask a local newspaper or radio station to help you produce the ad.

As a general rule, an advertising budget should not exceed 3 percent of your gross income.

Plan well in advance for holidays and special yearly events such as proms, New Year's Eve, or the wedding season.

Here are some advertising venues that may prove fruitful for you.

- Newspaper ads and coupons, or coupon books (Figure 22–14).

- Direct mail to mailing lists and your current salon client list.

- Classified advertising in the local phone book or yellow pages directory.

- Email newsletters and discount offers to all clients who have agreed to receive such mailings. Always include an "unsubscribe" link.

- Website offerings.

- Giveaway promotional items such as combs, emery boards, key chains, refrigerator magnets, or calendars.

- Window displays that feature and attract attention to the salon and your retail products.

- Radio advertising.

- Television advertising.

Spring Specials
at
The Manor Day Spa

Celebrate the coming of spring!
Let us pamper you with one of our new deluxe packages

The Getaway: Swedish massage, facial,   **$200**
manicure, pedicure, makeup,
haircut and styling (includes
complimentary lunch)

The Refresher: deep cleansing facial, makeup,
haircut and styling   **$100**

Body Sensations: aromatherapy massage, facial, makeup   **$75**

Tips and Toes: spa manicure, hot stones pedicure   **$55**

Feb. 15 through May 15 only

Deep conditioning treatment with every haircolor service!
Call now to reserve an hour, two hours, or a whole day
of relaxation and pampering at the Manor.

Bring in this ad to receive a 5% discount on any service.

The Manor Day Spa, 123 Main Street, Hometown, USA 12345
(300-555-1111)

Open Tuesday - Friday 10-6,
Saturday 10-4

Figure 22–14 Newspaper advertisement for services at a salon.

---

o Community outreach by volunteering at women's and men's clubs, church functions, political gatherings, charitable affairs, and on TV and radio talk shows.

o Client referrals.

o Contacting clients who have not been in the salon for a while.

o Telemarketing to tell your customers about products and services. (You need permission in advance to do this.)

o Videos may be used in the salon to promote your salon and its goods.

SELLING IN THE SALON

An important aspect of the salon's financial success revolves around the sale of additional salon services and take-home or maintenance products.

Figure 22–15 Selling retail products benefits everyone.

Whether you own or manage a large salon with several employees, or you are a booth renter with only yourself to worry about, adding services or retail sales to your service ticket means additional revenue. Beauty professionals, in general, seem to feel uncomfortable about having to make sales of products or additional services. It is important to work at overcoming this feeling. When practitioners are reluctant to sell, it is often because they carry a negative stereotype of salespeople—pushy or aggressive—and they do not want to be seen this way themselves. While there are salespeople like that, remember that there are also very helpful and knowledgeable sales professionals who make customer care their top priority. These people play a major role in the lives of their customers, and are very valuable to them because they offer good advice (Figure 22–15).

REVIEW **QUESTIONS**

1. What are the two ways in which you may go into business for yourself?

2. List five factors to consider when opening a beauty salon.

3. Name three types of ownership under which a business may operate.

4. What purpose do accurate records serve?

5. What two types of supplies make up a beauty salon's inventory?

6. Why is the reception area of a salon important?

7. Why is the receptionist called the "quarterback" of the salon?

8. Explain the elements of good telephone technique.

9. List six different kinds of advertising.

10. What is the best form of advertising? Why?

CHAPTER **GLOSSARY**

booth rental	Renting a booth or station in a salon (also known as chair rental).
business plan	Written plan of a business, as it is seen in the present and envisioned in the future.
capital	Money needed to start a business.
consumption supplies	Supplies used in daily business operations.
corporation	Business whose ownership is shared by three or more people called stockholders.
demographics	Information about the size, average income, and buying habits of the population.
partnership	Business structure in which two or more people share ownership, although not necessarily equally.
personnel	Employees; staff.
retail supplies	Supplies sold to clients.
sole proprietor	Owner and manager of a business.

A SPECIAL MESSAGE FROM ROBERT CROMEANS, International Artistic Director of Paul Mitchell Systems

Use Your Time Wisely

Many times in school, all we're focused on is getting out. The reality is that we need to focus every single day on making the right choices so that we can be the best beauty professional possible.

One thing that I remember from being a student is the idle time, the down time, and if there's anything I wish I had done differently, it's this: I wish I had done more techniques and services while still in school.

So instead of taking off till three o'clock, or hanging out and waiting for somebody to come in to teach you something, you should be focusing on creating more opportunities to do nails, whether it's your neighbor's nails, your friend's nails, or your family's nails. Get them in and do their nails.

Form Good Habits

Many times we think that when we're in school, we can dress or act a certain way. But these are the first habits that you're going to form in your new profession. So why not start forming habits now that will change your whole attitude when you get into the industry? Your professional life starts when you walk into school. From day one, you are a nail technician. Think forward to the end result—you want to be a good nail technician. You don't want to be mediocre. That means that you dress up, you apply makeup, and if you don't like makeup, be a nurse. You're in the beauty business. Do not treat school like a backstage rehearsal. Treat school like you're on stage. Start being the person you want to be while you're in beauty school.

Seek Mentors

While I was in beauty school, I picked a few mentors who helped me. The first was a company, Paul Mitchell, which may not sound like it's a mentorship, but the reality is; companies can give common knowledge to an industry. I think it's very important to use a company as a mentor for information and ideas.

Being connected into something bigger is just smart business. The business values are the enterprise it operates on. So find a company to believe in by looking out in the industry to see what inspires you, what seems to make the most connection to you.

Explore the Possibilities

I think the most important thing for new nail technicians is to find the right salon environment to work in. Start today on your homework—targeting salons you want to work for. We want you to stay in the business. There are far too few nail technicians, and we want to keep each and every one of you and show you how to make it.

Look around and pick one or two salons you'd like to work in—not when you think you're going to take your license, not when you plan to graduate, but many months before. Many of these salons would like to meet you in advance.

You could already be working in there after hours, not doing nails but just serving coffee and water. That way you can start to feel the vibe, start to see what professional nail care is truly about.

Communication, connecting with people, is the key. Start while you're in school.

Young kids sometimes say to me, "I'm working through school. What do I do?" I tell them the best thing to do is wait tables, because by waiting tables you get to blend with lots of different types of people, and you're there to serve them. It's very similar to cosmetology—not that we're waiters or waitresses, we're professionals, but with a human attitude. We're not working on mannequins. We're working on human beings, and our job is to make them feel beautiful inside and out.

Learn the Business

Business may seem like the farthest thing from your mind while you're in school. I'm not talking about balancing your checkbook; I'm talking about starting to understand business as it applies to professional beauty.

Business skills can be learned, and the information is out there. It's on websites, in industry journals; Milady business books; even the large companies are a source. Remember, the point here is that you have to accelerate your education, and the way you accelerate is not by studying harder, but by doing more. That will make a tremendous difference.

Continue to Learn

Advanced education is one of the most important things you can do, while in school and definitely when you're first beginning. DVDs are a good way to learn because you can fast forward, stop and go back, or watch it again a day later and find those missing clues that didn't make sense the first time. Websites like *www.behindthechair.com* are an incredible way to get information and ideas. A friend of mine, Winn Claybaugh, tapes interviews with successful beauty professionals and markets them as the Master Series. You want to sign up for those because the people he interviews will give you tons of working tools.

Distributors do some of the most important education for our industry. They're at the local level, so you don't have to be tied into a national program. Distributors are looking for people like you. My first connection with Paul Mitchell was via one of my distributors in Memphis, who started utilizing me for local classes while I was in beauty school. Make a point of getting to as many of their local events as you can. It's not a case of which company you love; anybody who is teaching at the level you're at right now will help you, either by showing you what to do or, in some cases, what not to do. Either way it's learning, and the quicker you can eliminate mistakes based on watching other people, the better.

There is so much going on, so get out and look around. Don't just look at the education you want; look at where in the world you haven't been yet. Find the education and make that your point of reference. You'll get to see other places, like the Italian streets, and it will make you think differently about style in America. Everybody in America has a certain way of thinking about Europe, and in Europe everybody wants everything American. Even in Japan they want a piece of America. You've taken on a license that gives you the language we all speak, the language of professional beauty. So get a passport and get ready. It's all about education, travel, having fun, and making money.

I want to be the first to congratulate you and welcome you into our incredible industry. You know the things we must do together to make things happen. Zig Zeigler, one of my favorite motivational speakers, said it the best: "If you do the things you ought to do when you ought to do them, the day comes when you get to do what you want to do when you want to do it." So pick your mentors, pick a target, and start thinking of school as a place where you learn your skills and develop a good work ethic.

Develop the habit of working hard in school; that will make things so easy when you become an employee of a salon because you'll fit right in. You'll already be up to speed. The thing about this industry that will blow your mind is how quickly you get to move closer to your goal. If you focus every day on taking a step in that direction, in no time at all you will realize your first goal—and then, my friends, you get to move on to the second one.

See you at a trade show soon!

Glossary

abductors   Muscles that separate the fingers.

abrasive board   A thin, elongated board, with a rough surface.

ABS   Acrylonitrile butadiene styrene.

acid   Solution that has a pH below 7.0 and turns litmus paper from blue to red.

acne   Skin disorder characterized by chronic inflammation of the sebaceous glands from retained secretions and Propionibacterium acnes (p. acnes) bacteria.

acquired immunity   Immunity that the body develops after it overcomes a disease, or through inoculation (such as vaccination).

acrylic (methacrylate) nail enhancements   A nail enhancement created by combining acrylic (methacrylate) monomer liquid with polymer powder.

acute disease   Disease having a rapid onset, severe symptoms, and a short course or duration.

adductors   Muscles at the base of each finger that draw the fingers together.

adhesion   A chemical reaction resulting in two surfaces sticking together.

adhesive   An agent that causes two surfaces to stick together.

AIDS   Acquired immunodeficiency syndrome; a disease caused by the HIV virus, which breaks down the body's immune system.

air hose   The hose that connects an airbrush compressor (the air source) to the airbrush itself.

albinism   Congenital leukoderma, or absence of melanin pigment of the body, including the hair, skin, and eyes.

alcohol   The class of cosmetic ingredients which ranges from ethanol and isopropanol, which readily evaporate and are colorless liquids, to cetyl alcohol, a white waxy solid that does not evaporate.

alkali   Solution that has a pH above 7.0 and turns litmus paper from red to blue.

alkanolamines   Substances used to neutralize acids or raise the pH of many hair products; often used in place of ammonium hydroxide.

allergy   Reaction due to extreme sensitivity to certain foods, chemicals, or other normally harmless substances.

alternating current (AC)   Rapid and interrupted current, flowing first in one direction and then in the opposite direction, the direction changing 60 times per second.

ammonia   Colorless gas with a pungent odor, composed of hydrogen and nitrogen; not used in the salon in gaseous form, but mixed with water to create ammonium hydroxide.

amp   Unit that measures the strength of an electric current (the number of electrons flowing through a wire).

anabolism   Constructive metabolism; the process of building up larger molecules from smaller ones.

anatomy   The study of the structure of the body's various parts.

anhidrosis   Deficiency in perspiration, often a result of fever or certain skin diseases.

anterior auricular artery   Artery that supplies blood to the front part of the ear.

antiseptics   Agents that may kill, retard, or prevent the growth of bacteria; weaker than disinfectants, so they are safer for skin contact.

aromatherapy   The use of aromatic fragrances to induce relaxation; therapy through aroma.

arteries   Thick-walled muscular and flexible tubes that carry oxygenated blood from the heart to the capillaries throughout the body.

asteatosis   Condition of dry, scaly skin due to a deficiency or absence of sebum, caused by old age or by exposure to cold.

asymptomatic   Showing no symptoms or signs of infection or disease.

atom   The smallest particle of an element that still retains the properties of that element.

atrium   One of the two upper chambers of the heart, through which blood is pumped to the ventricles.

autonomic nervous system   The part of the nervous system that controls the involuntary muscles; it regulates the action of the smooth muscles, glands, blood vessels, and heart.

axon   The extension of a neuron by which impulses are sent away from the nerve cell.

bacilli (singular: bacillus)   Short, rod-shaped bacteria; the most common bacteria; they produce diseases such as tetanus (lockjaw), typhoid fever, tuberculosis, and diphtheria.

bacteria   One-celled microorganisms; some are harmful, most are harmless.

bactericidal   Capable of destroying bacteria.

bacteriology   The science that deals with the study of microorganisms.

basal cell carcinoma   The most common and least severe type of skin cancer; often characterized by light or pearly nodules.

basal cell layer   The bottom, live layer of the epidermis, where cells divide and begin the keratinization process.

Beau's lines   Visible depressions running across the width of the natural nail plate.

bed epithelium   Thin layer of tissue between the nail plate and the nail bed.

belly   The midsection of the brush bristles; the area of the brush that retains the most paint.

belly (muscle)   The middle part of a muscle.

bevel   To slope the free edge of the nail surface to smooth any rough edges.

biceps   Muscle producing the contour of the front and inner side of the upper arm.

bit   Attachment to the machine, that actually does the filing.

blood   Nutritive fluid circulating through the circulatory system (heart, veins, arteries, and capillaries) to supply oxygen and nutrients to cells and tissues, and remove carbon dioxide and waste from them.

blood vascular system   Group of structures (heart, arteries, veins, and capillaries) that distributes blood throughout the body.

bloodborne pathogens   Disease-causing bacteria, viruses or fungi that are carried through the body in the blood or body fluids.

booth rental   Renting a booth or station in a salon (also known as chair rental).

brain   Part of the central nervous system contained in the cranium; largest and most complex nerve tissue; it controls sensation, muscles, gland activity, and the power to think and feel emotions.

bromhidrosis   Foul-smelling perspiration, usually noticeable in the armpits or on the feet.

bruised nails   Condition in which a blood clot forms under the nail plate, forming a dark purplish spot, usually due to injury.

bulla (plural: bullae)   Large blister containing a watery fluid; similar to a vesicle but larger.

business plan   A written plan of a business, as it is seen in the present and envisioned in the future.

callus softeners   Help to soften and smooth calluses, especially on heels and over pressure points.

capillaries   Thin-walled blood vessels that connect the smaller arteries to the veins.

capital   The money needed to start a business.

cardiac muscle   The involuntary muscle that is the heart.

carpus   The wrist; a flexible joint composed of a group of eight small, irregular bones held together by ligaments.

carrier oil   A base oil used in aromatherapy, that is added to an essential oil to dilute the concentration of the essential oil. The carrier oil adds slippage and makes massage easier to perform.

catabolism   The phase of metabolism that involves the breaking down of complex compounds in the cells into smaller ones, resulting in the release of energy to perform functions such as muscular movement or digestion.

catalyst   A substance that speeds up chemical reactions between monomer liquid and polymer powder.

cell membrane   Part of the cell that encloses the protoplasm and permits soluble substances to enter and leave the cell.

cells   Basic units of all living things; minute masses of protoplasm capable of performing all the fundamental functions of life.

central nervous system   The brain, spinal cord, spinal nerves, and cranial nerves.

chain reaction   A process that joins together monomers to create very long polymer chains. Also called a "polymerization reaction."

chamois buffer   An implement that holds a disposable chamois cloth, used to add shine to the nail and to smooth out wavy ridges on nails.

chemical change   Change in the chemical composition of a substance, in which a new substance or substances are formed, having properties different from those of the original.

chemical compounds   Combinations of two or more atoms of different elements united together chemically.

chemical properties   Those characteristics related to chemical reactions and causing chemical change in a substance.

chemistry   Science that deals with the composition, structures, and properties of matter, and how matter changes under different conditions.

chloasma   Condition characterized by increased pigmentation on the skin in spots that are not elevated.

chronic disease   Disease of long duration, usually mild but recurring.

cilia   Slender, hair-like extensions that permit locomotion in certain bacteria; their whip-like motion moves bacteria in liquid.

circuit breaker   Switch that automatically interrupts or shuts off an electric circuit at the first indication of overload.

circulatory System   System that controls the steady circulation of the blood through the body by means of the heart and blood vessels.

clarify   To make clear.

client base   Those customers who are loyal to a particular cosmetologist.

client consultation Verbal communication with a client to determine desired results.

coatings Products, including nail polish, top coats, artificial nail enhancements, and adhesives, that cover the nail plate with a hard film.

cocci Round-shaped bacteria that appear singly or in groups.

collagen Fibrous protein that gives the skin form and strength.

color fade (color blend) An airbrushing technique of applying subtle color combinations across the same nail at the same time.

color wheel A color guide that illustrates and identifies the primary, secondary, tertiary, and complementary colors.

combustion Rapid oxidation of any substance, accompanied by the production of heat and light.

comedo (comedone) Hair follicle filled with keratin and sebum. When the sebum of the comedone is exposed to the environment, it oxidizes and turns black (blackheads); when the follicle is closed and not exposed to the environment, comedones are a white or cream color (whiteheads).

commission A percentage of the money that a salon takes in from sales.

communication The act of accurately sharing information between two people, or groups of people.

complementary colors Colors located directly opposite each other on the color wheel.

complete circuit The path of an electric current, from the generating source, through conductors, and back to its original source.

concentric Balanced bits that do not wobble or vibrate.

conductor Any substance that conducts electricity.

congenital disease Disease that exists at birth.

connective tissue Fibrous tissue that binds together, protects, and supports the various parts of the body, such as bone, cartilage, and tendons.

consumption supplies Supplies used in daily business operations.

contagious disease Disease that is communicable or transmittable.

contaminants Substances that can cause contamination.

contraindication Any condition or disease that makes an indicated treatment or medication inadvisable.

converter Apparatus that changes direct current to alternating current.

corporation A business whose ownership is shared by three or more people, called stockholders.

corrosive A substance capable of seriously damaging skin, eyes, or other soft tissues on contact. Some corrosives have delayed action (minutes) and others affect the skin almost instantly.

cosmetology The art and science of beautifying and improving the skin, nails, and hair; and the study of cosmetics and their applications.

cross-linker A monomer that joins together different polymer chains.

crust Dead cells that form over a wound or blemish while it is healing; an accumulation of sebum and pus, sometimes mixed with epidermal material.

curette A small, spoon-shaped instrument used for cleaning debris from the edges of nail plate.

cuticle The dead tissue which tightly adheres to the natural nail plate.

cyst Closed, abnormally developed sac, containing fluid, semifluid, or morbid matter, above or below the skin.

cytoplasm All the protoplasm of a cell except that which is in the nucleus; the watery fluid that contains food material necessary for growth, reproduction, and self-repair of the cell.

decontamination Removal of pathogens and other contaminating substances from tools and surfaces.

deductive reasoning Process of reaching logical conclusions by employing logical reasoning.

deltoid Large, triangular muscle covering the shoulder joint, which allows the arm to extend outward and to the side of the body.

demographics Information about the size, average income, and buying habits of the population.

dendrites Tree-like branching of nerve fibers extending from a nerve cell; short nerve fibers that carry impulses toward the cell.

dermatitis Inflammatory condition of the skin.

dermatitis venenata Also known as contact dermatitis, an eruptive skin infection caused by contact with irritating substances such as chemicals or tints.

dermatologist Physician engaged in the science of treating the skin, its structures, functions, and diseases.

dermatology Medical branch of science that deals with the study of skin and its nature, structure, functions, diseases, and treatments.

dermis Underlying or inner layer of the skin; also called the derma, corium, cutis, or true skin.

diagnosis Determination of the nature of a disease from its signs and symptoms.

diaphragm Muscular wall that separates the thorax from the abdominal region and helps control breathing.

digestive system The mouth, stomach, intestines, and salivary and gastric glands that change food into nutrients and wastes.

digit A finger or toe.

digital nerve Nerve that, with its branches, serves the fingers or toes.

diplococci Spherical bacteria that grow in pairs and cause diseases such as pneumonia.

direct current (DC) Current that travels in one direction.

disease Abnormal condition of all or part of the body, organ, or mind that makes it incapable of carrying on normal function.

disinfectants Agents used to destroy most bacteria and some viruses and to disinfect implements and surfaces.

disinfection Second highest level decontamination; it is nearly as effective as sterilization but does not kill bacterial spores.

double loading   Placing two different colors of paint on either side of the brush; usually a darker color on one side and a lighter color on the other.

eczema   Inflammatory, painful itching disease of the skin, acute or chronic in nature, presenting many forms of dry or moist lesions.

efficacy   Effectiveness.

effleurage   A light, continuous-stroking massage movement applied with fingers and palms in a slow and rhythmic manner.

eggshell nails   Noticeably thin, white nail plates that are more flexible than normal.

elastin   Protein base similar to collagen which forms elastic tissue.

electric current   Flow of electricity along a conductor.

electricity   Form of energy created by a flow of electrons.

element   The simplest form of matter, which cannot be broken down into a simpler substance without a loss of identity.

employment portfolio   Collection, usually bound, of photos and documents that reflect your skills, accomplishments, and abilities in your chosen career field.

emulsion   Mixture of two or more immiscible substances united with the aid of a binder or emulsifier.

endocrine (ductless) glands   Organs (such as the thyroid or pituitary glands) that release hormonal secretions directly into the bloodstream.

endocrine system   Group of specialized glands that affect the growth, development, sexual activities, and health of the entire body.

epidemic   Occurrence of a disease that simultaneously attacks a larger than normal number of persons living in a particular location.

epidermis   Outermost layer of the skin; also called cuticle.

epithelial tissue   Protective covering on body surfaces, such as the skin, mucous membranes, and the lining of the heart, digestive and respiratory organs, and glands.

eponychium   The living skin at the base of the nail plate covering the matrix area.

ergonomics   The study of how a workplace can best be designed for comfort, safety, efficiency and productivity.

essential oils   Oils used in aromatherapy, which are extracted by various forms of distillation from various parts of plants, including seeds, bark, roots, leaves, woods, and resin.

esthetician   Specialist in the cleansing, preservation of health, and beautification of the skin and body; one who gives therapeutic facial treatments.

ethics   Principles of good character, proper conduct, and moral judgment, expressed through personality, human relation skills, and professional image.

ethyl acrylic (methacrylate)   The monomer used in most acrylic (methacrylate) monomer and polymer powder systems.

etiology   Study of the causes of disease and their modes of operation.

evaporate   To change from liquid to vapor form.

excoriation   Skin sore or abrasion produced by scratching or scraping.

excretory system   Group of organs including the kidneys, liver, skin, large intestine, and lungs that purify the body by the elimination of waste matter.

exfoliating scrubs   Used to remove dry or scaly skin.

exhalation   The act of breathing outward, expelling carbon dioxide from the lungs.

exocrine (duct) glands   Organs that produce a substance that travels through small tube-like ducts, such as the sudoriferous (sweat) glands and the sebaceous (oil) glands.

exothermic   Chemical reactions which produce heat.

extensors   Muscles that straighten the wrist, hand, and fingers to form a straight line.

fabric wraps   Nail wraps made of silk, linen, or fiberglass.

fiberglass   A very thin synthetic mesh with a loose weave.

fissure   Crack in the skin that penetrates the dermis, such as on chapped hands or lips.

flagella (singular: flagellum)   Slender, hair-like extensions that permit locomotion in certain bacteria; their whip-like motion moves bacteria in liquid.

flexors   Extensor muscles of the wrist, involved in flexing the wrist.

floating the bead   A technique used to seal nail art where a bead of sealer is dropped onto the nail surface and the brush floats across the surface and completely covers it with sealer.

fluid nozzle (tip)   A small cone-shaped nozzle at the end of an airbrush that holds the needle that releases the paint.

flutes   Long, slender cuts or grooves found on carbide and Swiss carbide bits.

foil adhesive   A special adhesive, just for foiling that is generally tinted white or pink and appears cloudy when it is wet.

foiling   One of the easiest and most cost-effective nail art techniques, it is applied after polish with a foil adhesive to create colors and patterns not available with standard polishing techniques.

foot files (paddles)   Large abrasive files used to remove dry, flaky skin and smooth calluses.

foot soaks   Products containing gentle soaps, moisturizers, etc., used in a pedicure bath to cleanse and soften the skin.

free edge   Part of the nail plate that extends over the tip of the finger or toe.

freehand painting (flat nail art)   Also referred to as flat nail art; a very expensive form of nail art using brushes and paint to create designs.

French manicure   An airbrushing technique that creates a natural looking nail with a smooth white tip at the free edge.

friction movement   Firm pressure applied to the bottom of the foot using thumb compression to work from side to side and toward the heel.

fungi (singular: fungus) Microscopic parasites, including molds, mildews, and yeasts.

fungicidal Capable of destroying fungi.

fuse Special device that prevents excessive current from passing through a circuit.

game plan Conscious act of planning your life rather than just letting things happen.

gas A state of matter different from liquid or solid. Gases are not formed by evaporation of liquids, as are vapors. Gases must not be confused with vapors or fumes.

gems Tiny jewels that add sparkle, dimension, and texture to any nail art.

general infection Infection that results when the bloodstream carries bacteria or viruses and their toxins (poisons) to all parts of the body.

glands Specialized organs that remove certain constituents from the blood to convert them into new substances.

glycerin Sweet, colorless, oily substance used as a moisturizing ingredient in cosmetic products.

goal-setting The identification of long- and short-term goals.

gravity-fed An airbrush system designed to pull the paint into the airbrush using gravity.

grit The number of abrasive particles per square inch.

hand movement The process of skillfully treating, working on, or operating with the hands.

hangnail or agnail Condition in which the eponychium or other living tissue surrounding the nail plate becomes split.

heart Muscular cone-shaped organ that keeps the blood moving within the circulatory system.

heel The point at which the bristles of a brush meet the ferrule.

hemoglobin Coloring matter of the blood; an iron-containing protein in red blood cells that binds to oxygen.

hepatitis Disease marked by inflammation of the liver; some types are caused by a bloodborne virus.

herpes simplex Fever blister or cold sore; recurring viral infection.

histamines Chemicals released in the blood that enlarge the vessels around an injury to speed removal of any irritating substance.

histology Science of the minute structures of organic tissues; microscopic anatomy.

HIV Human immunodeficiency virus; virus that causes AIDS.

hormones Secretion produced by one of the endocrine glands and carried by the bloodstream or body fluid to another part of the body to stimulate special activities.

humerus Uppermost and largest bone in the arm, extending from the elbow to the shoulder.

hydrophilic Water loving.

hyperhidrosis Excessive sweating, caused by heat or general body weakness.

hypertrophy Abnormal growth of the skin.

hyponychium Thickened skin between the fingertip and free edge of the nail plate, which forms a protective barrier that keeps pathogens from infecting the nail bed.

immiscible Not capable of being mixed.

immunity Ability of the body to destroy any pathogens that have gained entrance to the body and to resist infection.

infection The invasion of body tissues by disease-causing bacteria.

infectious Communicable by infection from one person to another person or from one infected body part to another.

infectious disease Disease caused by pathogenic microorganisms that are easily spread.

inflammation Condition of some part of the body as a protective response to injury, irritation, or infection, characterized by redness, heat, pain, and swelling.

inhalation The breathing in of air.

inhibition layer A tacky surface left on the nail once a UV gel has cured.

initiator A special ingredient found in monomer liquids, used to deliver a boost of energy needed to start a chemical reaction that joins monomers together to create polymers.

inorganic chemistry Branch of chemistry dealing with compounds lacking carbon.

insertion Parts of the muscle at the more movable attachments to the skeleton.

insulator or nonconductor Substance that does not easily transmit electricity; not a conductor.

integumentary system The skin and its accessory organs, such as the oil and sweat glands, sensory receptors, hair, and nails.

ion Atom or molecule that carries an electrical charge.

ionization The temporary separation of an atom or molecule into ions.

job description A document that outlines all the duties and responsibilities of a particular position in a salon or spa.

joint Connection between two or more bones of the skeleton.

keloid Thick scar resulting from excessive growth of fibrous tissue.

keratin Fiber protein that is the principal component of hair and nails.

keratoma Acquired, superficial, thickened patch of epidermis commonly known as callus, caused by pressure or friction on the hands and feet.

kilowatt 1,000 watts.

Latissimus dorsi Broad, flat superficial muscle covering the back of the neck and upper and middle region of the back, controlling the shoulder blade and the swinging movements of the arm.

leafing (gold leafing)   Also known as nuggets or nugget sheets; a thin, fragile foil-like material, available in gold, silver, and a variety of other colors; used to create a quick and easy form of nail art.

lentigenes   Technical term for freckles.

lesion   A mark on the skin. Certain lesions could indicate an injury or damage that changes the structure of tissues or organs.

leukoderma   Skin disorder characterized by light abnormal patches; caused by a burn or congenital disease that destroys the pigment-producing cells.

leukonychia spots   Whitish discoloration of the nails, usually caused by injury to the matrix area; white spots.

ligament   Tough bank of fibrous tissue that connects bones or holds an organ in place.

linen   A closely woven, heavy material used for nail wraps.

lipophilic   Oil loving.

liquid tissue   Body tissue that carries food, waste products, and hormones, e.g., blood and lymph.

local infection   Infection that is confined to a particular part of the body and may be indicated by a lesion containing pus.

lungs   Organs of respiration; spongy tissues composed of microscopic cells in which inhaled air is exchanged for carbon dioxide.

lunula   Whitish, half-moon shape at the base of the nail plate, caused by the reflection of light off the surface of the matrix.

lymph   Clear, yellowish fluid that circulates in the lymph spaces of the body; it carries waste and impurities away from the cells.

lymph nodes   Special structures found inside the lymphatic vessels that filter lymph.

lymph vascular System   Body system that acts as an aid to the blood system and consists of the lymph spaces, lymph vessels, and lymph glands.

macule (plural: maculae)   Spot or discoloration on the skin, such as a freckle.

malignant melanoma   Most serious form of skin cancer, often characterized by black or dark brown patches on the skin that may appear uneven in texture, jagged, or raised.

marbleizer (stylus)   A tool with wooden handles and a rounded ball tip that can range in size and is excellent for dotting small circles of color on a nail.

mask knife   A one-sided knife used to cut designs out of mask paper or plastic to create nail art stencils.

mask paper   Paper that is used to create nail art design stencils.

masques   Usually composed of mineral clays, moisturizing agents, skin softeners, aromatherapy oils and beneficial extracts.

massage   A method of therapeutic manipulation of the body by rubbing, pinching, kneading, and tapping.

massage oils   Blends of oils used to lubricate, moisturize, and invigorate the skin during a massage.

matrix   Area where the nail plate cells are formed; this area is composed of matrix cells that make up the nail plate.

matter   Any substance that occupies space and can exist as a solid, liquid or gas.

median nerve   Nerve that supplies the arm and hand.

melanin   Tiny grains of pigment (coloring matter) deposited in the basal cell layer of the epidermis and the papillary layers of the dermis.

melanocytes   Melanin-forming cells.

melanonychia   Darkening of the fingernails or toenails; may be seen as a black band under or within the nail plate, extending from the base to the free edge.

metabolism   Chemical process taking place in living organisms whereby the cells are nourished and carry out their activities.

metacarpus   Bones of the palm of the hand; parts of the hand containing five bones between the carpus and phalanges.

microbiology   The science that deals with microorganisms and their effects on other forms of life.

microorganism   Microscopic plant or animal cell.

mild abrasives   Substances used for smoothing nails and skin, e.g. pumice.

mildew   A type of fungus that affects plants or grows on inanimate objects.

milia   Benign, keratin-filled cysts that can appear just under the epidermis and have no visible opening.

miliaria rubra   Prickly heat; acute inflammatory disorder of the sweat glands, characterized by the eruption of small red vesicles and accompanied by burning, itching skin.

milliampere   One-thousandth of an ampere.

miscible   Capable of being mixed with another liquid in any proportion without separating.

mission statement   A statement that sets forth the values that an individual or institution lives by and that establishes future goals.

mitosis   Cells dividing into two new cells (daughter cells); the usual process of cell reproduction of human tissues.

mold   A type of fungus growth that usually grows in dark, damp places and on inanimate objects.

mole   Small, brownish spot or blemish on the skin, ranging in color from pale tan to brown or bluish black.

molecule   Two or more atoms joined chemically.

monomers   Individual molecules that join together to make a polymer.

motility   Self-movement.

motor nerves   Nerves that carry impulses from the brain to the muscles.

MSDS   Material Safety Data Sheet; information compiled by a manufacturer about its product, ranging from ingredient content and associated potential hazards to flammability and storage requirements.

muscular system   Body system that covers, shapes, and supports the skeleton tissue; it contracts and moves various parts of the body.

muscular tissue   Tissue that contracts and moves various parts of the body.

myology   Science of the nature, structure, function, and diseases of the muscles.

nail art   An add-on service offered at many salons that applies creative and unique custom designs to the finished nail.

nail bed   Portion of the skin which supports the nail plate as it grows toward the free edge.

nail disorder   Condition caused by an injury or disease of the nail unit.

nail folds   Folds of normal skin that surround the nail plate.

nail grooves   Slits or furrows on the sides of the nail.

nail plate   Hardened keratin plate covering the nail bed.

nail psoriasis   A condition which affects the surface of the natural nail plate, causing it to appear rough and pitted, as well as causing reddish color spots on the nail bed, and onycholysis.

nail pterygium   An abnormal growth of the skin that stretches into a winglike structure, on the nail plate, it may be a result of severe injury or allergic reaction.

nail rasp   A metal file with an edge that can file the nail plate in only one direction.

nail tip   An artificial nail made of ABS or tenite acetate polymer that is adhered to the natural nail to add length.

nail tip adhesive   A liquid or gel-like product made from cyanoacrylate monomer and used to secure a nail tip to the natural nail.

nail unit   All the anatomical parts of the finger nail necessary to produce the natural nail plate.

nail wraps   Nail-size pieces of cloth or paper that are bonded to the top of the nail plate with nail adhesive, often used to repair or strengthen natural nails or nail tips.

natural immunity   Natural resistance to disease, partly inherited and partly developed through hygienic, healthy living.

needle   The piece that fits into the fluid nozzle of an airbrush and controls the amount of paint released when the trigger is depressed.

nerve   Whitish cord made up of bundles of nerve fibers held together by connective tissue, through which impulses are transmitted

nerve tissue   Tissue that controls and coordinates all body functions.

nervous system   Body system composed of the brain, spinal cord, and nerves; it controls and coordinates all other systems and makes them work harmoniously and efficiently.

neurology   Science of the structure, function, and pathology of the nervous system.

neuron   Nerve cell; basic unit of the nervous system, consisting of a cell body, nucleus, dendrites, and axon.

nevus   Small or large malformation of the skin due to abnormal pigmentation or dilated capillaries; commonly known as a birthmark.

nippers   An instrument used for manicures and pedicures to trim tags of dead skin.

no-light gels   Thickened cyanoacrylate monomers.

nonpathogenic   Not harmful; not disease-producing; organisms that perform useful functions.

non-striated muscles   Also called involuntary or smooth muscles, muscles that function automatically, without conscious will.

nucleus   Dense, active protoplasm found in the center of the cell; it plays an important part in cell reproduction and metabolism.

objective symptoms   Symptoms that are visible, such as pimples, pustules, or inflammation.

occupational disease   Illness resulting from conditions associated with employment, such as coming in contact with certain products or ingredients.

odorless acrylic (methacrylate) products   Nail enhancement products that are slightly different from acrylic (methacrylate) products. These systems use monomers that have a very low odor and do not have the strong smell of ethyl acrylic (methacrylate) based products. If others in the salon cannot smell the monomer liquid when in use, it is considered odorless.

ohm   Unit that measures the resistance of an electric current.

oil-in-water (O/W) emulsion   Oil droplets suspended in a water base.

oligomer   A short chain of monomers that is not long enough to be considered a polymer.

oligomers   Short chains of monomers that have had the growth of their chains halted before they became polymers.

ology   Suffix meaning "study of " (example: microbiology). This can be associated with both scientific and nonscientific studies.

one color method   Gel is applied over the entire surface of the nail.

onychia   Inflammation of the matrix of the nail with shedding of the nail.

onychocryptosis   Ingrown nails; nail grows into the living tissue around the nail.

onycholysis   Separation of the nail plate from the nail bed, often caused by injury or allergic reactions.

onychomadesis   The separation and falling off of a nail from the nail bed; it can occur on fingernails and toenails.

onychomycosis   Fungal infection of the natural nail plate.

onychophagy   Bitten nails.

onychophosis   Any disease or disorder of the natural nails.

onychorrhexis   Abnormal brittleness with deep, rough grooves in the of the nail plate.

onychosis   Any disease or disorder of the natural nails.

onyx   Nail plate of the fingers or toes.

organ   In plants and animals, structures composed of specialized tissues and performing specific functions.

organic chemistry   Study of substances that contain carbon.

origin   Part of the muscle that does not move; it is attached to the skeleton and is usually part of a skeletal muscle.

os   Bone.

osteology   The study of the anatomy, structure, and function of the bones.

oval nail   A nail shape that is square with slightly rounded corners. This shape is attractive for most women's hands.

overexposure   Prolonged, repeated, or long-term exposure that can cause sensitivity.

oxidation   A reaction that chemically combines a substance with oxygen.

oxidize   To combine or cause a substance to combine with oxygen.

oxidizing agent   Substance that releases oxygen.

paper wraps   Temporary nail wraps made of very thin paper. Not nearly as strong as fabric wraps.

papillary layer   Outer layer of the dermis, directly beneath the epidermis.

papule   Pimple; small circumscribed elevation on the skin that contains no fluid but may develop pus.

paraffin bath   Used to stimulate circulation and to reduce inflammation and promote circulation to the affected joints.

parasite   Organism that lives in or on another organism and draws its nourishment from that organism.

parasitic disease   Disease caused by parasites, such as lice and ringworm.

paronychia   Bacterial inflammation of the tissues surrounding the nail; pus, redness and swelling are usually present.

partnership   A business structure in which two or more people share ownership, although not necessarily equally.

pathogenic   Causing disease; harmful.

pathogenic disease   Disease produced by disease-causing microorganisms, such as staphylococcus and streptococcus (pus-forming bacteria).

pathology   Science that investigates modifications of the functions and changes in structure caused by disease.

pectoralis major and pectoralis minor   Muscles of the chest that assist the swinging movements of the arm.

pediculosis capitis   Skin disease caused by infestation of head lice.

pedicure   Standard service performed by nail professionals that includes care and massage of feet and trimming, shaping, and polishing toenails.

perfectionism   A compulsion to do things perfectly.

pericardium   Double-layered membranous sac enclosing the heart.

peripheral nervous system   System of nerves and ganglia that connects the peripheral parts of the body to the central nervous system; it has both sensory and motor nerves.

personal hygiene   Is the daily maintenance of cleanliness by practicing good sanitary habits.

personnel   Employees; staff.

petrissage   A kneading movement in massage performed by lifting, squeezing, and pressing the tissue.

pH   Relative degree of acidity and alkalinity of a water-containing solution.

phalanges (singular: phalanx)   Bones of the fingers or toes.

phenolics   Powerful tuberculocidal disinfectants.

physical change   Change in the form or physical properties of a substance without the formation of a new substance.

physical mixture   Combination of two or more substances united physically, not chemically.

physical presentation   A person's physical posture, walk, and movements.

physical properties   Those characteristics that can be determined without a chemical reaction and that do not cause a chemical change in the substance.

physiology   Study of the functions or activities performed by the body's structures.

pincer nails   Increased crosswise curvature throughout the nail plate caused by an increased curvature of the matrix.

plasma   Fluid part of the blood and lymph that carries food and secretions to the cells.

platelets   Blood cells that aid in the forming of clots.

pledgets   Small, fiber-free squares often used by nail professionals to remove polish because the cotton fibers from the squares do not adhere to the nails, which can interfere with the polish application.

plicatured nail   Disorder in which one or both of the edges of the nail plate are folded at a sharp 90-degree (or greater) angle down into the soft-tissue.

pointed nail   A nail shape suited to thin hands with narrow nail beds. The shape is tapered and somewhat longer; however, these nails are often weak and may break easily.

polymerization   Chemical reaction that creates polymers; also called curing or hardening.

polymers   Substances formed by combining many small molecules (monomers) or oligomers, usually in extremely long, chain-like structures.

porous   Having pores or openings that permit liquids or gases to pass in.

position   The way a brush is held to create nail art; the brush can be positioned straight up-and-down or laid down with the bristles pulled across the paint surface.

pressure   The amount of force an artist applies to a brush while in the stroke motion when applying nail art.

primary colors   Colors that cannot be obtained from mixing together any other colors.

primers   Substances that improve adhesion.

prioritize   To make a list of tasks that need to be done in the order of most to least important.

procrastination   Putting off until tomorrow what you can do today.

professional image   The impression projected by a person engaged in any profession, consisting of outward appearance and conduct exhibited in the workplace.

prognosis   Estimating and predicting of the probable course of a disease.

pronators   Muscles that turn the hand inward so that the palm faces downward.

proprietor   The owner and manager of a business.

protoplasm   Colorless jelly-like substance found inside cells, in which food elements such as protein, fats, carbohydrates, mineral salts, and water are present.

Pseudomonas aeruginosa   One of several common bacteria that can cause nail infection.

psoriasis   Skin disease characterized by red patches covered with silver-white scales, usually found on the scalp, elbows, knees, chest, and lower back, rarely on the face.

pull   The flow of a brush across a painted nail surface, giving it a fluid movement and avoiding a rough, spattered look.

pulmonary circulation   Blood circulation from heart to lungs and back to heart.

pumice powder   A white or grayish powdered abrasive derived from volcanic rock, used for smoothing and polishing.

pure substance   Containing one type of molecule; not mixed with other substances.

pus   Fluid product of inflammation that contains white blood cells and the debris of dead cells, tissue compounds, and bacteria.

pustule   Inflamed lesion containing pus.

pyogenic granuloma   Severe inflammation of the nail in which a lump of red tissue grows up from the nail bed to the nail plate.

quaternary ammonium   Disinfectant that is considered odorless, highly effective, and fast-acting.

radial artery   Artery that supplies blood to the thumb side of the arm and the back of the hand; it supplies the muscles of the skin, hands and fingers, wrist, elbow, and forearm.

radial nerve   Serves the thumb side of the arm and back of the hand.

radius   Smaller bone in the forearm, on the same side as the thumb.

rebalancing   A method for maintaining the beauty, durability and longevity of the nail enhancement.

rectifier   Apparatus that changes alternating current to direct current.

red blood cells   Blood cells that carry oxygen from the lungs to the body cells and transport carbon dioxide from the cells back to the lungs.

redox   Contraction for reduction-oxidation; chemical reaction in which the oxidizing agent is reduced and the reducing agent is oxidized.

reduce   To subtract oxygen from or add hydrogen to a substance.

reduction   The subtraction of oxygen from, or the addition of hydrogen to, a substance.

reflective listening   Listening to the client and then repeating, in your own words, what you think the client is telling you.

reflex   Automatic nerve reaction to a stimulus that involves the movement of specific muscles as a response to impulses carried along a motor neuron to a muscle, causing a spontaneous reaction.

repair patch   A piece of fabric cut to completely cover a crack or break in the nail during a four-week fabric wrap maintenance procedure.

reproductive system   Body system responsible for processes by which plants and animals produce offspring.

respiration   Act of breathing; the exchange of carbon dioxide and oxygen in the lungs and within each cell.

respiratory system   Body system consisting of the lungs and air passages; enables breathing, supplying the body with oxygen and eliminating carbon dioxide wastes.

resume   Written summary of a person's education and work experience.

retail supplies   Supplies sold to clients.

retailing   The act of recommending and selling products to your clients for at-home hair, skin, and nail care.

reticular layer   Deeper layer of the dermis that supplies the skin with oxygen and nutrients; it contains cells, vessels, glands, nerve endings, and follicles.

retinoic acid   Retin-A; prescription cream for acne.

revolutions per minute (RPM)   The number of times a bit rotates in one minute.

ridges   Lines running the length of the natural nail plate, usually related to normal aging.

rings of fire   Grooves carved into the nail caused by filing with bits at the incorrect angle.

rosacea   Chronic congestion appearing primarily on the cheeks and nose, characterized by redness, dilation of the blood vessels, and the formation of papules and pustules.

round nail   A nail shape that is slightly tapered and extends just a bit past the tip of the finger. This natural looking shape is common for male clients.

sanitation or sanitizing   The first step in the decontamination process, designed to significantly reduce the number of pathogens or disease-producing organisms found on any surface

saprophytes   Nonpathogenic bacteria that normally grow on dead matter.

scabies   Contagious skin disease caused by an itch mite burrowing under the skin.

scale   Any thin plate of epidermal flakes, dry or oily, such as abnormal or excessive dandruff.

scar or cicatrix   Light-colored, slightly raised mark on the skin formed after an injury or lesion of the skin has healed.

seasonal disease   Disease influenced by the weather.

sebaceous glands   Oil glands of the skin, connected to hair follicles.

seborrheic dermatitis   A skin condition caused by an inflammation of the sebaceous glands. It is often characterized by inflammation, dry or oily scaling or crusting and/or itchiness.

secondary colors   Colors resulting from mixing equal parts of two primary colors, positioned midway between the primary colors on a color wheel.

sensitization   A greatly increased or exaggerated sensitivity to products.

sensory (afferent) nerves   Nerves that carry impulses or messages from the sense organs to the brain, where sensations of touch, cold, heat, sight, hearing, taste, smell, pain, and pressure are experienced.

serratus anterior   Muscle of the chest that assists in breathing and in raising the arm.

silicones   Special types of ingredients used in hair conditioners and as water-resistant lubricants for the skin.

silk   A thin, natural material with a tight weave; it becomes transparent when adhesive is applied.

simple polymer chains   The result of long chains of monomers that are attached from head to tail.

skeletal system   Physical foundation of the body. It is composed of 206 bones that vary in size and shape and are connected by movable and immovable joints.

skin tag   A small brown or flesh-colored outgrowth of the skin.

sodium hypochlorite   Common household bleach; disinfectant used on implements.

solute   The dissolved substance in a solution.

solution   Blended mixture of a solute in a liquid solvent.

solvent   A substance, usually liquid, that dissolves another substance to form a solution.

spirilla   Spiral or corkscrew-shaped bacteria that can cause diseases such as syphilis and lime disease.

squamous cell carcinoma   Type of skin cancer more serious than basal cell carcinoma, often characterized by scaly red papules or nodules.

square nail   A nail shape that is completely straight across with no rounding at the edges. The length of the nail can vary.

squoval nail   A nail shape that extends slightly past the tip of the finger with a rounded free edge.

stain   Abnormal brown or wine-colored skin discoloration with a circular and irregular shape

staphylococci   Pus-forming bacteria that grow in clusters like bunches of grapes, can cause abscesses, pustules, and boils.

steatoma   Sebaceous cyst or fatty tumor.

stencil   Precut designs made of plastic, paper, or fabric, used to create nail art.

sterilization   A highly effective type of decontamination that completely destroys every organism on a surface, whether beneficial or harmful.

stratum corneum   Outer layer of the epidermis.

stratum germinativum   Deepest layer of the epidermis, also known as the basal layer.

stratum granulosum   Granular layer of the epidermis.

stratum lucidum   Clear, transparent layer of the epidermis under the stratum corneum.

stratum spinosum   The spiny layer just above the basal cell layer.

streptococci   Pus-forming bacteria arranged in curved lines resembling a string of beads; they can cause infections such as strep throat and blood poisoning.

stress   The inability to cope with a threat, real or imagined, to our well-being, which results in a series of responses and adaptations by our minds and bodies; a situation that causes tension.

stress strip   A strip of fabric, 1/8" long, applied during a four-week fabric wrap rebalance to repair or strengthen a weak point in a nail enhancement.

striated muscles   Also called voluntary or skeletal muscles; muscles that are controlled by the will.

stripette or short striper   The shorter version of the stripe brush.

striping tape   A tacky-backed tape available in an assortment of colors that is applied over nail polish or other nail art to create bolder designs.

subcutaneous tissue   Fatty layer found below the dermis that gives smoothness and contour to the body; it contains fats for use as energy, and also acts as a protective cushion for the outer skin; also called adipose or subcutis tissue.

subjective symptoms   Symptoms that can be felt, such as itching, burning, or pain.

sudoriferous glands   Sweat glands of the skin.

superficial temporal artery   Supplies blood to the muscles of the front, side, and top of the head.

supinator   Muscle of the forearm that rotates the radius outward and the palm upward.

surfactants   Surface active agents; substances that act as a bridge to allow oil and water to mix, or emulsify.

suspension   State in which solid particles are distributed throughout a liquid medium.

system   A group of bodily organs acting together to perform one or more functions.

systemic circulation   Circulation of blood from the heart throughout the body and back again to the heart; also called general circulation.

systemic disease   Disease that affects the body generally, often due to under- or overfunctioning of the internal glands.

tactile corpuscles   Small epidermal structures with nerve endings that are sensitive to touch and pressure.

tan   Change in pigmentation of skin caused by exposure to the sun or ultraviolet rays.

tapotement   A massage movement using a short, quick hacking, slapping, or tapping technique.

telangiectasias   Dilation of the surface blood vessels.

tertiary colors   Colors resulting from mixing equal parts of one primary color and one of its nearest secondary colors.

test-wise   Having a complete and thorough knowledge of the subject matter and understanding the strategies for taking tests successfully.

ticket upgrading or upselling services   The practice of recommending and selling additional services to clients.

tinea pedis   Medical term for the condition known as athlete's foot.

tip   The very end of a brush's bristles, furthest away from the handle.

tip cutter   An implement similar to a nail clipper, designed especially for use on nail tips.

tissue   Collection of similar cells that perform a particular function.

toenail nippers   Professional instruments with curved or straight jaws used for cutting toenails.

torque   The power of a machine or its ability to keep turning when applying pressure during filing.

toxins   Any of various poisonous substances, some of which can be produced by certain microorganisms.

transferable skills   Skills mastered at other jobs that can be put to use in a new position.

trapezius   Muscle that covers the back of the neck and upper and middle region of the back; it rotates and controls swinging movements of the arm.

triceps   Large muscle that covers the entire back of the upper arm and extends the forearm.

trumpet nail   Disorder in which the edges of the nail plate curl around to form the shape of a trumpet or sharp cone at the free edge.

tubercle   Abnormal rounded, solid lump above, within, or under the skin, larger than a papule.

tuberculocidal   Capable of destroying the bacteria that causes tuberculosis.

tuberculosis   A disease caused by a bacteria that is only transmitted through coughing, and not by salon implements or services.

tumor   A swelling; an abnormal cell mass resulting from excessive multiplication of cells, varying in size, shape, and color.

two color method   Two different colors of gel are applied to the surface of the nail, in different places, as in a French manicure.

ulcer   Open lesion on the skin or mucous membrane of the body, accompanied by pus and loss of skin depth.

ulna   Inner and larger bone of the forearm, attached to the wrist and located on the side of the little finger.

ulnar artery   Artery that supplies blood to the muscle of the little finger side of the arm and palm of the hand.

ulnar nerve   Nerve that affects the little finger side of the arm and palm of the hand.

ultraviolet (UV) rays   Invisible rays that have short wavelengths, are the least penetrating rays, produce chemical effects, and kill germs; also called cold rays or actinic rays.

ultraviolet bulb   A special bulb that emits UV light and is used to cure UV gel nail enhancements.

universal precautions   Set of guidelines and controls, published by the Centers for Disease Control and Prevention (CDC), that require the employer and the employee to assume that all human blood and specified human body fluids are infectious for HIV, HBV, and other bloodborne pathogens.

urethane acrylate or urethane methacrylate oligomers   The main ingredients used to create UV gel nail enhancements.

UV gel   A type of nail enhancement product that hardens when exposed to an ultraviolet (UV) light.

UV lamp   A specialized electronic device that powers and controls UV lights to cure UV gel nail enhancements.

valve   Structures that temporarily close a passage or permit flow in one direction only.

vapor   Formed when liquids evaporate into the air.

veins   Thin-walled blood vessels that are less elastic than arteries; they contain cup-like valves to prevent backflow and carry impure blood from the various capillaries back to the heart and lungs.

venereal disease   Contagious disease commonly acquired by contact with an infected person during sexual intercourse, characterized by sores and rashes on the skin.

ventricle   One of the two lower chambers of the heart.

verruca   Technical term for wart; hypertrophy of the papillae and epidermis.

vesicle   Small blister or sac containing clear fluid, lying within or just beneath the epidermis.

virology   The study of viruses and viral diseases.

virucidal   Capable of destroying viruses.

virus   A submicroscopic organism capable of infesting plants and animals; infectious agent that lives and reproduces only by penetrating cells and becoming part of them.

vitiligo   Milky-white spots (leukoderma) of the skin. Vitiligo is hereditary and may be related to thyroid conditions.

volatile   Easily evaporating.

volatile organic compounds (VOCs)   Substances containing carbon which evaporate quickly and easily.

volt   Unit that measures the flow of electrons forward through a conductor.

water-in-oil (W/O) emulsion   Droplets of water suspended in an oil.

watt   Measurement of how much electric energy is being used each second.

wattage   A measure of how much electricity a light bulb consumes.

well (small color cup or reservoir)   Also known as the color cup or reservoir; a hole in the top of the airbrush where drips of paint are placed and stored.

wheal   Itchy, swollen lesion that lasts only a few hours, caused by a blow, the bite of an insect, urticaria, or the sting of a nettle.

white blood cells   Blood cells that perform the function of destroying disease-causing microorganisms.

work ethic   Taking pride in your work, and committing yourself to consistently doing a good job for your clients, employer and salon team.

Index